# DOCTOR WHO:
# THE PANDORICA OPENS

## Exploring the worlds of the
## Eleventh Doctor

# DOCTOR WHO:
# THE PANDORICA OPENS

### Exploring the worlds of the
### Eleventh Doctor

## FRANK COLLINS

First published in England in December 2010 by

Classic TV Press

103 High Street, Cherry Hinton, Cambridge, CB1 9LU, England

e: classictvpress@live.co.uk

w: http://www.classictvpress.co.uk/

ISBN: 978-0-9561000-2-3 (paperback)

Doctor Who: The Pandorica Opens © 2010 Frank Collins

Internal design and layout by Classic TV Press

Printed and bound in Great Britain by

CPI Antony Rowe, Chippenham and Eastbourne

1 2 3 4 5 6 7 8 9 10 11 12 13 14 15

British Library Cataloguing in Publication Data

A catalogue record for this book is available from the British Library

## ACKNOWLEDGEMENTS

This book would not have been possible without the support, advice and guidance of a particularly fine group of people.

Firstly, I am hugely indebted to Andy and Marisa Priestner of Classic TV Press for being both foolish and brave enough to ask me to write the thing in the first place. Their faith in the work and the contributions and suggestions made in the development of the volume you hold in your hands have certainly eased the birth pangs of delivering the first book from a wet behind the ears freelance writer. Their efforts have made the rambling manuscripts of the original chapters so much better than they actually were. It has been a pleasure to work with them.

I must also thank a number of contributors, including those who welcomed requests for images and those who had chapters thrust into their hands and were asked for, and gave, honest opinions. To begin with, I must applaud the efforts of a smashing bunch of *Doctor Who* fans, particularly those that act as unofficial reporters from the location filming of *Doctor Who* and capture in images, tweets and blogs the creation of the series as it happens. Their images, both on the cover and in the various chapters, greatly enrich the content and reading experience. So, thanks especially to Alun Vega, Rob Clarke, Catherine Cranston, Scott Frankton, Lee Tucker and Gareth Price for the use of their superb photography and particularly to Simon Watkins for his help in suggesting and tracking down images and people. They are the epitome of generosity that can be found within fandom.

My gratitude to Neil Perryman at *Behind the Sofa* and to Gareth Bundy for reading some of the initial drafts of chapters and to friends and *Doctor Who* fans, including Tony Jordan, Ian Smith, Kate Priestley, Stephen Witkowski, Richard Evans, Cameron McEwan and Steve Haywood who have supported this book, commissioned writing or just simply provided warm, funny conversations and good advice. It has long been a pleasure to make contact with other fans via Twitter, *Behind the Sofa* (thanks to my fellow writers Stuart Ian Burns, John Williams, Tom Dickinson, Paul Kirkley and Damon Querry), the *Doctor Who* Appreciation Society and various *Doctor Who* events, fora and blogs, and many whose names would fill an entire book in itself. They know who they are and will understand if I am unable to exhaustively list each and every one of them here. Thanks also to the many readers of my blog *Cathode Ray Tube*. After all, that's how it all started.

Finally, a debt of love and gratitude to Geoff Carter, a husband whose life was turned upside down for about six months as a result of this commission, and to our friends Cameron, Stuart, Andy, Louise and Denise whose love and laughter more than made up for my vanishing social life during the summer of 2010.

And of course, this book would not exist without the efforts of Steven Moffat and his production team and writers, ensuring that *Doctor Who* remains one of the best shows ever made for British television.

# TABLE OF CONTENTS

# INTRODUCTION

Never mind 'the girl who waited' branding tagline that accompanied the introduction of new companion Amy Pond to the latest series of *Doctor Who*. What about the boy who waited? Steven Moffat is a life-long *Doctor Who* fan, a man who, on the DVD commentary for *The Empty Child* and *The Doctor Dances*, professed that he had waited forty years to see his name appear over the titles and music of a show he had loved since he was a child. The Hugo and BAFTA award winning writer achieved a long-cherished ambition in May 2008 when it was announced that he would be stepping into the executive producer job vacated by the man the BBC had trusted to revive *Doctor Who* in 2003, Russell T. Davies. Media and fandom speculation went into overdrive about the future of *Doctor Who* and about the man who would, from 2010 onwards, be responsible for the adventures that appeared on screen. After all, it was a significant moment in the history of the show and represented the first passing of the torch from a production team that breathed new life into the programme. It signalled and initiated a production regime change, including the casting of a new actor to play the Doctor, which would perhaps significantly alter the look and feel of a popular drama that was right at the top of its game in terms of success. Moffat was about to steer a series regarded as a flagship drama for the BBC, a massive commercial and international success and, crucially, an example of how a television drama production could become a multi-platform, multi-media juggernaut. As well as spawning the spin-off shows *Torchwood* (2006- ) and *The Sarah Jane Adventures* (2007- ), the series still represents the BBC's commitment to media convergence, merchandising and interactivity as one of the purest examples of three hundred and sixty degree broadcasting in the twenty-first century. Looking back to 2003, when Russell T. Davies was commissioned to produce and write *Doctor Who*, this particular media monolith did not exist. Any producer now following in Davies's footsteps not only has to ensure that the series maintains, or indeed surpasses, the standards achieved by him and his team in storytelling, spectacle and characterisation, but also has to manage the way *Doctor Who* appears via multiple delivery technologies, ensuring that the series engages in new ways with media audiences and offers them opportunities to participate in the *Doctor Who* universe through as many products as possible. In response to this, Moffat and his producers oversaw: the distribution of 3D cinema trailers; a BBC Outreach tour to launch the new series and screen the first episode *The Eleventh Hour* to local schoolchildren in Belfast, Inverness, Sunderland, Salford and Northampton; a major promotion for the series in America; three newly developed, downloadable computer game episodes, *City of the Daleks*, *Blood of the Cybermen* and *TARDIS*; two BBC Proms featuring the music of composer Murray Gold; and a touring arena show *Doctor Who Live*.

While the *Doctor Who* franchise continues unabated in 2010, the first tangible cosmetic changes unveiled were always going to be received with some trepidation by critics and fans alike. The opening episode *The Eleventh Hour* is also the inauguration of a redesigned title sequence, a re-scored version of the iconic Ron Grainer title music by Murray Gold, and new series branding, including a dramatic logo incorporating a TARDIS motif. This repackaging of the series, the evident renewal of the programme that would then resonate through other aspects of the production, is the first indication to the audience of new executive producer Moffat's intentions for *Doctor Who*. An inevitable process of change for the forty-seven-year-old franchise, it is the customary way many new producers and their production teams initially stamp their own vision onto the series. Supporting Moffat, the 2010 series is produced by a new executive production team in the form of: Piers Wenger, who replaced Julie Gardner as Head of Drama at BBC Wales; incoming executive producer Beth Willis, the former producer of *Ashes to Ashes* (2008-10); and producers Tracie Simpson, who had been with the show since 2005 as production manager and then producer of the 2009 specials, and Peter Bennett, another veteran of the revived series as, initially, first assistant director, then production manager, and fresh from producing *Torchwood: Children of Earth* (2009).

Many fans remain divided about the changes to the opening titles and other design alterations made throughout the series, some of which are addressed in this book. The new titles and the revised title music, symbolic of how a new era of the series arrives on the screen, are radical in both the way that they honour the past and introduce new elements; the graphics allude to the scudding clouds and vortexes of past sequences but then incorporate a 'travelling TARDIS struck by lightning' element, and the music is arranged with a new bridging motif that stalls the signature 'scream' opening of the familiar Ron Grainer composition. They signal that the new production team is willing to tinker extensively with established motifs. The intention of the revamped titles is unclear, even though *Doctor Who* is seen as a programme that thrives on change, and beyond showing the TARDIS having a typically bumpy ride, unfortunately there is a sense that they resemble an advertisement for antacid (some fans refer to the sequence as the 'reverse Gaviscon' titles) rather than a plunge into the time vortex. Murray Gold's revision of the classic theme, in an attempt to mark further changes by delaying that all-important opening scream used to declare the start of an episode so effectively, rather wrong-foots the viewer with a rumbling brass section before striking up the unearthly original. He also seems to have introduced more of the Peter Howell electronic flavourings from the 1980 realisation of the theme, toned down Delia Derbyshire's famous ululations and whirls, and added more percussive elements and a choir. Overall, it is a somewhat disappointing title sequence that lacks impact because certain iconic, familiar elements have been neutered in the drive to produce something new, to offer change for the sake of change. However, it does explicitly signify the difference in tone that I will explore in this book.

In a year of transition, how did Moffat ensure he added his own signature to the narrative and visual discourses that form *Doctor Who*? Did the stories produced in his first year as show runner and executive live up to the benchmark, award-winning drama of *The Girl in the Fireplace*, *Blink*, *The Empty Child*, *The Doctor Dances*, *Silence in the Library* and *Forest of the Dead*? The object of this book is to examine each episode of the 2010 series, identifying the course that Moffat and his fellow executives plot for the programme but, more importantly, to reveal the intricacies of storytelling and characterisation, especially relevant with the introduction of a new Doctor, played by actor Matt Smith, and his latest companion, Amy Pond, played by relative newcomer Karen Gillan. Amy is the first companion in the revival of the series not to be from London, and is a strikingly different female character and another conscious sign of the modifications that Moffat and his production team wanted to apply to the new series. The development of the Doctor and Amy is traced through my critique of the stories, reflecting on the series's narrative arc and the already established lore and continuity that inform our appreciation of the Time Lord's adventures. One of the key areas the book examines is genre. From the outset, Moffat has alluded that the series he wants to make, according to his interview with *SFX* in March 2010, should resemble "a big, fabulous fable – it's a fairytale. Fairytale sounds weak and insipid but fairytales are actually scary, dark and terrifying, and everybody loves those." Throughout, I will be looking at how the connection with fairy tales is evidenced in the series and its relationship with the horror and fantasy genres, and how history, politics, nostalgia and Britishness impact on the narratives and characters.

The opening chapter on *The Eleventh Hour* focuses on the introduction of a new Doctor, his relationship with Amy Pond and the world of Leadworth, including Amy's boyfriend Rory Williams. The broader themes of the 2010 series are outlined here, as are the first hints provided of Moffat's dictum for change. While it may look like business as usual on the surface, with a number of recurring motifs that emphasise many of the established tropes from Russell T. Davies's tenure on the series, the first episode is seeded with what will eventually turn out to be a distinct pattern of discourse, blossoming into very particular and often quite rigorous depictions of the Doctor and Amy, and their relationship to the series's grand narratives. Here, the characters specifically inhabit a *Doctor Who* that is less like the broader, comic book epic and melodrama of previous series and more like a Tim Burton-esque fantasy realm, influenced by fairy tale, Gothic horror and mythology. The template that Moffat constructs is also examined in relation to the male and female protagonists in his previous comedy and drama output. Briefly, the chapter also looks at other cosmetic changes made by the production team, with contentious decisions about design aesthetics eventually discussed further in the chapters on *Victory of the Daleks*, *The Hungry Earth* and *Cold Blood*.

With *The Beast Below*, I take the opportunity to reveal and then delve further into the political subtexts that dominate this and many other episodes in the series. The chapter also deconstructs the idea of 'Britishness' and how national identity is an intrinsic element of the satire in *The Beast Below*. Here, the Doctor and Amy become versions of Peter Pan and Wendy wandering the Neverland of a future United Kingdom, just as the electorate were about to alter the political landscape of Britain in May 2010. The nostalgic seduction found in the myth of the Blitz and in the indomitable British spirit on the home front during the Second World War, as personified in the series's use of the iconic figure of Churchill, also becomes the discourse under the spotlight in the chapter on *Victory of the Daleks*. By the time we get to Moffat's two-part story featuring the return of his extraordinary creations the Weeping Angels, the focus shifts onto *Doctor Who*'s long-established relationship with all things Gothic. The symbolism of monsters and religion, the power of the gaze and the complexities and traumas of travelling in time with the Doctor are subjects that form the focus on genre in *The Time of Angels* and *Flesh and Stone*. I also unravel some of the associations between River Song, the Doctor and Amy, highlighting one of the continuing themes of the book that suggests Moffat has returned the Doctor to his original status as innocent, eternal explorer, as the Time Lord who never grew up.

The episodes *The Vampires of Venice*, *Amy's Choice*, *The Hungry Earth* and *Cold Blood* alter the dynamic of the relationship between the Doctor and Amy, and Moffat's reintroduction of Rory Williams into the series forms much of the discussion central to the chapters on these stories. Amy's perceived abandonment issues and her phobia to commitment, and how these affect Rory and the Doctor, are core concepts addressed in these sections of the book. Equally, the ramifications of these relationships are later examined in the final chapter on *The Pandorica Opens* and *The Big Bang*. The men in Amy's life and her own attitudes towards them are seen as a major signature of Moffat's first series as showrunner, central to the narrative and psychological journey that the companion undertakes. The course of this psychological journey clearly reaches a crossroads in *Amy's Choice* as the desires and aspirations of both companions are held in stark contrast to the darker side of the Doctor. *The Vampires of Venice* also provides the book with a specific contextualisation of the vampire genre and the politics of racial identity, while *The Hungry Earth* and *Cold Blood* further reflect on this as well as commenting on the nostalgia of *Doctor Who* for itself, where homage and pastiche re-create significant tropes of the Pertwee era.

The two episodes *Vincent and the Doctor* and *The Lodger* are seen as specifically authored texts, and the chapters examine the output of Richard Curtis and Gareth Roberts in relation to the episodes. A complex examination of creativity, madness, the authenticity of the artist and the commodification of the life and art of Vincent van Gogh is seen in relation to the use of history and iconic cultural figures of the past within *Doctor Who*. Gareth Roberts's *The Lodger* is perhaps the most atypical episode of

4

the series and, while it harks back to the 'Doctor/companion lite' episodes of the Russell T. Davies era, this chapter focuses on a noticeable mission to reconfigure the Doctor as an asexual innocent abroad in the universe and examines how the episode achieves this through its associations with queer theory and the idiom of queer television. Finally, the last chapter on *The Pandorica Opens* and *The Big Bang* attempts to draw together the major arcs of the series and the character development of Amy as seen through the prism of 'epic' storytelling and the cinema of Steven Spielberg. It also returns to the complex discussions about time paradoxes and the current series's reflection of postmodern theories about the end of history.

The book is a veritable Pandora's box (or Pandorica box if you will?), with the contents revealing the folklore, mythology and symbolism ingrained in the stories. Throughout, I will touch on debates about television itself, how *Doctor Who* is positioned as quality family viewing and as a televisual British cultural export. I also apply cultural and media theory, psychoanalytical perspectives, and a blend of literary, film and television criticism to dig below the surface of shiny, new *Doctor Who*. Similar academic study or scholar-fan appreciation of *Doctor Who* has often met much resistance in the fan community because of the use of what James Chapman refers to, in *Inside the TARDIS: The Worlds of Doctor Who*, as the "impenetrable critical language of high theory." Notably, I am not an academic but I am a fan of the series. Although I am familiar with much cultural and media theory, this dissection of the series is therefore partly a layman fan's perspective, informed by a background in contemporary fine art and design, and wherever possible I have introduced the many different theoretical perspectives into these chapters at a level which I hope fans will intellectually appreciate and feel comfortable with. I tend to agree with Matt Hills that the combined use of theoretical jargon and a passionate knowledge of the series to critique the programme is possible without descending into obfuscation. As he suggests in *Triumph of a Time Lord*, "we should refrain from assuming that this hybrid identity somehow detracts from 'innocent' enjoyment of the TV series, or that it is some sort of 'spoiling' activity, as expressed in the common sense, anti-intellectual notion of 'over-analysis'." More importantly, this deconstruction of the series is purely my own and the opinions and theories ventured about *Doctor Who* here are not presented as the definitive argument about the intended discourses played out in the thirteen episodes of the series. They are my interpretations and I do not claim them to be essentialist in nature. If, after reading this book, you feel the urge to return to the episodes and watch them again in the context of the layers of meaning offered here, whether you disagree with them or not, then I will consider this publication a success.

## Chapter One

# THE ELEVENTH HOUR

Written by: Steven Moffat
Directed by: Adam Smith
First broadcast: 3 April 2010

---

"What have you got for me this time?"

Running at 65 minutes, the opening episode of Series Five, *The Eleventh Hour*, covers a lot of ground. Its major task is to introduce a new Doctor, in the form of actor Matt Smith, whose debut had been awaited since the announcement of his casting in January 2009 and his brief appearance at the conclusion of *The End of Time – Part Two*, broadcast on 1 January 2010. As well as introducing us to the eleventh incarnation of the Doctor, this episode is also our first encounter with a new companion, Amelia Pond, or Amy as she is formally known throughout the series.

The episode opens with a pre-titles sequence. This was shot after the production block for this episode had wrapped and was separately produced by Nikki Wilson and directed by Jonny Campbell, who had been working on the production of the episodes *The Vampires of Venice* and *Vincent and the Doctor*. The pre-titles pick up directly from the conclusion of *The End of Time*, with the TARDIS exploding, in flames, and hurtling back to Earth whilst carrying the newly regenerated Doctor. Before the new title sequence crashes in, this opening clearly operates as a 'handing of the baton' from one era of the show, that overseen by Russell T. Davies, to the next, the newest as produced by Steven Moffat. With an action sequence that shows the Doctor clinging on to the TARDIS for dear life as it spirals out of control across the cityscape of London at night, Moffat here clearly desires to assure viewers that they are watching the same series that had made its triumphant return back in 2005.

The sequence is very typically styled in the way many similar action scenes had been incorporated into the Davies era, opening with the oft-repeated visual motif of 'God's eye view' of the Earth in space before plunging down towards England as a brassy, insistent score from Murray Gold accompanies the TARDIS spinning across several familiar sights of London. London landmarks, including the Swiss Re building (the 'Gherkin'), the Tower of London, the Houses of Parliament and Buckingham Palace have been a recurring visual watermark in the series, firmly placing the adventures into a recognisable location, acting as a form of cultural tourism and visual shorthand for the series's place within English heritage. English icons, including recognisable landmarks, will continue to appear in the series and perceptively reflect the UK government's *Icons of England* project from 2006 that asked the public to nominate those icons which they felt best represented the nation. Looking down the list we see that Moffat does exceptionally well in featuring many of them in this and later stories: *Alice in Wonderland*, Big Ben, Queen's head stamp, the Spitfire, St George's Flag, Stonehenge and the Tower of London. The opening scene includes Big Ben, a landmark that has had some significance within the establishment of the series since 2005, having been partly demolished by a crashing spaceship in *Aliens of London* and then rebuilt by the time of *The Christmas Invasion*. It and the Houses of Parliament will reappear in *Victory of the Daleks* as a visual motif summarising Britain's indefatigable stance against the Nazis during World War II.

The Doctor hangs onto the TARDIS as it narrowly swoops over the spire of Big Ben, the chimes from the tower matching the doom-laden peal of the TARDIS's own Cloister Bell that can be heard here and later when the ship has crashed in Amelia Pond's garden. Clearly the sequence is designed to indicate 'business as usual', offering an assurance that huge, sweeping changes are not on the agenda at this stage of the episode. As a writer, Moffat does not entirely slough off the previous era as masterminded by Russell T. Davies. Beyond the cosmetic changes of the opening titles, *The Eleventh Hour* continues to reference the previous producer's work as well as provide nods to the classic series of *Doctor Who* (1963-89). The Shadow Proclamation, introduced by Davies in his very first episode *Rose* (when the ninth Doctor attempts to reason with the Nestene Consciousness) and then later with mentions seeded throughout the revival of *Doctor Who* (2005-) in episodes *The Christmas Invasion*, *Fear Her*, *Partners in Crime*, and most prominently, with an actual appearance, in *The Stolen Earth*, is cited by the new Doctor as he confronts the Atraxi. The Tenth Doctor's ability to click his fingers and open the TARDIS doors as recalled by River Song and first seen in Moffat's *Forest of the Dead* from 2008's Series Four is used again when the Doctor finally asks the adult Amy aboard. Moffat's oft-quoted 'wibbly-wobbly-timey-wimey' line, first heard in his script for *Blink* in 2007, again makes itself heard. The now familiar golden glow of the Time Lord's regeneration energy is also seen as the Doctor explains to the young Amelia that he is "still cooking" as his hands glow and a stream of energy is released from his mouth in precise correlation with scenes in David Tennant's first story, *The Christmas Invasion*.

More important is the way that references to the revived series bleed into references to the series's past with two very striking sequences in the final encounter with the alien Atraxi. Here the Doctor demands of the aliens threatening to boil the Earth that they search their databases: firstly, to put their own plans into perspective with those attempted by previous invaders; and secondly, to determine that they are aware that the Earth remains defended (another nod to Tennant's first episode). For the former, Moffat includes a sequence of aliens past and present including the Sea Devils, Sontarans, Cybermen, Hath, Ood and Daleks to illustrate the point, although technically Hath and Ood have never actually invaded the Earth, and for the latter he inserts a thrilling sequence of all previous ten incarnations of the Doctor, ending with a dramatic and significant moment where David Tennant's image as the Tenth Doctor is burst open as Matt Smith's Doctor proudly declares his status as the Eleventh. It is a very strong visual message that states Matt Smith is picking up the torch from those that have formerly played the part as well as underlining that this new Doctor is the very same man who we were introduced to in 1963. The sequence of monsters also foreshadows the alliance of evil that will trap the Doctor in the Pandorica in *The Pandorica Opens*. The two sequences also reflect Reinette's line in Moffat's Series Two episode, *The Girl in the Fireplace*: "That's the way it's always been. The monsters and the Doctor. It seems you cannot have one without the other."

What these 'flashback' sequences also do, and blatant continuity was something that Russell T. Davies was initially very cautious about using as he started work on 2005's Series One, is enable Moffat to declare that his series as producer is very definitely and permanently linked to all those that have gone before. As Series Five progresses there are more reminders of this legacy drip-fed into future episodes and it is clear that Moffat is not shy about referring to the rich history of the programme and is confident that the audience built up since 2005 will now easily take such references in their stride. It marks a difference between him and Davies, where Davies often worried that such continuity might be alienating to a non-fan audience or to an audience only aware of the show since its 2005 revival.

Finally, the series's most iconic object, in the form of the TARDIS, also undergoes a process of renewal, as part of the episode's narrative that parallels the Doctor's own regeneration, and a redesign within the new series's production team's remit of change. The exterior of the police box is transformed into one that clearly resembles the prop used by the makers of the two Dalek films in the mid-1960s and the original TARDIS prop seen in the first season of Hartnell stories, now looking chunkier and in a brighter shade of blue with white-lined windows and the return of the St John's Ambulance badge on the door. It proposes that Moffat is as nostalgic about the appearance of the TARDIS as the fan audience and in hindsight the changes he makes aptly fit within the characters' own affections for the police box as "something old, something new, something borrowed, something blue" when the Doctor plants memories in the young Amelia's head as a way of bringing him back from the void in *The Big Bang* at the end of the series.

The interior of the TARDIS undergoes a more radical change. The set is bigger and multi-levelled with stairways leading off into other areas of the ship and with the console set up on a glass-floored dais above which hangs a concentric series of copper circles. It more reflects the original Peter Brachacki design from 1963 as well as many of the elements introduced by designer Ed Thomas in 2005. The general feeling is of a vast but warmly inviting space, with a retro mid-1970s aspect to some of the sloping walls, lighting design and a large round viewing screen, and featuring a console packed with a very cluttered and odd assortment of controls that has developed from the bric-a-brac approach of the 2005 design. Visually, there is a lot for the viewer to take in and there is a richer feel to this environment.

## "Little Amy Pond. Waiting for her magic Doctor to return"

After the opening titles and before the Doctor crashes the TARDIS in Amelia's garden, director Adam Smith opens the first scene with a close-up of a toy windmill. There is a gust of wind and the sails spin violently as the camera pans to the right and tracks through the moonlit gardens, past beehives, benches and to the front door of Amy's house where there is an abandoned swing gently swaying in the breeze. The camera then tracks forward towards the house.

The shot of the windmill, blown by a seemingly non-existent wind, gains significance at the end of the series, as the Doctor's life unravels and he find himself back at Amy's house with young Amelia. In *The Big Bang*, director Toby Haynes replicates exactly the same shot of the windmill to open that final scene set in Amelia's house. It is clear this must be a specific direction in Moffat's opening and final scripts for the series and that the repeated shot of the windmill acts as bookends to the odyssey that the Doctor and Amy eventually go on. The windmill might represent the circle of time taking us from the beginning of Amy's story in Leadworth, with the character's development through the remaining episodes of the series, and then to the end of that journey which, clearly in Moffat's view of the series, is also the beginning, a new beginning. The Doctor's role is to understand the nature of the orphaned young Amelia, and the adult Amy, together with the strange, empty house she lives in, where life is gradually being eaten away by the forces emanating from the crack in her bedroom wall. At the end of the series he returns her to the same point at which he met her in *The Eleventh Hour* but with her life, home and memories restored as result of triggering the reboot of the universe.

The young Amelia, who we have not yet seen or identified, narrates a prayer to Santa over director Adam Smith's opening shot, thanking him for her Christmas presents. But it is a communication that is months late because, as she explains, it is Easter. This cleverly reflects the story's comedic effects of the Doctor constantly being late in reuniting with Amy. However, this little girl is praying because she is more worried about a crack in her bedroom wall. It immediately suggests that Moffat is restating a number of the child's point-of-view narratives that were present in both *The Girl in the Fireplace* and *Forest of the Dead,* featuring respectively the young Reinette in fear of the monsters under her bed, and CAL and the young girl with the incurable disease preserved in the computer core of a planet-sized library. He is also keen to reiterate his interest in childhood fears: the monsters under the bed, the shadow on the floor and the living statues are joined by the crack in the bedroom wall. This is something highlighted by Moffat in his interview with *The Guardian's*

Gareth McLean, 22 March 2010: "For me, *Doctor Who* literally is a fairy tale. It's not really science fiction. It's not set in space, it's set under your bed. It's at its best when it's related to you, no matter what planet it's set on."

Amy's chat with Santa supposes that she has a child's ordinary, well-adjusted fantasy life and the answer to her prayer, the crash landing of the Doctor, could be a mimicry of the similar arrival of Santa with his sleigh. However, the world of her inner imagination is about to be severely affected. Certainly, as we discover later, the Doctor becomes a vital fantasy figure to her as she grows up and one as important as all the other imaginary figures likely to figure in her developmental progression such as Santa, the Easter Bunny or the Tooth Fairy. This also dovetails with one of the major themes of Series Five, the symbolic importance of fairy tales.

Amy, even at the age of 7, clearly has a somewhat ambivalent attitude towards figures of authority. On her initial encounter with the Doctor, he having climbed out of the smoking ruins of the TARDIS, she immediately enquires "Are you a policeman?" and demands, when he replies that he is the Doctor, "if you're a doctor, why does your box say police?" As far as she is concerned he is either a doctor or a policeman and Santa is either too busy to investigate the crack in the wall or has sent someone else to carry out the work. Her relationship to authority figures and fantasy figures becomes a major factor in the construction of her identity. Later in the episode when we first see her as an adult, she appears as, and impersonates, a policewoman and reveals in her conversation with Mrs Angelo (Annette Crosbie) that she has also impersonated a nurse and a nun. It is part of a more significant masquerade as, gleaned from her other confession to Mrs Angelo, further revelations from her boyfriend Rory and the episode's concluding tracking shot of her bedroom full of drawings and handmade figures of the Doctor and the TARDIS, we see that as a child she re-created the Doctor (as the Raggedy Doctor) and the alien that emerged from the crack in the wall. These were used as fantasy figures for role-play, the role-play she continues as a kissogram in adult life, including dressing Rory up as her imaginary friend the Doctor. Again this aspect of the character reflects the themes of storytelling and fairy tales that dominate the series and, because no one believes that she ever met the Raggedy Doctor, it may also explain her defensiveness and lack of respect for figures of authority by the very fact that she pretends to be some of them.

When Amy, as policewoman, curtly tells the Doctor "Amelia Pond hasn't lived here in a long time," it is clearly part of her act, a role-playing where she lies to him about Amelia having not lived in the house for six months. She does in fact hoodwink him into thinking she is a policewoman and certainly does not let on that she knows who he is. It is only when the alien threat is revealed to her and the Doctor demands she call for backup that the pretence is dropped. "But you're a policewoman," says the Doctor. "I'm a kissogram!" she shouts in reply and as if to underline this partial emergence of Amy Pond she whisks off her hat and unfurls her long hair. However, the audience is ahead of the Doctor, because we know it is Amy Pond but he hasn't quite figured it out yet. Part of the illusion is that Karen actually drops her Scottish accent whilst portraying the policewoman, hiding the character's heritage. This Scottish heritage is also something of a running gag in the series and is later mentioned in *The Beast Below*, *Victory of the Daleks* and *Vincent and the Doctor*. Only when the Doctor makes the connection with the once-demolished shed in the garden, deducing its replacement is 12 years old by 'tasting' it (a moment of orality in the episode which we will expand on later), does he realise that he is 12 years late returning to Amelia's garden and that the policewoman standing in front of him is lying. "Why did you say six months?" he questions her. "Why did you say five minutes?!" she screams in her broad Inverness accent. And with that the masquerade is over and the scales fall from the Doctor's eyes.

It is also clear that her independence from adults at an early age and, crucially, her disappointment in them stems from her orphaned life with Aunt Sharon, from the fact that her parents have seemingly vanished and her perceived abandonment by the Doctor. He breaks a promise to her that he'll be back in five minutes as he disappears to re-phase the TARDIS's engines and then does not return for 12 years. As "the girl who waited" not just for the Doctor but for the reappearance of her parents, she has obviously acquired the psychological scars to fuel this inner frustration, especially after biting the four psychiatrists that have tried to deal with the symptoms of her personality disorder. Taking this into consideration, Karen Gillan's performance here and throughout the rest of the series is certainly a departure from the choices of previous series. Amy is not an immediately appealing character and she is often seen as reactionary, secretive, impulsive, defensive and emotionally quite cold. The thirteen stories are therefore as much an analysis of this young woman's anxieties as they are adventures in time and space, exploring her relationship with Rory and her capacity to love him, as well as her attitudes towards authority figures and the fantastical brother/father figure of the Doctor.

There is a very quixotic, aggressive quality to Karen Gillan's portrayal of Amy and it is too easy to categorise her simply as 'feisty' – a word that has been in media circulation since the announcement of her casting and her character was described – because in the end it is clear that Amy is actually emotionally damaged rather than independent. This is again a new departure for the series and potentially offers up a more complex, even if often unsympathetic, female character that takes us beyond the simple classifications of Rose as 'the romantic soul-mate', Martha as 'the unrequited lover' and Donna as 'the best mate' that the Davies era explored. With Moffat as head writer on the series, the Amy Pond character is surely an extension of the Lynda Day character he created in children's series *Press Gang* (1989-93), where the girl's self-sufficiency and toughness hides a great deal of complex insecurities, and an analogue of Susan, Sally and Jane, the sexually confident but utterly paranoid lead women characters in his sit-com *Coupling* (2000-4). Many of his female characters have emotional hang-ups and anxieties and it would seem that Amy Pond is no exception.

As the series progresses, her attitudes towards Rory and the Doctor will also reflect some of the male–female relationships from those earlier Moffat series, but above all there is the allusion of the state of Amy's psyche to the crack in the bedroom wall that is the driving force to the series's development of the character. The crack in the wall is not only a visual clue to the damage the exploding TARDIS has inflicted upon the universe but it is also a symbol of Amy's childhood fears and her antagonism towards adults. This includes adults such as her parents and the Doctor who might leave and promise to come back but often never do. "People always say that," says the young Amelia, already prepared for the disappointment that is to come when the Doctor promises to return. The episode also ends on a moment of revelation where it is suggested that Amy is about to be married, about to take on the role of a wife, and her impulsive decision to run away from this duty and responsibility again highlights her insecurity about being an adult. She qualifies her 'elopement' with the Doctor with a requirement that he and the TARDIS get her "back in time for… stuff." Her wedding is simply 'stuff' to her. Amy is literally containing, or keeping the lid on, the anxieties and anger of her abandonment, but the veneer of the front she presents is also cracking and her brittleness, echoed in her cynical attitude, makes her less empathetic to audiences. One of the biggest issues that Karen Gillan faces during this series is how to make that appealing and, as we will see, she is not entirely successful in that endeavour.

Conversely we also have Matt Smith in his first episode as the Doctor. In parallel to the on-screen maturation of Amy from her 7-year-old to her 21-year-old self, the episode also provides a slowly developing persona for the latest incarnation of the Time Lord. A key sequence, and this also links into the discussion about fairy tales, is the Doctor's first meeting with Amelia in her house. After getting out of the TARDIS, still wearing the 'raggedy' clothes of his previous incarnation that will be part of Amelia's fixated vision of her Raggedy Doctor fantasy figure, he collides with a tree ("steering's a bit off") and explains that he is still in the throes of his regeneration. Later, they sit down to indulge in a frenzy of eating, the illicit 'midnight feast' of so many children's books. Much of it is what you would describe as staple, 'child-friendly' food – apples, beans, bread and butter, ice cream, custard, fish fingers – and as she helps herself to ice cream the Doctor settles on that ultimate child wish fulfilment of combining two 'child-friendly' favourites, fish-fingers and custard, in the appropriately named 'fish-custard'. It is an indication that the Doctor is regressing, following his own advice from the past, where in 1975's *Robot* he commented, "What's the point of being grown up if you can't be childish sometimes?" However, he is also playing a game with young Amelia Pond. It is a stratagem to get round her defences and work out what exactly she is doing all alone in a deserted house. Smith's affability shines through the performance and he is subtle enough to play the Doctor as a mix of newborn infant looking at the world in wonder and wise old man who can spot someone is in trouble. This is underlined later in *The Beast Below* when he confirms to Amy that he "never interferes unless there's children crying." There is a mercurial, Peter Pan-like quality to his interpretation of the Doctor that matches the impression that we have of young Amelia as a Wendy 'wannabe', desperate to fly off with him into the universe. The imagery and themes of Peter Pan are a major component of how Moffat sees the relationship between the Doctor and Amy and we'll explore that further in Chapter 2, *The Beast Below*.

As the episode leaps forward 12 years, his apparent innocence about his delay is blunted by the realisation that Amelia has grown up into Amy. "Growing up – you never want to do that," he claims when he becomes aware that Amy's rites of passage into adulthood has been at the hands of four psychiatrists (some of whom she has bitten) and a village who all humour her for her obsession with the imaginary friend of the Raggedy Doctor. The Doctor, still having post-regeneration seizures, gradually becomes the authority figure of old, puzzling out the mystery of Amy's house, Prisoner Zero and the impending Atraxi destruction of the Earth. He positively relishes the idea that he has only 20 minutes to save the Earth and the episode's title *The Eleventh Hour* playfully combines the adjacent meanings of saving the Earth at the last minute, at the eleventh hour as it were, with the length of an episode (just over an hour) which also features an Eleventh Doctor.

Director Adam Smith also tries something new and with the aid of Moffat's script he demonstrates how the Doctor sees the detail in the ordinary with a stop-motion camera sequence that travels into the Doctor's eye and then observes the activity on the village green. It is a Doctor-centred 'what's wrong with this picture' point of view that demonstrates his instant deduction that Rory is not photographing the sun burning up but is in fact taking images of Prisoner Zero. Very different in tone as an example of how the Doctor's quick mind operates, the sequence works as a one-off instance in this episode but would have been hard to bear if endlessly repeated throughout the series. However, a very similar sequence occurs in *The Beast Below* where it is Amy that learns to appreciate the detail in their surroundings and deduces the truth behind the origin of the star-whale and the alternate solution to killing or stunning the beast in order for Starship UK to continue on its way.

As the Doctor walks through Leadworth, Moffat also begins to outline his desire to place the Doctor in isolated, more intimate locations rather than cities like London or Cardiff. Clearly the Doctor now feels slightly out of his depth in an idyllic English village, with Leadworth emulating a vision of pastoral Britishness under threat that *The Avengers* (1961-9) made its stock-in-trade, and is frustrated when Amy tells him there are no power stations, airports or cities nearby. Leadworth also later becomes an important part of *Amy's Choice* where the idyll of country life becomes the location that determines which man she will choose to have in her life –

Rory or the Doctor. Its magical landscape contains illogical elements for the Doctor that are epitomised in the duck pond that has no ducks and where Amy herself does not ever remember it populated by ducks. Disappearing parents and disappearing ducks are signifiers for the effects of the crack in time as we partly discover in *The Big Bang* and perhaps also suggest something of the emptiness at the centre of Amy's life in Leadworth. The village and the local hospital also recall the environs of *Spearhead From Space*, the Third Doctor's introductory story in 1970, and not only is there a reflection of that Doctor's exile, of his time thwarting alien invasions in the 'home counties', but the manner in which the Doctor disposes of the Raggedy Doctor ("to hell with the raggedy") that is in effect borrowed from his predecessor's appearance and assembles his wardrobe from clothes at the hospital also recalls *Spearhead From Space* and the 1996 *Doctor Who* TV Movie. His final chosen appearance seems to be a mixture of college professor and indie rock star with a distinct nod towards the costume worn by Patrick Troughton: tweed jacket complete with elbow patches, bow tie, braces, rolled up trousers and boots. He retains the huge quiff of hair that most observers remarked upon when they saw his first interview after being announced in the role. "The hair of an idiot," remarks Liz 10 in the following episode *The Beast Below* and her description is very near the mark as Smith's hair is often seen in mock Stan Laurel disarray.

Finally, Moffat repositions the Doctor as both a fantastical and mythological figure. Amy has mythologised him through her drawings, cartoons, handmade figures and the games she has played with Rory. Rory, as a nurse, is by extension a projection of the Doctor and a figure that Amy has settled on as 'second best' to the original. The 'fantastical' version of the Doctor, her Raggedy Doctor, is well known to the majority of the village's population to the extent that he is clearly recognised by Jeff and Mrs Angelo as the imaginary friend she has fixated upon since a child. The approach here is very different from the Earth-based stories that Russell T. Davies wrote for the previous four series, that tended to position the Doctor, rather uneasily it has to said, as a God-like figure.

Ordinarily, Davies would often pair the Doctor up with UNIT or Torchwood, where he was always a known quantity to both organisations, and alien invasions would be framed by a faux news report trope, often fronted by Lachele Carl as Trinity Wells, to signify that the events were of global importance. Here, Moffat's only concession to the Davies era is to have the Doctor hack into a video conference between various scientists, that includes a cameo from Sir Patrick Moore, and get them to spread a computer virus across the world, as seen in various tricked-up stock shots of the New York Stock Exchange and the centres of London and Tokyo. Here there is no UNIT, no Torchwood and no Trinity Wells. The globalising of the threat is not repeated again in this series and marks another shift in the way Moffat sees the Doctor's relationship to his activities on Earth.

The Doctor is referred to as the 'magic' Doctor on a number of occasions and this emphasises a desire to shift the stories into the realm of fantasy and fairy story where the Doctor is more of a wise old wizard than he is an all-powerful God substitute. The 'magic' Doctor is also inextricably linked to Amy's fantasies about him and her inner child when, in the confrontation with Prisoner Zero in the hospital, the multi-form taunts, "Little Amelia Pond, waiting for her magic Doctor to return," and later in the scene, when the multi-form takes on the guise of little Amelia it continues to chide, "Poor Amy Pond. Still such a child inside. Dreaming of the magic Doctor she knows will return to save her." Smith certainly communicates a complex mix of child-like wonder and eccentric wisdom and his is a more physically exaggerated performance where the use of his hands, body and legs are as much an expression of the new Doctor as are his often very subtle facial movements. It is a sophisticated and enthralling debut and he exudes charisma enough to constantly light up the screen.

## "The Pandorica will open. Silence will fall"

Steven Moffat has made no secret about the direction and tone of the series under his stewardship. In any number of interviews he has suggested that his intention is to take the series into the realm of magic and fairy tales where, according to Gareth McLean in *The Guardian*, "his instinct led him towards a more 'storybook quality'."

*The Eleventh Hour* and its director Adam Smith provide the benchmark here in setting the visual tone which accords with the series's proposition as fairy tale. Immediately, he pulls our attention to the garden of Amy's house with his deliciously slow pans through the moonlit shrubbery. He invests it with mystery, a certain menace and a sense that this is a place where magic is about to happen. It conjures up echoes of Frances Hodgson Burnett's *The Secret Garden* or Philippa Pearce's *Tom's Midnight Garden*. In *Children's Literature*, Peter Hunt comments on Pearce's symbolic idea of the garden as "a powerful image of childhood... representing the sheltered security of early childhood." Anne H. Lundin, in her *Constructing the Canon of Children's Literature: Beyond Library Walls and Ivory Towers*, regarded Hodgson's book as one containing "the mythic imagery of a restored garden, of something submerged awaiting discovery, of the secrets we bear." The garden in *The Eleventh Hour* is the stage from which Amy and the Doctor launch their journey through the following twelve episodes. It is the place in which they are both shaped and changed uniquely, that influences their feelings and thinking, a space in which they are redefined and, as previously mentioned, to which they both return in *The Big Bang*, completing the cycle of the journey. The garden also represents the forest of so many fairy tales and Moffat himself uses the forest as another site of primal mystery later in the series in *Flesh and Stone*.

16

The TARDIS crash lands in the garden, demolishing that great British institution and national symbol, the shed. It is a symbolic box that mirrors that other box in the series finale, the Pandorica, and where both are containers that are simultaneously instruments of time, transporting the occupants into and out of the chronology of the stories. The TARDIS, and the Pandorica particularly, are also representations of Hesiod's ancient myth of Pandora and her box which, depending on the crux of your interpretation, is a vessel or a prison that either contains all the evils of the universe or the very last hope for mankind. The exploding TARDIS is eventually pinpointed as the cause of the cracks in the skin of the universe, a metaphor for the evil force inadvertently released into the universe, and conversely the Pandorica, referred to as a "fairy tale" by the Doctor on several occasions, is depicted both as a prison and a device by which the Doctor can repair the cracks in the universe. "The madman with a box!" therefore has a double meaning in the series and we will talk about the Pandorica in more detail in the chapter on *The Big Bang*.

When the Doctor eventually pops his head out of the TARDIS, Murray Gold's incidental music cleverly emulates the crescendo of Strauss's *Also Sprach Zarathustra* as his head appears in the smoke. Donald Ferguson, in his *Masterworks of the Orchestral Repertoire*, sees Strauss's music as "dealing with the motives that impelled the descent of (Nietzsche's) philosopher from his contemplative heights." It suggests the new Doctor has fallen to Earth and is ready to enlighten us as to his own moral philosophy. An interesting moment here is that little Amelia is present at the opening of the crashed TARDIS in her garden and is later instrumental in opening the Pandorica in *The Big Bang*. She is a symbolic key, an emblem of childhood curiosity, used to initiate the circular narrative of causality as depicted by the turning windmill, and to resolve it in the concluding episode of the series. Amelia in the garden is also symbolic of many other storybook tropes. Dressed in her red dressing gown and gingerly treading through the undergrowth she is the epitome of both Red Riding Hood about to step off the path and an immature Eve about to taste the first fruits of knowledge.

The first thing the Doctor requests is an apple. The apple is one of the most powerful symbols in the episode because in many of the distinct mythological interpretations available it is always seen as a key to knowledge. Whether it is the Greek myth of the 'Apple Of Discord', where the fruit is seen as symbolic of the core or the crux of an argument; the apple eaten by Adam and Eve as a symbol of the acquisition of the knowledge of good and evil, the fall of man into sin and redemption from sin; or the traditional gift for a teacher or a symbol of love, the episode uses the apple in a number of metaphorical ways.

After popping his head above the TARDIS door, with Matt Smith for all the world looking like Michael Palin in a Gilliam-esque fantasy as he hurls a grappling hook out of the ship, he is given an apple but only to bite into it and spit it out undigested. He later accuses Amelia of trying to poison him when she serves up all the various items of food he requests.

17

The implication of the poisoned food or apple has a direct root in classic fairy tales and could form a link to Snow White's seven-year sleep as a consequence of taking a bite of the poisoned apple. It is another symbol of "the girl who waited". There are a number of elements in the story that resonate here with the idea of 'waiting' and the sleeping princess. There is the 'missing' 12-year period between the Doctor leaving young Amelia and then meeting the adult Amy. We have the coma patients all in a state of unconsciousness whilst the multi-form psychically intervenes and we also have the suggestion that Amelia and/or Amy has descended into sleep and is emerging out of a dream of the 'someday my prince will come' variety. It is through a dream state that Amy also inadvertently assists the multi-form, taking on the form of her younger self and projecting an idealisation of the Doctor and her as Amelia when it sends her into unconsciousness. Only through suggestion can the Doctor get Amy to recall the creature she saw in the room in her house and thus reveal its true form to the searching Atraxi. The concept of waking from a dream is clearly implied in the climax where, after frightening the Atraxi away, the Doctor leaves in the TARDIS witnessed by Amy and Rory, and Amy closes her eyes. The sound of the TARDIS engines is then laid over the image of her closed eyes and an image of young Amelia, sitting on her suitcase in the garden, that then dramatically cuts to the adult Amy waking up and finding the TARDIS at the bottom of the garden. "The girl who waited" and who endured "14 years since fish-custard" revives like Snow White or Sleeping Beauty, after shutting out the world but clinging to her fantasy of the Raggedy Doctor.

The apple is also an emblem to Amy of a forgotten or lost mother who used to carve smiley faces into the fruit to encourage her daughter to eat some of her five-a-day. In a direct parallel to the scene where the Doctor pockets the apple and casually remarks to young Amelia, "She sounds good, your mum. I'll save it for later," he is later reunited with the adult Amy, presenting to her the same apple that she gave him 12 years previously as proof that he is the same man that she met as a child. It is the core symbol that settles their argument in Leadworth when she refuses to believe that he is real. When he is trapped by Amy, after she deliberately shuts his tie in a car door, he throws her the apple with the smiley face and says, "I'm the Doctor. I'm a time traveller. Everything I told you 12 years ago was true. I'm real. What's happening in the sky is real and if you don't let me go now, everything you've ever known is over." Director Adam Smith does something quite extraordinary at that moment in the scene and he frames the Doctor and Amy in profile, holding the shot for quite a long time as he bathes them both in a golden glow and allows a white-blue lens flare to slash across the image as the Doctor holds her hand clutching the apple and says, "Amy. Believe for 20 minutes." The apple is a visual acknowledgement of Amy's choice in the episode, whether to trust the Doctor or not, and her own desire, one she has struggled with since childhood, for the Raggedy Doctor to be real, and finally it is an object that helps her to remember an absent mother. As the series progresses, her choices and her beliefs become a central element in the drama.

As an object it also reflects a number of other elements in the story. As a circular, spherical shape, as a closed circle, it extends to the presence of Prisoner Zero as signifying the beginning of the adventure and the very solution to its removal from the real world. Prisoner Zero is therefore 'Year Zero', the base point in time that signifies the beginning and the end of the story but also zero as a void, as representative of the space between the universes. This idea could also equate with the way that *The Eleventh Hour* and *The Big Bang* also feature the sun, as a circle, as zero, where both episodes depict it as burning up in the sky. The idiom 'the apple of your eye' also seems an appropriate context to bring in here. Not only does the apple also symbolise love – the parental love missing from Amy's life, the feelings she has for Rory and the Doctor – but the episode, and much of the series, is also concerned with perception, with seeing the detail, seeing the truth. This request applies to the characters in the story and to the audience at home. After the Doctor and young Amelia listen to the warning about Prisoner Zero and the Doctor dashes off to fix the TARDIS whilst Amelia packs her suitcase, the audience is given some specific visual clues. There is the open door on the landing in the background of the shot as Amelia rushes to and fro to do her packing. When she gets to the garden, there is a shot out of her bedroom through the curtains where a dark figure passes very quickly in front of the camera. The implication is that Prisoner Zero is in her house and freely moving about. Did Prisoner Zero kill Amy's parents or did they get absorbed by the crack in the universe? These guessing games get more complex as the series continues.

During the scene at the dinner table, Moffat also puts front and centre the concept of the series as a storybook or fairy tale. The Doctor is impressed with Amelia's name. "Amelia Pond. Like a name in a fairy tale." Later this is something she is rather bitter about as an adult when they meet again 12 years later and Mrs Angelo refers to her as Amy. "Who's Amy? You were Amelia," demands the Doctor. "Yeah, now I'm Amy." "Amelia Pond. That was a great name," he insists. "Bit fairy tale," she rebukes cynically to his observation of some 12 years previous. It is a rejection of his romanticisation of her name and hints that perhaps her journeys with him in the TARDIS will be a way of repairing the damage and reigniting in her the imagination that fairy tales possess.

The crack in the bedroom wall is also another familiar device from children's fiction. It is a recycling of the idea of the secret door or portal into other spaces and other dimensions and the notion that Prisoner Zero has escaped through the crack and into Amy's house is a reference to all those secret gardens and wardrobes that occupy classic children's literature. "You've had some cowboys in here. Though not some actual cowboys. Though that can happen," confirms the Doctor as he examines the crack in the wall. This not only suggests that the crack has allowed forces through from other universes, conjuring up Gilliam-esque images such as those from *Time Bandits* (1981) – of men on horseback leaping from wardrobes – but it also refers back to Moffat's script for *The Girl in the Fireplace*. There the Doctor is in mind-link with Reinette and his dialogue on the state of her psyche is precisely the same. The multiple meaning here is that by extension the Doctor acknowledges Amelia's fear that something has come through the crack, prefigures her psychological trauma and dryly comments on the quality of Leadworth's builders.

In *The Eleventh Hour* we are also told that there is a perception filter over the sixth door in Amy's house and that you can only see it in the corner of your eye. Moffat brings out his box of tricks again to activate the audience's fear of looking. Like the act of blinking in *Blink* will seal your fate with the Weeping Angels, in this episode he entreats you to look "where you don't want to look" in order to discern the truth and for Amy to realise, "that's a whole room I've never noticed before" when the Doctor advises her how to perceive the unknown properly. As soon as she sees the hidden room, the mood of the scene darkens dramatically and evokes the familiar tropes of horror films where characters approach the door to a realm of anxiety in disregard of their own common sense. The story is full of distorted ways of seeing, of detecting reality both consciously and unconsciously in the 'corner of your eye'. The episode is full of visual tropes that underscore the theme of 'seeing' – the huge eye staring out through the crack in the bedroom wall; the ever-probing huge eyeball of an 'all-seeing eye' at the centre of the Atraxi starship that simultaneously appears on all the world's television channels; a big close-up of Dr Ramsden (Nina Wadia) examining Barney Collins's eye in the hospital ward; the previously mentioned Doctor's point of view and Rory's photographing of Prisoner Zero's various identities. Bizarrely, in the final confrontation between the Atraxi ship and the Doctor there is even an eyeball that sniffs, reminding us that not just sight but taste, touch and other senses are also ever present in the episode. Two of the biggest visual clues in the episode – the wedding dress hanging up in Amy's bedroom and the waveform of the crack on the TARDIS scanner – are both more or less seen from an audience perspective, with the implication that the Doctor does see the latter but chooses to ignore it, signaling further complexities to character and story development as the series progresses.

The entire eating scene in Amelia's kitchen suggests that the Doctor continues to rationalise the world, the universe, as much through his senses as he does through his accumulated wisdom and keen intelligence. He tastes and rejects a variety of foods, sniffs and tastes the demolished shed to realise the error of his 12-year hiatus, and sensitively runs his fingers over the cracked surface of the bedroom wall. Prisoner Zero and its gaping maw or maws are a prime symbol of this orality, and are further examples of the abject and the uncanny in the series. The abject as the principle function of the modern horror film is evoked here with the multi-form's undisguised appearance. An image of the abject – a slimy, putrefying, rather phallic creature constantly baring its fangs – is represented as the monstrous 'other' threatening to cross the border into our reality and disrupt the social and cultural order of Leadworth and the hospital, passing between the human and the inhuman both symbolically and visually as it takes on the identities of the village's various residents. Barbara Creed, writing in *Fields of Vision: Essays in film studies, visual anthropology, and photography* – 'Horror and the Carnivalesque – The Body Monstrous', describes the mouth as "another aspect of the abject. The mouth represents the inside and outside plane of the body; its lips are on the outside; the other side of the lips leads into the body's inner recesses." The multi-form's habit of opening its maw wide, whether in semi-human or non-human form, and screaming, "signifies a renunciation of speech and a blurring of boundaries between animal and human."

This blurring or slippage between animal and human is further exemplified by the way it physically and psychically confuses Barney Collins and his dog as it attempts to impersonate him and ends up with Collins barking and gnarling and both man and dog in symbiotic action as "one creature disguised as two". The multi-form's impersonation, through the psychic links to the coma patients, confuses and then swaps orality between man and dog and later between a mother and two daughters. As the mother realises her error in her use of the two daughters to speak to Amy and Rory she pointedly remarks, "I'm getting it wrong again. So many mouths." The mother too is a component of the abject, as a representation of the monstrous-feminine, absorbing the unconscious Amy to ridicule her fantasy of the Raggedy Doctor by having a facsimile Amelia tell him, "what a disappointment you've been," to wound her psychologically with an image of mother and daughter as a reminder to her of the absence of her own parents ("I watched you grow up. 12 years and you never even knew I was there"), and to impart to the Doctor, and the audience, the series's referential meme, "The Pandorica will open. Silence will fall." The mouth, the maw, the crack in the bedroom wall and the final opening of the Pandorica itself express the abject and impart secrets to us about the unfolding story, the psychological states of the Doctor and Amy and the series's continuing fetishism of the monstrous 'other'.

The phallic creature that prowls after Amy in the room "that shouldn't be there" also suggests a powerful iteration of the horror movie iconography of the killer stalking a victim. The scene acts as a formal introduction to the adult Amy and her role in the narrative, wherein Moffat's re-engineers the concept of the 'final girl' in a manner akin to the way Buffy Summers subverts the role of female protagonist in *Buffy the Vampire Slayer* (1997-2003). Amy exhibits some of traits of the typical 'final girl' that Carol Clover describes in *The Dread of Difference: Gender and the Horror Film* – 'Her Body, Himself – Gender in the Slasher Film,' where the female protagonist is often "compromised from the outset by her masculine interests, her inevitable sexual reluctance, her apartness from other girls, sometimes her name... (with) her exercise of the 'active investigating gaze'... (she) *looks* for the killer, even tracking him (the killer) to his forest hut or his underground labyrinth, and then *at* him, therewith bringing him, often for the first time, into our vision as well." Certainly Amy acts as the investigating gaze here and eventually acknowledges the presence of the multi-form, but she is not the 'final girl' that Clover describes.

As Jason Middleton points out in 'Buffy as Femme Fatale: the Cult Heroine and the Male Spectator', in Elana Levine and Lisa Parks's *Undead TV*, Buffy herself mitigates against the compromises of the 'final girl' figure in slasher films. She defies Clover's definition of a final girl "as boyish, not sexually attractive, favouring 'practical' clothing, and not sexually promiscuous, and often having a unisex name." Like Buffy, Amy is visually very sexualised and challenges the monsters that threaten her whilst also actively desiring male characters. It is defined in the flatteringly exiguous policewoman uniform she wears throughout this episode, then upon introducing Rory to the Doctor as a 'friend' she suggests an availability that Rory denies by repeating his own status as "Boyfriend!" and she does not avert her gaze when the Doctor undresses, suggesting she really desires to see him out of his Raggedy Doctor uniform. This sexualisation of the companion did not go unnoticed with a number of viewers, with the *Daily Mail* reporting about complaints posted on an online forum that the producers had "completely demeaned *Doctor Who* by replacing good episode stories with slutty girls," and with another asking "Why did she dress up as a tarty policewoman? Surely that's not fitting for a family show." It is clear that both had missed the point that Amy's job was as a kissogram and that she was dressed up for work – "I go to parties and I kiss people. It's a laugh!" she explains. At no point is it suggested that she is a prostitute or a slut. However, the relationship between Amy and Rory is ambiguous in this first episode and the final reveal that her wedding is an impending event and that she is deliberately travelling in the TARDIS in a state of denial about it does provoke some interesting story developments later in the series centring on the dynamic between Amy, the Doctor and Rory.

## "That's just the beginning. There's loads more"

In conclusion then, *The Eleventh Hour* succeeds in providing the audience with a confident handing over from the previous Doctor and series production team. It often plays to audience expectations with plenty of familiar visual tropes and references but it also confidently sets out its own prescription for the series. The opening episode clearly establishes a number of ongoing themes and potential character developments and looking at it with the hindsight of watching a full series there is much that mirrors the climax of the series in *The Big Bang*. The major themes about the complexities of time travel and its psychological impact on humans are seen from a very different angle as embodied in the character of Amy. The episode also sets up the series-long mystery of the Pandorica and the cracks in the skin of the universe.

The references to fairy tales and children's literature to inform the series's overall tone are also in the foreground, through the symbolic resonance of characters, objects, costumes and mood or through specific references in dialogue and in Owen McPolin's deep focus cinematography and lighting. Murray Gold's music also plays a major part in establishing this ambience. He not only refers back to established themes for the Doctor, as used in previous series, but also creates themes for Amy and her environment that resonate with plenty of Danny Elfman-style choral sections that bring to mind the music for *Edward Scissorhands* (1990) or *The Nightmare Before Christmas* (1993). Many reviewers picked up on the Tim Burton quality to the visuals and music in *The Eleventh Hour* and in a BBC America press release Moffat confirmed this, "If you look at the stories I've written so far, I suppose I might be slightly more at the fairytale and Tim Burton end of *Doctor Who*, whereas Russell is probably more at the blockbuster and *Superman* end of the show." Appropriately, Helena Bassil-Morozow's summary, in *Tim Burton: The Monster and the Crowd*, of what she describes as the "Burtonian postmodernist subject-individual" could well be describing Moffat's own vision of the series and its central character: "Refusing to grow up, rejecting any authority, clinging to his creativity-generating complexes for dear life, voluntarily fragmented but pining for wholeness, hating the unconscious but feeling overpowered by it... searching for the lost God inside and outside himself, cursing his lonely fate."

This is also, in effect, the fairy tale of how a woman grows up and sadly disconnects from her own inner child. It reflects Moffat's interest in the inner fantasy lives of children, something he has thematically exploited in his earlier episodes with specific childhood scares – the monster under the bed, the monster creeping up behind you. The episode shows how a child's creative imagination sets out to deal with abandonment issues as formalised in young Amelia's fantasy role-playing of adventures with the Raggedy Doctor. Her stories, drawings and dolls, so much like those created by any child that is watching who then goes on to write and act out their own adventures with the Doctor, become sublimated into an adult life where the yearning for such adventure still exists but has not been acted upon. No wonder she likes dressing up and kissing people for a living. The final scene is of Amy, in her nightie, as a substitute Wendy joining the Peter Pan-like Doctor in the TARDIS. "You wanted to come 14 years ago," he says. "I grew up," Amy replies. "Don't worry, I'll soon fix that," he responds. He clicks his fingers and the TARDIS, that glowing magic box, opens and its light fills her face with wonder. Significantly, the burdens and anxieties of moral responsibility that were the inner turmoil of the Tenth Doctor, as represented by the revived series shibboleth 'sole survivor of The Time War', have also been dissipated. Its major achievement then is to debut an instantly charismatic Doctor, unfettered from such ideology and iconography, and, not since Tom Baker skipped on the spot with Ian Marter in *Robot*, have we had an actor who so physically owns the role. Big, gangly Matt Smith is a fireball of sheer presence and simply commands you to watch him. To embrace the child-like, to rediscover it in yourself, to get back to the essence of your being is one of the main themes here whether it is the Doctor eating fish-custard in Amy's kitchen, Amy remembering apples with smiley faces, the Doctor and the TARDIS getting a facelift or the significance of Prisoner Zero and the millennium bug virus that resets all the counters in the world to zero. It is about going back to the beginning which, when we get to *The Big Bang*, is also concurrently the end.

## Chapter Two

# THE BEAST BELOW

Written by: Steven Moffat
Directed by: Andrew Gunn
First broadcast: 10 April 2010

---

"Gotcha!"

*The Beast Below* restates Steven Moffat's intention that the series should be seen within the framework of children's fiction and in specific alignment with classic children's literature. In the previous chapter I suggested that the early scenes set in Amelia's garden in *The Eleventh Hour* evoke the early to mid 20th Century works of Frances Hodgson Burnett and Philippa Pearce. In *The Beast Below* the implications of the relationship between the new Doctor and Amy and the series as a fairy tale narrative are embellished by Moffat's cues from influences as diverse as J. M. Barrie, Lewis Carroll and other classic texts such as *Pinocchio* and *The Snow Queen*. *The Beast Below* also embraces elements of political satire with timely nods to Orwell's *Nineteen Eighty Four* and Terry Gilliam's own interpretation of his dystopian vision in *Brazil* (1985). His story of an entire country living on the back of a sentient, kindly space creature also evokes Terry Pratchett's *Discworld* series of comic-fantasy novels and an aborted *Doctor Who* script by Pat Mills and John Wagner, *The Song of the Space Whale*, where the TARDIS crashes in the belly of a giant whale, that was intended for Season 20 of the show in 1983.

It is ironic that Moffat looks to Pratchett as an influence here. Moffat clearly states that he believes the series is a fairy tale, as emphatically underlined in his interview with Adrian Lourie of *The Scotsman* in March 2010: "Maybe this isn't new but it is my view: *Doctor Who* is a fairy tale – not sci-fi, not fantasy but properly a fairy tale. And I don't mean Disney-style where the endings are changed and everyone lives. *Doctor Who* is how we warn our children that there are people in the world who want to eat them." Pratchett's own guest blog with *SFX* magazine of May 2010 argues that the series is not science fiction and its use of science is very dubious. Whilst Pratchett could rightly argue that the perception of *Doctor Who* as science fiction is wrong, his blog then criticises the series for suggesting the science in the stories is legitimate: "I just wish that it was not classified as science fiction. Much has been written about the plausibility or otherwise of the *Star Trek* universe, but it is possible to imagine at least some of the concepts becoming real. But the sonic screwdriver? I don't think so. *Doctor Who*'s science is pixel thin." The series has never concretely made a claim that the denouement of its stories are realistically solved with 'hard' science and Moffat's own views of the series as fairy-tale fantasy clearly suggest it is never ever likely to try and make that claim. Pratchett's views that some episodes have relied on Deus Ex Machina to solve their plots or presented the Doctor as a Christ-like figure are pertinent but his labelling of the series as "not science fiction" flies in the face of Kim Newman's definition of the series in the BFI's TV Classics book *Doctor Who*: "*Who* originally see-sawed between British science fiction and BBC period drama. Voracious for material, ideas and moods the programme expanded to take in modes as variant as the surreal British trendiness of *The Avengers*, the blood and thunder Gothicism of Hammer horror, panto humour, conspiracy thriller, studio bound fantasia, social satire-comment, design-led futurism, deliberate and unintentional camp, even ambitious philosophising." Moffat's view also indicates that he is going back to the 'pre-Disney' horror, violence and death of Grimm's original tales as the source of his inspiration. Whilst Pratchett may have some issues with plotting and bad science in the series, *Doctor Who* has long been held up as an example of a British television series that can be what ever it wants to be, including, but not exclusively limited to, science fiction, fantasy and fairy tale. Certainly the series under Moffat, and *The Beast Below* is a good example, blends the science fiction elements of spaceships and monsters with fairy-tale characterisation and a dark, dream-like mood.

The pre-titles sequence of *The Beast Below* opens with a shot of the creaking, groaning hull of Starship UK and initially validates the robotic Smilers, dispensing their authority over the schoolchildren, as this episode's statement of *Doctor Who*'s own decades-long obsession with the 'monster of the week'. From the fade-out of the titles, the story immediately emphasises the 'fairy tale' theme of the series. This is clearly seen in the sequence where Amy floats outside the TARDIS, almost 'flying', as the Doctor holds her by the leg. With Amy in her nightie and the Doctor demonstrating to her that he has the ability to show her the vistas of space, this is again another replay of those symbols of Wendy and Peter from Barrie's *Peter Pan*. Barrie never allowed his character of Peter Pan to grow up and, in a sequel to his original play, *When Wendy Grew Up*, the narrative describes Wendy as a grown woman telling bedtime stories to her daughter Jane. She tells Jane of Peter's regular visits over the years until he eventually forgets to come. When Jane goes to sleep, Peter reappears and asks Wendy to fly away with him. Fearing she is now too old, she refuses. Peter weeps and wakes up her daughter Jane who then flies off with Peter. In the conclusion of the story, Wendy turns to the maid Nana and confirms that this cycle will continue with generations to come, "forever and ever, dear Nana, as long as children are young and innocent." The motifs that Moffat establishes with the Doctor and Amy, formed within the power of storytelling to reclaim lost youth and innocence, are reinforced in the opening scene above Starship UK. The Doctor is himself, in Amy's eyes, a storybook character and it is established in *The Eleventh Hour* that her life has been shaped by the fictional analogue of the Raggedy Doctor, and that the fiction has returned to her and her imaginary friend is no longer a distant myth that she has re-created in her own fictions, storytelling and role-playing. Her triumphal cry of "It really is a spaceship!" as she floats outside the TARDIS confirms that she now believes in the 'madman with his box'.

The series's own emphasis on storytelling, myth and fantasy is also a key concept in Barrie's book, where the story of Peter Pan is a fiction within a fiction, a memory of the adult Mrs Darling and the older Wendy in its sequel. The Doctor, like Peter Pan, has returned to Amy and looks no different to her, 'staying young' like Barrie's character. As Ann Yeoman summarises in *Now or Neverland: Peter Pan and the Myth of Eternal Youth*, "Peter Pan... is the spirit of perpetual youth and joy associated with Neverland, Barrie's country of childhood. The captivating image of Peter Pan at the nursery window, enticing Wendy and her brothers to fly away with him to Neverland, inevitably resonates differently in the child than in the adult. For the child, Peter Pan means, perhaps more than anything else, freedom." It is an image that has continually played out in the *Doctor Who* series as each Doctor invites each new companion into the TARDIS. Moffat offers a reading of the Doctor as a similar symbol of freedom, of creative, youthful energy as well as the eternal wise, old man. Both he and Amy could also be symbolised as 'high flyers' who desire to see beyond the limitations of everyday life, with the transposing of the staid Edwardian England of Barrie's book for the rural life of Leadworth and his fantasy Neverland for the Time Lord's wanderings in the vistas of time and space. The theme of eternal youth and ancient wisdom is also reflected in the figure of Liz 10, the Queen of Starship UK, whose body clock has been slowed down ("keeps me looking like the stamps") and whose obsession with the central symbol of the glass of water drives her to keep investigating the government she suspects of undermining her authority. Liz is also a character who dons a disguise and impersonates one of her subjects to delve into Starship UK's secrets and this continues the use of disguise, masks and impersonation as a theme that is repeated throughout this series.

The distinction between youth and age is also given a political context where children under 16 are aware of what is happening on Starship UK but are powerless to prevent the adults from 'forgetting' the secrets of the ship when they vote. The adults flying aboard Starship UK could therefore be seen as trapped in an ephemeral adulthood, where their retrospection – knowing of but not responding to the silent crying of a child, knowing of but not willing to understand the plight of the Star Whale – is powerless to do anything to re-create what once came naturally: to be youthful and wise. But as Wendy observes in *Peter Pan*, "It is only the gay and innocent and heartless who can fly," and *The Beast Below* and the following episodes examine the darker aspects of the Peter Pan mythology where the re-ignition of the irrepressible spirit of childhood and innocence are checked by the painful decisions and choices that adults must make. There is also an element of sexual fantasy for Amy when she realises that she has been whisked away by a strange man, beguiled by the man's bravado and twinkling eyes, and that seems to quicken her pulse. Her reverie is briefly halted by Mandy's mention of a boyfriend as they investigate the road works, instantly reminding her that she is supposed to be getting married. The impending wedding, and its significance as a commitment to adulthood is later underlined when the Doctor rushes back to the TARDIS exclaiming, "Big day tomorrow!" blissfully unaware of its context to Amy. It is enough to stop her in her tracks and confess, as much to herself as to the Doctor, her desire not to leave childhood behind just yet: "Have you ever run away from something because you were scared, or not ready... or just, just because you could?" This line emphasises that Amy is the latest in a long line of female characters that Moffat has written about, all running away from their lives as adults and clinging on to the freedom and independence they had as children. Immediately the Doctor senses this and sees her statement as a summary of his own desire to run away "once... a long time ago" from the cloying society of the Time Lords, not ready to join them in their role purely as observers. This neatly brings us back to his earlier explanation to her in the TARDIS, and his subsequent debunking, of his alleged non-interference in the affairs of other planets and people.

Here the Doctor and Amy hover above the industrialised space-faring remnants of humanity, an image of "whole nations migrating to the stars," and a voiceover narration from Karen Gillan creates a recap of the story so far with the rarely used form of interior monologue for the character, linking back to similar devices used in the Russell T. Davies era of the show, particularly those used in *Army of Ghosts* (with "My name is Amy Pond" a direct reflection of the "My name is Rose Tyler" opening eulogy), *The Family of Blood* (Son Of Mine's narration of the Doctor's punishments), *The Last of the Time Lords* (Martha Jones's narration) and *The End of Time* (Rassilon's history of events). She confirms here that she has 'eloped' on the night before her wedding, but beyond an obvious delight in taking the trip of a lifetime, we do not yet know what her feelings towards the Doctor are and whom it was she was intending to marry. In the *Introducing The Beast Below* video posted on the official BBC website, Moffat underlines the main theme of the story as one in which Amy "is going to understand the man she is travelling with." These subplots will be revealed in her choices leading towards maturity because Amy's odyssey, as we pointed out in Chapter 1, is one of self-discovery and her identity crisis, as in most children's literature and fairy tales, is embodied by her status as an orphan and her childlike nature. In Hans Christian Andersen's story *The Snow Queen*, in particular, this idea is shown by Helene Høyrup in 'Childhood as a Sign of Change' – *Change and Renewal in Children's Literature* as "an expression of nineteenth century double vision, whereby the adult self ascribes meaning to childhood which in turn serves to revitalise adult culture." Most tales complete this odyssey with the process of marriage or finding a father figure and as we will see this is very much a component of Amy's story in forthcoming episodes as well as the conclusion of this series.

Following the allusion to *Peter Pan*, one of Amy's tasks on this sophomore voyage is to reunite the Doctor with his own shadow. In Barrie's book Peter is left incomplete, without his shadow, after his first visit to the nursery. Wendy recovers the shadow and sews it back on to Peter's feet. The shadow is his tie to the human world of the Darling family and a symbol of his responsibilities. The eternal figure of the Time Lord who does not always recognise when a 'leap of faith' is required is a key concept in *The Beast Below*. His inability to see an alternative way out of the problem at the end of the story is finally resolved by Amy. The story proposes that the newly regenerated Doctor, whilst espousing that 'God is in the details' when he and Amy survey the police state of Starship UK, fails to see the solution, symbolised by Amy's revelatory moment of recall, to the dilemma of the Star Whale's survival. A key word of dialogue is "gotcha" and it represents the Peter Pan-like shadow that both Amy and the Doctor must mutually 'sew onto their feet'. It is a trope that the revival of the series and the classic series has often re-emphasised – that the Time Lord needs the company of humans to temper his hubris; that those that travel with him also learn to see beyond their own narrow realities to attain a sense of their essential humanism within the vast scope of the universe. Both the Doctor and Amy use "gotcha" as a way to indicate that both of them have uncovered and confirmed the other's failure to recognise some home truths. When the Doctor rounds on her and says she has a choice – "it's this or Leadworth" – after she complains that she is not dressed for exploring Starship UK, he knows intuitively that she will choose the adventures with the 'madman and his box'. It is based on simple, human curiosity and a desire to investigate the unknown. At the moment of truth, "what will Amy Pond choose?" he confirms with a point of his finger and says, "Ha, ha! Gotcha!" when her face betrays her attempt to hide a response to this question. This "gotcha" will be repeated in *The Big Bang* and accompanies the theme of choice that threads throughout the series.

At the end of the story, the Doctor stumbles towards his own moment of self-realisation, that he is as old, wise and kind as the Star Whale, and that, like the Star Whale, he will always help those children crying silently amongst the stars. When Amy points this out to him and reminds him that his own kindness is rooted in the misery of longevity, loneliness and pain, she offers him a choice between loneliness and companionship with a responding "gotcha" as they physically embrace and he confirms his choice of her as a suitable companion. This self-realisation is in the very "shadows – whatever they're afraid of – they're nowhere to be seen," that the Doctor identifies as symptomatic of living in the dystopian police state: the refusal to acknowledge your responsibilities and act upon your choices. The Doctor and Amy can only reveal the true mission of the Star Whale to the Queen, the Winders and the population of Starship UK when these shadows, representing the fear of the truth, can be acknowledged by their owners. This reality is illuminated by Amy's bold risk assessment of the situation. The final scene where Amy and the Doctor debate the recklessness of her actions and the potential consequences mirrors a similar scene in Russell T. Davies's *The End of the World*. Both scenes depict the Doctor and his companion framed by the vastness of space as seen through the observation decks of both Platform One and Starship UK. Not only is the visual signature of these scenes duplicated, but both are about the human impulse to survive and how this impulse reflects, in the first instance, the Doctor's survival guilt as the last Time Lord in *The End of the World* and, in contrast to his eternal renewal, how transient human existence can be; and in the second instance the Doctor's capacity for kindness borne out of wisdom, age and loneliness.

### "That's not just a ship. That's an idea. That's a whole country"

In the week that *The Beast Below* was transmitted, Gordon Brown announced on 6 April 2010 that, after formally asking the Queen to grant the dissolution of parliament, there would be a General Election on 6 May 2010. After pointedly saying, "I know where I came from and I will never forget the values... instilled in me by my parents," Brown confirmed he was off on a tour of the UK, travelling "the length and breadth of our land" to bring the people "a very straightforward and clear message." In the opposition corner there was much talk from David Cameron about bringing to an end 13 years of Labour's 'big government' and replacing it with the Tories' concept of the 'big society' where essentially the government abdicates from engineering civic responsibilities and places the task with communities and individuals. In both instances *The Beast Below* satirises these gestures. These values are clearly forgotten by the generations living on Starship UK and the story acknowledges that this desire to 'forget' is a generational rites of passage where 12-year-old Mandy explains, "Everyone chooses the forget button." She is not yet eligible to vote, but "anytime after 16, you're allowed to see the film and make your choice," she continues, "and then once every five years..." inferring that after the adults watch this party political broadcast it wipes their memory of what they have seen. The collusion between society and state about the use and abuse of power is also tied into this cycle.

The timing could not have been better and Steven Moffat's script for *The Beast Below* is both an examination of the British psyche, its relationship to nationalism and tradition, the development of our cities and towns, and of the nature of politics itself. The political climate in which this series is broadcast will have further significance in the following episode *Victory of the Daleks*. "Life on a giant starship, back to basics. Bicycles, washing lines, wind-up streetlamps. But look closer, secrets and shadows. Lives led in fear. Society bent out of shape, on the brink of collapse," whispers the Doctor. Starship UK is analogous, with its post-solar flare survivors (with the solar flares neatly fitting into *Doctor Who* continuity proposed by the events in 1975's *The Ark in Space*) and their quotidian existence, to Clement Attlee's post-war consensus of the mid to late 1940s. As David Kynaston states in *Austerity Britain*, "the concept began to be accepted that the British people, in return for all their sufferings in a noble cause, deserved a new start after the war." Starship UK represents that period of privation and is also both a symbol of make-do and mend and of the post-war attempt to regiment the lives of citizens in the UK through progressive town and city planning. The 'bolted together' nature of the ship suggests a diverse population, segregated by differences in class and wealth, literally flung together in an act of desperate survival. In *The Spiv and the Architect*, Richard Hornsey describes how the "fragmented and aesthetically disordered post-war city" of the late 1940s is subjected to radical planning that not only sought to repair the devastation wrought by wartime bombs but also desired to impose order in "a design for community living within the reformed urban environment, as a set of collective engagements and activities that would interpellate all citizens into a performance of civic participation." Starship UK is a set of rather uniform buildings thrust together to house the surviving UK population of the Earth. Its design, modernist and efficient, is linked directly to the structure of the society within it and echoes the futurist zeal of 1951's *Festival of Britain*, where the Southbank Exhibition informed visitors of "the story of British contributions to world civilisation through the medium of tangible things." The population of Starship UK appears to have a fatalistic attitude to what happens around it and is ordered and contained by the very structure of the urban environment built for it and the higher authority that controls it. No one is allowed 'below' and this configuration mirrors the way the populace behaves, outwardly mobile but inwardly too intimidated by the secrets of that society to acknowledge a crying child in the street. Keep moving and don't ask questions.

The society they live in is visualised as a synthesis of British historical and cultural icons, those "tangible things" – the Union Jack, red telephone boxes, bakelite television sets, lollipop ladies, city gents in bowler hats, Underground transport signage, military field-telephones – a blend of distinct periods in British economic and cultural history depicting an era of cultural inertia in parallel with its political stagnation. A clever piece of continuity also lies in the use of the Magpie Electricals logo above the workmen's hut, linking thematically back to the 1953 period of *The Idiot's Lantern* as well as to its previous appearances in other episodes of the series and in *The Sarah Jane Adventures* (2007- ), seen on the back of television sets, computers, on phones, and recently on items attached to the TARDIS console in *The Eleventh Hour* and *Vincent and the Doctor*. Here social history is melded with iconography to depict a Britain that appears to be almost self-consciously celebratory about its survival from the solar flares, a John Bull idée fix of a mythological Britain and yet one that is, as the Doctor observes, "bent out of shape." It is a blend of the post-war austerity under Labour's Attlee government and the pre-Falklands period of recession under Thatcher in the early 1980s.

As the story develops, Moffat turns the contentious vision of a 'great' Britain, with its hubristic nationalism, into one that describes a police state run by a single monarch and her acolytes. It is both the depressing totalitarian vision of Orwell's *Nineteen Eighty Four* coupled with the Machiavellian underbelly of the Elizabethan world of the 16th Century. This dichotomy of ideologies suggests the conflicted political and economic milieu that viewers themselves were surrounded by whilst watching *The Beast Below* and during the aftermath of the election in May 2010. As Amy sits in the voting booth, she is shown an electoral broadcast where the screens are full of BBC idents, using the UK map and a familiarly nostalgic typeface introduced to the television service in 1962, whilst a hi-tech mind-wipe takes place as one of the silent, grinning Smilers, the Tony Blair of Starship UK, looks on. Visually and conceptually it is a powerful scene. However, the edit assembled by director Andrew Gunn and editor John Richards with its depiction of the booth, the voting procedure, the mind-wipe and Amy recording a message, seems rather ambiguous and slightly unclear as to when she did record the message. On initial viewing it appears as though Amy hits the 'forget' button *immediately* after seeing the film. We are given no indication that she recorded a message until it actually starts playing after she presses the button and recovers from the mind-wipe. This implies that perhaps Amy recorded the message in the booth earlier. However, a careful viewing of Karen Gillan's performance does indicate, in her puzzled reaction to the tears on her face, that we have seen the sequence from Amy's point of view. Immediately after she sees the film there is a direct cut to her pressing the 'forget' button and it is only when you see the shot of her wiping away her tears and then compare it to her tearful video message that you have any indication that she recorded the message just *after* watching the broadcast and *before* she had her mind wiped. It is also not clear from the script and direction as to whether there are record buttons in all the voting booths and whether the rest of the adult population could also have discovered the darkness at the heart of the ship by recording similar messages to remind themselves of what they had seen.

When the episode transmitted, and also post-broadcast, the parties reminded us that 'Broken Britain' desperately needed bolting back together, just as the various English counties were re-created in metal for the exodus from Earth. *The Beast Below* chimed with voters faced with the legacies of Labour and Tory policy, of a society disenchanted and alienated after social and economic collapse, where civic responsibility had failed to emerge in the face of rampant capitalism. With its voting booths where the populace always forget and rarely protest, *The Beast Below* is also an analogy of Orwell's *Nineteen Eighty Four* where those that lead the country and profess to champion the underclass against the effects of a polarising capitalism are in reality concerned only with establishing and perpetuating their own power. The five-yearly plebiscite in *The Beast Below* keeps the populace from questioning and maintains their enforced ignorance of what they may have discovered in the five-year period. They learn to forget through a weird form of Orwellian doublethink. This peculiar cognitive dissonance, 'remember to forget, forget to remember', is precisely the way propaganda works in Orwell's Oceania – war is peace, freedom is slavery, ignorance is strength. Would voters, the episode gently mocked, 'forget' to 'protest' or 'protest' to 'forget' on 6 May 2010? The hung parliament, and the Con-Lib alliance eventually created from it, are as much symbolised by the episode's own contentious bricolage of cultural, historical and political signs. Here the alliance between an absolute monarchy and a state police force that terminates children and dissenters is forged on the back of ideological and iconographic contradictions and the underclass represented by the beast below.

Liz 10, as the highest authority, needs to be reminded by the floor she fills with glasses of water that "every single day my government is up to something." As a result of the Doctor's intervention, she is then presented with the paradox of either forgetting or abdicating, to know better than what the video message of herself is telling her, to believe and doubt at the same time. "The impossible truth in a glass of water... not many people see it," whispers Liz and her aphorism connects us to the story's themes of observation and self-deception. It is all about seeing the truth, "the impossible truth." For the UK this is a familiar scenario, a general election every four years, the same parties to choose from, the same beliefs and doubts. *The Beast Below* contends that we know better than what any of the parties are telling us but we vote and hope otherwise. Agencies – the police, the monarchy and government – debase history, trivialise the truth and annihilate the past on a daily basis. Protest and you are fed to the Star Whale, sent to Room 101 or quietly retired. "Then once every five years everyone chooses to forget what they've learned. Democracy in action," summarises the Doctor. This may be the series's least ambiguous attempt at political satire so far. Russell T. Davies had certainly laced his era with some acerbic views, namely with the Downing Street-set farce of *Aliens of London*, complete with tongue-in-cheek reference to the sexing up of the WMD dossier that provided the case for war in Iraq, and the downfall of Harriet Jones in *The Christmas Invasion*, incurring the Doctor's anger by destroying the retreating Sycorax ship, mirroring Thatcher's order to sink the Belgrano. Davies also satirised media and politics in Series One, as Matt Hills outlined in *Triumph of a Time Lord*: "If *The End of the World* deals with media society metaphorically and moralistically chastising decadent, insulated responses to what we see on our screens then *The Long Game* and *Bad Wolf* tackle media culture more literally." The classic series of *Doctor Who* was also no stranger to political satire and interest in the series's familiarity with the genre was piqued nearly two months previous to the transmission of *The Beast Below*. *Newsnight* picked up on comments from Sylvester McCoy in Marc Horne's 'Doctor Who at War with Planet Maggie' article reported in *The Sunday Times* on 14 February 2010. Whilst this could be seen simply as the further efforts of a right-wing media spinning stories about a 'lefty' biased BBC by stating the obvious about *The Happiness Patrol,* a *Doctor Who* story made in 1988, it is interesting to compare it with *The Beast Below.* After McCoy stated that, "Our feeling was that Margaret Thatcher was far more terrifying than any monster the Doctor had encountered," the *Newsnight* feature, with a rather bemused Gavin Esler, looked at the 1980s era of the show and its relationship to the Thatcherite politics of the day. It confirmed that *The Happiness Patrol* was a thinly disguised critique of Thatcher's policies. A sense of déjà vu is therefore elicited with the Doctor telling us that we are about to "hear the sound of Empires toppling" as he brings Helen A's administration to a grinding halt in that story then being reflected some 22 years later in the Doctor's "We're bringing down the government," as he thumps the 'protest' button in the voting booth in *The Beast Below.*

Moffat's script not only critiques a flawed voting procedure (perhaps in a not so veiled attack on the current 'first past the post' system) as coercion to ensure the populace maintain the regime on Starship UK, out of fear for its destruction nevertheless, but it also depicts a monarchy entrenched on the throne as a nationalist figurehead. Her 'constitutional' power works against her ever making the proper choice, abdicating her responsibility to herself, the people and the Star Whale. "I hope I keep the strength to make the right decision," she implores herself in the Tower of London video message. It is a decision to keep forgetting what she has learned every ten years of her reign. The Queen Elizabeth we see here is rather like her Tudor ancestor, a monarch protected by a nest of observers and spies with Hawthorne (a brief but effective performance from Terrence Hardiman) dutifully carrying out her orders as a Walsingham-like figure running his own branch of the secret service. The brotherhood of Winders and Smilers install Liz 10 as a perpetual and absolute monarch not legally or historically bound to any real form of constitution. "Be again the heart of this nation, untainted," she reminds herself on the video recording as history looks like repeating itself in service to misguided purposes. *The Beast Below* posits a choice between Britain maintaining its nationhood either as a republic or unifying under the allegedly politically neutral figure of the Queen ("Never voted. Not even a British subject"). The Winders and Smilers definitely have one protocol, 'God Save the Queen' because they believe she is the only one who can maintain the current course of Starship UK, but in this instance it is obvious that is from herself that she really needs saving. The relationship between the Doctor and the British monarchy has also been a running theme in the current revival and as Liz 10 reveals to the Doctor, "I've been brought up on the stories. My whole family was. The Doctor. Old drinking buddy of Henry XII. Tea and scones with Liz II. Vicky was a bit on the fence about you, weren't she? Knighted and exiled you on the same day. And so much for the Virgin Queen, you bad, bad boy." Again, this places the Doctor as a mythical figure at the heart of British consciousness and complements established continuity links in *Tooth and Claw, The Shakespeare Code* and *The End of Time.* Nationalism is also wittily commented on with more

34

references to Amy's Scottish heritage. When Amy suggests to Mandy that "Scotland's got to be here somewhere," she is told that they wanted their own ship. "Good for them. Nothing changes," concludes Amy. Later this is a counterpoint to the Doctor's own revelation to Amy about his Time Lord origins when Mandy asks him of the voting system, "How do you not know about this? Are you Scottish too?" He warns her, "Oh, I'm way worse than Scottish," and then confirms his pro-republican or pro-democracy stance by hitting the 'protest' button and fearlessly voting for regime change.

## "Welcome to London Market. You are being monitored"

The world of Starship UK is enmeshed in surveillance. As Amy and the Doctor arrive and begin to explore, Amy is suddenly overwhelmed by the realisation that she is in the future. On the plaza where the TARDIS has landed she can see up into the heavens and tannoy voices announce that she is in London Market and being watched. She has emerged from the TARDIS into a culture and society founded on, and fuelled, by secrets hidden from view, beyond the range of normal perception as much as the painful screams of the Star Whale are beyond the range of human hearing. The Doctor insists that Amy look deeper, beneath the surface, and describes the society around them as a "police state", nodding towards the strange automata standing in their booths that are dotted all around the market area and, as we see later, throughout the ship. The Doctor notices that the Smilers are clean and well maintained in contrast to the rest of the dirty, faded and crumbling plaza that he and Amy walk through. These automata have already been introduced to the audience in the pre-titles sequence, acting as OFSTED inspectors to a group of children in a classroom and rewarding each for their achievements of the day. These creatures, with their smiling faces, are not as benign as they seem. They police this state of 'bolted together' Britain, preventing crime, protecting areas of the ship from investigation, acting as educational arbiters and constantly on guard. They are mobile CCTVs, the grinding gears of a 29th Century 'Big Brother', dishing out punishments on the spot and attacking anyone who penetrates into restricted areas of the ship where surveillance of ordinary citizens has entered the mainstream of police activity, where reasonable search and seizure is probably a joke. Their smiling faces twist and turn into grimacing, almost screaming visages if they detect any form of failure or any kind of non-conformity. Timmy, a Blyton-esque name if ever there was one, has already been labelled as a 'bad boy' and has disappeared down into the depths of the ship.

The Smilers are in essence the offspring of Moffat's clockwork men as featured in *The Girl in the Fireplace*. He seems fascinated with the grind of machinery, the aesthetic of whirring, clicking mechanical gears and the idea of machines working in the service of a higher power. The Smilers resemble the fortune-teller, clown and laughing policeman automata of fairgrounds, ensconced and framed in their curtained booths. They clearly link to a childhood memory of visits to seaside resorts and fairgrounds where the young Moffat might have encountered these sinister machines in their coin-operated cases. The imagery of their grimacing, angry faces resembles certain figures depicted in some of the works by painter Francis Bacon. There are elements in his work that isolate the subject in space within frames, boxes, platforms and cage structures and this device is said to directly link to the photo booths that Bacon used to frequent in his 1950s and 1960s Soho heyday. The photographic images from the booths influenced many of his works such as *Head I-VI* and the infamous 'Screaming Popes'. Bacon's paintings obsessively depict open and screaming mouths, are an art of abstraction wherein he captured a powerful sense of post-war existential despair in the twisted distortions of the face and figure. As Andrew Graham Dixon comments in his *Sunday Telegraph* review of Tate Britain's 2008 retrospective, "Bacon was a carnivalesque dramatist of despair with an almost Baroque sense of colour and composition. His pictures might be fundamentally gloomy, but there is an exuberance about them too, a decadence and hilarity bordering on outright hysteria." A sense of exaggerated carnival is imbued in the grimacing and twisting faces of the Smilers, as is the abject of the horror film, something we touched upon in Chapter 1. Bacon's twisted faces and seated forms are imbued in the Smilers and the distorted human figures in their carnivalesque booths suggest a sympathy with his work where, as *The Socialist Review* offered in their review of the 2008 retrospective, "he uses cage structures to suggest his subjects are prisoners or creatures on display; the way, often, they are placed on plinths, or beds, with a sense of space around them, so that they appear served up like meat or specimens on a dish; or the way he used cubist forms, in his portraits, to knead the flesh round the bones of the skull. But if these are some of the means by which Bacon achieved his effects they leave the driving force of those effects unidentified." Bacon was something of a reactionary and, like the Smilers who patrol the ship and liquidate dissent, casting them into the abyss of the underclass on behalf of an absolute monarchy, "he was a kind of Nietzschean, adhering to a sort of 'exhilarated despair', and a positive supporter of social inequality as part of 'the texture of life'."

It is intriguing to note that the Smilers change their expressions from smile to frown to evil grimace by twisting their heads round. When Liz 10 is ordered to go to the Tower of London, yet another of those British icons that the series has used, she questions the Winder who has come to fetch her. In response, his human head twists round, to the sound of machinery whirring, to reveal the threatening visage of a Smiler. He is half human, half Smiler. A cyborg 'other' that, as Christine Cornea suggests in *Science Fiction Cinema: Between Fantasy and Reality*, is a "literal melding of human self with mechanical other... as a kind of self-projection or uncanny reflection of the self." The befanged visage of the Smiler and its double-headed cyborg identity brings together a number of symbols. There is that of Janus the Roman god who was an emblem of change and transition, the progression of past to future, of beginnings and endings, which suggests the cycle of the story, the rise and fall of an empire, the right or wrong decision made. Finally, there is the symbol of the contorted mouth, and Mark Dery in *The Pyrotechnic Insanitarium: American Culture on the Brink* offers that the scream itself, as also embodied in Edvard Munch's painting *The Scream*, is representational of the "introverted, alienated psychology of modernism." The Smilers are the embodiment, within the narrative, of what was once outside that is now inside, is now machine and flesh, Star Whale and spaceship, human and inhuman. They are totems of alienation where the silent crying of children and a broken political system capture the kind of despair that would become endemic in a society after a major period of conflict, economic collapse or a significant disaster.

### "It refuses to eat the children"

Once again, children and the child-centred narrative are central to the story in this second episode of the series. From the opening pre-titles sequence with the lined up school pupils receiving their adjudication from the Smiler, to the episode's conclusion where the Star Whale reaches out a friendly tentacle to Mandy Tanner and Amy understands the 'nature of the beast', children are key to interpreting the Doctor as protector of the innocent and Amy as innocence in respite. Amy is "still a child inside", and through her 'innocent' eyes, innocent that is to the complex moralities of living in space and time, the truth about Starship UK is revealed. *The Beast Below* also continues to develop the idea that the series is a dream fantasy, part of a story told to, and involving, children. The dream-like quality of *The Beast Below* is embellished with another very striking score from Murray Gold. Gold's approach here is to add more of a texture to the images rather than a recognisable set of themes. The tinkling, shimmering quality of the music here contains some dissonant fragments of Tchaikovsky's *Dance of the Sugar Plum Fairy* from *The Nutcracker* and the haunting glissando piano elements of *The Aquarium* by Saint-Saëns, from *The Carnival of the Animals* suite. Both are classical pieces that particularly appeal to children.

The milieu that the children exist in is a synthesis of iconography that most adults over 40 would recognise. The schoolroom looks like something created from an adult memory, populated by wooden school desks and end of lesson bells. Timmy clutches onto a leather satchel and Mandy is dressed in a simple gingham pique dress with a cardigan that might suggest she is growing up in a time of privation. If children fail their lessons the punishment is banishment 'below', evoking the spectre of Dickensian workhouses and satanic mills. We later see Mandy reunited with Timmy in the 'torture chamber' of the Tower of London where the children, rejected from being eaten by the Star Whale, seem to be allocated menial tasks by the Winders. Strangely, there does not seem to be an explanation as to why Timmy fails to recognise Mandy when they meet again. Before his journey 'below', Timmy is addressed by a young girl, speaking on screen from within a mock-up of the BBC's Test Card, with a curious Lewis Carroll-like rhyme. This is a 'Vator Verse' – Starship UK's version of 'Poems on the Underground' presumably – sponsored by a brand of candy-burgers (another emblem of the child-like way that two food favourites are combined, like 'fish-custard'). The girl speaks of a "horse and a man, above below; one has a plan but both must go; mile after mile, above beneath; one has a smile and one has teeth; though the man above might say hello; expect no love from the beast below." It is cryptic and clearly refers to the Star Whale, the Smilers and the topsy-turvy world in which they exist. It implies a Lewis Carroll-like universe where everything is transposed – man and beast, man and machine, adult and child – and it is symbolically stabilised at the end of the episode with Amy reciting a new verse over the floating image of Starship UK and the Star Whale: "In bed above, we're deep in sleep; while greater love lies further deep. This dream must end. This world must know; we all depend on the beast below." The verses bookend the episode, suggest a symbolic journey, out of a chaotic world and, by the conclusion, to a return to normality that implies the end of a bad dream. This is accompanied by Liz 10 announcing, "there will be no more secrets on Starship UK" and handing over her mask to Amy and the Doctor. The Lewis Carroll influence can also be seen in the sequences where Amy investigates the hole in the road and where Amy and the Doctor plunge down a tunnel into the mouth of the Star Whale, rather like Alice down the rabbit hole. The mouth of the Star Whale also recalls the heroic journeys of Jonah and Pinocchio into the belly of the great whale, and in 'the beast below' the Doctor and Amy come to understand Liz 10's observation of Starship UK, that "there's a darkness at the heart of this nation."

Central to the story is the transposition of the Doctor and the Star Whale. The comparison that Moffat provides is clearly his version of Davies's more angst-ridden psychological profile of the Doctor as a survivor of the Time War. It is an explanation and revelation of the Doctor's nature for both Amy and the audience at home, acting as a restatement of the character's heroic purpose in the series. Amy summarises with, "What if you were really old and really kind and alone? Your whole race dead, no future. What couldn't you do then? If you were that old, and that kind, and the very last of your kind, you couldn't just stand there and watch children cry." This again affirms the Doctor's raison d'être at the opening of the episode when he and Amy observe Mandy crying on the plaza and where he offers the caveat to Amy's earlier question in the TARDIS about being observers only. He "never interferes unless there's children crying," and by the conclusion of the episode her doubts about being detached from such situations, "like a wildlife documentary," are resolved.

Judging by Mandy's situation on Starship UK, children remain 'undigested' by the society they live in until they are of age to vote. The fear of being eaten by a witch, monster, ferocious wolf, wicked stepmother, or threatening animal has survived for centuries as a familiar theme in fairy tales and childhood fantasies. Starship UK's mythology suggests that children are asked to be good for fear of being consumed by the Star Whale. This fear, in reality, is unfounded when Timmy and other children are found alive in the Tower of London and Hawthorne confirms that the Star Whale's diet does not include the youngsters sent 'below' by the Smilers because they scored Zero on their test results. Again, what the script is not clear about in the episode is, when the Star Whale refuses to eat the children provided for it, what exactly the Winders get the children to do as slave labour. We see children in the Tower of London but what exactly are they doing down there? It is clear that adult protestors are not reprieved from such a fate and to be consumed, either by the fear of the beast below or by the beast itself, is therefore the end of hope. In *The Beast Below*, to 'forget', whether you're the Doctor, Liz 10 or Amy, is part of learning to be an adult. This fits in with the increasingly obvious use of the child's viewpoint that the new series has started to embrace and the childish need to forget the bad things we know we have done or our potential rejection from parents. In the plaza sequence the Doctor points out that the parents are so afraid of the secret at the heart of this society that they are unwilling to comfort a crying child.

The primal fear of being consumed, another symbol of orality that the series uses, again links into the sequences in the whale's mouth, of Amy and the Doctor being regurgitated, of the grinning visages of the Smilers that reflect the horror-film tropes and visual motifs about the monstrous carried forward from *The Eleventh Hour* and used throughout much of the *Doctor Who* series itself. The mouth of the whale is also likely to be a reference to the fairy-tale and mythological science fiction of *Star Wars* (1977), bearing a resemblance to the trash compactor scene in that film, and also a nod to the sequence in *The Empire Strikes Back* (1980) depicting the Millennium Falcon trapped in the belly of the space slug. *Star Wars* is also quoted in Liz 10's dialogue when she first meets the Doctor in the engine room of the ship as, in a manner akin to Princess Leia addressing Obi Wan Kenobi, she pleads, "Help us, Doctor. You're our only hope."

## "What's wrong with this picture?"

Whilst they observe the scanner screen in the TARDIS the Doctor describes Starship UK to Amy as, "The United Kingdom of England and Northern Ireland, all of it, bolted together, floating in the sky. It's Britain, but metal… living and laughing…and shopping," but when they finally leave the TARDIS to explore he immediately informs Amy of his observations to the contrary. "Isn't it wrong?" he asks her. Here, he wants her to emulate the same deductive reasoning borne out of careful observation that he demonstrated in *The Eleventh Hour*. Once again, the truth is in the detail. "Actually look," he demands. Looking and observing are central elements to the story, as much as they were in *The Eleventh Hour*. That first episode of the series emphasised the Doctor's ability to sift through the vast amounts of information presented to him to pinpoint a vital piece of data, depicted atypically in Adam Smith's stop motion sequence on Leadworth village green. Here, director Andrew Gunn creates a montage of Amy's experiences and observations on the ship to produce a more traditional flashback sequence. It is a deductive vision that pushes Amy into making a decision about the Star Whale's survival, the outcome of which redeems her in the eyes of the Doctor. It comes after a pivotal moment in the Tower of London where the Doctor berates Amy for ignoring the message she recorded. She had pleaded with herself to persuade the Doctor to leave but then voted to forget the secrets in the broadcast and turned off the message as it played. He believes she was wrong to do that even though she was not aware that she had done it because her mind had been wiped.

"You don't ever decide what I need to know," he demands. This of course is the serious repercussion of his jokey claim to her in the TARDIS that they are "observers" only and he is now angry that she did not properly heed his warning and that he has been forced into a choice between the survival of humanity or the continuing existence of the whale. He is also angry at the barbarism that the humans have inflicted on the Star Whale. There is a very pointed remark, "You're only human," levelled at her that condemns her along with those that manage Starship UK. It is his bleak view of humanity, showing they can often make terrible errors of judgement, which has been threaded into the revival of the series since the Ninth Doctor referred to the inhabitants of Earth as "stupid apes". However, it is only through Amy's act of remembering, as opposed to the act of forgetting this society asks of its citizens, that an alternative to the three options on the table – to kill the whale, to let it continue in agony or to destroy humanity – is offered. "Nobody human has anything to say to me today!" he shouts, clearly unable to see any other way forward. It is only when Amy notices the gentle greeting to Mandy from the Star Whale that we hear the Doctor in voiceover ask, "C'mon, use your eyes. Notice everything." The camera zooms into her eye, just as the camera zoomed into the Doctor's eye in *The Eleventh Hour*, to emphasise further the symbolic importance to the series of exterior and interior vision, and a whole sequence plays out that gathers together all the visual and aural evidence she needs. Not only is it as though the broadcast in the voting booth had not been forgotten after all, that Starship UK's real secret is being revealed to her, but it is also her flouting of the rule that the Doctor outlined at the start of the episode, one which he was never serious about himself: "In fact – thing one – we are observers only." She is an observer but an active rather than a passive one.

The analogue of the Star Whale to the Doctor is very heavily signposted and lacks subtlety through over-repetition, suggesting the director and writer were not confident the audience would get the analogy. It seems odd considering director Andrew Gunn has used much sleight of hand throughout the episode to either throw the audience off guard with ambiguity, as in the voting booth scene, or defy logic to keep the Star Whale secret where, in the opening scene, even the TARDIS scanner does not detect it as Amy and the Doctor view the ship on the screen. Arguably, the episode suggests the Star Whale is tethered to the underside of the ship and is only released after Amy presses the 'abdicate' button but this is again something that remains unclear. The Smilers are also promoted at the top of the episode as the 'monster of the week' but do not actually feature in the episode very much as traditional *Doctor Who* monsters. Their presence and origins are ambiguous and we never really understand what they are beyond their role as threatening guardians, as tools of the state. The defining virtue of kindness, in the Doctor and the Star Whale, is also something clearly missing from the British residents of Starship UK and we do not get a sense of how the adult citizens relate to their plight. Perhaps Moffat is also tapping into the notions of Mervyn Peake's own phantasmagorical depiction of England, in *Gormenghast* for example, as a decaying citadel where the oppressive weight of tradition blots out any form of empathy. However, it does reflect a difference between Moffat and Davies in the way that supporting characters are formed within, and support, the power of the narrative. Davies often used them to underline the emotional impact of disastrous situations on 'ordinary' people. *The Beast Below*, a story that particularly focuses on the plight of the citizen under the heel of a harsh regime, fails, in some respect, to communicate the psychological and emotional consequences on other human beings simply because the 'ordinary' citizen is rarely seen. Here, a girl in a nightie, a schoolgirl, a black Cockney Queen ("I'm the bloody Queen, mate. Basically, I rule") and a bow-tied, gangly-limbed Time Lord remove that weight of tradition from a population conspicuous by its absence in the episode. Sophie Okonedo's performance as Liz 10, particularly in the final scenes where the chirpy Cockney mask really does fall away and she is genuinely horrified by what she has done in the name of duty and loyalty, is one of the highlights of the episode. *The Beast Below* sadly says that we would rather prefer our society to develop off the back of the suffering of others and that we endlessly repeat this exploitation by forgetting and not protesting. The lull of warm and fuzzy nostalgia filling the minds of those on Starship UK, that disguises a heavy-handed "big government" and that harks back to an illusory "you've never had it so good" culture, underlines the uncomfortable accusation that anything strange and alien has to be exploited as a virtue of imperial power. Moffat's script does ask some questions about post-imperial British identity and nationalism and the events in *The Beast Below* reflect Chris Rojek's ideas in *Brit-Myth*, where he sees "British values as slippery abstractions. Many people find it hard to identify with the ideals of free speech, identity and tolerance. Often it is only when these ideals are infringed or violated that they become a *cause celebre*."

This theme, and how it reflects the configuration of a post-war British identity, extends into the following episode *Victory of the Daleks*. Unusually for the current series, the next episode is previewed in the final scene in the TARDIS through the use of an overlapping story mechanism that has not been seen to this extent in the series since the early 1960s.

Normally, new episodes are previewed just before the end titles and are formatted as specific 'next time' segments. As *The Beast Below* concludes, the Doctor chats to Churchill on the phone and behind the Prime Minister looms the familiar shadow of a Dalek. Finally, the TARDIS dematerialises and rushes to his aid whilst Amy narrates the closing rhyme. The final shot is of what will become the familiar reiteration of the series's major visual symbol. It is the crack in time, the crack in Amy's bedroom wall, appearing wherever they go and here shown on the hull of Starship UK.

## Chapter Three

# VICTORY OF THE DALEKS

Written by: Mark Gatiss
Directed by: Andrew Gunn
First broadcast: 17 April 2010

"What does hate look like, Amy?"

The aftermath of the Second World War looms like a shadow over *Doctor Who*. The 'collective memory' of the era, including the trauma of the Blitz and the bombing of Hiroshima and Nagasaki, can be found in sublimated form in the earliest of the *Doctor Who* stories to feature the Daleks. In both *The Daleks* and *The Dalek Invasion of Earth* the Doctor's oldest enemies can be seen in their purest forms. The former tells a tale of nuclear war and the survivors – the Daleks and the Thals – who are placed in binary opposition to each other in its aftermath. The Daleks have been mutated by the effects of the war and protect themselves in mobile armour, whilst the Thals are blond, peace-loving humanoids. The story rehearses the fears of a nuclear conflict fresh in the minds of viewers that had experienced the atomic bombs that brought the war to a conclusion in 1945, the tensions of the Cuban Missile Crisis of 1962 and the xenophobia fuelled by a drive towards racial purity projected by the Nazi rise to power in Europe. The latter serial restages a devastated London with its population traumatised by the Blitz (viewers at the time were still witnessing the clearing up of bombsites in the early 1960s) and a fantasy projection of what a Nazi-occupied Britain might actually feel and look like. As writer Mark Gatiss himself summarised in an interview with *SFX* in April 2010, "They [the Daleks] are, weirdly, an inherently World War II feeling creature. The Nazi connection is there, and also the world of the early '60s is very heavily post-War – they feel like they belong to it. There's a nice match to it."

During the 1960s and 1970s, in the classic series of *Doctor Who*, Dalek stories tended to underplay many of these initial ideas and themes and instead the Daleks were positioned as a generic race of evil aliens bent on galactic dominance. Their appearance in the *TV Century 21* comic between 1965-7 echoes Frank Hampson's *Dan Dare* strips, and this aesthetic and their role as conquerors of time and space are further expressed on television in *The Chase* and *The Daleks' Master Plan*. The two Dalek films made in 1965 and 1966 also take the pulp form of the comic book as the basis for adapting the first two Terry Nation serials and the Technicolor, widescreen clashes between the Doctor and the Daleks position this relationship firmly within a children's action-adventure story

45

context. As we will see later, the influence of the two Dalek films is integral to how the Daleks appear in *Victory of the Daleks* in 2010. With *The Power of the Daleks* and *The Evil of the Daleks* in the late 1960s it is David Whittaker's influence that sees the Daleks elevated from their comic book machinations to make a brief return to the themes of their genetic inheritance, presaging much of the Dalek civil war narratives of the mid to late 1980s. *Victory of the Daleks* quotes extensively from both serials, with the camouflaged, Union Jack Daleks paraphrasing the claim of "I am your servant" from the former as "I am your soldier" in the reveal on the rooftop of the Cabinet War Rooms and masking their crafty behaviour by serving tea and doing the filing whilst prowling round corridors up to no good. The Doctor, as played by Matt Smith, also reiterates "the final end" as uttered by Patrick Troughton's Doctor from the latter serial as he too prepares to witness the premature destruction of the Daleks. The Dalek stories of the early to mid 1970s such as *Day of the Daleks*, *Planet of the Daleks* and *Death to the Daleks* are more a reflection of the complex operations and guerrilla style tactics in the theatre of the Vietnam conflict. Aptly, *Planet of the Daleks* is set on the jungle planet Spiridon and *Death to the Daleks* plays out much of its chase narrative within the framework of the planet Exxilon's ancient culture and temple-like city, evoking the ongoing war in Cambodia. In all three serials humans or humanoids are involved in galactic wars and are pitched against the Daleks in a desire to expunge the influence of their dogma and ideology. It is not until *Genesis of the Daleks* that Terry Nation's original themes are more blatantly married to Nazi ideology and iconography, and to the use of science as a tool to prop up a xenophobic, racist and totalitarian rule. The serial also plays out as if we are witnessing both the last days of Hitler struggling to ensure the survival of the Aryan legacy of his party *and* the bitter end of the Vietnam War. This decades-long war, coincidentally concluding in April 1975 just as the six episodes of the serial were being transmitted, is a subtext in the story "microcosmically reflecting upon tendencies in the viewer's world," as Jonathan Bignell and Andrew O'Day observe in their book *Terry Nation*.

*Victory of the Daleks* can be seen foremost as an attempt to reset Dalek continuity back to these 1960s and 1970s roots, having been further complicated with the binary oppositions between the Daleks and the Time Lords in Russell T. Davies's saga of the Time War, and proposes a cleansing of the vestiges of the current series's proposition of a Doctor psychologically driven by survivor guilt versus Dalek refugees and insurgents created by the War. This scenario has been driven by, in the first instance, a racially impure army created by an Emperor with a God complex in *The Parting of the Ways*, the activities of a terrorist cell – the Cult of Skaro – in *Doomsday* and *Daleks in Manhattan/Evolution of the Daleks* and, in the final instance, by Davros instigating a jihad against the whole of reality during *The Stolen Earth/Journey's End*. Russell T. Davies even postulated in the *Doctor Who Annual 2006* that the Time War saga had itself been provoked by the Time Lords and with respect to *Genesis of the Daleks* he suggested, "The Time Lords fired the first shot." It would seem that Steven Moffat and the writer of *Victory of the Daleks*, Mark Gatiss, both decided that this particular iteration of Dalek history had run its course and to close it down in favour of a new one. As I suggested in Chapter 1, the commissioning of Series Five and the installation of a new production team has provoked a revisionist agenda for the established 'icons' of the series, including the TARDIS, the theme music and opening titles and now an opportunity to reboot Dalek history and continuity. Hence, Gatiss creates a "new paradigm" for the Daleks, much as Terry Nation and Robert Holmes had set out to redefine the story of the origins of the Daleks in *Genesis of the Daleks*, where Dalek history was also set on a new course. In *Victory of the Daleks* there is a parallel between the writer and production team's desire for change and the new Daleks' own defiant extermination of their smaller, gold and khaki Time War namesakes. "The restoration of the Daleks," barks the white Supreme Dalek, inviting us to complete a chain of similarly titled stories that ran from *Resurrection of the Daleks* to *Remembrance of the Daleks*, whilst also witnessing the gunning down of its impure brothers as "the resurrection of the master race." As the new Daleks destroy the old, where the unclean are cleansed, the story pulls continuity back to themes of 'racial hygiene' linked to the eugenics programs of the Nazis that sought to eliminate defective or impure citizens. The irony in *Victory of the Daleks* is that prior to the Dalek Progenitor's creation of these purest of pure Daleks, their Union Jack-wearing Time War cousins are blasting the Luftwaffe's finest, and by extension removing the Nazis, that they ideologically relate to, from the skies above England.

Although the story uses a number of established and successful tropes to portray the Daleks' cunning and deviousness – picking up on *The Power of the Daleks* as a primary example of how duplicitous they can be – *Victory of the Daleks* is saddled with a contrived subplot as a mechanism to establish the new series's boldly coloured, shiny replacements. It is interesting to see that the Doctor's role as binary opposite to the Daleks is used as the primary device to trigger this re-engineering. It is not until the Doctor cries, "I am the Doctor and you are the Daleks!" that this opposition, this "testimony" can be confirmed, the very link that has always been an element of the series's own long history. The Daleks bait and set a trap for the Doctor because he would appear to be their only salvation through a declaration of his true, pure identity in relation to their mongrel origins. Seen as impure and tainted, they are unable to start the Dalek Progenitor and for some unfathomable reason the voice recognition and activation of the Progenitor will only register when this testimony is produced. It must validate that they are Daleks, that they are his sworn enemy because only the Doctor can claim it to be so. It seems a very complicated plan for the Daleks: to plant a robot agent, Edwin Bracewell, in Churchill's bunker to 'create' the Ironside combat versions of the Daleks; for them to await the arrival of the Doctor which is totally dependent on a phone call from Churchill; then get him angry enough to state the obvious and use a recording of his voice to activate the Progenitor. Beneath these contrivances, there are some interesting themes about ideology and nationalism as forces that shape decisions about life and death. The suggestion here is that the Doctor gives 'birth' to the new Daleks as a mythological reversal to his continuing determination to halt their genesis, as first seen in one of the most iconic moments of *Doctor Who*, the "if I touch these two wires" speech from *Genesis of the Daleks*. His hatred of the Daleks drives the Doctor throughout most of *Victory of the Daleks* and here it becomes a form of self-fulfilling prophecy whereby the Doctor, trying to evidence their true nature to Churchill, Amy and Bracewell, allows his hatred of them to signify as the one thing that defines them. The Doctor is tricked into giving his greatest enemy a new lease of life and the upper hand in the narrative. This underlines Mark Gatiss's own proposition for the episode, from the March 2010 edition of *Doctor Who Magazine*, when he states: "the reason it's called *Victory of the Daleks* is cos they win. They *win*." It is an ironic reversal of the established 'Doctor always defeats the Daleks' trope that the majority of previous serials and stories have usually employed.

## "Broadsword calling Danny Boy"

*Victory of the Daleks* also provides a discourse on the respective ideologies the Daleks and their human opponents use to either disrupt or protect the process of democracy. The original series of *Doctor Who* has made no bones about associating the Daleks with Nazi ideology and iconography. It has often reflected in its stories the after-effects of the Second World War on late 1950s and early 1960s British society and culture. From 1963 through to the mid-1970s, the spectre of the war and how it shaped British consciousness and culture continued to be played out in the series as well as the deep fears borne of the then escalating Cold War. As late as *Genesis of the Daleks* in 1975, writer Terry Nation and script editor Robert Holmes were still blatantly using visual signifiers of the war such as uniforms, the Iron Cross on the costume for Nyder, the setting of most of the drama in underground bunkers and the imagery of gas-masked soldiers haunting the churned up battlegrounds of conflict between the Thals and the Kaleds. In *Remembrance of the Daleks*, the Daleks are also associated with the post-war rise of fascism and racism, with the legacy of Oswald Mosley extended into the character of Rattigan and societal attitudes towards immigrants in the London of 1963. One of the key issues with *Victory of the Daleks* is not the alliance of the Daleks to a Second World War context which as Gatiss has indicated was always a given. It is the presentation of the war itself. Gatiss has done his research and in an interview with *SFX* in April 2010 he stated his intentions for the script:

> "I've certainly tried to be careful in terms of taste. It's not like Agincourt – it's in living memory and it's a very strong and vivid

memory. So I wanted to have all the fun of a bank holiday war movie without taking the piss. And I have to say, in my research for it my respect for the people who went through the war only increased even further. It's very hard to get any of that research into the episode because you don't want to look didactic, but I was very careful to try and make it feel that the real war was still going on, and that it didn't just stop for a fortnight to have a bit of fun in space!"

Evidently, Gatiss tries to emulate a genre of British war movie, one that would traditionally have been shown in a holiday period. The likes of *The Great Escape* (1963), *Where Eagles Dare* (1968), *The Dam Busters* (1954) and *633 Squadron* (1964) are all films that would eventually come to epitomise this genre and viewing tradition and the "Broadsword to Danny Boy" call sign used in the Spitfire assault is a direct lift from *Where Eagles Dare*. Much as many of them were constructed from actual events and incidents, in the main they are framed as action-adventure films that seek to rework wartime memories into popular culture. *Victory of the Daleks* follows in this tradition with its gung-ho heroics, dogfights, stiff upper lips and the 'backroom boys' saving the day, but it very rarely troubles the viewer with the real horrors of the Blitz, the effects of it and the war on the home front. In choosing to be less didactic about the subject matter, *Victory of the Daleks* has only minor success in attempting to convey the human hardship and sacrifices of the times. The type of films Gatiss references all emerged during the Cold War period as the Soviets and Americans issued threats and counter-threats to one another. The likelihood of winning any war that resulted would be at the exclusivity of Britain, as the propagandist revival of Empire, which the war had used to prop up national identity, had already diminished. These films could be seen as, as Neil Rattigan explains in his essay 'Last Gasp of the Middle Class: British War Films of the 1950s' in *Reviewing British Cinema 1900-1992*, "the myth of the British at war, which emphasised the 'British can take it' syndrome and a certain masochistic satisfaction in hardship." *Victory of the Daleks* draws very heavily on 'war as nostalgia' and the mythological idea that the Second World War was, as Rattigan suggests, "The last time in which the British stood together in their various social positions, united in common goals and community." It also uses the nostalgic power of the Cabinet War Rooms setting and the vistas of a war-torn London to underline this mythology. The episode seems intent on maintaining this view, repackaging the dominant ideology and iconography of the period at the expense of realism, certainly the realism of suffering that those fighting the war endured. In the pre-titles sequence to the episode, Gatiss attempts to address the human cost of the conflict by showing us Breen, one of the service women working in the Cabinet War Rooms – the character's name a little nod to *Quatermass and the Pit* (1958-9) – worried about her fiancé Reg going into battle against the Luftwaffe. Later, Churchill sees that she is "down in the dumps" but emphasises to her the need to concentrate on the action of the day. It is only at the end of the episode that we learn anything more about this situation, with Churchill in a matter-of-fact manner explaining to Amy, as they observe Breen crying and being consoled by a colleague, that Reg was "shot down over the Channel." It is rather a tokenistic registration of the losses incurred and we know nothing about Breen or any of the other military personnel in the story, making it exceptionally difficult to emotionally engage with their plight. Whilst Gatiss seeks to balance realism with taste, and with transmission on an early Saturday evening obviously requiring that balance, it is interesting to contrast his use of characters to articulate the horrors of war with those that Moffat used in *The Empty Child* in 2005. Moffat, through the central character of Nancy, a teenager terrified of revealing that the brother she cares for is in fact her young son, better articulated something of the terrible lives and hardships that orphaned children endured during the Blitz and its impact on the so-called 'dead end kids' who had prematurely returned from evacuation or remained behind in the cities.

*Victory of the Daleks* uneasily, and rather contentiously, assumes the mantle of the 'Dunkirk spirit' that continues to epitomise the consensus view of the British at war, at a time when our society has shifted away from this collectivist accord into an era where the individual is of more importance within a post-Thatcherite age of enterprise, privatisation and free competition. The danger here is that its use of this 'spirit' simply regurgitates the many sources of propaganda that were in fact part of the era's consensus creating process. It joins Pathe News, Picture Post, the radio and cinema of the time in their promotion of a certain frame of citizenship and nationhood. In 'You and I – All of Us Ordinary People: Renegotiating 'Britishness' in Wartime' in Nick Hayes and Jeff Hill's *Millions Like Us? British Culture in the Second World War*, John Baxendale indicates that despite the consensus of national identity "the overall effect of the war was to prop up an Imperial power which was already in irreversible decline." Going back to Gatiss's comment in the *SFX* interview about his use of the Second World War background ("It's not like Agincourt – it's in living memory and it's a very strong and vivid memory") it is hard not to find the episode's articulation of Britishness as a living memory within the context of Empire as somewhat naïve. The memory he refers to is not necessarily a memory shared by the different generations and communities now watching *Doctor Who*. The depiction of the Blitz and Churchill's command attempts to revive, perhaps in a parodic way, a nationalism that now seems much at odds with the multi-cultural and multi-ethnic Britain of 2010. Chris Rojek proposes in his book *Brit-Myth* that there are deeply polarised views about the legacy of Empire and that "nations have the strongest sense of themselves as nations only when they are imperilled. In Britain, the key moments in this respect occurred when the nation regarded itself as white, Christian and implacably affiliated to Anglo-Saxon/Celtic values." Furthermore he believes the opposite of Gatiss's view is now in the ascendant: "the imagery that appeals to national virtue in the face of Nazi fascism seems as remote and meaningless as Agincourt. The nation of 1940 is scarcely recognisable today."

It is interesting to note that *Victory of the Daleks* was transmitted during a politically volatile month in Britain. The election campaign for 2010 was underway and the depiction of Britishness in the episode became part of the narrative of national identity that each party was desperately attempting to map out. From being an event in which cultural production occupied a key role, for reasons of propaganda, the war itself has become a cultural product, especially embedded in popular culture, in the post-war world. Much of the reworking of wartime memories into popular culture, especially the invocation of a 'Britain Can Do It' nationalism, often acquires further meaning in moods of national uncertainty and change at specific historical moments. As Cameron, Brown and Clegg invited the British to cast their votes, the country was in deep recession, it was a 'broken Britain' according to the Conservatives and the *Radio Times* decided to feature the 'new paradigm' Daleks, in red, blue and yellow variations, on three exclusive covers declaring 'Vote Dalek!' in the week of the episode's transmission. In its coverage of the 2005 election and to promote the Series One episode *Dalek*, the *Radio Times* previously used images of the Daleks patrolling the Houses of Parliament. In 2010 the newly redesigned Daleks, assigned their party colours, could be seen again, dominating the iconic London landmark but this time on a cover augmented with searchlights and diving Spitfires. The image also chimes with the series's own mythology, of the Daleks crossing Westminster Bridge in the 'what if the Nazis had invaded' proposition of *The Dalek Invasion of Earth* in 1964. At the end of April, The Green Party also got in on the act and released an election campaign video that playfully demarcated the differences in ideologies between parties whilst also offering an ironic reversal of the Daleks' hatred for anything unlike them. It depicted a screen divided into four quadrants; three quadrants contained a coloured Dalek (red, blue, or yellow), and the fourth contained a green rabbit. The tune of the *Sesame Street* song "One of These Things is Not Like the Others" played on video. As the tune finished, the rabbit shot and destroyed the Daleks with red laser beams from its eyes. In *Victory of the Daleks* this continuum of propagandist imagery is further embellished with Churchill's reveal of a wartime poster showing the Ironside Dalek surrounded by searchlights and a 'To Victory!' exclamation.

Media production both within and without the framework of the episode uses the myth of the war to represent a moral certainty that seems all too absent in the election time clash between Right and Left but one that, as Jose Harris suggests in *The World War Two Reader*, in her chapter 'War and Social History: Britain and the Home Front in the Second World War,' does not really speak to the "sheer diversity of the wartime experience of different individuals, different localities, different organisations and different social groups beyond the march of nationwide social democracy." Yet again this series uses motifs from popular culture, especially paying homage to *Star Wars* (1977) where the Spitfire dogfight with the Dalek saucer above the Earth is very reminiscent of certain visual effects sequences in Lucas's film. The irony is, of course, that the film's 'Death Star trench run' scenes were inspired by the heritage of Second World War cinema in both *The Dam Busters* and *633 Squadron* and the bombing runs shown in both films. When the Dalek saucer finally takes off down the time corridor the sequence is also highly reminiscent of the Millennium Falcon's jump into hyperspace, complete with a stretching, elongating star field. These sequences are made more evocative through Murray Gold's use of fittingly rousing music that is firmly in the vein of *The Dam Busters* and *633 Squadron* composers Eric Coates and Ron Goodwin, respectively.

## "We will return"

Perhaps the most controversial element of the story is the redesign of the Daleks. It would be an understatement to say that the new design of such iconic figures has divided viewers and fans alike. As *The Sun* reported on 19 April 2010 in "New-look coloured Daleks 'like toys'," the reaction from fans, in particular, has been vociferous and likens the latest incarnation to, amongst other objects of derision, Teletubbies, Power Rangers, Fisher-Price toys, Ikea kitchenware and disabled toilets. "A poll on the biggest *Who* fan site, Gallifrey Base, gave the new look a big thumbs down," states the article and the reaction is to an extent understandable. The Daleks are one of the very few icons of the series that have remained more or less unchanged throughout the tenure of the original series and its revival in 2005. Both the TARDIS exterior and the Daleks have endured as design statements within the series, undergoing the slightest of variations over time but maintaining their easily identifiable and original visual cohesiveness.

The original Raymond Cusick design is a triumph of modernist 1960s stylisation. It epitomises the way that streamline design stood for mobility, speed, efficiency and luxury, all concepts that were identified with modernity and a positive vision of the future. Cusick was probably inspired by a generation of designers born in the United States at the end of the 1920s that included Raymond Loewy, Norman Bel Geddes, Henry Dreyfuss, Harold van Doren and Walter Dorwin Teague. The new breed of industrial designers in the 1930s were more open to the suggestions of science and practical technologies, but were less restricted by aesthetic traditions. Concepts such as speed and change, exploration of new materials, together with new modes of transport and appliances were common to their aesthetic that in turn influenced many science fiction writers, illustrators and filmmakers. It is not therefore too great a leap to see the link from the streamlined designs of Bel Geddes, Loewy et al. directly influencing Saturday morning serials such as *Flash Gordon* (1936-40) and, later, Frank Hampson's artwork for comic strips such as *Dan*

*Dare* and Cusick's design thinking for *Doctor Who*. The Dalek extends the streamlined machine age motif and incorporates a range of aesthetic influences from design of the 1950s, particularly design influenced by the early Atomic Age. An anthropomorphic quality is evoked in the skirt, with its organic-looking bumps, and the accompanying gun stick and plunger arms. This mirrors the Catherine Winkler and Richard Whipple Predicta television set from 1959, where the set is poised on what looks like two feet and topped with a screen resembling an enormous eye. The series of bumps that stud the skirt are also perhaps an homage to the way plastic was then being used for packaging, particularly the pharmaceutical industry and its introduction of blister packs for medication, and also to Earl Tupper, who found a way to mould polyethylene plastic into bowls, dishes, and cocktail shakers, creating Tupperware. The Dalek design inhabits an era that, as the *New York Times: Art Review – Form Followed Fission Through The Atomic Age* on 26 October 2001 reported, "makes use of organic forms popular in the decades after World War II – especially the human figure and its components, but also boomerang, plant, teardrop, kidney, amoeboid, cellular and mushroom-cloud shapes, along with those of molecular structures – in mediums from highbrow painting to popular consumer products."

Cusick's legendary design is therefore an amalgamation of influences. It embodies the machine age streamlining of American design in the 1930s and 1940s and incorporates the legacy of the Bauhaus and the futurism of the new Atomic Age, both aesthetically and philosophically. Cusick's genius lay in making a mobile bomb shelter-cum-tank both an object of curvilinear beauty and of stark, elemental terror. It is also ironic that post-war industrial design produced by a generation of exiled Europeans in America would go on to provide the inspiration for the design of a creature that represented the very fascism they had escaped from. As Piers Britton and Simon Barker observe in *Reading Between Designs: Visual Imagery and the Generation of Meaning in The Avengers, The Prisoner and Doctor Who*, "their squat forms were full of latent menace" and their relative size remained unchanged for decades with only minor variations in colour, sizes of fenders, angles of skirt, gun, plunger and eye stalk detailing. Most importantly of all, the original design was effective, attractive and had fluidity to its configuration. Britton and Barker also see the Daleks possessing "the power of stylish design to excite – and therefore to sell." It is acknowledged that the introduction of the Daleks into the series in 1963 made *Doctor Who* a popular success that endures to this day and sparked the 'Dalekmania' of the early to mid-1960s that generated a whole merchandising industry.

It was the original design configuration that the 2005 revival of *Doctor Who* faithfully returned to in the creation of the Dalek props for the series that would feature in all the Dalek stories until 2009. Concept designer Matthew Savage was instructed by Russell T. Davies to retain the classic Dalek silhouette but to 'beef it up' and the design therefore incorporated rivets and machine elements. In *Doctor Who – The Inside*

*Story*, model effects expert Mike Tucker explains further: "Russell was also sharp enough to know that if the design of the Dalek changed too much, was too radically different to what had gone before, it might end up looking more like a toy and less like the most fearsome thing in the universe." A prophetic quote it would seem because that is one of the criticisms levelled at the new Daleks making their debut in *Victory of the Daleks*. Since the return of the series, *Doctor Who* has been transformed into a global, multi-million pound brand, a cross-platform transmedia storytelling experience with an associated merchandising industry that constantly needs feeding with new ideas and formats. Many fans see the development of the new Daleks as a cynical exercise to sell more products and more toys and it was also noted by the *Doctor Who* site *Kasterborous* on 30 April 2010, and by many other sites and forums that month, that *Private Eye* had alleged "in return for investment in this year's series, BBC Worldwide suggested that a new Dalek would come in very useful – and in return it is getting nothing less than a full set of entirely redesigned models in day-glo colours. The red, blue, yellow, orange and white Daleks – collect 'em all because your kids are going to nag you to death to do so! – will be unveiled in this Saturday's episode and will appear in shops soon afterwards."

Obviously, BBC Worldwide are interested in commercially exploiting the *Doctor Who* brand but the allegation from *Private Eye* does throw up some interesting questions on how much and how far the commercial arm of the BBC should influence the direction of the series and the creation and design of one of its most iconic assets. Is *Doctor Who* now becoming nothing more than the BBC's version of those other television goldmines *Transformers* (1984-7) or *He-Man and the Masters of the Universe* (1983-5) where, as Katalin Lustyik describes in 'Going Global? Children's Television in Transition in Central-Eastern Europe' – *European Film and Media Culture*, such programmes are used "as a centre of gravity to drive the development and growth... of consumer products such as toys, merchandising, home videos and on-line business"? Considering the *Private Eye* suggestion that the multi-coloured Daleks are simply toy collectibles infers that the design of the new Daleks also aligns itself with the latest range and colours of, for example, Apple's iPods. Nick Briggs, the actor who provides the voices of the Daleks, interviewed by Nick Griffiths on the *Radio Times* website said, "They're so brightly coloured and bouncy and delightful, they almost look good enough to eat." This also indicates a number of other factors at work in the way the Daleks are redefined in the Moffat era of the series. As well as the allegiances to brand development where the Daleks are aimed at a market driven by children as consumers, the production itself seems to view the new Daleks as a fusion of childhood nostalgia (probably inherent among fans within the production team such as Moffat, Gatiss and Briggs) for the Daleks featured in the Technicolor widescreen Dalek films of the 1960s, and the childlike oral gratification that the Daleks now seem to generate and that is also corroborated by designer Peter McKinstry in an interview in *Doctor*

*Who Magazine* in April 2010: "I think the new colours were influenced by the films too. Steven's note was that they should make kids want to go up and lick them." This begs the question as to when and why did the Daleks transform themselves from one of the most terrifyingly evil creatures in the universe into a bag of sweets. Oddly enough this child's point of view of the Daleks chimes with many of the other themes in the series and it feels as if Moffat wants to shoehorn them into his concept of it as dark fantasy for children. The emphasis on 'devouring' the new Daleks suggests parity with the use of child-friendly food within the series itself ('fish-custard', 'candy-burgers') that is further symbolised here by the Doctor's bluff against the Daleks with the Jammie Dodger biscuit. It also connects well with the Fourth Doctor's own threat in 1977's *The Face of Evil*, "Now drop your weapons, or I'll kill him with this deadly jelly baby!" The series has also been no stranger to glorying in a sense of Roald Dahl-like childishness in its stories, and many would point to the burping bin in *Rose* and the farting Slitheen in *Aliens of London* as the latest examples, but to whom these are addressed and at which audience the programme is aimed became even more of a moot point in the week leading up to the transmission of the finale episode *The Pandorica Opens*. In the question and answer session after his BAFTA Annual Television Lecture on 15 June 2010, Stephen Fry criticised *Doctor Who* as an example of the infantalism of British television. "The only drama the BBC will boast about are *Merlin* and *Doctor Who* which are fine but they're children's programmes. They're not for adults. And they're very good children's programmes, don't get me wrong, they are wonderfully written... but they are not for adults. They are like a chicken nugget. Every now and again we all like it. Every now and again." Bearing this context in mind, arguably the new Daleks could be seen as the latest variation of chicken nuggets being sold back to the child and adult audiences of *Doctor Who*.

Understanding the design of the new Daleks offers an intriguing insight into the use of nostalgia and retro in postmodern culture. Making them bigger, dominant, taller, to apparently match Matt Smith's eyeline, is not a bad idea but clearly rejects the established principle that their threat lies in the depiction of them as squat, mean concentrated lumps of evil feeding off their hatred of the unlike. The lines of the original design become distorted as the skirt section is pushed in and upwards. The thick base they move upon is reminiscent of the 1960s film Daleks, and replaces the tapered, angular and smaller base of the 2005 design. The original Daleks used to point like an arrowhead, giving the design a sense of aggressive kinetic motion. The latest design is more of a blunt instrument with the skirt panels now a series of thicker, punched out sections, rather like prefabricated car design sections. It is worth noting that the rear of the Dalek now resembles the spoiler of a sports car with a series of vents enclosed in a slightly hooded assembly. Until 2010, the panels and skirt ordinarily flowed straight up into the shoulder section and the encircling band of iconic slatted panels. A new and fairly ugly, dark grey plastic-looking shoulder section, housing the new sucker arm and gun, runs around the Dalek's body and now hangs over the skirt in a rather unflattering 'muffin-top' effect suggesting an over-spilling waist-line. Instead of a design that flows naturally from the skirt to the dome of the Dalek, the lines are interrupted by, and clash with, the bulging shoulder section. The effect this has is to make the creature look as if it has hunched shoulders and is about to topple forwards. The removal of the slatted detailing from the shoulders is obviously a referral back to the early 1960s television version of the Dalek but it is a perfunctory one at best because it does not balance with the skirt section and the overall effect, particularly when viewed from side on, is of a Dalek with a bad back. The sucker and gun emplacements stick out, no longer recessed within the shoulder, suggesting a look based on, ironically enough, the Louis Marks toy Daleks of the 1960s.

The neck and head are now pushed forward, completely out of line with the sweep of the skirt, emphasising the effect that the whole Dalek is about to pitch forward. Overall, all extraneous detail such as rivets, bolts, slats, struts and sharp angles have been removed altogether or smoothed away. Wearing their bright colour schemes, they appear less threatening and the whole redesign suggests a radical rethinking of the Dalek, shifting it from 'armoured tank' to 'nippy hatchback'. Big, in this case, is not always better and whilst I understand designer Peter McKinstry's desire to remove all the rivets and bolts from the 2005 design because they suggest something 'hand built', I believe the design the production team has come up with breaks up the classic silhouette of Cusick's original and, as Russell T. Davies warned Mike Tucker back in 2005, if you go too far you end up with a toy. The design incorporates a nostalgia for the 1960s that suggests a retro sensibility described by Ryan Moore in *Sells Like Teen Spirit: Music, Youth Culture and Social Crisis* as having "no qualms about taking objects or images out of their original context and reusing them inconsistently in the present." If the new design of the Dalek is a retro-inspired and nostalgic imitation of the original Cusick design of the 1960s as well as its simulations in the Dalek films and toys of the period, there is a danger that the 'new paradigm' introduced in *Victory of the Daleks* is simply fulfilling Jean Baudrillard's view of retro, in *Simulacra and Simulations*, as "the death pangs of the real and of the rational."

## "If wishes were kisses?"

The pre-titles sequence is a flurry of Cabinet War Room activity as the Germans begin their attack and the RAF scrambles their aircraft in response. Sirens are wailing. Someone wishes they could be turned off. "If wishes were kisses?" the service woman Breen operating the radio quickly responds, suggesting that it will be unlikely and that she would be a very lucky girl if all their wishes could come true. Interestingly, this idea of wishes and desires being granted, planted rather subtly here, is developed fully in the denouement of the episode. Bracewell, assisted by Amy, will perhaps be the recipient of such wishes as he recalls his unrequited love for Dorabella and his humanity begins to emerge. The new Daleks, threatening to destroy London with the Oblivion Continuum in Bracewell's body, are preparing to leave. The Doctor is desperately trying to 'defuse' this living bomb. Bracewell has already been revealed as a man-machine constructed by the Daleks as part of the lure for the Doctor. His role in the story has so far been as an analogue to the many 'backroom' boys, the boffins and scientists that enabled the defeat of the Nazis during the Second World War. He is the story's version of various scientists and engineers: Barnes Wallis, who as well as inventing the 'bouncing' bomb of *The Dam Busters* fame also designed airships and the Wellington bomber; Sir Robert Watson-Watt who worked on radar at Bawdsey Research Station; or Alan Turing who worked at Bletchley Park on German cryptanalysis and, ironically, developed and proposed a number of ideas about computers and machine intelligence. Layered on top of this homage to British ingenuity is a darker analogy to Nazi scientists, such as Wernher von Braun who worked on the V2 rockets that were fired upon London in 1945, many of whom later were recruited by the USA to work on their space programme.

Bracewell is also the latest in a long line of artificial beings that have not only been featured in *Doctor Who*, in both the classic series and the revival, and here especially relevant to the cyborg nature of the Smilers in *The Beast Below* that we looked at in Chapter 2 and the overall theme of which we will revisit in the essays on *The Pandorica Opens* and *The Big Bang*, but also in a plethora of science fiction films, television programmes, books and comics over many decades. He is a key metaphor representing our own burning questions about the body and identity and how technology might impact on our minds and physicality. As J. P. Telotte clearly suggests in *Replications: A Robotic History of the Science Fiction Film*, our fascination with artificial beings in science fiction is to be found in the way the genre has of "employing the figure of artifice as a trope or lead for addressing those issues that press most insistently on the culture and to opening up the far larger... question of human *being*, of what it is we are." Bracewell's other ancestor is the Tin Man in *The Wizard Of Oz*, particularly as they are both man-machines missing that essential human element, a heart. Like the wooden boy who wants to be human in *Pinocchio*, the robotic Maria in *Metropolis* (1927) and the Replicants in *Blade Runner* (1982), Bracewell does 'grow' a human heart, does acquire a human response when he accesses the implanted memories in his machine brain and connects to a feeling, an emotion that one assumes that the original Bracewell had once coveted. With this the episode asks questions about personal identity, about human desire, reason and memory. It is interesting to note that this transformation begins when one of the Ironsides shoots off Bracewell's hand. We later see this hand, perhaps rebuilt or reconstructed temporarily, and covered in a black glove, suggesting visual links to the German scientist Rotwang in *Metropolis*, the similarly attired, eponymous 'mad scientist' of *Dr No* (1962) and the parodic, wheelchair-bound figure of what is, in relation to

Bracewell's humanisation in the story, the wryly titled *Dr. Strangelove or: How I Learned to Stop Worrying and Love the Bomb* (1964). The journey taken to Bracewell's emotional awareness and emergence begins with that fateful attack from the Daleks where their machine dominance over him reaches a revelatory crescendo, leaving him damaged, as both Daleks chant "Victory! Victory! Victory!" Their chant, echoing the equally ebullient rhetoric of those Churchillian propaganda posters, defines them as his masters, his creators rather than he being theirs and it mirrors the way they also use the Doctor to then create the 'new paradigm' on the Dalek saucer.

These events lead Bracewell into a crisis over his mental and physical identity (in a particularly good scene for actor Bill Paterson where he recalls memories of the misery of the First World War) and he is seen to be contemplating suicide, offering to Churchill and Amy that, "My life is a lie and I choose to end it." When he asks them both, "What am I?" it is Churchill who emphasises one of the series's major themes in asking him to contemplate the several choices before him – to either be on the side of humanity or the side of the Daleks, to either be a machine or to be a man. "I don't give a damn if you are a machine, Bracewell. Are you a man?" demands Churchill. This manliness that he requests is then emphasised by the innuendo implicit in director Andrew Gunn's close-up of actor Ian McNiece as he chomps down on a very large, phallic-looking cigar and archly raises his eyebrows, practically winking at Bracewell in acknowledgement of this suggestive meaning. The ideals of sexual potency and masculine power here tie in with the man-machine body of Bracewell as a centre of repression where his very human body is about to erupt out of its alienating machine trappings as his emotional responses are freed from the programming in his brain. Amy, whose role in the story has been quite peripheral until this point, is the agency through which Bracewell reconnects with his subjectivity as it undergoes its transformation. She reminds him of his superiority as a piece of advanced technology in order to devise solutions to counteract both the Nazis and the Dalek forces. "Bracewell! It's time to think big," orders Churchill as they sift through ideas about rockets and gravity bubbles. Within ten minutes he has Spitfires hurtling into space and has established communications to the Dalek saucer just as the new Daleks announce their own composite of subjectivity in the roll call of "Strategist. Scientist. Drone. Eternal. And the Supreme."

In the true spirit of 1950s and 1960s pulp science fiction, the Daleks claim "the Earth will die screaming" (a nod to the title of Terence Fisher's 1965 British science fiction film noir) and that the Doctor must choose between allowing them to escape and the destruction of the planet. As if to emphasise this and this series's themes again the white Supreme Dalek barks, "Choose, Doctor! Choose! Choose!" The Doctor's compassion, his humanism, is seen as a weakness by the Daleks and they set Bracewell on a countdown to destruction and, rather like the TARDIS exploding in *The Pandorica Opens*, causing time to vanish through cracks in the universe, the Oblivion Continuum will see the Earth bleed into another dimension. When the Doctor reveals and opens the interface between man and machine after knocking Bracewell to the floor, we are presented with a mechanical body that bears an uncanny resemblance to the comic book character Iron Man and the Oblivion Continuum device looking similar to the 1980s game phenomenon, Simon. Described as an 'electronic game of memory skill', it was marketed with the slogan "Simon's a computer, Simon has a brain, you either do what Simon says or else go down the drain," which certainly sums up what would happen to the Earth if the Oblivion Continuum is allowed to progress. The 'memory skill' in this scene is Amy's ability to connect with Bracewell's memories, which the Doctor, not being human and therefore perhaps not in touch with the same emotions and desires, initially fails to do. Bracewell's thoughts and memories, stolen and planted into his positronic brain, become an exploration of the fashioning of subjectivity as Bracewell attempts to recall his life and his humanity in order to cancel out the effects of his machine body and his relationship to the Daleks as an unfeeling machine creature.

Critically, it does become a rushed and clichéd 'love conquers all' solution to the plot, but the themes remain interesting as Bracewell uploads his memories and explores body, soul and thought, transforming himself through an act of painful confession. Amy, already seen as a character who desires and is desired, sexualised by her role as a kissogram policewoman and actively gazing at the Doctor's body in *The Eleventh Hour* and revealed to have 'eloped' on her wedding night in *The Beast Below*, connects with and understands the nature of Bracewell's repressed desires for Dorabella. She does this by first appealing to their mutual nationalist connections with "Hey, Paisley" – established earlier in the episode when they each recognised their Scottish origins – and then by paraphrasing her own line to Mandy about not being allowed to talk about 'below' in *The Beast Below*, "And because you're not supposed to, you don't?" Here she evokes hidden desire with "Ever fancied someone you know you shouldn't?" and we are allowed access to Bracewell's feelings for Dorabella. Murray Gold reintroduces the glissando, dream-like theme used in *The Beast Below* as the scene plays out and it suggests that Bracewell and Amy have entered a personal, private space to make these connections. Dorabella is a curious name and possibly relates to Dora Penny, the recipient of a mysterious coded letter from the composer Edward Elgar. The 22-year-old daughter of the Rector of Wolverhampton who had known the Elgar family for about 2 years, Elgar would later (in 1898-9) immortalise Dora in the *Dorabella* of the *Enigma Variations*. She was apparently very interested in the industrial revolution of the period and possessed a keen interest in machines and the emerging technologies of the period, and with her diary decorated in Morse code, Elgar perhaps assumed that she could crack the cryptogram in the letter. With Bracewell as an analogue of those Second World War scientists, particularly Turing, this is possibly a playful reference by Gatiss to code cracking and the work at Bletchley Park that successfully decrypted the Germans' Enigma machine codes. It may also suggest that Amy's way into Bracewell's heart is in itself some kind of emotional cryptography.

In *Uncovering Lives: The Uneasy Alliance of Biography and Psychology* by Alan C. Elms, the male characters in L. Frank Baum's *Oz* books are seen as a way for young male readers to be assured "that their nurturant tendencies are valuable and that they (like the Tin Man, Jack Pumpkinhead and others) will live through their physically oriented self doubts to become whole people in the end." As the Doctor triumphantly says to Bracewell, after the emotional upheaval of remembering his passion for Dorabella has deactivated the bomb, "Welcome to the human race!" Bill Paterson quietly impresses as Bracewell, managing to convey well the confusion at discovering his non-human origins and the conflict between machine intelligence and human emotion. However, the episode's coda where the Doctor and Amy heavily suggest that he goes in search of his desire, his Dorabella, seems to go on for longer than is necessary and feels like padding when it could easily have been reduced to a couple of effective lines.

## "Keep buggering on"

One of the major themes of the story is the use of advanced science, military science in particular, to define national ideologies. The Daleks construct Edwin Bracewell, a technologically superior man-machine, to 'assist' Churchill with the development of weaponry to defeat the Luftwaffe. He is also a walking bomb, an Oblivion Continuum, which the Daleks then use to delay the Doctor as they make their escape down a time corridor. We also have a Progenitor device, a fabled object of Dalek super-science that creates genetically pure Daleks in a new paradigm to supersede the remaining mongrels of the Time War. Bracewell, as well as constructing the Ironside Daleks for Churchill, also provides the British with a methodology to achieve 'out of the atmosphere' flight for Spitfires that also appear to be armed with laser cannons to knock out the Dalek energy beam. The Daleks can also magically counteract switched off mains electrical generators and power stations to cancel the effects of the blackout, thus inviting the Luftwaffe to bomb London with even greater precision. This use and misuse of science also reflects many of Dalek creator Terry Nation's own stories for the classic series, particularly where such themes focus on the very creation of the Daleks. As Jonathan Bignell and Andrew O'Day point out in *Terry Nation*, "Several of his *Doctor Who* stories are premised on the misuse of scientific knowledge and scientific and technological discourse and iconography are especially important in the creation of the evil, machine-like Daleks in *The Daleks* and even more explicitly in *Genesis of the Daleks*."

All these stratagems are bound up with reinforcing nationalist ideology, be it British, Nazi or Dalek, and within the binary opposition of the Daleks' rigid allegiance to control and dominance through a calculated use of science versus the serendipitous, altruistic and often irrational creative thinking in the use of technology that the Doctor employs. *Victory of the Daleks* does offer an analogue to the stalemate between the Western and Eastern nuclear war machines that emerged during the Cold War as a result of the end of the Second World War. Its discourse depicts the way that advanced technology and the power behind it defines nationalism and the post-war self-image of Britain, its allies and enemies. The Daleks are both a symbol of German technological might that emerged after the First World War and the National Socialist doctrines that empowered it and they also suggest in their avowal of a 'new paradigm' the post-war Soviet and NATO arms escalation and ideology that emerged from the aftermath of the conflict. Hugh Macdonald, in 1982's *The Crisis in Western Security*, sees the struggle between Daleks and humans in *Doctor Who* as representative of the way "we have set technology to serve political objects by means of military power but we have forgotten that the problem of power in politics is manageable only by an understanding of interests and will, rather than by surrogate organisations that impose technically and doctrinally narrow attitudes upon us." Macdonald sees military science, here codified in the nascent Cold War tensions of the nuclear arms race expressed in Churchill's obsessive need of the Daleks' superior fire-power and in the Daleks' desire to become better, faster and stronger, articulated as a transnational ideology. The East-West divide and the emergence of other nuclear states are emblematic of a belief in what Macdonald sees as "the efficacy of scientific weapons development" and these nation states each think of one another as possessing the "dangers and dysfunctions of Dalek-like thoughts."

It is interesting to note how some of these dysfunctions play out in the human attitudes towards the Daleks as a technologically superior race. Churchill is quite unequivocal in his use of the Daleks to "win me the war" and there is clearly pressure on him to repel the Nazi invasion at any cost. "If Hitler invaded Hell, I would give a favourable reference to the Devil," he tells the Doctor. Ironically, this is a paraphrase of a statement he actually made in June 1941 in response to Hitler's invasion of the Soviet Union. Churchill's hostility to the Communists was well documented and when he proposed sending in British troops to aid Stalin he was criticised in Parliament and then responded with that infamous retort. Gatiss at least in this instance captures something of his attitudes and by 1946, after the Yalta Conference and witnessing the Soviets installing a Communist government in Poland, Churchill would again be highly critical of their regime. Gatiss's script certainly showcases the man's self-expression and the idea that practically for most of his political life he, as David Cannadine states in *In Churchill's Shadow: Confronting the Past in Modern Britain*, "turned out words and phrases in tumultuous torrent and inexhaustible abundance." Cannadine also explores the other side of the bullish rhetoric that arguably only ever proved effective at the peak of the war in 1940. Whilst he may have inspired many during the toughest year of the war, he never entirely endeared himself to the public. "Churchill's oratory was far more important and interesting to himself than it was to the British political classes or to the British people in general... he was often rude and vituperative, bullying and overbearing, apocalyptic and irresponsible," offers Cannadine. These qualities do bubble to the surface only very occasionally in Gatiss's script and there is certainly an indication of Churchill's war-mongering in the story especially when he gloats exultantly over Bracewell's Ironsides and says, "Death to our enemies, death to the forces of darkness and death to the Third Reich!" and where, ironically, his rhetoric starts to resemble that of a Dalek. This mirrors an earlier scene in the story where the Doctor himself confronts Churchill over his doubts about the Ironsides and asks him to "Destroy them. Exterminate them!"

There are many controversial views of Churchill and certainly the bombing of Dresden in 1945 created an immense unease within the British intelligentsia and the public where for the first time questions were being asked about the methods being used to end the war. His changing attitudes towards Stalin and the Russians, at first knowing he would have to bring them into the War as Allies, however much he detested their regime, and then conceding to their demands at Yalta only to then realise that Stalin would not honour the agreements made at the conference, also came in for much criticism and a vote of no confidence in the House. Gatiss acknowledges that Churchill is a controversial figure in Dan Berry's interview with him in *Doctor Who Magazine*, April 2010, "Churchill is still a very controversial figure, a very complex man. But *Doctor Who* is not the place to talk about any of his policies. You've got to print the legend and that's what we're doing really." Again, Gatiss does suggest something of the man's complex nature by showing him as a Prime Minister determined to roll back the oncoming Nazi forces at any cost and perhaps more interestingly, he is shown to covet the Doctor's TARDIS, knowing that as a time-travelling device it would enable him to change history and save millions of lives. "Think of what I could achieve with your remarkable machine, Doctor. The lives that could be saved," he begs. When the Doctor denies him with, "It doesn't work like that," suggesting that Churchill's darkest hours must be allowed to play out as a fixed point in history, Churchill then ominously announces, "Must I take it by force?" This also foreshadows the speech in the lift as they go to the rooftop to witness the Ironside exterminating the oncoming German bombers. "I will grasp with both hands anything that will give us an advantage over the Nazi menace," states Churchill and perhaps here Gatiss is quietly reminding us that the Ironsides are a symbol of that eventual decision to ally Britain with Stalin as Hitler invaded the USSR in 1941. As a side note, the naming of the camouflaged Daleks as Ironsides evokes more British history with 'Ironside' being the nickname given to troopers in the Parliamentary cavalry as part of the New Model Army formed by Cromwell and used during the English Civil War that eventually saw the shift of political power from monarchy to parliament. It also suggests the steam-powered ironclad warships of the Nineteenth Century and the Iron Curtain that Churchill indicated had descended across Europe in his

'Sinews of Peace' address in 1946.

The problem here is that the use of Churchill is often tokenistic and, combined with Ian McNiece's somewhat over-wrought portrayal, the character steadfastly refuses to come to life as a three-dimensional human being. Whilst historically Churchill was the quintessential 'the man and the hour' where, as David Cannadine explains in *In Churchill's Shadow: Confronting the Past in Modern Britain*, "Between May and December 1940, he talked his way into immortality and [his] magnificently defiant words were soon accompanied by equally defiant deeds [that] acquired an iconic status and historic significance they retained to this day," the Churchill we see in *Victory of the Daleks* is more or less a caricature of a very complicated man. It raises the argument that perhaps the revival of *Doctor Who* should not incorporate into its stories certain historical figures from recent memory about whom we know a great deal, particularly their personal politics and psychology. When you look at the difference between the depiction of Churchill here and that of Shakespeare in *The Shakespeare Code*, it suggests that while artistic licence can be granted to national icons such as Shakespeare, about whom there is more speculation than hard facts, it also can be a hindrance to debates about the use of such figures and whether the stories they feature in can address some of their personal complexities. In the end, Churchill, despite his legendary status, is used to prop up a now rather clichéd view of Britain where the real dilemma and challenge of nationhood today is, as Chris Rojek suggests in *Brit-Myth*, "to embrace the multi-cultural, multi-ethnic and global realities of the world in which we now live. An esprit de corps will not be achieved by appealing to Churchill, Dunkirk or VE Day. This is because some of the people called upon to celebrate these historical icons in British history regard themselves and their ancestors to be victims of British hubris and insensitivity."

## "All right, it's a Jammie Dodger. But I was promised tea!"

*Victory of the Daleks* is problematical in that it also does not know whether to invoke the 'pseudo-historical' sub-genre of the series where, as Daniel O'Mahony defines it in '"Now how is that wolf able to impersonate a grandmother?" History, Pseudo-history and Genre in Doctor Who,' within David Butler's collection *Time and Relative Dissertations in Space*, "the historical period has been invaded by a science-fictional presence before the Doctor shows up or turns out to be a fabrication mocked up by the villains for their own dubious purposes" or the 'historical' sub-genre where "the Doctor, his companions and the TARDIS are the only science-fictional intrusion into a narrative that otherwise features historical elements." With the former O'Mahony is saying, "history is up for grabs" and in the latter that "history itself is a topic for debate within the story." Gatiss invites us into history in that emblematic sequence on the rooftop where Amy and the Doctor gaze out at the London skyline crowded with barrage balloons to the aural accompaniment of bombs dropping and air-raid sirens (itself a nod back to Rose's trip across war-torn London as the Germans conduct a nighttime bombing run in *The Empty Child*). "Doctor, it's..." begins Amy, only to have her declaration completed by the Doctor: "History." But that is as far as we are allowed to understand history in the story, at least the British history of the period, because its use switches to a form of historical tourism that, as Gatiss has indicated, he does not want us to debate too closely. This tourism and use of iconography reaches an apotheosis in the mimicking of the flag raising on Iwo Jima that is staged on the rooftop of the Cabinet War Rooms and is completed with a juicy close-up of the Union Jack flapping in the breeze. This re-enactment within the episode is in itself playing into the controversy that surrounded the photograph taken on Iwo Jima by Joe Rosenthal. Rosenthal was falsely accused of staging the flag raising and posing the troops featured in the photograph and spent most of his career rightly refuting the accusation. It is a propagandist image that has been replicated ever since and most recently was emulated in the "Raising the Flag at Ground Zero" photograph by Thomas Franklin in the aftermath of the 9/11 attacks.

*Victory of the Daleks* also see the series make another bid for 'quality television' status in the way that it faithfully re-creates the London and Cabinet War Rooms of the Blitz period and, as we have already indicated, the use of Churchill as a 'sign' of British heritage within the story. At the same time it attempts to tell a story about the Daleks which hyperbolises the 'Nazi mythologising' of their race within a Second World War setting but also offers a 'restoration' of the Daleks that revises, by returning to a kind of Dalek Year Zero with the use of the Progenitor device, the entire Time War phase of their history and offers an equally questionable re-visioning of a 1960s design icon. The science-fictional aspect of the story is more dominant and relates an altogether different history to us. It is the continuing history of the Daleks and their relationship to the Doctor. An important moment in Dalek history is crammed into an already packed narrative and what should be the triumphant reveal of the new Dalek paradigm is rather squandered despite director Andrew Gunn's best efforts and they finally emerge at a point some twenty minutes into an episode that runs only forty-two minutes in length. There is also little time given to develop the Doctor and Amy's relationship and Amy only actively participates in the last half of the story. Pointedly, her encounter with the Daleks emphasises both a major plot point in the series when it is revealed that she has no memory of the Dalek invasion of the Earth in *Journey's End* when clearly she should have, and the fact that she now understands the jeopardy her journeys with the Doctor will place her in. "And here's me thinking we'd be running through time, being daft and fixing stuff. But, no, it's dangerous," she summarises her observations of their lifestyle in time and space. This also foreshadows the arc of the series that is one very much geared around "running through time" and "fixing stuff" when dealing with the consequences of the crack in time, here seen again as the TARDIS departs. When Bracewell's bomb is deactivated and the Doctor hands out praise to those involved, he kisses Amy on the forehead – this "if wishes were kisses" motif is symbolised later in a similar gesture from him during *Flesh and Stone* where the wider series arc is finally revealed. Beyond this, there is still a captivating performance from Matt Smith to savour, whose physicality is a pure delight and who manages to deliver a number of lines that could easily have been lost on the page. The TARDIS destruct button bluff with the Daleks ("Don't mess with me, sweetheart") with the Jammie Dodger is wonderfully played and his anger in trying to get a reaction from the camouflaged Daleks is genuinely realised. He holds much of this together and is clearly a fine asset to this series. Andrew Gunn's direction is, at times, very cinematic. The shots of the Doctor looking over his shoulder as the Daleks prowl the War Rooms are beautiful examples of the deep focus cinematography the series has now embraced, one shot mirroring a very similar shot of Amy looking over her shoulder in *The Beast Below*, but he only achieves a minor success in bringing life and movement into the new Daleks even though he tries hard to shoot them from various angles and distances.

Structurally the episode is uneven, squashing in short-handed storytelling into a very limited running time. As a two-part story this would have worked far better, with the first half properly examining Churchill's character and his use of the Ironsides, better establishing Bracewell and then leading up to the reveal of the new Daleks as the cliffhanger to the first part. The second half of the story could then have shown Bracewell working on the Spitfires over a longer period of time rather than the scant ten minutes indicated in the finished episode, then delivering a far more satisfying threat from the new Daleks, heavily underscoring the idea that whilst the Doctor saves the Earth, the Daleks escape him and maintain their 'victory'. A longer running time would then have allowed the development of the supporting characters like Breen and could perhaps have included sequences of the Blitz, conveying the awful realities of the War that Gatiss was obviously keen to portray. We are shown or told about the Blitz at a distance, amidst Churchill's constant restating of the high stakes, and connections to personal stories are kept to a bare minimum. It would have been interesting to see characters in air raid shelters or sleeping in the Underground to give us a real sense of what was at stake. There is much talk of incendiary bombs and strikes but we never see them or the aftermath. The story as it is neither offers us 'history up for grabs' nor 'history itself as a topic' and it somewhat short-changes what should be a huge development for the Daleks into the bargain.

Chapter Four

# THE TIME OF ANGELS
# FLESH AND STONE

Written by: Steven Moffat
Directed by: Adam Smith
First broadcast: 24 April & 1 May 2010

---

"Catacombs, probably dark ones. Dark catacombs. Great!"

The Gothic genre and *Doctor Who* have been comfortable bedfellows for some time and many would agree that the pinnacle of this relationship was no better realised than in the three seasons of the original series produced by Philip Hinchcliffe and script-edited by Robert Holmes between 1975 and 1977. The Hinchcliffe and Holmes partnership used a wide range of Gothic characteristics to define their era. Their Gothic fiction offered a 'pleasant terror', supplementing it with melodrama and parody, even self-parody (something that Holmes exploited to the full), that embodied extreme emotion, the vicarious thrills of fearfulness, atmosphere and an appreciation of the sublime. Edmund Burke described the sublime as anything that "is productive of the strongest emotion the mind is capable of feeling" – and therefore by example the coexistence of terror, pain and delight within the Gothic genre. The Gothic style uses extremes of the mysterious and fantastic that David Punter in *The Literature of Terror: A History of Gothic Fictions*, in part, summarises as: "an emphasis on portraying the terrifying, a common insistence on archaic settings, a prominent use of the supernatural, the presence of highly stereotyped characters and the attempt to deploy and perfect techniques of literary suspense." When we get to Steven Moffat's *The Time of Angels* and *Flesh and Stone* we see the series continue and expand upon *Doctor Who*'s long engagement with the Gothic. Whilst references to the genre appeared earlier in *The Eleventh Hour* and *The Beast Below*, the Gothic previously manifested itself to a greater extent during stories as diverse as 2005's *The Unquiet Dead*, *The Empty Child* and *The Doctor Dances*, 2006's *Tooth and Claw*, *The Impossible Planet* and *The Satan Pit*, 2007's *Blink*, and finally with 2008's *Silence in the Library*, *Forest of the Dead* and *Midnight*.

The use of the genre in a modernist context is examined by Catherine Spooner in *Contemporary Gothic*: "Gothic texts deal with a variety of themes just as pertinent to contemporary culture as to the eighteenth and nineteenth centuries, when Gothic novels first achieved popularity." She sees the genre capable of offering multiple narrative possibilities where the relationship between the past and the present, the nature of the

67

monstrous 'other', the disassembly and reassembly of the self and the examination of grotesque and mutating physicality all come into play. She also suggests that the genre is not fixed and has a fluidity that allows for a Gothic presence to appear in other, non-related texts as a participant in it rather than as a dominating and single influence. Thus Russell T. Davies and Moffat use their *Doctor Who* to codify certain elements within stories as Gothic, such as werewolves, demons, zombies and supernatural forces, but also place them within drama that explores the issues of trust between the Doctor and his companions, their sense of self and identity, anxieties about childhood, religion, death and sexuality whilst simultaneously employing comedy, space opera, history and satire as genre structures. Series Five has already touched upon well-known and well-used tropes: the image of Amy's haunted house and her role as the 'final girl' pursued and impersonated by the multi-form in the English pastoral of Leadworth, and the Gothic carnivalesque represented by the Smilers and the Winders demarcating the political limits of a broken society. In *The Time of Angels* and *Flesh and Stone* Moffat uses space opera and Gothic horror in combination with fairy-tale elements to address contemporary anxieties about the culture of fear generated by the war in Iraq and Afghanistan. Gothic has recently, according to Spooner's analysis of the genre's drive to fictionalise the past as a way of sanctifying the present, "performed a particular kind of cultural work, a means through which Western culture could displace its fears into an exotic, distanced other and thus feel safe."

*The Time of Angels* and *Flesh and Stone* adopt a number of Gothic motifs and themes and comment on the nature of the genre itself. The Weeping Angels are reintroduced to the series after their startling success in *Blink*. Gothic monsters par excellence, they are stone angels, statuary and symbols associated with both Muslim and Christian faiths, the ubiquitous stone guardian seen standing over the graves of loved ones in every city cemetery and functioning as powerful symbols of faith and redemption. The brilliance of *Blink*, in this use of such a familiar image to terrorise, was to suggest that any statue, not just benign-looking angels, could come to life and plunge its victims into a quantum hell and, rather like vampires, feed off their potential life energy. The Doctor describes them to Amy as "the deadliest, most powerful, most malevolent life form evolution has ever produced" and this underlines Moffat's assertion that his scripts for *The Time of Angels* and *Flesh and Stone* are to *Blink* as James Cameron's *Aliens* (1983) was a sequel to Ridley Scott's *Alien* (1979). In *Alien* the robot Ash, talking to Ripley, Parker and Lambert about the creature that is stalking the crew of the spaceship Nostromo, admires it as a "perfect organism. Its structural perfection is matched only by its hostility." Scott's film uses Gothic horror within a space opera context to explore the monstrous nature of the beast, with the maze of corridors in the ship substituting as the archetypical haunted house, mansion, cellar or dungeon of Gothic literature. The same can be said of the Doctor and Amy's journey through the Aplan Mortarium, its vast caverns filled with statuary and lined with the bodies of the dead, where typically, as David

Punter explains in *A Companion to the Gothic*: "Gothic takes place – very frequently – in crypts. The Gothic speaks of, indeed we might say it tries to invoke, spectres. Derrida, in for example *Spectres of Marx* chooses the same rhetoric to talk about what we might term, the 'suppressed of Europe.'" With the 'war on terror' iconography that Moffat places within the context of the Gothic genre, the "spectre haunting Europe," in Derrida's description, evokes a deep anxiety that that is generated in cycles of violence in wars and civil conflict with the phantom 'other'.

The journey through the catacombs then is a ripe opportunity to use the trappings of the Gothic to allow characters to reveal secrets, wrongdoings and, in reflecting Freud's 'return of the repressed', exorcise their own psychological phantoms. As the Doctor, Amy, River and the Clerics led by Octavian penetrate the maze, which River describes as "six levels and represents the ascent of the soul," all manner of confessions are overheard where the truth is as hard to find as "a stone angel on the loose amongst stone statues." One of the major secrets revealed is that the Doctor is unaware of River's true identity and purpose. Octavian grabs her by the arm and interrogates her, "He doesn't know yet, does he? Who and what you are." River acknowledges that it is too early in the Doctor's time stream for him to know the truth about her. Secrets, lies and the truth permeate the story from this moment on and the caveat to this confession is, as she reassures Octavian that the Doctor will not discover her crime, that later it is Octavian's death that partly reveals to the Doctor her imprisonment and precipitates her own confession about the man she killed.

During *The Time of Angels*, Amy is infected by her encounter with the Angel that the Church has tracked down and as she rubs her eye, a torrent of dust pours out of it in an arrestingly surreal image that suggests the legends of Medusa turning her victims to stone. Continuing with the use of the Gothic mode to map out secrets, Amy lies to River about her condition as River lies to her about the maze of the dead being "not really that bad. " River similarly offsets the truth about the pain she inflicts upon Amy with the viro-stabiliser and its efficacy at protecting her against any pollutants. This encounter is also the setting for further enquiries from Amy about the Doctor, her qualification to River of "Cos you know him in the future, don't you?" alerting us to Moffat's use of the Gothic to tell narratives from different points in time and to create comic obfuscation about River's actual relationship with the Doctor. "You're *so* his wife," accuses Amy in a brief scene where they behave like gossiping housewives as the Doctor attempts to listen in on their conversation. "Do you really think it could be anything that simple?" responds River. This conversation neatly alludes to the notion that gossip and storytelling are part and parcel of the way the Gothic can open up discussions about human fears and grapple with subject matter that is best left undisclosed. The mystery of River's true identity and relationship with the Doctor becomes a narrative reflection of Amy's future confession to the Doctor about her own relationship with Rory. River's ambiguous response is: "You're good. I'm not saying you're right..." and the mystery of whether she is the Doctor's wife, mother or other relation is left unresolved. Even Alex Kingston is not privy to straight answers from Moffat about this relationship, as she explained in her interview with Jason Arnopp in the April 2010 edition of *Doctor Who Magazine*: "Whenever I ask him direct questions about River's relationship with the Doctor, he goes towards answering, then... doesn't completely fulfil that promise! I think Steven always likes to have a door slightly ajar in case he decides to make a left-turn! I was very sure that River was the Doctor's wife. Very, very sure. Then for some reason, I suddenly thought, 'Oh my god, is she his mother?' So now, I don't know any more... but I still think she's his wife."

The catacombs are a psychopathological space that has an adverse effect on the living human explorers who must not only deal with the revelation of their innermost confidences but also struggle with fear of the dark, claustrophobia and dread of the unknown in an architecture that seems to have no boundaries, physically or morally. Gothic space has also been a major visual component of *Doctor Who* since the 1960s and the caves and catacombs here have their antecedents in everything from, amongst many examples, *An Unearthly Child* to *Doctor Who and the Silurians*, from *The Ribos Operation* to *The Caves of Androzani*. The closest analogue in terms of story and visuals, a battle between space marines and monsters, is *Earthshock*. The fear inscribed in Gothic narrative and space is also perfectly encapsulated in Moffat's use of word play. Bob, one of the jumpier Clerics who fires at what he mistakenly thinks is an Angel, is 're-christened' by the Doctor when Octavian claims that they have all been given sacred names by the Church. "Sacred Bob. More like Scared Bob now, eh?" comforts the Doctor. This overemphasis on fear is also part of the genre's knowingness and its ability to accommodate self-parody and comic relief as part of its repertoire. After Octavian describes the route into the Aplan temple to the Doctor, he conjures up this sense of parody in his ironic summary, "Oh good. Catacombs. Probably dark ones. Dark catacombs. Great." He at once acknowledges that the space we are about to enter is both a cliché of the horror film and of *Doctor Who* itself but, even so, it is a forbidding prospect and a place where fear is a positive emotion to be cherished because "scared keeps you fast." Octavian underlines this parodic approach to managing fear in catacombs filled with statuary and dead bodies by advising Bob to "remain calm in the presence of décor."

The Angels are figures that use the Gothic to make sense of contemporary fears and concerns. They also operate as opponents within what, Moffat seems to suggest, is a futuristic religious jihad where 'the Church', presumably the Christian one, is a militarised force sent out to extinguish evil. Kelton Cobb, in the *Blackwell Guide to Theology and Popular Culture*, emphasises this relationship between the Gothic and the demonising of non-Christian religious figures within media and news culture where he suggests that the Gothic is now being used as a "narrative form for divining the meaning of real events" and where

"Gothic elements have been ascribed to Osama Bin Laden, the emaciated but austerely handsome Bedouin who, driven by stern principles, destroys buildings associated with our most consequential institutions – buildings filled with innocent women and children that melt in fiery conflagrations. He relentlessly pursues us, haunting us at every turn. Whenever rumours of his death begin to circulate he makes ghostly appearances on mysterious tapes to rally the forces of evil and remind us of his invincibility." This could be read into how the ghost-like Angel on the video loop haunts Amy, reaching out to consume and possess her and also in the revelation that the Aplan Mortarium is full of Weeping Angels who "relentlessly pursue" the Church's Clerics and their Father Octavian. As the first part of the story unfolds in the catacombs this threat refuses to be fully described, pinned down, its ambiguity filling the characters with a sense of great uncertainty. If anything, *The Time of Angels* articulates some of our own fearful distraction with national and global security. The desert combat gear worn by these troops is another iconographic element that links the story into the Iraq War genre of films and television dramas such as *The Hurt Locker* (2009) and *Generation Kill* (2008) and news media narratives of the wars in Iraq and Afghanistan. The use of modern war tropes sees the Weeping Angels crudely represent what Cobb refers to as "the hydra-like dispositions of global terrorism" and wherein the Angels as demonised and monstrous insurgents become "intractable forces of hatred arrayed against us." There is also the Milton-esque quality of *Flesh and Stone* where the 'war in heaven' of *Paradise Lost* is here retold as the 'Fall of the Weeping Angels' and their banishment from the tree-borg 'Garden of Eden'. It forms part of the episode's eschatological vision of the end of time, flirting again with 'war on terror' ideology and iconography that also describes the 'sleeper' nature of the reviving Angels as the "difference between dormant and patient."

This view of an enemy seemingly impossible to destroy is one that dominates James Cameron's *Aliens* too, itself a cinematic treatise on the Vietnam War. Its milieu of marines battling alien monstrosities within the darkened, smoke- and moisture-filled labyrinthine corridors and vaults of an outpost established to terraform a hostile alien world is visually referenced here in the conflict between the Church's troops and the emerging Angels. There is even a direct reference to it in the dialogue as Father Octavian notes that Alfava Metraxis "has been terraformed. Six billion colonists." Ironically, Octavian is also a Bishop, second class, which further reinforces the story's links to *Aliens* and its own Bishop, the 'artificial person' played by Lance Hendrikson. The religious context of the story with its troops of Clerics and Bishops all donning desert camouflage gear also echoes Vincent Ward's original treatment for *Alien3* (1992) in which Ripley's struggle with the alien takes place on a wooden planet inhabited by monks and where, during their conflict, the alien is seen by them as a representation of the devil. Finally, the aesthetics of the 'war on terror' are complemented by Adam Smith's epic, widescreen pan down the hull of the wrecked Byzantium in collision with the Aplan temple, which

71

resembles a much larger version of ancient Petra, that immediately suggests various associations to images of the widespread damage and cultural vandalism inflicted upon Babylon and the ancient buildings of Basra and Baghdad in the war with Iraq and of the planes that were flown into the Twin Towers. Indeed, calling the spaceship the Byzantium is also perhaps a reference to the disastrous Christian crusades of the 13th Century where they sacked the eponymous city, with the story replaying that Crusade through Father Octavian and his Clerics as they seek to wipe out the evil Angels.

The catacombs are not the only example of how the story utilises Gothic space. The story in *The Time of Angels* is initiated by the Doctor's discovery of the Home Box flight recorder from the Byzantium on display at the museum of the Delirium Archive. The museum is church like, suggestive of a Gothic architecture, and again is a fittingly mausoleum-like setting for the Doctor to go digging around in relics of the past, present and future. Gothic stories litter their plots with clues placed or hidden in artefacts and letters, usually left for, what would be in nineteenth century Gothic novels, the heroine to interrogate and interpret. Right from the opening sequence, Moffat constructs *The Time of Angels* from non-linear, multiple-perspective subplots and begins within the drug-induced dream of a Byzantium crew member, shifts to River's escape, then jumps to the Delirium Archive with the Doctor receiving her message and returning to the Byzantium where he affects River's rescue. It emulates the characteristic of Victorian Gothic in its use of fragmented storytelling and is later seen in much greater changes to the series's overall arc by both confronting the Doctor with the crack in the skin of the universe and inserting into the story the future Doctor travelling back through his own time stream from the events of *The Big Bang*. By the beginning of *Flesh and Stone*, Moffat shifts the location of the story to the interior of the Byzantium, a seemingly conventional science fiction spaceship setting. Not only does the visual framework of the story completely change but we also see him use a trademark structure that is repeated in the other Moffat two-parter in this series. That structure sees Moffat effectively replacing the threat of the Weeping Angels, built up to a fitting cliffhanger in the opening part of the story, with the primary narrative of the time-eating crack in the universe. This new stage of the story again undergoes Gothic fragmentation and as the crack in the universe manifests itself on the flight deck of the ship, the Doctor, Amy and River escape into another layer of the puzzlebox narrative. A vast bulkhead opens, with a visual symmetry to the opening of the Dalek Progenitor, the mouth of the Star Whale and the widening of the crack in Amy's bedroom wall, to reveal an entire forest, another archetypical Gothic setting, within the bowels of the ship and into which the characters flee. The forest in a spaceship image also parallels the way characters interact with the jungle environment of the planet Eden, captured within a projection machine on board a spaceship, in *Nightmare of Eden*. This is also part of a consistent visual trope within both episodes that shows various characters, including the

Weeping Angels, leaving or entering spaces via holes, airlocks, doorways, cracks and screens. In delayed response to Amy's demand that they visit a planet at the beginning of *The Time of Angels*, the Doctor adroitly summarises the changing complexity but fragmentary nature of both the narrative and the visual staging of the story: "A forest in a bottle on a spaceship in a maze. Have I impressed you yet Amy Pond?" In a way, this also sounds like Moffat directly asking the same question of the audience.

The pre-titles to *The Time of Angels*, where one of Alistair's crew wanders dazed under the influence of River's lipstick, shot in surreal wide angle by Adam Smith, amidst the rolling greens and deep shadows cast by trees of some imagined garden or glade, prefigures the next landscape of the psyche within which Moffat places his characters. Ironically, that brief moment of sunlit greenery also acknowledges the heavenly 'afterlife' that River and her crew ascend to in the conclusion of *Forest of the Dead*. The cathedral of trees revealed inside the Byzantium also connects back to the Gothic arches of the Delirium Archive. The forest of tree-borgs, a mythical deep, dark wood, is where Moffat best explores the relationship between the Doctor and Amy. The image of Amy alone in the forest is again another symbol of her abandonment and of the adults, her parents, whom she has forgotten about. As Jack David Zipes points out in *The Brothers Grimm: From Enchanted Forests to the Modern World*, "the forest allows for enchantment and disenchantment, for it is the place where society's conventions no longer hold true." He sees the German forests of the Grimm stories as the setting where law and truth can be rediscovered to provide us with a deeper understanding and representation of society and the people within it. They become a psychological testing ground for Amy, the Doctor, River and Octavian and, as the setting for many eighteenth and nineteenth century tales, Zipes suggests they "keep alive our longing for a better, modern world that can be created out of our dreams and actions."

In Chapter 2 we talked about the relationship between Amy and the Doctor as mutually necessary in the same way that Peter Pan and Wendy must cooperate in order to understand the darker aspects of themselves and the world around them. For Peter Pan, it is his detached shadow that prevents him from achieving psychological insight and for the Doctor and Amy it is the fear of the unknown that threatens their ability to conquer their own shadows, to deal with the unconscious. In *Now or Neverland*, Ann Yeoman regards the defeat of the shadow, or the subsumation of it to create a fully rounded personality, as "the courage and humility that enables it [the personality] to maintain a sacrificial stance in the face of life, without which there can be no hope of transformation and spiritual growth." The Doctor and Amy seem to constantly be prepared to sacrifice themselves and cause the sacrifice of others in order to escape the confines of the Gothic narrative into which they have descended. Priya Jaikumar succinctly summarises this release from the Gothic narrative in *Cinema at the End of Empire*: "escaping from this world often involves a sacrifice, magical helpers and talismanic objects that restore memory and rightful status." *The Time of Angels* and *Flesh and Stone* not only depict the sacrificial deaths of Octavian and his Clerics, the use of familiar and unfamiliar talismans such as the Weeping Angels, the sonic screwdriver, River's diary, the Home Box, the gravity globe and the communicators to restore order, but they also show Amy and the Doctor developing a relationship to help them conquer their own fears and acknowledge that they may have to sacrifice themselves to deal with the death of time itself. This requirement is highlighted by Angel Bob's request of the Doctor that the crack will be sealed if he throws himself, as a massive space-time event, into the fire at the end of the universe. The talismanic Home Box, looking like a miniature version of the Pandorica, is representative of the many secret messages and letters in Gothic stories and its antiquarian symbolism is further embellished when the Doctor confirms that its message is in old High Gallifreyan, the lost language of the Time Lords, linking us further back to the similarly Gothic *The Five Doctors*. The Angel in the belly of the ship is said to have been "pulled from the ruins of Razbahan," which confirms the object with an Eastern European or Arabic exoticism. The use and depiction of talismans, artefacts, catacombs, forests, gardens, archives and museums also foreshadow settings such as the hyperbolised Gothic palaces of *The Vampires of Venice*, the church in *Vincent and the Doctor* and the museum in *The Big Bang*, whilst also referring back to similar visual and narrative cues from *Silence in the Library*, *Forest of the Dead*, *Blink* and *The Girl in the Fireplace* that include libraries, abandoned houses and the palace at Versailles and their fractured subplots that unfold events from different points in time.

Fear, and not overt horror, is *The Time of Angels*'s stock in trade and the sequences in the maze of the dead are beautifully shot, the darkness constantly pierced by torches, with Adam Smith's cinematic framing and cutting rehearsing much of the similar hand-held material present in *Alien* and *Aliens*, and cementing the episode's desire to paralyse with anxiety and dread. *Flesh and Stone* is a pure adrenalin rush generated by the fusion of the traditional *Doctor Who* 'base under siege' default narrative and the childhood memories of playing Blind Man's Buff. However, this version of the game, (it originally dated back to the Greeks), is definitely the biggest test of the trust that tenuously exists between the Doctor and Amy to this point. Director Smith demonstrates that he fits this material like a glove with many visually impressive moments scattered through the story: the camera twirling round to show the Doctor, Amy, River and the soldiers all sticking to the skin of the Byzantium via the artificial gravity and then the Doctor's disorienting climb into the ship; the staccato visual flourishes and pressure cooker atmosphere of the Angels breaching the airlock and then some lovely hand-held shots as they begin attacking the control room; the impressive reveal of the forest and the pulsing and strobing lights in the trees accompanied by some amazing focus pulls as the Angels advance.

Visual lyricism and fantastic use of the Puzzlewood locations support the references to childhood memories of Blind Man's Buff and counting games that inform Amy's fate but they also connect to the symbolism of forests in fairy tales and romance legends the world over. The very earthiness of the tree-borg environment is described to us by Smith's close-ups of Amy's shoes trudging through the muddy ground, by her fall and by her near death as she curls up in the greenery. Her dilemma evokes Dante at the start of *The Divine Comedy* ("In the middle of the journey of our life I found myself in a dark wood where the straight way was lost"). Her losing the path in the impenetrable forest of Angels depicts her uncertain trust for the Doctor and, like all fairy tales set in the 'deep, dark wood', her questionable trust in him must be resolved by finding the true path. With two parts to the story there is plenty of time to create a thick soup of atmosphere, to develop the story and invest emotionally in the supporting characters, particularly the return of River Song. Cinematography, production design, visual effects and music all adeptly infuse the story with Gothic power and in director Adam Smith the producers have found a talent who seems more than capable of bringing this mix of Guillermo Del Toro and James Cameron, screwball comedy and spy-fi, spectacularly to life.

## "Do I look that clingy?"

*The Time of Angels* and *Flesh and Stone* continue the series's exploration of Amy's insecurities and further develop the sense that no matter how hard she strives for her independence it is the fragmented aspects of her psyche, outwardly evidenced in her misanthropy, that then force her into a childlike overcompensation throughout the story. In the sequence in the drop ship, where she is almost possessed by the Angel, she craves an affirmation of her own cleverness from the Doctor after she eliminates the Angel by pausing the video loop during a microsecond of static. "It was, wasn't it? That was pretty good," she offers and the Doctor ignores her and asks River to hug Amy as his admission by proxy that she has done well. "Cos I'm busy," he replies to her after she questions his reluctance to hug her and it is left to River to enthusiastically tell her how brilliant she was. This also extends the supportive camaraderie between the two women and positions River as a mother symbol to whom both Amy and the Doctor must refer over the course of both episodes.

The surrogate parents that River and the Doctor become to Amy is a theme that is repeated in various scenes. The discussion with Amy in the maze of the dead about River's future with the Doctor as River administers her with the stabiliser and the later scene where they both attempt to help Amy deal with her possession by the Angel in the forest further highlight Amy and River's mother-daughter symbolism. Her abandonment issues return whilst escaping from the Angels at the end of *The Time of Angels*. She believes she is turning to stone, refuses to move, and the Doctor has to deal with a girl whose physical impairment is now mirroring her emotional dysfunction. Their breathless debate about the Doctor's fate not relying on her own survival culminates in a revealing accusation from Amy, "I don't need you to die for me Doctor. Do I look that clingy?" Her defensiveness here suggests her ambivalent reluctance to admit to any emotional and physical dependency on her part. This changes by the end of *Flesh and Stone* and this aspect of the character is further examined in the relationship with Rory from *The Vampires of Venice* through to *Cold Blood*. Whilst she often physically places those that bond with her at arm's length, possibly fearing their disloyalty, deep down she craves intimacy. Here, the Doctor's solution is to bite her to snap her out of her nightmare and this is strikingly the reverse of young Amy's attacks on the psychiatrists who attempted to unpick her neuroses about the Raggedy Doctor. Whereas Amy bit those experts to distance them from her, the Doctor bites her to try and bring her closer and back into his protection – "You bit me!" she cries, "Yep, and now you're alive," concludes the Doctor defiantly. Her claim that she will not need him to die for her is of course the antithesis of the major story arc of the series. He *has* to die for her in *The Big Bang* in order to restore to her the loving relationship she had with her parents and secure the marriage with Rory.

The Doctor and Amy's destinies are wrapped together over the course of the series and our first inklings of the real importance of this are scattered through this two-part story and with some references back to similar clues in previous episodes. Trust and faith are important themes here, naturally evolving from Amy's issues with the Doctor in *The Eleventh Hour* where the Time Lord took twelve years to return to Leadworth to deal with Prisoner Zero. Sacred Bob's murder at the hands of the Angel, the death of a soldier "who died in fear. In pain and alone" even after the Doctor had reassured him about the nature of fear, is a further example of the Doctor's flawed heroics. "You made me trust you and when it mattered you let me down," accuses Bob with a line that could well have come from Amy after twice being abandoned in *The Eleventh Hour*. His reliability is questioned and Angel Bob's comments taunt him into action. He insists on a vote of confidence from Amy, River and Octavian. Octavian sums it up well with "We have faith, sir" in that the Doctor, just as Peter Pan in Disney's film version advises the Darling children that all they require to fly is "faith and trust, and something I forgot... just a little bit of pixie dust," will achieve not only a leap of faith figuratively but literally as he shoots down the gravity globe and they all 'fly' to the surface of the Byzantium to escape the Angels. The entire speech about the trap that the Angels put him into is a triumphant affirmation of his own trickster-like nature and the symbolism of the Doctor caught in a trap is one that will be repeated with the greatest of all traps – the Pandorica. Similarly, as the Doctor attempts to guide Amy back through the forest to the Byzantium using just the sonic screwdriver and her communicator in *Flesh and Stone*, River's blunt "it's never gonna work" is met with a tirade of angry abuse from him: "What else have you got? River, tell me!" certainly underlines the fragile nature of trust and the need for faith from all three characters. His anger continues to drive him when he suggests that the crack in time could be fed with a "big, complicated space time event" and she asks, "Like what, for instance?" and he yells, "Like ME... FOR INSTANCE!" His explosive anger suggests a momentary projection of his negative traits, his shadow self, onto River at the very moment that he needs her and Amy to trust him more than ever.

A significant moment in *Flesh and Stone* is where Amy is completely alone and blind in the forest after the Clerics that were protecting her have been devoured by the crack. This is beautifully emphasised in a brief wide shot used by director Adam Smith that shows Amy, wearing red incidentally, symbolically alone like Little Red Riding Hood or one of the Babes lost in the middle of the wood. It evokes all the Gothic connotations attached to primeval fears and childhood memories of the forest, the mythical beings that inhabit them and the cautionary tales attached to this heritage. Typically, Little Red Riding Hood is seen as a Gothic fairy tale about a young girl achieving sexual maturity and seems an appropriate link here to Amy's impending wedding about which she still remains in denial. Her fear for her own life in the forest is eventually translated into a full-blown confession to the Doctor about her marriage to Rory at the end of the episode and her temporary blindness in the story could therefore be seen as not just a physical impairment but also a moral or spiritual blindness that she emerges from. The Greek words for 'sight' and 'knowledge' are semantically linked and Amy's physical and mental state is best summed up by Chad Hartsock's examination of Plato's allegory of the prisoner in the cave in *Sight and Blindness in Luke-Acts: the Use of Physical Features in Characterization*, where the prisoner believes he can *see* reality in the shadows on the cave walls. Hartsock suggests, "Socrates repeatedly declares that for the prisoner to understand the true reality rather than simply the shadows, the prisoner must 'look towards the light' and his eyes must 'become steady' and truth is represented by the light and by the sun." As Amy opens her eyes to face the blinding light at the edge of the forest, she is confronted with the truth of the crack in time and the true nature of the threat it poses. Her temporary blindness is also linked into the child's fear of abandonment and her own adult separation anxiety. As in so many fairy tales, the blindness is also suggestive of a punishment for her own curiosity, where quite clearly the Doctor told her to remain in the TARDIS and she, like so many companions before her, blatantly refused to conform to his conventions.

At the conclusion of *Flesh and Stone*, in the TARDIS Amy confesses to the Doctor, after suggesting that he is running from River, that "I'm running too." They sit in her bedroom, having been gone five minutes since the end of *The Eleventh Hour*, and she shows him her wedding dress, finally admitting that she is getting married in the morning. This moment of trust and openness between them is suddenly disrupted by Amy's libidinous need for a one-night stand with the Doctor. Whilst this may be one way in which a traumatised subject might attempt to recover from a life or death situation, it still suggests Amy's sense of trust is somewhat misplaced, where the revelation of "running" from the wedding dress is a cue to seduce the Doctor. She is distancing herself from her intended husband-to-be in a clear disavowal of the planned marriage and the adult relationship that it signifies. Previously, we have argued that Amy's cynical, offhand demeanour is just a projection of a dysfunctional personality coping with abandonment issues, but at this point in the series what could be regarded as her feisty defensiveness is transformed into behaviour that problematises her as a character and plays directly into those criticisms from fans that she is too sexualised, is seen as a "slut", that we highlighted in Chapter 1. In hindsight, it is clear that Moffat is playing against the audience's identification with the character, defying our expectations of her by imbuing her with a sexual worldliness that would not be unremarkable in some of the female characters in *Coupling* (2000-4). The Doctor is, presumably, summarising most of the audience's thoughts at this point with his exclamation of "you're getting married in the morning!" as she starts to seduce him and he demonstrably repels her. The consequences of her 'elopement' with, and desire for, the Doctor is explored in the following episodes, crucially timed with the introduction of Rory as a regular character. However, the way she is presented here does the character no favours, simultaneously offering her as very gratuitous 'eye candy' in the retrogressive idiom of many past female companion characters, often described as 'something for the dads' within the history of the show, whilst seriously impairing what was initially our willingness to empathise with the character, her emotions and her background. There is also a sense that Moffat is using this scene to try and unburden the series of its post-2005 romanticisation and sexualisation of the Doctor's relationship with his companions. He seems intent on disassociating the Doctor from the humanising, romantic and unrequited love entanglements of the Tenth Doctor's era. He restates the Doctor's separateness from them in the way the Eleventh Doctor is endearingly clueless about Amy's staggeringly obvious emphasis "about *who*... I *want*" and in how he points out Amy's questionably moral actions on the night before her wedding with an emphatic "and this can't ever work" as he fends off her attentions. Whilst it is a much-needed clearing of the decks, inviting in a reinterpretation of the Doctor as a potentially morally asexual character, in the process it inadvertently damages the character of Amy by making her less likeable.

## "The eyes as the windows of the soul"

In Chapters 1 and 2 we looked at how the series and the characters used perception, the act of looking, of deducting and seeing the true meaning of events within different stories, using many visual tropes such as the Atraxi eyeball, the eye looking through the crack in the wall, the zoom of the camera into the Doctor and Amy's eyes and the omnipresent screens of Starship UK to suggest obsessive looking and watching. It has also been used as a symbolic counterpoint to the maturing relationship between the Doctor and Amy. The Doctor has taught Amy how to navigate her way through the perils of time travel and encounters with alien and inhuman societies through noticing the important details and using them to find a solution to a particular trouble or problem.

In *The Time of Angels* and *Flesh and Stone* this theme is developed further and sparks a crisis that threatens Amy's life. Inevitably, with the reintroduction of the Weeping Angels, the inherent dangers of looking and not looking are again of concern to the series. Previously in *Blink*, Moffat played with the conventions of the children's game Grandmother's Footsteps to create a monster that only moved when you blinked and remained 'quantum locked' in stone if you kept looking at it. With these two episodes Moffat gets the opportunity to take the concept further and imbues the Weeping Angels with ferocious new attributes and abilities whilst also embedding them within a symbolic and psychological order of meaning that examines the complex nature of our curiosity and desire to gaze. Amy's curiosity and interrogating gaze replicates our own fascination with viewing the fearful and the horrific that is implicated in the *Doctor Who* obsession with monsters, fear and death. Ultimately, this intense interest becomes an instrument of possession as the image of the Angel burned into Amy's retina enters her consciousness and changes the nature of the threat from what is initially the physical materialisation of the Angel to something more troubling: her loss of control and loss of humanity. Moffat's use of devices to scare children by turning their own fears against them, with monsters under the bed or danger lurking in the corner of your eye, is here augmented by Weeping Angels literally manifesting themselves from our television sets and later by a deadly game of Blind Man's Buff. Symbolically, we are also concerned with what would be termed the 'evil eye', where the gaze of the Weeping Angels is now akin to Medusa turning her victims to stone, and with the image of an Angel on the back of the retina itself becoming an Angel in the 'mind's eye' and possessing the soul of the character and, suggestively, the viewer too. These are powerful and ancient concepts and if we are to assign the Angels as figures of insurgency in a religious war with Christianity, as represented by Father Octavian and his Clerics, then the widespread belief in the Muslim world of 'the evil eye' as symbolic of having power over someone or something through evil intent is an apposite one to use. However, virtually every culture has referred to it and the oldest references appear in the cuneiform texts of the Sumerians, Babylonians, and Assyrians, around 3000 BC. The 'mind's eye' suggests the visualisation of ideas, of creating images in the mind as part of the memory, and River, reading from the book about the Angels, underlines the significance of Moffat's concept: "What if we had ideas that could think for themselves? What if one day our dreams no longer needed us? When these things occur and are held to be true the time will be upon us. The time of Angels." The power of images to come alive in the mind as a theme reaches an apotheosis when the Doctor realises that all the statues surrounding them are dying Angels, "losing their image" as Amy notes, but then with the power of those images rejuvenated by the radiation spilling out of the crashed Byzantium.

With these symbols in mind, it is fascinating to see how Adam Smith and Moffat use these concepts and marry them to tightly edited sequences that might suggest a layer of meanings and perceptions transmitted by the character of Amy and to the audience. It is important to look at the scene where Amy is trapped in the drop ship with the video loop of the Angel and consider Laura Mulvey's 1975 article *Visual Pleasure and Narrative Cinema* as well as an understanding of the different ways of looking or gazing, offering a counterpoint to her arguments, that are occurring in the sequence in *The Time of Angels*. Mulvey's highly influential article was a study in the meaning of cinematic spectatorship and used Freudian psychoanalytic theory to argue that cinema viewing allows the viewer (essentially male in her analysis) to engage in a voyeuristic objectification of female characters and a narcissistic identification with an idealised image seen on the screen. Her argument was based on her assertion that "pleasure in looking has been split between active/male and passive/female" and that it is purely a male spectator that is viewing in a voyeuristic and fetishistic manner. Her contention was that classic filmmaking objectified women in relation to a "controlling male gaze" and therefore men do the looking whilst women are there to be looked at. The problem with this view is that it assumes the female spectator is completely passive, that passivity is purely female and activity is purely male. Neither does it take into consideration that female and male viewers may engage both passively and actively at subjects on the screen nor does it consider that there are gay, lesbian and transgender spectators and that the male body is now increasingly sexually objectified in mainstream cinema and television.

There is an interesting opening line to the scene. Amy hangs out of the doorway and asks, "Anybody need me? Nobody?" as the Doctor and River are preoccupied. It is both a call out to the characters in the story and a request of the desires of the audience watching at home. Unconsciously, we ask ourselves if we do need Amy and naturally the active male, heterosexual viewer will definitely find some correlation there as an attractive Karen Gillan/Amy posits that question to them. However, there is no response to her from the human characters in the drama. We are all, as viewers, now alerted to the fact that she is alone with the image of the Angel in the ship. The only response Amy gets is from the four-second clip of the Angel in the hold of the Byzantium. It has turned its head and is glancing at her whereas seconds before it hid its face in its hands. She moves towards the camera, her interest piqued. Amusingly, Smith then intercuts a short scene between River and the Doctor as they discuss the definitive work on the Angels, written by a madman. "Ooh, not bad. Bit slow in the middle. Didn't you hate his girlfriend?" mocks the Doctor as he hurriedly skims through the book. The joke about the girlfriend is a rather appropriately tongue-in-cheek barb about lack of male identification with female characters and ironically could be a view directed at Amy's pairing with the Doctor. The madman and his book is also a clever correlation to the 'madman with his box' motif and also prefigures the madness of

Vincent van Gogh in the later episode *Vincent and the Doctor*, especially the lines about ideas thinking for themselves and coming alive. Later, when Octavian asks River if she trusts the Doctor and she says she does, he has to confirm, "He's not some kind of madman then?" She can only repeat, "I absolutely trust him" and in doing so confirms that the Doctor is probably a madman you *can* trust.

The Angel is now facing Amy directly with its arms in supplication. Their mutual gazes are reflected in Smith's use of shots to suggest Amy's point of view and the Angel's point of view both layered into the identifying gaze of the audience. On top of this we must also remember that other modes of viewing are taking place – the CCTV camera that views the Angel in the hold of the ship and the camera that Smith is using to film the scene. There is a multiplicity of viewing and gazing occurring in this scene. Smith switches from a medium shot of Amy, now engrossed in the image of the Angel, to her gazing out of the screen directly at the audience. She glances at the time code on the video clip and our point of view becomes hers as a close-up of it appears on the screen. The audience actively becomes Amy's point of view, the Angel's point of view, the camera and the security CCTV in this scene. In close-up, Amy jumps back. There is a cut back to the Angel, which has now moved closer on the screen, the previous shot corresponding with its closer view of Amy. This spell is broken by a quick insert shot of Amy's left profile and this immediately restores the audience point of view as dominant for a moment before the next shot which is a mid-shot of Amy gazing directly at the Angel on the screen and at the audience through their television screens.

Back outside, River is consulting her diary and tells the Doctor she knows who he is because she has pictures of all his faces. There is a further joke about him never showing up in the right order and that she always requires the Spotter's Guide. The Doctor, leafing through the book on the Angels, demands, "Why aren't there pictures?" as Smith dramatically intercuts a close-up of the Angel in the video loop. Amy is still gazing at it and us. She attempts to shut off the screen with a remote control and having failed to do so peers at the images, "You're just a recording. You can't move," she says disbelievingly. She then tries to unplug the monitor. Smith cuts in more and more close-ups of Amy and the Angel. She gets worried and tries to leave the drop ship but finds the doors locked and starts shouting for the Doctor's help as, from her point of view, we see the Angel now with an open, befanged mouth. At precisely the same moment the Doctor quotes from the book, "That which holds the image of an Angel becomes itself an Angel" and confirms what inevitably the audience has already been speculating about and dreading. A number of subtexts here suggest the breaking of the fourth wall (a familiar television trope where a programme acknowledges the presence of the audience and often directly addresses them and is more often used in comedy and only experimentally in drama) where Smith and his editor Will Oswald emulate the act of blinking, as if the audience is Amy looking at the Angel, and the progressive movement of the Angel is a result of that communal blink, and where Amy is directly looking at the Angel but also looking right at the audience. They compound this suggestion when, after River has questioned the Doctor's quote from the book, there is a cut back to Amy who turns to look again and she/we see the Angel now materialising out of the monitor screen and fulfilling the prophecy of the book. This emphasises Moffat's use of childhood fears by suggesting that the Angels can pop out of the television screen after their victims, adding a further symbolic complexity to the audience's relationship with the images they see on the screen. The complex interweaving, and consequent ownership, of the image of the Angel in the vault and the gaze at the image is also wittily referred to in the pre-titles where River is preparing her message to the Doctor and our viewpoint is that of the security camera, with its monochrome, indistinct footage later duplicated by the footage of the Angel, where she both knowingly winks to the Doctor as a character within the drama and acknowledges the pleasures of gazing to the audience. Amy's encounter with the Angel on the monitor screen also mirrors the similar scene in *The Beast Below* where Amy is sat inside the voting booth and is 'brainwashed' by images displayed on a screen and routed directly into her cortex through the vivid motif of speeded up imagery playing over her eyes.

The sequence is visceral, full of tension and anxiety, cleverly using the act of looking and the art of capturing images to provide what Barbara Creed refers to as "the uncanny gaze" that she believes is central to experiencing horror films. In *Phallic Panic: Film, Horror and the Primal Uncanny*, Creed suggests that the uncanny, which in horror films may be codified as ghosts, spirits, bodies, doubles and monsters that remain hidden and then are suddenly revealed, relies on the gaze to conduct this revelation. "As the horrified spectator focuses on the scenario unfolding on the screen, the uncanny gaze is constructed at that point at which the familiar becomes unfamiliar. The spectator experiences a sense of fractured identity, of the self in 'bits and pieces'," she explains and her further investigation of the embodiment of the uncanny in male and female monsters and doubles is certainly suggested in the way that Adam Smith has shot the sequence. His imagery suggests that the figure of the Angel is virtually mirroring the figure of Amy in the scene and this reflects the Gothic theme of the double as an agent that threatens the integrity of the self, a malevolent other that destabilises the identity of the individual. One of the interesting aspects of the Angels is that they remain of unspecific gender, appearing female but also very androgynous and again this aligns with the 'monstrous-feminine' that we discussed in Chapter 1. The opening maw of the Angel, as it materialises out of the screen, relates to Creed's definition of it in *The Monstrous-Feminine: Film, Feminism, Psychoanalysis*, as "woman as vampire" or "woman as witch". One of her other definitions of the 'monstrous-feminine' also seems to be referred to later after the revelation that the image of the Angel is now in Amy's mind and where Amy herself thus becomes "woman as possessed body".

It also alludes to Nakata Hideo's *Ringu* (1998) and its story of an urban legend surrounding a videotape that curses the viewer to an untimely death. The story of a vengeful female ghost seeking some kind of rest reaches its climax when the film's central character, an investigative journalist, witnesses the spirit's emergence from the playing videotape, out of the television screen itself, and into the 'real' world. Eric White, in describing Hideo's themes in his case study on *Ringu* and *Ringu 2* for *Japanese Horror Cinema*, also summarises much of this chapter's observations about the similar sequence in *The Time of Angels*: "the film thus associates ubiquitous technological mediation – that is the cameras, television sets, videocassette recorders, telephones and other such hardware foregrounded throughout the film – with the intrusion of 'posthuman' otherness into contemporary cultural life." In *Ringu*, the spirit spreads its curse through its own urban legend and, because the videotape that contains it becomes a much sought after and copied item, virally possesses those that watch it. The image of an Angel becoming an Angel fulfils the same function, the creature multiplying itself through images and possessing victims simply through the locked gaze. This reproduction of the Angel from a video loop also seems to become part of the Gothic pastiche of the story where the reuse and simulation of Gothic conventions in themselves become, as Allan Lloyd Smith outlines in *American Gothic Fiction: An Introduction*, "a progression of increasing distortion... a ghosting of the original Gothic." The pastiche is also specifically evident in Murray Gold's music where his atonal registers and eerie ambiences recall Danny Elfman's scores for *Batman* (1989) and *Sleepy Hollow* (1999), Kubrick's use of Penderecki and Bartok in *The Shining* (1980) and some of James Horner's string motifs from *Aliens* (1983).

Equally, the theme of the locked gaze as a possessive force is repeated when the stone Angel on the loose lures in the patrolling Clerics Angelo and Christian with a false hope by using their fallen comrades' voices to entreat them to "Come and see." The request to see the image of an Angel is achieved through the further "technological mediation" of the two-way radios that the Clerics use to communicate with each other. As each Cleric is murdered, his consciousness is in turn used by the Angel to entrap his colleagues. This process eventually culminates in the creation of Angel Bob as the mouthpiece for the rapidly growing army of the Weeping Angels. The use of the dead man's consciousness is an extension of Moffat's own creation of the data ghosts in *Silence in the Library* and suggests that humanity's fate is to become a simulation of itself in death. Moffat assigns new powers to the Weeping Angels, their evil spreading like a virus and where Fred Botting, discussing the use of Gothic tropes in *Gothic Romanced*, describes evil as "boundless, unconstrained by structure or location, diabolically intent on reversal, subversion and multiplication." This is confirmed in the Doctor's realisation that the images of the Angels consume us in the very act of our looking at them that, originally in *Blink*, was the only way we could immobilise them. "The eyes are not the windows of the soul, they are the doors. Beware what may enter there," he quotes from the madman's book on the Angels, confirming the earlier description of the Angel as "a thing in the belly of that ship that can't ever die." This is an analogue to the curse of the videotape in *Ringu* and the symbolism of the eye, as a two-way conduit between universes, between the unconscious and the conscious, that neatly ties into the Atraxi and Prisoner Zero's use of the crack in Amy's wall and how she was mind-wiped in *The Beast Below*. Seeing is also not quite believing in *The Time of Angels* and the statuary that fills the Aplan Mortarium is later revealed to be an army in waiting, covertly masking its true identity with a "low level perception filter" until one of them arrives in the Byzantium on a rescue mission. Again, the use of filters by the Angels to camouflage their activity is suggestive of a subversive enemy operating beyond the knowledge of the Doctor, as it was with Prisoner Zero in *The Eleventh Hour*, and feeds into the fears of a phantom-like Al-Qaeda 'other' operating across many boundaries, infiltrating the recesses of Western culture and of our own minds through the crackling, indistinct, proselytising video messages sent from a frontline of the Weeping Angel jihad, emphasising the story's subtextual interpretation of religious indoctrination via media and warfare.

## "Hello sweetie"

Amy, as we have discussed in Chapter 2, is very much analogous of Wendy to the Doctor's representation of Peter Pan in this series. The relationship that Amy has with the Doctor until this point has been one of mutual discovery, where Amy has proved herself to the Doctor by solving the dilemmas posed by the Star Whale and the Daleks. As a result of this the Doctor has exorcised his shadow side, the negative traits of himself, and has learned to respect the human, emotional perception of his companion. This development is to some extent thrown into disarray by the arrival of River Song. Her ambiguous status intriguingly reveals to Amy that this strange man she ran away with on the night of her wedding is certainly capable of human desire, perhaps of heteronormative relationships with women. The triad of Amy, River and the Doctor is also reflected in Barrie's *Peter Pan* with the interrelationships between the characters of Peter, Wendy and Tinker Bell. Barrie's book is also, ironically, a warning to parents to act responsibly in the way they bring up their children, that finds its resonances in the way that Amy relates to the Doctor and River and in the Doctor's family background. Peter is one of the Lost Boys of Neverland as much as the Doctor is the Last of the Time Lords of Gallifrey. We have had hints of the Doctor's lineage and relationships, including references to his childhood home, his family and an actual 'granddaughter' Susan in the original series, and in the revival we have his 'daughter' Jenny in *The Doctor's Daughter*, a mention of a brother in *Smith and Jones*, and the appearance of a mysterious Time Lady in *The End of Time* that many, including Russell T. Davies, have speculated is his mother. The Doctor's status as a runaway has been part of the series since 1963, with the First Doctor immediately asking, "Have you ever thought what it's like to be wanderers in the fourth dimension? Have you? To be exiles? Susan and I are cut off from our own planet, without friends or protection." It transpires later that the Doctor actually stole the TARDIS and ran away from Gallifrey. Like Peter Pan, the eternal, childlike Doctor prefers freedom and exile to stuffy, adult conformity, and Jason Marc Harris describes Barrie's portrayal of adults in *Folklore and the Fantastic in Nineteenth-Century British Fiction* as "not superior to children developmentally; adults' imaginations are diminished as well as their spontaneity and their morality, if it seems improved, depends more on convention than it does on compassion. These characters do not carry their childhood journeys into Neverland on through into adulthood." In *Doctor Who*, the companions are emblematic of the journey from immaturity to maturity and Amy is no different. Her journey is, as we have stated, one that sees her reconnect to her childlike imagination and her own Neverland, one she contains within her in order to make sense of her self in the face of parental abandonment and her impending adult life with Rory. Unfortunately, as Harris concludes, *Peter Pan* does not offer this "ethical amelioration or reconciliation between the childish imagination and adult rationality." It is equally questionable if *Doctor Who* can achieve the same reconciliation.

The relationship between Amy and the Doctor, posited thus far as one of shared and innocent adventure, dramatically shifts in *Flesh and Stone*. Amy is highly sexualised in the role of companion and it is intimated that she is less sexually repressed than Rose, Martha or Donna, unafraid to articulate her desire to others despite her impending monogamous relationship with Rory. At the end of the episode, Amy's sexual desire for the Doctor, earlier emphasised in her desire to gaze upon the unclothed Time Lord in *The Eleventh Hour*, is allowed release as a side effect of the trauma she suffers in the forest. Amy's 'Red Riding Hood' experience, with the fairy tale itself representing a symbol of libidinal curiosity, is exacerbated by undertaking the dangerous task of walking without seeing amongst the predatory Angels in a story overloaded with the importance of seeing and perception. Karen Coats, discussing *Peter Pan* in *Looking Glasses and Neverlands: Lacan, Desire, and Subjectivity in Children*, sheds light on the sexualising of the relationship between Amy, the Doctor, River and, later, with Rory: "Wendy desires him [Peter Pan] sexually, upon their first meeting she asks for a kiss and offers one as well. In Neverland, she sees herself as the mother of the Lost Boys." This correlates with the various innuendos and questions that Amy keeps bombarding the Doctor with upon their first meeting with River, particularly the explicit moment when River requests the Doctor's help using the sonic screwdriver and she exclaims, "Oooh, Doctor. You sonic-ed her!" It also underlines Amy's later assertion that the Doctor and Rory are "my boys" in *The Vampires of Venice* and that she has by osmosis taken on a mothering role to them both, rather like the adult version of Wendy.

85

The Doctor is embarrassed and uncomfortable in the presence of Amy and River, despite his symbolic similarity to Harris's description of Peter Pan as a "chaperone between childhood and adulthood. He is a marker between the two worlds, or rather, he is a conflicted being that embodies aspects of both." Both women clearly find a certain *jouissance* in his suffering as Amy, reflecting the latent sexuality of Wendy, and the more experienced River, as femme fatale Tinker Bell, enmesh the Doctor in their dynamic interplay. This dynamic between the characters, also inclusive of Rory when he joins the series as a regular character in *The Vampires of Venice*, resembles the classic male/female attraction repulsion that maps out power as an explicit theme in the Katherine Hepburn and Spencer Tracy romantic comedies of the 1940s and 1950s and one that is also a hallmark of Moffat's writing for *Coupling* in which a number of male and female characters undergo a mutual ritual humiliation through various exchanges of power in a quest to delineate what, in essentialist terms, is a 'real man' or what is a 'real woman'. In *Coupling*, the tendency is for Moffat to depict the male characters as subordinate to each other whilst developing a form of homosocial bonding in opposition to the peer group of women in the series. This bonding will be later reflected in the way the Doctor and Rory will iron out their differences and construct their united front of masculinity in opposition to Amy's fairly dismissive view of them as "my boys".

However, this front is easily dismantled by Moffat's female characters and, like *Coupling*'s Steve Taylor, played by Jack Davenport, the Doctor is briefly shown, on the surface at least, as a weak and incompetent man in the face of so much female power. In much of Moffat's work, the stronger female characters set out, whether deliberately or by chance, to demean male characters, sometimes for very good reasons, until men demonstrate their ability to deal with problems that women themselves have failed to resolve, often achieving this victory either by accident or by design. This 'battle of the sexes' attitude would seem to have been applied to the Doctor, River and Amy in *The Time of Angels* and *Flesh and Stone*. River Song assumes an attitude that the Doctor is not as good as he thinks he is and she therefore seeks to trip him up deliberately in front of Amy, encouraging Amy in her own insouciance towards the Time Lord. This process is framed by the comedy fencing between the Doctor and River. River, again mirroring the female characters in *Coupling* and emulating Hepburn's sparring with Tracy in films like *Adam's Rib* (1947), uses her superior piloting skills to belittle the Doctor, turning him into a sulking quasi child figure. When the Doctor is told he leaves the blue brakes on, he violently addresses them as "blue boring-ers" because they stop the TARDIS from making that keynote, special noise the audience is familiar with. His reduction to child status is further emphasised by him demonstrating that "brilliant noise" to a puzzled Amy and River. This impression of the wheezing and groaning noise of the TARDIS landing is one that every child viewer has at one time or another made a stab at impersonating when re-creating the televisual experience of *Doctor Who* during play. The Doctor's freer, unorthodox methods are couched in less repressive terms compared to River's stricter, tightly controlled procedures which might accomplish the task more efficiently but are only half the fun.

The game of TARDIS one-upmanship continues when the Doctor turns the tables by rattling off an environmental reading and identifying the planet they have landed on not by referring to the instruments but by popping his head out of the TARDIS door. His instinctive and unfettered approach is regarded by River as part of his sexual charm: "He thinks he's so hot when he does that." When Amy asks how River learned to fly the TARDIS and she responds, "Oh, I got lessons from the very best," the Doctor sits back, full of pride and assuming she is praising him, only to have her then deflate that hubris with "It's a shame you were busy that day." Later in the series, in *The Pandorica Opens*, she reveals that it was indeed the Doctor that taught her to fly the ship. In mimicking the romantic comedy dialogues of Tracy and Hepburn, these scenes propose a scenario of sublimated seduction between the Doctor and River and are helped by superb performances from Alex Kingston and Matt Smith. It also parallels the similar desire for Peter Pan by Wendy, Tinker Bell and Tiger Lily in Barrie's book. Like Peter, the Doctor eventually submerges himself in disavowal and this is at its strongest in the conclusion of the episode when Amy's burgeoning desire emerges back in her bedroom and the Doctor rejects her advances.

River Song is the tomboyish femme fatale, a meld of Tinker Bell and Tiger Lily, who keeps returning to the Doctor at various points in his time stream. Moffat embellishes her character by positioning her as an enchantress with a secret, a film noir character best summed up by Mary Ann Doane's concept of the femme fatale as "the figure of a certain discursive unease, a potential epistemological trauma. For her most striking characteristic, perhaps, is the fact that she never really is what she seems to be." *The Time of Angels* and *Flesh and Stone* place key emphasis on River's relationship to the Doctor and the mystery at the centre of her incarceration in the Stormcage facility. River plays with her identity, first appearing as a glamorous, beautifully coiffed and dressed blonde spy, working undercover on the Byzantium for the Church, and then later emulates the masculinity of the Clerics with her desert camouflage gear whilst operating within a conspicuously male environment. In effect, she is the troubling return of the Great Mother symbol, the female aspect of the Doctor that he himself attempts to outrun. Amy succinctly enquires, "Are you basically running away?" as he abandons River on the surface of Alfava Metraxis and prepares the TARDIS to leave. When Amy confronts him about this, he anxiously responds, "Yep. Cos she's my future," and she questions if he really can run away from the future. "I can run away from anything I like. Time is not the boss of me." He may well be equating 'time' with River, underlining that it is her that he will not allow to dominate him. "That woman is not dragging me into anything!" he cries, referring to River but perhaps also subtextually to Amy after she has used her own influence to ensure she gets five minutes on the planet surface. Later, Amy and River bond after River acknowledges what Amy has already witnessed – the Doctor's childlike way of "keeping score" by visiting museums. Moffat also uses River in several moments of bathos during the story to highlight this domination. The Doctor makes his grand speech in the Delirium Archive about the old Gallifreyan language on the Home Box and, as Amy asks him to translate the glyphs on the Box, there is a swing from the escalation and expectation of the epic in his description, "There were many days when these words could burn stars, raise up Empires, and topple Gods," to the amusingly mundane translation of the message as "Hello sweetie." When the Doctor has a rant at Amy about the terrible danger they are in and what kind of a day he is facing in order to destroy the Angel without first dying of radiation poisoning or blowing up the ship, he ends with, "That's my day, that's what I'm up to. Any questions?" Amy clearly sees that he is aggrieved at being dragged into this situation by River and she ignores the perilous schedule he has ahead of him and asks, "Is River Song your wife?" Again, Amy observes her as a woman who has dominance over the Doctor ("the way she talks to you, I've never seen anyone do that. She's kinda like, you know, 'Heel boy!'") and then reaches the conclusion many characters and viewers have since made with "She's Mrs Doctor from the future, isn't she? Is she gonna be your wife one day?" The Doctor, again assuming a childlike petulance and wearing his "Mr Grumpy Face", responds with what clearly is a clever line scripted by Moffat and then read by Matt Smith in such a way as to be ambiguous, that seems to reply in the affirmative to her question but with the line also simply agreeing that he is "Mr Grumpy Face today". Amy extends his misery by jibing at him, "Oops! Her indoors!" as River calls for him from the doorway of the drop ship.

River is simultaneously lover, wife and mother, but the story introduces an anxiety at the heart of this definition, a darkness that only she and Octavian can eventually shed light upon. Clearly, time is not the boss of the Doctor but River might well be when we learn that she could have caused his death in the future. The Great Mother is a projection of the Doctor's own inner feminine nature and is a vital part of his fully individuated self. River's femme fatale imagery is just one aspect of this female nature, just one aspect of her character, because as we have seen earlier in *Silence in the Library* and *Forest of the Dead*, here in both of these episodes, and later in *The Pandorica Opens* and *The Big Bang*, they both care for and rely on each other. As Erich Neumann states in *The Great Mother: The Analysis of an Archetype*, the Great Mother "inspires an emotional response in both positive and negative measure. She may be experienced as *femme inspiratrice*, a loving creative muse, or as *femme fatale*, a snaring seductress." The seductress is a projection of River that we see in the pre-titles sequence, handled by director Adam Smith as if it were the opening stunt in a James Bond film, where spectacle meets camp excess. As a fifty-first century Mata Hari, she has managed to evade Alistair and his henchmen (a nice bit of metatextuality occurs by having

Simon Dutton, who played super sleuth *The Saint* in a number of television movies in the late 1980s, as the dinner-suited Alistair) with her hallucinogenic lipstick and found a way of sending a message to the Doctor. The lipstick might be something that the Q of the Bond films would supply to a female agent in the field and the frivolity of Alex Kingston's performance in these scenes reaches a climax of camp expression when she dictates her coordinates into the Home Box, pausing coquettishly to primp her hair as she emphasises "slash acorn" in reading off the last of the coordinates. In a scene that would give Bond's ski-jump off the Alps to outrun his adversaries in *The Spy Who Loved Me* (1977) a run for its money, she is jettisoned out of the airlock of the Byzantium into the waiting arms of the Doctor. As she departs, River reminds Alistair, "Like I said on the dancefloor. You might want to find something to hang on to!" which in itself refers back to Moffat's euphemistic use of 'dancing' as representative of sex, particularly in *The Doctor Dances*, and confirms her own role as proto-Bondian spy temptress. Her role as adventurer and her status as archaeologist for hire mirrors the Doctor's own freelance explorer status. With the possible exception of the second Romana, she is the closest analogy to a female Doctor the series has yet produced and we already know that her relationship to the Doctor will become one of intimate trust because, above all else, including her ability to fly the TARDIS, her TARDIS-shaped diary that intimately logs all their adventures together and which she describes as "our diary" to Amy, and the sonic screwdriver bequeathed to her by a future Doctor in *Silence in the Library*, she knows the Doctor's true name.

However, the theme of trust, as discussed earlier, is a strong one in these episodes and is intrinsically linked to the figure of River Song and to the dominating subplot of the crack in time, which returns to the fore in *Flesh and Blood*. Octavian initially warns River that she must not let the Doctor know who she truly is or he will likely not help them on their quest. Sacrifice, trust and faith are crystallised in the major scene between Octavian, being strangled by one of the Angels, and the Doctor who is desperate to free him. He warns the Doctor, "You can't trust her. You think you know her but you don't. You don't understand who or what she is." She is what Helena Bassil-Morozow, in *Tim Burton: The Monster and the Crowd*, calls "a female creature who offers [the hero] her knowledge and experience. Alternatively she can be a dangerous witch who cunningly devises to devour him." Octavian even confirms her darker side in his dying words: "She killed a man. A good man. A hero to many," after the Doctor asks why River was imprisoned in the Stormcage facility. Octavian's own perception of faith and courage intermingle here with his acknowledgement that both qualities must be tested in order to maintain their validity. The Doctor, seen as a figure who stands on the cusp of the paradoxical relationship of suffering and sacrifice, encourages faith and trust to help create new possibilities and restore order to chaos. It is the path that Octavian refers to in: "I will die in the knowledge that my courage did not desert me at the end. For that I thank God and bless the path that takes you to safety." The last scene between the Doctor and Octavian gives the story a much-needed emotional coda. "I wish I'd known you better," the Doctor says, as he sadly leaves him to his fate. Matt Smith and Iain Glen, as Octavian, are quite superb as both characters reach a crossroads in their relationship, mutually respectful of courage as the Angel prepares to strangle Octavian. Smith's performance in this scene is the icing on the cake and the very profound sadness in Smith's eyes is a moving contrast to the scenes with Angel Bob and their mixture of witty banter (the "I made him say 'comfy chairs'" joke is lovely) and gallows humour ("Get a life, Bob") combined with the eccentricity of his analysis of the crack ("Oh, that's bad. Oh, that's extremely not very good") and his rage at the Angels when they find delight in making Amy count down to her death ("I'm five... *fine!*" is a wonderful Freudian slip about Amy's childlike mental state) and at River on the Primary Flight Deck.

The idea of a life being lived by the Doctor, River and Amy as a way of testing their faith and imagination, which Ann Yeoman in *Now or Neverland* sees as binding "past, present and future, out of which synthesis we make a cohesive story and so imbue life with meaning," is central to Moffat's often complex plotting that involves multiple character points of view and different parts of the story taking place at different times and often out of order. His notion of River's 'spoilers' in the diary of her encounters with the Doctor is a central motif, where the Doctor states, "The diary – her past, my future. We keep meeting in the wrong order." There are untold stories yet to come, obviously addressing her fall from grace where she "killed a very good man, the best man I've ever known" (suggesting the victim is the Doctor), but we are prevented from leaping ahead in the diary and revealing these as 'spoilers'. River powerfully structures the expectancy of the narrative, "Long story, Doctor. Can't be told. Has to be lived." Ironically, we have already seen her live and die in *Forest of the Dead* and we know her fate, this irony symbolised in the handcuffs she wears at the end of the episode, having used handcuffs to restrain the Tenth Doctor in *Forest of the Dead* and thus prevent him from interfering in her self-sacrifice. "You, me, handcuffs. Must it always end this way?" foreshadows her death. Her acknowledgement that she will see the Doctor again soon "when the Pandorica opens" also symbolises her as harbinger, fully aware of what will, and must, happen ("I remember it well") when they reach the Pandorica. Their last scene together underlines the whole fairy-tale ethos of the series too. "That's a fairy tale," he counters at her mention of the Pandorica. "Oh, Doctor. Aren't we all?" she replies with a twinkle in her eye. Either good witch or bad witch, she vanishes in a veritable puff of smoke.

### "Time can be *un*written"

Trust, faith and the way Moffat uses quantum uncertainty in his narratives will become major themes when we reach the end of the series. In *Flesh and Stone* he lays the groundwork, with River's story becoming a schizophrenic blurring between the past informing the present and the present deciding the future. This blurring is in Moffat's referral to the crash of the Byzantium as an event in River's diary in *Silence in the Library*; an adventure in the 'Bone Meadows' which we have yet to see; her reappearance in *The Pandorica Opens*; the many references to her future crime; and her previously witnessed death. We become hyperconscious of Moffat's use of temporal ambiguity and the crack in time motif, whilst illustrating this, also suggests that any part of the *Doctor Who* canon is up for reinterpretation or, indeed, erasure through an act of his own rewriting. What many fans contested was either a continuity error or a deliberate manifestation of a 'future' Doctor, which it indeed turned out to be, also forms part of the major sequence between Amy and the Doctor in the forest. The Doctor arrives back from the explosion of the Pandorica, travelling along his own time stream and towards non-existence in our universe, to implore Amy to "start trusting" him. They debate his inability to tell the truth to which the Doctor replies, "If I always told you the truth I wouldn't need you to start trusting me." Amy is concerned about the reappearance of the crack from her bedroom wall, that symbol of anxiety over the parents she does not remember, but the future Doctor is "working it out" and instead asks her to "Remember what I told you when you were seven?" The key word here, as the Doctor himself emphasises, is 'remember' in a beautifully played, very tender scene where the Doctor takes Amy's hand and then rests his head on her forehead, encouraging her to trust him, to remember the trust she had in him as a seven year old. She is, however, gradually abandoned again as the Clerics escorting her wink out of existence. The fate of the universe ultimately boils down to her simple faith in the Doctor to help her make her way back to the ship. This scene will resonate with the climax of *The Big Bang*, where the Doctor, as storyteller, will help the sleeping Amelia to reconstruct the narrative of her childhood and bring her parents back to life. The series to date has built up a disorientating *Last Year at Marienbad* (1961) influenced concept of truth, a terror of recalling things out of order and the loss of memories where the out of sync relationship between River and the Doctor, the notions of remembering and forgetting who you are and how you perceive reality are again reiterations of the series's themes. Likewise, as the soldier Clerics forget each other whilst they investigate the crack in time on the edge of the forest, Amy's warning to Marco, "There won't be any *you* if you go back there," touches on the similar crisis she will face with Rory at the end of *Cold Blood*. The Angels laughing at the Doctor, referring back to the mockery of him by the multiform in *The Eleventh Hour*, with their "The Doctor and the TARDIS hasn't noticed yet" and director Smith's pulling back of the camera to reveal the symbolic glowing crooked smile of the crack in time is also a deliberate use of Proustian memory to try and bring order to the story arc of the season.

The looping back of narrative, with time paradoxes at the heart of it, is prefigured in the Doctor's brief moment of realisation as he leaves the forest and returns to the Byzantium. Before Octavian's death, the Doctor begins to understand the nature of the problem and his significant recall of the duck pond without its ducks and Amy's inability to recognise the Daleks parallels the growing unease in the forest as Amy realises that the Clerics protecting her are vanishing, erased from history and with each remaining Cleric instantly forgetting about their missing comrades. As the Doctor pauses before the airlock, he mutters "Time can be *un*written!" and, mimicking the round shape of the hatchway, he draws a circle in mid-air and then reverses it. There is even a 'swishing' sound effect on the soundtrack to emphasise this movement and highlight the significance of his deduction. It is also a zero, his hand movement visually resembling the motion of the windmill and symbolically linking it to Prisoner Zero and the resetting of every clock and counter to zero in *The Eleventh Hour*, to Amy's counting down to the zero of her death in the forest, that defines the entire series's story arc. It is an arc that ends and begins in *The Big Bang* as the Doctor throws himself into the sun to reverse the "fire at the end of the universe," to rewind the story, and return the timeline to the night before Amy's wedding. The clock in her bedroom turning midnight as they depart in the TARDIS at the end of the episode is full of symbolic fairy-tale meanings where 'magic' is undone at the stroke of midnight and could be a metaphor for what Spencer R. Weart describes as the "clock of doom" in *Nuclear Fear: A History of Images* where an atomic countdown featured on every issue of *Bulletin of the Atomic Scientists*, set at seven minutes to midnight in 1947 and then by 1953 the editors had moved it to two minutes to midnight, "when hydrogen bombs arrived. The image, ignoring what would happen after the hour had struck, had a clear symbolism: nuclear midnight meant the end of time."

The time-devouring crack in the universe gobbles up history, for all the world becoming a parody of Jean Baudrillard's postmodernist assertion that we are living at the end of history itself where, as Jonathan Bignell explains in *Postmodern Media Culture*, Baudrillard's concept of the end of history can be explained as, "Either the acceleration of modernity has increased to the extent that 'we have flown free of the referential sphere of the real end of history,' or because the 'masses' produced by the media have nullified the discourse of history by 'deceleration, indifference and stupefaction,' or because events are so imbricated in representation that linear time, cause and effect, and the difference between real and representation become unsustainable, so that *Apocalypse Now* (1979) or *JFK* (1991), for example, become more 'true' accounts of events than non-fictional representations." Time running out as a result of some colossal explosion which occurred in Amy's time is also used to explain why humanity has such a terrible time recalling notable events like "a Cyberking, a giant Cyberman walks all over Victorian London and no one even remembers" and it suggests a playfulness at work where Moffat amusingly offers a solution to fan critiques of major portions of *Doctor Who* 'history' that questions why multiple alien invasions and incursions in Earth's past are conveniently only ever remembered by the Doctor and his companions and never by the populace. Moffat not only has the crack in the universe as the major threat in the series providing a convenient if not apocalyptic solution to wiping out all of the marauding Angels but he also has it threatening the fabric of the series itself as it gradually erases events and people in the *Doctor Who* universe. To cap it all he even arranges for the transmission of *The Pandorica Opens*, the date of Amy's wedding and when the TARDIS explodes to be one and the same, 26 June 2010. This Baudrillard-like 'cause and effect' unravelling of time, the referencing and then erasure of history and the reorganisation of key events using Moffat's distinctive script structuring wittily reflects an essence of the fan constructions and erasures within *Doctor Who* canonicity itself. His use of the crack in the universe story to justify or not these re-constructions (or 'ret-cons' as they are familiarly known) within fan perceived canonicity is something we will return to in the last chapter. With time being re-written and un-written in *Flesh and Stone* we also get a taste of what Moffat has in store for the finale. The erasure of the Clerics does not seem to have any consequences for the rest of history, and they are in effect cannon (or indeed canon) fodder if this is the case, but with the Doctor warning Amy that "if the time energy catches up with you, you'll never have been born. It will erase every moment of your existence. You will never have lived at all," the ramifications of her erasure do seem to be of greater importance. The Doctor's realisation about Amy, as he sees the clock in Amy's room strike midnight, is that "it's you, it's all about you. Everything. It's about you. Amy Pond. Mad, impossible Amy Pond. I don't know why, I've no idea, but quite possibly the single most important thing in the history of the universe is that I get you sorted out right now." The connection between the time-devouring crack in the wall, the obsession with the 'remembering' and 'forgetting' of people, places, events and times and the disruption of the wedding day of an abandoned child-woman all weave together in this scene. And Moffat throws in a bit of bathos after this grand speech by having Amy misconstrue the "get you sorted out right now" of this major plot development as the promised fulfilment of her own sexual desires, with her assuming that the Doctor is bundling her into the TARDIS to have his way with her rather than 'sort' the problem with the universe. She seems to have forgotten that travelling with the Doctor is one of the most dangerous things you can ever do and, as the Fourth Doctor so succinctly put it in *Pyramids of Mars*, "one false move and you'll never know the time again."

## Chapter Five

# THE VAMPIRES OF VENICE

Written by: Toby Whithouse
Directed by: Jonny Campbell
First broadcast: 8 May 2010

---

"Then I take it you're a refugee, like me?"

Monsters as troubling metaphors for race, ethnicity and immigration are inextricably part of the lifeblood of the original series of *Doctor Who*, symbolically itself a project conceived in the twilight of Empire. James Chapman, in *Inside the TARDIS: The Worlds of Doctor Who*, clearly sees such subtexts emerging from narratives about intruding aliens as early as 1967's *The Ice Warriors* that attempt "to characterise the monster as a form of 'Other' that represents cultural anxieties around race and immigration." With that story transmitted contemporaneous to Enoch Powell's infamous 'rivers of blood' speech in Birmingham in 1968, and with later serials such as *The Mutants* tackling the post-war dismantling of empire and the acknowledgement of the evils of colonialism, it is evident that *Doctor Who* often commentates, whether explicitly or implicitly, on political, social and cultural concerns. Alec Charles has already explored many of these issues with *Doctor Who*'s past and present in his essay, 'The Ideology of Anachronism: Television, History and the Nature of Time' in *Time and Relative Dissertations in Space*. Whilst he praises Russell T. Davies for "resurrecting *Doctor Who* within a socially and sexually aware world of council housing and flamboyant sensuality" and observes that "the 2005 series... breathed life, real life, into the format for the very first time and thus began to overcome the stagnant decadence of postcolonial nostalgia in which the series had been steeped," he also understands some of the problems that Toby Whithouse's *The Vampires of Venice* represents within this revival. One of the obvious changes that Moffat and his writers have made to the format's newly-acquired social awareness is signposted here by this series's rather nostalgia-fueled retreat into the programme's past. Whilst we see the return of classic monsters in new guises, such as the Daleks and the Silurians, restaging much of the political content of the original series, gone are the extended families of the companions who often reinforced Davies's agenda for real-world verisimilitude, and absent are some of the stories set in recognisable, modern-day, city environments that provided tangible touchstones of the ordinary world within which the extraordinary often took place. The only element that resembles Davies's world is the relationship between Amy and Rory, and bringing them back together in this story is the most successful aspect of Whithouse's script. Understandably, there is a conscious effort to move away from Davies's format to prevent the series from a stagnation of a different kind, but is a retreat into a nostalgic reverence of the series a good move? As Alec Charles argues, this vision is based on a reading of the series as "a televisual text that offers itself in the guise of anti-imperialist human liberalism [that] ends up as a paradigm of ideological and ontological conservatism." The ideas and themes lurking under the surface of *The Vampires of Venice* suggest the revival of the series is also not immune to offering a conservative view of moral and ethical issues whilst simultaneously peddling the format's liberalism.

As early as Mark Gatiss's script for *The Unquiet Dead*, the subtext, that Charles might see as a retrogressive reminder of the original series's stagnation, can be detected about the influx of Eastern immigrants into the West and whether they should be welcomed into British communities. His alien refugees, the Gelth, could be seen as analogous to Polish, Serbian and Russian citizens facing entrenched British prejudices about foreigners. Troublingly, the Gelth turn out to be the Trojan horses in an evil attempt to possess all of the Earth and the story is reduced to a rather uncomfortable alignment of the monster with the immigrant. In effect, both his and Toby Whithouse's scripts share a similar plot and themes. An alien race, here the Saturnynes and originally the Gelth in Gatiss's story, flee from a disaster that affects space and time – with 'the silence' and the Time War as more or less the same proposition – and seek shelter and a desire to establish a colony on Earth. Whithouse chooses to use vampires, symbolic figures already saturated with dense and multiple meanings, as the invading monstrous force in his story but he also clearly defines them as evil from the outset, whereas the Gelth's real motives are not revealed until the climax of *The Unquiet Dead*. The drama reflects many readings of the vampire coded as an anxiety about immigration and racism. As Dale Hudson argues in 'Vampires of colour and the performance of multi-cultural whiteness' in *The Persistence of Whiteness*: "vampire films... reflect changes in immigration laws and public perceptions of immigrants and immigration. Vampires are represented as sexually predatory immigrants who infect and enslave the weak and unwary. Vampires contaminate flesh and blood, they disrupt national and racial certainty." The fear of the foreign immigrant encapsulated in the invading vampires of this story could also be linked to a number of debates taking place in the period leading up to the episode's transmission. Certainly, with the General Election having just taken place days before this episode was shown, the issue of immigration was a major point of debate, where, lest we forget, Gordon Brown had just been hoist by his own petard at the end of April 2010 with 'bigot-gate', caught calling a Labour supporter, sixty-five-year-old Gillian Duffy, who had challenged him over the economy and immigration, a "bigoted woman."

This incident and the BNP's election manifesto calling for "no further immigration from Muslim countries as it presents one of the most deadly threats to the survival of our nation," are the latest arguments in a decades-long debate that has clouded the modern British political landscape since the late 1940s. Such arguments often reflect the way immigrants are frequently seen by the right wing as a drain on national resources whilst also spreading their own undemocratic ideas. Joe Feagin's 'Toward an Integrated Theory of Systemic Racism' in *The Changing Terrain of Race and Ethnicity* by Maria Krysan and Amanda E. Lewis considers this reactionary opinion within the powerful image of the vampire as: "sucking blood from many victims, while rather harsh, does strongly suggest the continuing *process* of extraction of resources from one group to the benefit of another." Whithouse acknowledges, in his use of the vampire, that the genre often expresses some of the discourses on race and nation within public opinions of immigrants and immigration. Vampires, particularly, are often treated in such narratives with much the same hostility as are actual immigrants from Eastern and Southern Europe. Rosanna's line about the death of her race as one more to add to the Doctor's guilty conscience disinters a number of contradictory views of the series as either white, post-colonial, post-imperialist apologia, multi-cultural propaganda or as conservative racism. The reactions to the first episode of the revival, *Rose*, and to Gatiss's *The Unquiet Dead*, both broadcast in 2005, illustrate how the series is often perceived from opposing political viewpoints. David Butler, in his introduction to *Time and Relative Dissertations in Space*, cites several posts made on the BNP's own website about the first episode, where *Rose* is seen as "the BBC [using] any opportunity to force multi-culturalism down our throats. Now we have a Dr Who assistant who has a black boyfriend," and where the depiction of alien refugees in *The Unquiet Dead* is described on his own website by science fiction author Lawrence Miles as "offensive, poisonous, xenophobic shit."

Whithouse also brokers an additional subtext about mixed-race heritage and the contamination of the human gene pool by alien 'Others', a pool literally symbolised in the offspring of the Saturnyne swimming about in the canals of Venice. The story's obsession with the monstrous 'Other' is seen in the vampirism of the Saturnynes as representative of a 'body politic' that attempts to annex an area of Renaissance Italy for its own purist colonial purposes as well as the conversion of human women into suitably bioengineered wives for the thousands of husbands waiting in the waters of Venice. The annexation of Venice in the story, codified as a form of Balkanism in the way the Saturnynes geopolitically attempt to divide the city into regions that could be potentially hostile or non-cooperative with each other, is ironically reinforced by the fact that the story was filmed in Trogir, Croatia, where borders and ethnicity became central to the post-Bosnian war era in what Jack David Eller describes in *From Culture to Ethnicity to Conflict* as a sense of "new 'pure' nation-states emerging from the ruins of Yugoslavia." *The Vampires of Venice* sets up a story of a refugee alien species and their desire for coexistence with the human race at a time when the figure of the vampire plays a central role in the modernising agenda of the genre itself where it is no longer constrained to the Gothic landscapes of pre-modernist Europe but is an unrestrained global, capitalist influence, crossing borders without prejudice. In *Vampire Legends in Contemporary American Culture*, William Patrick Day also proposes that "tales of the vampire in search of community have a tangential relation to the political and social movements of this era, particularly feminism and gay rights." Whithouse's script for *The Vampires of Venice* also arrives during a period of interesting and rapid development for the vampire genre and how it is currently explored in cinema and television. Indeed, Whithouse has significantly added to a modernist re-contextualising of the genre with the complex, psychological examination of the often-indistinct divide between supernatural creature and mortal human and the quixotic nature of good and evil in his much-celebrated series *Being Human* (2008- ). That series is very much a part of the explosion in the post-modern fascination with vampires represented, to an extent, by the teenage vampire romances of Stephanie Meyer's *Twilight* series and the highly sexualised tales of Southern vampire and human integration in Charlaine Harris's Sookie Stackhouse novels, now adapted for television as *True Blood* (2008- ). While he is restrained by the audience and the time-slot he is writing for in *Doctor Who*, Whithouse nevertheless reflects the multiple readings of the genre, using the monstrous Saturnynes to comment on the fluidity of sexuality, racial purity and ethnicity and this is signified in several key scenes of the story.

In the processing chamber, the theme of the vampire as immigrant 'Other' polluting the bodies of human beings and as a creature problematising gender identification and sexuality is synthesised in the confrontation between Amy and Rosanna. It is also where the vampire as representative of the 'deadly threat to nationhood' is conflated with Amy's loss of humanity. Judith Halberstam describes this theme in *Skin Shows: Gothic Horror and the Technology of Monsters*: "the monster itself is an economic form in that it condenses various racial and sexual threats to nation, capitalism and the bourgeoisie in one body." In the scene, Amy is made aware of this process in literal and metaphoric terms. "This is how it works. First we drink you till you're dry. Then... we fill you with our blood. It rages through you like a fire, changing you, until one morning you awake and your humanity is a dream... now faded," explains Rosanna after she has bitten Amy. The purpose of this conversion, that the girls at the school are simply fated to be concubines to male alien monsters, is then revealed when Amy asks what will happen if she survives this transformation. "Then there are ten thousand husbands waiting for you in the water," Rosanna confirms. During a later scene, when the Doctor finally confronts Rosanna in the throne room, he provocatively wolf-whistles at her, simultaneously mocking her human disguise but also implying that she looks desirable, framing her as a potential sexual threat to the citizens of Venice. She asks him, "Then I take it you're a refugee, like me?" after deducing he does not originate from Earth and is the owner of the psychic paper that gained him access to the city. She further explains that the Saturnynes are running from the "silence," reminding us again about one of the series's story arcs, and that their home planet is now lost. Her proposal is to get the Doctor to help her establish the colony on Earth, where "we can build a new society here, as others have." She follows this with a coquettish, flirtatious proposal, "What do you say? A partnership. Any which way you choose." The Doctor is more concerned with the fate of Guido's daughter Isabella and dismisses her request, "I don't think that's such a good idea, do you? I'm a Time Lord. You're a big fish. Think of the children." This also supports his later definition of Rosanna's purpose, "She's going to sink Venice and repopulate it with the girls she's transformed." When Rory points out that she will need "blokes" to repopulate the sunken city and Amy recalls Rosanna's claim about the "husbands waiting in the water," the Doctor realises that Rosanna is making the male children "some compatible girlfriends." His final reaction to this plan is, "I mean, I've been around a bit, but really, that's... that's... ew," as if, to him, the whole idea of mixing the human and alien gene pools is beyond the pale.

Morally, he will not entertain the idea of her inter-species alliance, his witty remark "think of the children" veiling a repugnance of a mixed-race partnership with her, condemning Rosanna for executing Isabella without even acknowledging her name. This dismissal of the girl is, for him, what marks the difference between Time Lord and Saturnyne ethics and negates any form of compassionate compromise on his part simply because she has failed, in return, to offer any for Isabella. The Doctor is particularly harsh to these survivors fleeing from the crack in the universe and at the end of the episode Rosanna bluntly questions his lack of compassion as she prepares to sacrifice herself in the lake with "One city to save an entire species. Was that so much to ask?" He attempts to argue his own position within the moral high ground, "I told you. You can't go back and change time. You mourn but you live. I know Rosanna, I did it," but this surely does not avoid the fact that he is about to be responsible for her suicide and for the genocide of the species? Without females to procreate with, one assumes that the "ten thousand husbands" will eventually die out and the Saturnyne lineage will come to a halt. Appropriately, she demands of him, "Tell me Doctor, can your conscience carry the weight of another dead race?" and this echoes the darker side of the Doctor's moral nature where his roles as victim and killer become interchangeable, a side of him that informed much of the Ninth and Tenth Doctor's survivor guilt regarding his role in the Time War.

To continue with the series's analogy to Barrie's *Peter Pan*, it is as if Rosanna and the Doctor are also elements of the same consciousness that informs the characters of Peter and Captain Hook. As Ann Yeoman explains in *Now or Neverland*, "Both Hook and Peter Pan enjoy extraordinary powers, yet each suffers a desperate and self-destructive loneliness. Hook would kill the youth and youthful creativity he envies; Peter Pan is as ruthless and cruel as the 'old man' he hates." Rosanna's final words to the Doctor, before she plunges into the water to be devoured by, what are in effect, her own children, are "Remember us. Dream of us." These words underline the common themes of remembrance and forgetfulness that weave through the series. The symbolism of Saturn, the word itself contained within the alien race's name of Saturnyne, evokes her final sacrifice in its meaning. Seen as the bringer of sorrow, Saturn represents the unrelenting aspect of reality, here seen as the rationalist Doctor, which forces the individual, here the sole survivor Rosanna, to become something that is not true to his or her nature. For Rosanna, it is the non-consummation of the brides and their husbands in the waters of Venice that leads to the consumption of her body by her own offspring. It is the final act of insatiable vampire consumers driven by a hunger for perpetual youth. The problem here is that Rosanna is also forced to disavow her Saturnyne appearance and nature, with the broken perception filter resulting in her fixed human identity, and the Doctor suggests that she can only continue to live in Venetian society by permanently passing as human, by outwardly being one of them. In this regard the episode is morally conflicted in its themes of speciesism and racism, and whilst it tries to paint a sympathetic picture of the Saturnynes as refugees, the story often goes to some extremes to depict them as a multi-cultural, mixed race bogeyman – where 'aliens' seek out humanity's innocent daughters, change them and then have sex with them – a suspicion that haunts some shadowy corners of post-colonial, multi-racial Britain. The Doctor is also depicted as a rather intolerant man and, despite his liberalism, is unable to offer Rosanna much more beside crude assimilation within human society, when he could have intervened earlier and perhaps taken the Saturnynes to another, uninhabited but suitable, world.

To deflect our attention from the spectre of miscegenation, Whithouse inserts the subplot of the Saturnynes' plan to sink Venice as an emblem of their evil insurgency, to underline to the audience and to the Doctor that these are evil fish aliens from space who must be fought and defeated. The Renaissance trappings of Venice are also used as a backdrop to the Doctor's attempt to chaperone Amy and Rory on a romantic date and the alien invasion story mirrors this with its tale of male fish aliens looking for compatible brides. Many other aspects of the Doctor's righteous determination to prevent their interracial conquest reflect the series's pre-2005 stagnation in its handling of themes and character. Rosanna, despite a very rich, fruity performance from Helen McCrory, is just the latest in a long line of female villains, an extension of those presented in *The Hand of Fear*, *Image of the Fendahl* and *The Stones of Blood*, where the Doctor is caught, as Alec Charles explains, "in the emasculating fantasies of female power... [with a] discomfort in the presence of female eroticism and his denial of his own sexuality [where] these repressions seem to stem from some colonial neurosis." As I pointed out earlier, there is indeed an adolescent distaste of sex as well as a fear of the 'Other' framed by the Doctor's reaction to the Saturnynes' desire to mate with their converted female brides and in Rosanna's eroticised proposal to him. Reflecting the use of Barrie's *Peter Pan* as an analogy to the character of the Eleventh Doctor, Charles also redefines the Doctor within this construction of post-imperial and post-colonial British nostalgia as "the boy who never grows up never has to watch the sun set on his Empire," and in Whithouse's script there is an anxiety within his liberal humanism in his opposition to the colonial ambitions of the Saturnynes. He eventually is forced to battle them as they try to sink Venice when he has failed to offer a benevolent alternative. "The storm is coming," shouts Rosanna after he rejects her partnership, recognising not only the Doctor's designation in the post-2005 revival as 'the oncoming storm' and the Saturnynes' plan to alter the climate of the planet, but also his reactionary, moral superiority as it boils to the surface in favour of his usual liberal platitudes. Maybe all that *Doctor Who* can do in this decade is wear its paradoxes on its (his) sleeve.

## "Step into the light, my dear"

In *The Vampires of Venice*, Whithouse puts much of the progressive and modernist transformation of the vampire genre aside in favour of a tongue-in-cheek pastiche of its conventions, taking what we see as formulaic and clichéd depictions of the vampire and their own representations of the post-imperial fears of the 'Other' from a number of Hammer productions of the 1960s and early 1970s, and uses these and the imagery associated with them to frame the story's unstable elements associated with sexuality, race and genetic impurity. Thus it resembles, partly in narrative and certainly visually, Terence Fisher's *The Brides of Dracula* (1960) and the later *Lust for a Vampire* (1971). In the former, a girls' academy becomes the target for a predatory aristocratic vampire, Baron Meinster, after he is inadvertently freed by one of the girls from the restraining shackles applied by his own mother. Until then, his mother provides him with a selection of young women on which to feast. Once on the loose, the film both suggests vampiric incest as he turns on his own mother to quench his blood lust and his nobility's rampant sexuality as he preys on a number of the girls at the school. Like most Hammer films of the period, it is very much a commentary on the so-called sexual corruption and liberties of the times. With the latter film, the setting is again a girls' school, where the sexual sensationalism shifts from the heterosexual predations of a male vampire to the then exoticism of Carmilla, a lesbian vampire. The film is the second in a trilogy based on J. Sheridan LeFanu's *Carmilla* and details the sex-infused vampire shenanigans at the school. A newly arrived English teacher discovers that Carmilla is not just interested in biting the necks of young girls, as Harry M. Benshoff eloquently summarises in *Monsters in the Closet: Homosexuality and the Horror Film*: "despite the abundance in these films of female nudity and woman-to-woman vampire sex, the films are not steeped in a lesbian sensibility but rather a heterosexual male one. Hammer's lesbian vampire films were all written and directed by men and in many ways are much more indicative of a straight man's fear of women's sexuality than they are representative of an expression of lesbian desire." *The Vampires of Venice* school setting and its very subtle insinuations about such desire, and particularly the male fear of female sexuality, by using the visual coding of Hammer's 'Carmilla' trilogy also parallels some of the exploitation films of the 1950s, particularly *Blood of Dracula* (1957), set in an all-girl boarding school, where the film, as Benshoff explains, "brings together many different strands of US post-war culture – especially fears of nuclear technology/holocaust, the rising power of the young, and the hint of forbidden sexuality." The film features a science teacher, Miss Branding, experimenting on the girls to harness their destructive power and bring peace to the world, mirroring Rosanna's conversion process on the Calvierri girls to make acceptable brides for their husbands in a bid for a peaceful coexistence with humanity. When Rosanna attacks Amy and bites her, challenging the girl with "Make sport of me, will you? Tease me as if I were your dog? Well, this dog has a bite, girl," the sequence also explicitly reflects the "quasi-lesbian/vampiric relationship" in Hammer's *Countess Dracula* (1971), "between predator and prey, wherein the younger, more innocent girl is drained of her life-force and/or blood by an older, but still feminine woman."

Thus the vampire brides of the Calvierri academy are dressed like the pupils at the finishing schools featured in Hammer's *The Brides of Dracula* and the 'Carmilla' cycle of films, complete with flowing white nightgowns accentuating their heaving breasts, and are described knowingly by the Doctor as, "pale creepy girls who don't like sunlight and can't be seen [in a mirror]. Am I thinking what I think I'm thinking?" In a metatextual moment, as the brides attack the Doctor, Amy and Rory at Guido's house, the Doctor reveals them to be fully converted into Saturnyne fish aliens but is unable to resist a comment on their décolletage: "Blimey, fish from space have never been so... buxom." In an earlier sequence, there is a subtle hint of the incestuous relationship between Baron Meinster and his mother depicted in *The Brides of Dracula* with Jonny Campbell's overhead shot of Rosanna and Francesco as he lies sprawled across his mother and she slowly strokes his hair. The story is full of these generic, conventional visual tropes, with the Venetian settings capturing some of the lush romanticism of Hammer's heyday and the work of its highly regarded production designer, Bernard Robinson. This is nowhere better expressed than in the scene in the crypt, a superbly realised Gothic space, where the Doctor is confronted by the exotic vampire brides whom, he discovers, do not cast a reflection in the mirror on the wall, thus echoing both Jonathan Harker's initial confrontation with Count Dracula and his eventual seduction by vampire brides in the original novel of *Dracula*. Hammer's 1958 adaptation of Bram Stoker's book, ending with the climactic fight between Van Helsing and Dracula, is also a source for a lovely visual pun where Rory grabs two candlesticks during his duel with Francesco and strikes a pose not unlike that made in the film by actor Peter Cushing to form them into a crucifix.

One of the contentious aspects of Whithouse's use of the genre and these familiar tropes is that halfway through the script he completely debunks them by rationalising the supernatural power of such figures – casting no reflection, their ability to fly, the appearance of their teeth, the deadliness of exposure to sunlight – as an iteration of the Saturnynes' own science. It is revealed that their technology provides them with the transgressive mystique of the vampire. When the Doctor confronts Rosanna about their ability to cast no reflection and yet bare their fangs whilst still in human form, the two engage in a dialogue that takes the mythology of the vampire and reduces it to the side effects of applied science. According to the Doctor, the perception filter, once again symbolising the trope of judging and misjudging by appearances that is often deployed throughout the series, "manipulates the brainwaves of the person looking at you. But seeing one of you for the first time in, say, a mirror, the brain doesn't know what to fill the gap with, so leaves it blank... hence no reflection." Vampire fangs are the source of much humour and horror in the episode, as well as being a repetition of the orality of the monster and the 'monstrous-feminine' themes that have featured in previous episodes. Prior to the Doctor's entrapment by the vampire brides in the crypt, he preens himself in the mirror ("Hello, handsome") that ultimately does not cast their reflection, baring his teeth comically during his moment of self-appreciation. Earlier, whilst planning to infiltrate the school with Amy, Rory and Guido, he emphasises both the hidden threat of the Saturnynes and their fanged appearance. The line "Makes you wonder what could be so bad it doesn't actually mind us thinking it's a *vampire*?" is made comical by the way actor Matt Smith puts a physical and vocal stress on 'vampire', as if he were a child pretending to be one, by again baring his teeth. The apparent horror of the vampires is exactly that, a pretence, and in their confrontation Rosanna and the Doctor confirm that all of Whithouse's allusions to vampire mythology and to the Hammer vampire films are simply a way of dressing up the rather standard alien colonisation/invasion plot, using surfaces and spectacle as a form of genre drag, to nullify the more potent sexual themes in the characters and performances. The fangs are real but the rest is faked and, as Rosanna so aptly puts it, "self-preservation overrides the mirage."

As soon as the use of such overfamiliar imagery is confirmed merely as visual pastiche, the possibility of the supernatural is wrenched away from the story. This shifts the romantic associations of the vampire figure, fully endorsed by the beautifully costumed, humanised versions of Rosanna and Francesco, to what William Patrick Day refers to as 'post-human vampire', where as Saturnynes they become "self-alienated, fragmentary beings who cannot define their own identities, feral intellects without a capacity for empathy or an ethic beyond need." This transformation occurs when Amy attacks Rosanna and damages the perception filter device that maintains her liberated, charismatic, erotic and romantic image. From this moment on, the Saturnynes are shown as completely monstrous, inhuman parasites that stink of fish and they are demystified as supernatural entities. The story seems to become a form of "disenchantment" where, according to Day, "emancipation from superstition brings freedom but such freedom has a corrosive side. Disenchantment takes the form of restless disillusionment when our desire for magic, for the supernatural, for transcendent order and power, is dismissed as mere childish atavism without being at all diminished." Whithouse rationally explains the vampires away, robbing the story of its gleeful, self-indulgent realm of romantic supernaturalism and magic just when the current series has shifted its position markedly towards fairy-tale romanticism. This places *The Vampires of Venice* more within the series's previous depictions of the traditional dichotomy between science and magic, where magic is often described as the effects of alien science, as in the linguistic science used as witchcraft by the Carrionites in *The Shakespeare Code*, and where the Doctor asks Ace in *Battlefield* if she recalls Clarke's Law – that any sufficiently advanced technology is indistinguishable from magic – and explains that the same can be held true in reverse – any sufficiently arcane magic is indistinguishable from technology – while justifying the possibility of a dimensional spaceship which has been grown, not built. The Doctor and Amy's childish joy at discovering vampires is replaced with the desultory term 'fish from space' to explain the 'monster of the week' Saturnynes as the aliens they anticipate to find and, inevitably, uncover. This is not an unfamiliar way of dealing with vampire mythology in *Doctor Who*, with the science versus superstition trope part and parcel of the vampire narratives in *State of Decay* and *The Curse of Fenric*, but in those stories the vampire creatures – the Three Who Rule in the former and the sea-dwelling Haemovores in the latter – are more successfully integrated into the storytelling. *State of Decay* manages to keep intact some of the transgressive sexual elements of Hammer's vampire films even though it too uses the genre as pastiche within a science fiction story, whereas the sheer breadth of *The Curse of Fenric*'s epic saga, greatly influenced by Norse mythology, makes the story of the Saturnynes rather a mundane one in comparison.

## "Then we will take your world"

The web of relationships between mothers and sons, fathers and daughters, wives and husbands described in *The Vampires of Venice* explores some interesting themes about abandonment, capitalism, class and morality. In the pre-titles sequence, the story establishes a number of familiar tropes. In many classic fairy tales the father, economically unable to support them, has to send his only son or daughter out into the world to fend alone. The morals within these tales were, as Jack Zipes indicates in *Fairy Tales and the Art of Subversion*, "used to justify a division of labour and the separation of the sexes. Certainly the growing proletarian class... could not think of keeping wives and children at home." We see Guido, the humble boat-builder, hand over his daughter Isabella to the care of

Signora Rosanna Calvierri, obviously one of the rich patrons of the city judging by her lifestyle and appearance. Guido describes to Rosanna that his daughter's prospects are poor and he can only see a future for her in the Calvierri school for girls where, he feels, she can find "a chance for betterment, escape." There is no exchange of money and Rosanna instantly enrols the girl, seemingly accepting her mere physical presence as payment enough, as a commodity to be exploited. "She is my world," Guido explains, and Rosanna avariciously responds, "Then we will take your world," thus implying that not only does the Calvierri household wish to possess Isabella but that it also wishes to contain within it Venice itself, the very world in which she exists, its economy, labour and production.

Guido's reaction is initially one of joy and Isabella also seems rather happy with this arrangement, even though it amounts to nothing more than the abandonment of a father's duties to his daughter by offering them to another authority. As Roger Salerno, in *Landscapes of Abandonment*, suggests, "In the beginning of the thirteenth century, abandonment's earliest uses described submission to authority, control or jurisdiction of another. It sometimes described individuals who gave themselves or their children into bondage. It denoted submission of the serf to his or her master. Abandonment could mean the surrender of someone or something to another or the total disregard of one's personal, familial, religious or civil obligations. The abandonment of children, for example, was frequently considered abdication of one's rights to them as possessions." Guido's joy soon evaporates when he discovers that the school wants possession of his daughter with immediate effect. After he is dismissed and his rights to Isabella are rescinded, she is left alone and presented to Rosanna's son Francesco as merely some fleshy commodity ripe for consumption. The idea that the vampire and the victim are analogous to breeders and prey is something that gains momentum further into the story when we discover that the prosperous house of Calvierri's victims are being converted into ideal wives for the alien husbands in the lagoon. Judith Halberstam, in *Skin Shows: Gothic Horror and the Technology of Monsters*, suggests a link between wealth, patronage and the figure of the vampire in her analysis of Stoker's *Dracula* in that the titular vampire "represents money, old and new, but he also releases a sexual response that threatens bourgeois culture precisely from below. Harker and his cronies create in Dracula an image of aristocratic tyranny, of corrupt power and privilege, of foreign threat."

When the Saturnynes are revealed and their process for transformation of the girls is applied to Amy, it could almost be described as a form of technological vampirism achieved through alien machines and science to replace the blood of the girls with the possessive power and lusts of these creatures. Interestingly, Karl Marx also used the vampire as a metaphor for capitalism: "Capital is dead labour, which, vampire-like, lives only by sucking living labour, and lives the more, the more labour it sucks." The Saturnynes become the phantasmagoria living in the capitalist machine of Venice that the Doctor describes as "one of the most powerful cities in the world" and where he and Amy, through the psychic paper, acquire the attributes of the aristocracy, with the Doctor described as "your Holiness" and Amy as "Viscountess" as they enter the city. Their encounter with the inspector also reinforces the Calvierri's patronage of the city as a way of isolating it from what turns out to be a non-existent plague. Rosanna wields her wealth and power, sealing off the city and recruiting the daughters of the proletariat, and shows that the human community can easily be bought off and convinced of their good fortune at the hands of the aristocracy. There is an ongoing theme about education in the story, providing much humour and further observations of the privileged over the bourgeois. The school of the Calvierri is definitely held in high esteem and the Doctor is puzzled by Guido's attempt to literally penetrate the veil of secrecy surrounding the girls and the disappearance of his daughter. The Doctor observes, "Parents do all sorts of things to get their children into good schools. They move house, they change religion. So why are you trying to get her *out*?" Guido has obviously realised that the girls have undergone a process of commodification that has released their basest lusts and instincts: "Something magical happens in there. Something magical, something evil. My own daughter didn't recognise me. And the girl who pushed me away, her face... like an animal." As Guido comes to terms with abandoning his daughter and how the school has affected her, this is contrasted with the intimate scene between Rosanna and Francesco ("Mummy's hydrating, Francesco") where it is revealed that they have "already converted more than enough" of the girls and formal introductions to Francesco's brothers are due. Rosanna tempers Francesco's eagerness and sees their beneficiaries as willing victims, and her declaration of "let them hammer on our door. Beg to be taken," adds an erotic allure to the 'gift' that they bestow on their chosen ones.

In the edgy and uncertain aftermath of the British General Election in 2010, with the electorate facing a period of financial restriction and drastically reduced public spending in the Coalition government's proposed £6.2 billion cuts as it makes a serious attempt to deal with a capitalist recession, the conservative retreat of the Calvierri aristocracy into their Venetian school and the use of authority and control over the populace parallels the way that both the Universal Studios and Hammer Films horror canon also reflected their own uneasy times. James Craig Holte sums this up in *The Fantastic Vampire: Studies in the Children of the Night*, where he sees the horror films of the 1930s reflecting "the unease caused by the Depression – the failure of patriarchal capitalism to provide a stable structure for families or communities," and the Hammer films of the 1950s and 1960s emerging during "the rise of consumerism, the failure of patriarchal structures to re-establish the pre-war order, the rise of the middle class and the changing role of women in society and the family." At the time of transmission you would also be forgiven for finding an equanimity between the hung parliament rhetoric of Brown, Cameron and Clegg, all pleading that we must think of the country's need for a strong, stable government, and Rosanna Calvierri as she matches this rhetoric with, "I believe protecting the future of one's own is a sacred duty." It carries a double meaning – ensuring the race of the Saturnynes survives genetically and the self-protection of monied aristocracy in favour of the bourgeoisie struggling to scrape two pennies together. The discussion of a pact between her and the Doctor uncannily echoes the various open offers that the Tory and Labour parties tried to tempt Nick Clegg with in the tense period of the hung parliament. Rosanna, as unlikely to go for proportional representation as Cameron ever is, suggests the Doctor is on a hiding to nothing trying to persuade her to rethink her policies. She instead goes for unleashing a very different kind of Eurozone crisis, using a device to fill the sky with thick vapour, visually akin to the drifting volcanic ash cloud that brought most of Europe's air transport to a halt in the same month, to boil the atmosphere and trigger earthquakes.

The Calvierri school, ironically, resembles one of the Coalition's propositions for academy schools to be set up away from the control of local government by charities, teachers and parents, but it is unlikely the Coalition envisaged "betterment and escape" as something quite like this. Amy, whilst exploring the hyperbolised Gothic space of the school, verbalises the class distinction between the Venetian working class and the environment that they place their daughters in with "Blimey, this is private education then," but it also demarcates her own not-so-privileged background back in Leadworth. When Amy, interrogated by Rosanna, is asked, "What are you doing in *my* school?" she wittily evokes the 'nanny state' of her own time, putting on a rather serious face and announcing: "OK. I'll tell you. I'm from Ofsted." Rosanna also positions herself in direct contrast to the local population by referring to them as a "world of savages," delineating her superior aristocracy with technological advancement over a 'humble boat builder' like Guido and further emphasising her role as the mother-goddess who will eventually sacrifice herself once denied the "one city" in which her kith and kin can also take shelter from the wild chasms of the universe where they "saw silence and the end of all things."

## "According to this, I'm your eunuch"

Vitally important to *The Vampires of Venice* are both the further development of the Doctor and Amy's relationship in light of the events shown at the conclusion of *Flesh and Stone*, and the reintroduction of the character of Rory Williams, last seen in *The Eleventh Hour*. His progression occurs within the script's themes about the interrelationships between wives and husbands, fathers and daughters, and mothers and sons. As we have discussed, the story maps out the associations between Rosanna and Francesco, where a son is conflicted by a mother figure who attempts to reign in his baser instincts and who will do anything to protect the future of her species, and Guido and Isabella, in which a father believes giving his daughter away to the Calvierri school will provide her with a better life.

Overlaid onto this dynamic of the supporting characters is the story of wife and husband *in potentia*, Amy and Rory. Their connection with these familial relationships is immediately prefigured in the pre-titles to the episode where, as director Jonny Campbell moves into a close-up of Isabella screaming, there is a jump cut to Rory screaming down his phone, professing his love for Amy at the stag do before their wedding. Desire is interlinked here, as Francesco makes his lusty intentions clear to Isabella while Rory announces over the phone to Amy, "I haven't told you for seven hours that I love you – which is a scandal!" as Campbell pans the camera slowly up the empty wedding dress hanging in her vacant room. Amy and the Doctor are absent at this moment, the empty dress and the abandoned bedroom a signifier of Rory's love having been deferred just as Guido, and his fatherly love for Isabella, is immediately dismissed from the house of Calvierri. Rory's mention of time and Rosanna's insistence that Guido must leave because "time ticks" foreshadows how time will affect Rory's future storyline. Seven hours is merely a shadow of the two thousand years he will wait as the guardian of the Pandorica in *The Big Bang* as, with the exception of dying *twice*, the ultimate declaration of his love for her. *The Vampires of Venice*, as well as reintroducing Rory, establishes him as a character within the journey of maturation that both he and Amy will undertake until the end of the series. It is a journey that will see Rory slough off his image as a proxy, reluctant Raggedy Doctor, as the second best to Amy's fantasy of the real man. He will finally prove his mettle to the Doctor, whom he sees as an immediate male rival, and to Amy, enamoured of the Doctor's virtues to the point of being blind to those of her husband-to-be. Throughout the first half of *The Vampires of Venice* he wears an emblematic red T-shirt with his and Amy's picture in a heart pierced by an arrow, a crude representation of what he believes the relationship between them is based upon at that point in the series. What he discovers is that this representation is unable to properly describe his real feelings for Amy and the sacrifices he must make for her.

The Doctor has also recognised that Amy's desires have been misdirected towards him. After his embarrassing clinch with her at the end of *Flesh and Stone* he has obviously set out on a mission to rectify this. Bursting out of the cake at Rory's party, the Doctor becomes both the comic disavowal of desire and the heightened locus of Rory's jealousy and annoyance at the Doctor's ill-timed interference in his life. He replaces the female stripper, as a symbol of the onlookers' by now confused sexual objectification, and is innocent of what his appearance to the strains of David Rose's 'The Stripper' could be construed as in the all-male environment of a stag do. Not for Rory then the pleasures of a one-night stand before the big day, something that Amy was more than happy to indulge in even if it was as a reaction to the stress and trauma she had endured on the Byzantium. He is even denied the indulgence of watching a stripper. "There's a girl outside in a bikini. Could someone let her in, give her a jumper? Lucy, lovely girl. Diabetic," explains the Doctor, once again suggesting that he has been returned to a state of innocence, where the sight of a semi-naked woman seems more likely to evoke concerns about her health and keeping her warm than any form of sexual desire. However, the Doctor's intentions soon become clear and he openly discusses Amy's seduction in front of Rory and his male friends, triggering Rory's deeper concerns with, "Tell you what though, you're a lucky man. She's a great kisser." Much gasping and smashing of glasses accompanies this revelation and the Doctor then realises that his social etiquette might need some fine-tuning and, even as a nine-hundred-year-old alien, he has much to learn about handling these delicate situations surrounding human desire. As we discussed in Chapter 4, Moffat and his writing team seem very keen to recontextualise the Doctor within what Alec Charles, in 'The Ideology of Anachronism: Television, History and the Nature of Time' in *Time and Relative Dissertations in Space*, regards as the image of "an objective, asexual saviour-explorer... a man who's neither out for himself nor for a bit of the Other." That project continues here and throughout the rest of the series and where, in parallel with Rory's experiences offering him maturity, the initial, misdirected focus on Amy and the Doctor as a couple, as boyfriend and girlfriend, definitely shifts back to Rory and Amy as husband and wife.

The Doctor, whilst busily repairing the TARDIS, emphatically describes to Amy and Rory the territory that the episode, and the series, will go on to explore: "The life out there – it dazzles. It blinds you to the things that are important. I've seen it devour relationships and plans." Amy has already been temporarily blinded by 'the life out there' in *Flesh and Stone* and the trauma of it sent her into the Doctor's, rather than Rory's, arms. Eerily, he also foreshadows Rory's fate in *Cold Blood* where adventures in time and space can literally gobble you up (and Rory is seen to shiver or jump with fright either deliberately or coincidentally at the timing of that line with an explosion in the TARDIS) and it reflects the real choices that Amy has to make in *Amy's Choice*. "For one person to have seen all that, to taste the glory, and then go back. It *will* tear you apart," warns the Doctor. His solution is to take them on a romantic trip to revive the relationship, to highlight the importance of their feelings for each other and psychologically repair their fragmented personas. Bizarrely, the Doctor is sat on a swing under the TARDIS console as he announces all of this, suggesting some associations with Jean-Honore Fragonard's eighteenth-century Rococo painting 'The Swing' which depicts a love triangle between two men and a woman. In a painting full of sexual symbolism, the woman, being pushed on the swing by her husband, is covertly observed by her lover. In the Russell T. Davies era of the show, the narratives pushed the Rose and Mickey relationship apart; both went their separate ways as characters while Rose formed a romantic attachment to the Doctor. Her final reward was a life on an alternate Earth, with a more-human simulacrum of the Tenth Doctor, in *Journey's End*. Here, the narratives push Rory and Amy together while repositioning the Doctor as the eccentric loner and wise father figure. Amy's reward will be to marry the man she genuinely grows to love and appreciate.

However, Rory remains unimpressed with the Doctor. This is evident when the Doctor attempts to show off the dimensional properties of the TARDIS and offers to patronisingly explain it to him, suggesting that Rory is like any other companion and does not comprehend the mind-boggling science behind it all. Rory pre-empts him with: "It's another dimension. It's basically another dimension," cutting him short in reeling off his standard litany. "I like the bit when someone says, 'It's bigger on the inside!' I always look forward to that," retorts the grumpy Doctor after Rory explains that he has been reading up on the latest scientific theories since their last encounter in Leadworth. His rationalisation of the mysterious TARDIS is part of his determination to become equal to the Doctor in Amy's eyes. However, this is something he fails to maintain when, in Venice, he is confronted by what appear to be vampires. Whilst the Doctor and Amy find the prospect of meeting supernatural creatures like vampires an overtly exciting one, his own reaction is, "What is wrong with you people?" astonished that they think this is all in a day's work or fun. He struggles to rationalise the illogic of the supernatural, exclaiming, "This whole thing is mental. They're vampires for God's sake!" only for the Doctor to suggest and then later confirm that they are in fact technologically advanced aliens.

The rivalry between the Doctor and Rory intensifies later in the episode as they endure a series of standoffs that recalls the male posturing of characters in *Coupling* and *Press Gang*. The complex weave of familial relationships, of confused identities and roles, turns into a piece of comic misdirection that would not be out of place in a Hollywood romantic comedy as Amy, the Doctor, Rory and Guido hatch a plan to break into the school. Amy suggests that they need someone on the inside, meaning her, but the Doctor refuses to let her do it. However, after rejecting Guido's idea of blasting their way in with gunpowder, the Doctor returns to Amy's plan, agreeing that they pretend to be father and daughter to gain access. "But you look about nine," observes Amy, in a tongue-in-cheek play on the media and fan criticism of Matt Smith's casting as the youngest actor to play the part, as well as a reminder of the Doctor's status as 'the boy who never grew up'. Further slippage occurs between roles and identities with the Doctor becoming at first brother ("Too weird," dismisses Amy) then fiancé, with the latter at Amy's insistence. Again, Amy's desire has an interchangeable point of identification, both unconsciously and consciously, between Rory and the Doctor. Rory is incensed and would rather not have the Doctor running around telling people that he is Amy's fiancé. He does not want another man usurping his role again. Amy then encourages Rory to go with her to the school but, oddly, impersonating her brother rather than actually being her lover/husband. Guido admits that he thought the Doctor *was* Amy's fiancé and the Doctor quickly steps in with "Yeah, that's not helping." Amy's perception of the fluidity of male roles for the Doctor and Rory underlines the insecurity, perhaps stemming from her own abandonment as a child, she has about the objects of her desire, about her final choice of parent, sibling or lover. She is as much a pre-Oedipal good mother as Rosanna represents the pre-Oedipal stepmother/witch and the episode demands Amy must conquer the negative aspect of the Great Mother symbol, embodied here by Rosanna, in order to formalise her real connection to Rory. Amy, in defeating the stepmother/witch figure, must then transfer her affections from the hero father figure of the Doctor (the nine-hundred-year-old wise man who looks nine, according to her) to her husband Rory, in the similar way that the character Beauty switches her affections in *Beauty and the Beast*. Rory is not actually the hero figure because that role belongs to the eternal explorer-saviour of the Doctor who must deal with the shadow side of himself as externalised by forces and threats such as Rosanna and the vampires. Rory is more akin to the lover where, as Ethel Spector Person explains in *Dreams of Love and Fateful Encounters*, he must "confront certain prohibitions and demons. But unlike the hero, whose demons are found in the external world, the lover's demons are frequently found to reside in his own unconscious." For Rory, this is about conquering his inadequacy (the psychic paper used to get them through the gates of Venice describes him as Viscountess Amy's eunuch which blatantly symbolises him as a castrated man) and devising a strategy that will see his personality "reorganised at a more complex level; as an adult that has come into his own and achieved a new maturity." This reorganisation also means engaging in a standoff with the Doctor to establish his masculine identity before Amy, on the unconscious level, will permit him to love her. Amusingly, Rory and Amy become brother and sister figures, a sibling match that parallels father and daughter Guido and Isabella, when they are presented to Rosanna and, like the fairy-tale figures of Hansel and Gretel, they too must face the cannibalistic, vampire anti-mother that the witch in the story, and the Signora here, represents. In *The Hard Facts of the Grimms' Fairy Tales*, Maria Tatar further expands on this: "the alien meddlers who make their way into households and attempt to divide a heroine from her father or husband are painted in the worst imaginable colours. As terrifying ogres and evil enchantresses, they take on almost mythical dimensions."

As the Doctor and Rory rush through the tunnels beneath the school, a dark, threatening space that lends itself perfectly to Rory's exploration of his own unconscious, the frustrated husband-to-be wastes no time in questioning the Doctor about the earlier revelation at the stag do. "What happened between you and Amy?" demands Rory. "You want to do this now? *Now?*" replies the Doctor as they hurry down the passageway with their torches. This mirrors the earlier scene where Rory initially attempts to reason with Amy about her life with the Doctor. She describes this as "running" and "fighting" and says how scared she has been but avoids the enquiries about missing him. Her reaction is to tentatively punch him on the shoulder at arm's length and then withdraw, still unsure about him and his exposed feelings, deflecting his attentions and questions with "Rory, this is our date. Let's not do this, not now." In the secret tunnels, an aptly Gothic arena for revelation and truth, he demands an explanation from the Doctor: "I have a right to know. I'm getting married in 430 years." The Doctor confirms his own diagnosis of Amy's desire for him in *Flesh and Stone*: "She was frightened. I was frightened, but we survived and the relief of it... and so she kissed me." Humour is used again to deflect the awkwardness of the emotions on display. "And you kissed her back?" asks Rory. "No. I kissed her mouth," quips the Doctor, who then goes on to confirm Rory's future role in the narrative with "She kissed me because I was there. It would have been you. It *should* have been you." The Doctor is determined to set things right, suggesting that Rory should have the status of companion after Rory concurs, "it should have been me," in the situation described. "Exactly. That's why I brought you here," the Doctor finally reveals. As the torches blow out in a sudden gust of wind and they are left stranded in the darkness, the time for emotional truth is over and as the Doctor whispers, in rather childlike tones, "Can we go and see the vampires now, please?" he requests the relationship issues should become secondary to hunting down monsters in a haunted house.

The scenes by the trapdoor offer some *Coupling*-influenced humour at the expense of Rory's physical endowments. There is the phallic symbolism in the male panic surrounding the comparison between the Doctor's ultraviolet portable sunlight, unfolding like a *Star Wars*-style lightsaber, and Rory's rather ineffectual penlight ("Yours is bigger than mine," he opines, whilst the Doctor glares at him and demands, "Let's not go there."). Blotting out the danger lurking in the surroundings of the Calvierri school, Rory also frets that his wedding is in danger of cancellation, with the loss of the deposit paid on the village hall and the hiring of a salsa band. However, he is abruptly snapped back from that possible reality when the Doctor discovers a number of drained corpses and intimates that the process used by Rosanna is unstable. Fearing for Amy's safety, he turns on the Doctor, accurately summarising how the Time Lord dangerously radicalises those that travel with him. "You know what's dangerous about you? It's not that you make people take risks. It's that you make them want to impress you. You make it so that they don't want to let you down. You have no idea how dangerous you make people to themselves when you're around," accuses Rory. He echoes the taunts about these 'children of time' that Davros made to the Tenth Doctor in *Journey's End*: "You take ordinary people and fashion them into weapons... How many have died in your name? The Doctor, the man who keeps on running, never looking back because he dare not, out of shame." Later, the Doctor does respond to Rory's accusations, as Venice is shaken by earthquakes and Rory and Amy come to his rescue, "So one minute it's 'you make people a danger to themselves,' the next it's 'we're not leaving you!'" he yells in frustration. "But if one of you gets squashed or blown up or eaten, who gets..." he continues, but his protestations are cut off by the effects of the next tremor. One assumes that sentence ends with the words 'the blame'.

Essentially, this is Rory projecting his own inadequacies and frustrations onto the Doctor out of fear that he will never be able to protect Amy from the dangers lurking in time and space and will never find the resourcefulness within himself to meet these forces head on. That these dangers are real and people get killed is proved by Isabella's death, where ironically she is made to walk the plank just as Captain Hook forced the Lost Boys to do likewise to face the crocodile in *Peter Pan*, and also by Guido's self-sacrifice in blowing up the vampire brides. When the Doctor seeks to stop Rosanna from initiating the final phase of her plan to sink Venice, Amy immediately springs up to join him but he demands that she goes back to the TARDIS, heeding Rory's earlier concerns. "We don't discuss this. I tell you to do something, Amy, and you do it!" Amy is annoyed at this turn of events and Rory is clearly relieved, but this is only a temporary respite because Rory then has to fend off Francesco on his own. In a story about the evil power of the Great Mother, Rory's only recourse to get Francesco's attention is to childishly insult his mother Rosanna: "The only thing I've seen uglier than you is... your mum!" The duel between them is a final vindication of Rory's bravery and the first indication that Amy and Rory can work together as a couple to face off against the alien monstrosities that the universe throws up. Amy despatches Francesco and rescues Rory, asking him "Why did you make the sign of the cross, you numpty?" when clearly the crossed candlesticks he brandished would have no effect on a fish from space. "Oh, oh, right! I'm being reviewed now, am I?" he complains, aware that in Amy's eyes he may be compared to the heroic and resourceful Doctor. His reward is the first real indication of intimacy between the two characters as Amy passionately kisses him.

The ultimate reward for Rory in *The Vampires of Venice* is the approval of him by the Doctor and Amy as a suitable travelling companion. After assuming his presence is surplus to requirements with "It's fine. Drop me back where you found me. I'll just say you've..." Amy asks him to stay, and the Doctor agrees. Amy assumes the role of mother, as the mirror image of Rosanna with her ten thousand sons, and she is now the matriarch slowly determining her relationship to the father-brother figure of the Doctor and the husband-lover figure of Rory. "Got my spaceship, got my boys. My work here is done," she claims satisfactorily. This suggests that beneath this, she has been part of a process, that also includes the Doctor and Rory, which Kenneth Lambert calls "the emergence of the self... that normally needs the support of a holding situation because of the powerful and frightening emotions involved – even more so when no adequate holding mother figure, or mother and father pair have become introjected during infancy and childhood," in *Analysis, Repair and Individuation*. Her mothering towards the two men ("Nice one. I will pop the kettle on") and her nomination of them as "my boys" is comically disputed by Rory, "we are *not* her boys," but then the Doctor deflates this by his honest acknowledgement that, actually, they are. This further confirms and builds upon the dynamic established between male and female characters by Moffat in the earlier episodes of the series.

*The Vampires of Venice* does rely very heavily on tried and tested, formulaic *Doctor Who* tropes. The climax of the episode, showing the Doctor switching off the Saturnyne terraforming device at the top of the bell tower, repeats the similar denouements of *The Idiot's Lantern*, where the Doctor defeats the Wire atop Alexandra Palace television tower, and *Evolution of the Daleks*, which sees him clinging to the top of the Empire State Building to direct lightning through his body. Even as the skies above Venice boil and obliterate the sun, Amy also very conveniently manages to use her compact mirror to burn Francesco with a ray of sunlight and achieves this after most of the story has shown the vampire Saturnynes managing to stroll about, with the scant protection of hats and parasols, completely unharmed by the daylight. The episode also demonstrates that, whilst it may be a case of continuing to sell the same ideas to an audience, it is even harder to sell them with some variable effects work which ranges from some very beautiful digital matte paintings of the Venetian skyline to stilted, amateurish studio-based green screen work showing the Doctor on the bell tower. The spectacle also offers a not-so-convincing CGI depiction of the Tim Burton-esque Saturnynes in their true forms, but where there is a lack of budget for visual effects there is a tendency here to describe rather than show, especially problematic in the sacrifice of Isabella where she thrashes about in the water and tells us what is happening to her rather than us actually seeing it for ourselves. The scene would have been rather more convincing if director Jonny Campbell had employed a couple of underwater shots of the Saturnyne creatures grabbing at her.

Supported by a very witty script, *The Vampires of Venice* succeeds, in part, with the development of the three main characters. Arthur Darvill fulfils the potential he displayed in *The Eleventh Hour* and makes Rory such a fresh presence as an audience identification figure in the series by dint of the character's very normality. A welcome addition to the TARDIS crew, Rory offers a much-needed balance to the overwhelming 'kookiness' and cynicism of Amy and the full-blown eccentricity of the Doctor. The sword fight between him and Francesco is a lovely bit of physical comedy and there are other very droll moments in the story too, including: the Doctor's confrontation with the vampire brides of Calvierri using the library card with the First Doctor's image; Rory and Amy's pretence as brother and sister to Rosanna Calvierri ("I'm a gondola... *driver*," explains Rory); and a witty allusion to the version of *Casanova* (2005) starring David Tennant, where the current Doctor is much relieved that he has arrived in Venice 145 years before Casanova's birth and will not run into him, and by implication the Tenth Doctor and Tennant. After all, he owes him a chicken. By virtue of the gloriously photographed locations in Trogir, the episode plays on 'quality television' as represented by prestigious period dramas and what Matt Hills regards in *Triumph of a Time Lord* as the series's flirtation with "historical citations and high cultural aesthetics," with additional visual nods to Visconti's *Death in Venice* (1971) amongst them. The episode also ends in a stylish manner, repeating the 'silence will fall' meme and using Rosanna's dialogue, "There were cracks. Through some we saw silence and the end of all things," over silent shots of the Venetian canals, accompanying Rory and the Doctor's puzzled reactions ("All I can hear is... silence"). Campbell then zooms his camera suggestively towards the TARDIS and straight through the keyhole in the door before the 'next time' trailer kicks in. However, these notable successes and minor failures are nothing compared to the story's conflicted and confusing re-enactment of an imperialist fantasy of defining and drawing frontiers, both the national (preventing the isolation of Venice by the Saturnynes) and galactic (the Doctor repelling those that wish to possess the Earth), and its troubled attempt to humanise the aliens without the whiff of racism or speciesism.

# Chapter Six

# AMY'S CHOICE

Written by Simon Nye
Directed by: Catherine Morshead
First broadcast: 15 May 2010

---

### "We have to grow up eventually"

Over the last five chapters we have been examining the development of
Amy Pond as a character, her relationship with the Doctor and how her
decision to travel with him on the night of her wedding has affected the
man she left behind, Rory Williams. Simon Nye's *Amy's Choice* is not only
an intricate summary of the tensions between them, of how their
motivations and desires have been illuminated to the audience thus far,
but it is also a super-narrative that turns the character of the Doctor inside
out and exposes his dammed up desires and anxieties about the two
humans he is traveling with, his failing to take responsibility for his own
actions whilst they are in his care. It is an emptying out of the skeletons in
his own closet, where the darkest aspects of his persona hold sway and
articulate the opinions, decisions and thoughts that he would ordinarily
leave unsaid.

These things best left unsaid are, for the benefit of the viewer, woven
into two dream states in the episode, although the revelation that both so-
called realities are actually fantasies does not emerge until the end of the
episode. They encompass a number of themes and symbols that the series
has, in previous episodes, articulated narratively and visually. In this
episode, they include the folly of youth over age, the fear of growing older,
the competition between a lover and a hero, choosing your friends,
admitting to your mistakes and deciphering the truth about yourself and
your real desires. It is important to remember that what happens in *Amy's
Choice* is all part of a dream landscape, the Doctor's darkest thoughts writ
large by his alter ego the Dream Lord. Eventually, the choices he makes
are those he believes Amy and Rory would, or should, make based within
events that are projections of his fears in conflict with his desires. They
explore both his doubts about his own track record and history of
relationships with his companions and his fears about the monsters that
seek to destroy them all. Yet, there is a suggestion that not all the traumas
suffered in the two dreams are of the Doctor's making and being provided
courtesy of his Dream Lord double. The episode suggests they are also
informed by the imaginations of Amy and Rory, as the Dream Lord
indicates, rather ambiguously, at the end of the story: "I hope you enjoyed
all your little fictions. It all came out of your imagination so I'll leave you

to ponder on that." The title of the episode, *Amy's Choice*, is itself indicative of the many emotional choices and decisions at the heart of the story that are inextricably bound up with Amy's relationship to "my boys," the Doctor and Rory. Nye's script therefore takes the process of symbolically, and literally, 'marrying' Rory and Amy, one instigated by the Doctor in *The Vampires of Venice*, and completes that episode's restructuring of the 'family' of characters. He does this by examining their roles, in counterpoint to the heroic figure of the Doctor, both as his companions aboard the TARDIS and as a married couple in a fantasised, dream version of Leadworth. The audience has already observed the progress of these characters as the series gradually builds a profile of them in relation to what Carl Jung referred to as the task of 'individuation'. As part of Nye's symbolic tying together of these characters, Amy, Rory and the Doctor are seen to deal with, and finally integrate, the shadowy areas of their personas both internally, with the conflicted love triangle between all three characters as a prime example, and externally, where anxieties and repressions are projected onto a fairy-tale landscape filled with monsters that need to be defeated. As Christopher Hauke explains in *Jung and the Postmodern: The Interpretation of Realities*, "Individuation is about the dual struggle of the subject with, on the one hand, the 'inner world' of the unconscious, with all its infantile, personal and collective aspects, and, on the other hand, the struggle with the 'outer world' of the collective society."

One of the major subplots in the story concerns Rory and Amy's lives in Upper Leadworth, as perceived by, and in opposition to, the Doctor's view of it as an outsider. It describes their life in Upper Leadworth (Rory points out that Leadworth has "gone slightly upmarket" as a signifier of his high estimation of the rural life they lead) and how they both come to reject its rural backwater vision of their future together (its anti-modernist space eventually summed up by Amy as "it's not really me though, is it? Would I be happy settling down in a place with a pub, two shops and a really bad amateur dramatics society?"). They eventually opt for a more nomadic existence as travellers in the TARDIS where, Hauke suggests, the wider universe is full of alternate "post-modern concerns [that] now focus on the effects of the global economy, mass media representation and the homogenisation of styles and values... which comprise equal and, to some extent, more hidden threats to the potential for subjects to become individual men and women." For the Doctor, Upper Leadworth is simply a place he arrives in by mistake, an echo of his "fourteen years since fish-custard" yo-yoing, in time and space, to and from the village in *The Eleventh Doctor*. There he despaired at its isolation from cities and airports, and here its mundane nature is further symbolised by the bench he sits on with Rory and Amy, "Look at this bench. What a nice bench. What will they think of next?" It is a place he describes, in a verbal slip, as a "nightmare... did I say nightmare? More of a good mare," and that is seen, with devastating honesty by his crueller alter ego the Dream Lord, as "the village that time forgot." When the pensioners of the village suddenly disappear, the Doctor finds that deducing their fate is difficult as Leadworth itself makes him slow down because of its sheer dullness. He ceases to operate effectively there and it is where, as we discuss later, he is faced with particular challenges that demarcate his functions within *Doctor Who* narratives.

For Rory and Amy, the idyll of Upper Leadworth is a landscape of their inner desires, hopes and dreams, where they are initially seduced by its charms and then torn apart by its destructive nightmare. Amy accepts Upper Leadworth for the sake of her relationship with Rory, their marriage and the imminent arrival of their baby, but Rory definitely sees Leadworth as an idealisation of how he wants to live his life. When they all suspect that nothing is quite what it seems, shunting between Leadworth and the TARDIS, the Doctor suggests that Upper Leadworth is Rory's particular fantasy, "your dream wife, your dream job, probably your dream baby. Maybe this is your dream?" Amy's pregnancy is symbolic of their aspirations to make a new life in the five years since they allegedly left behind their travels with Doctor. After director Catherine Morshead sets the idyllic scene with lyrical shots of the countryside and the cottage, with Amy's domesticity framed by baking in sunlit kitchens, she and Rory are disturbed by the sound of the TARDIS's arrival. The Doctor's arrival is heard and seen both as a technological disruption into their countryside ideal ("Leaf blowers. Use a rake!" yells Rory) and as a physical act when he disturbs Amy's flowerbeds. In a way this interruption symbolises what Susanna Paasonen, in *Figures of Fantasy: Internet, Women, and Cyberdiscourse*, sees as the "dualism of culture and its two gendered modes: the aesthetic and the technological." When the Doctor arrives outside their cottage, he finds the idea that his former companion is pregnant rather a difficult one to come to terms with, where his implied innocence of such matters is couched in avoiding an admission that she is pregnant. Instead, he describes her "huge" condition as the result of having "swallowed a planet" or as an outcome of "when worlds collide." This firmly positions him as a man more concerned with the vastness of the universe, the outer world, rather than as someone sensitive to the domestic scene now presented to him, embedded in a natural intimacy and fecundity of reproduction. Paasonen's dualism, where "the aesthetic mode means imagining and creating unforeseen things, [and] the technological mode means controlling nature through technology and turning ideals into reality," suggests that the unfettered, pastoral world of Leadworth, a place where the randomness of biology and nature reigns supreme, is in contrast to the Doctor's life in the TARDIS and his desire to see the wonders of the universe via technological means, to rationalise and to some extent control them.

Further, Paasonen sees these two modes "correspond to the rational (male) and the subjective, intuitive, introverted, wishful, dreamy or fantastic... emotional, even temperamental (hysterical) female." The Doctor comments to Rory and Amy, "So what do you do around here to stave off the, you know..." and he finishes the sentence with "self-harm"

119

while Amy completes it with "boredom." Rory counters, "We relax. We live, we listen to the birds. We didn't get a lot of time to listen to birdsong back in the TARDIS days." This suggests that he, more than Amy perhaps, has embraced the introverted, dream-like fantasy of Leadworth, whereas back in the rational world of the TARDIS the Doctor believes they have returned to reality, that what they witnessed was the result of having "probably jumped a time track." These opposing modes are further explored when the Doctor attempts to rationalise Leadworth, which they all begin to suspect is an alternate reality, as a technological creation by "looking for motion blur, pixilation," and proposing, "It could be a computer simulation." The birdsong that heralds the switch between each dream state is a symbol of the natural world, a marker used by birds to signal alarm or to advertise territorial ownership and it delineates the borders between Leadworth and the TARDIS. Ironically, it also resembles, as the Doctor, Amy and Rory slump into unconsciousness upon hearing it, the sound effects used in classic cartoons when a character is hit on the head hard enough to daze or knock them out. The switching between the fantasy life in Leadworth and their journey in the TARDIS immediately creates concern for the Doctor: "Trust nothing. From now on trust nothing you see, hear or feel." He begins to rationalise and map out these dream states in the TARDIS: "We could still be in Upper Leadworth dreaming of this, don't you get it?" Amy blames the malfunctioning technology of the TARDIS for creating side effects in reality that even the Doctor is unable to diagnose because he threw the TARDIS manual into a supernova. He may be a rationalist but he often disagrees with the orthodoxy of the finer technical details and he suggests to them that they should "look for all the details that don't ring true" in determining which 'reality' is the real one. Rory and Amy challenge the reality of the TARDIS, probably because initially they see the Leadworth scenario as the preferred choice out of the wish fulfilments on offer. "We're in a spaceship that's bigger on the inside than the outside," Rory advises, and "with a bow tie wearing alien," adds Amy. "So maybe 'what rings true' isn't so simple," he suggests, emphasising the deceptive nature of perceived reality by using his fingers as quotation marks. The dream in Leadworth is also a quotation of Rory's desires where he has become a doctor ("Unlike you, I've passed some exams," he notes of the Doctor) and has a wife and child. However, at the very moment that the Doctor claims that Leadworth is Rory's fantasy alone, his insecurities rise to the surface again. "It's Amy's dream too. Isn't it, Amy?" She acknowledges it is but the Doctor has already moved on, seeing "the details that don't ring true," and questions her about the old people's home where the inhabitants live to a very ripe old age. As a rationalist he is keen to investigate: "There's something here that doesn't make sense. Let's go and poke it with a stick."

The precipitation of Rory's insecurities at this moment leads into a complex unravelling of both Amy's and Rory's characters. Their personalities fragment as soon as the Dream Lord materialises in the dead TARDIS. When the Doctor asks for Amy's opinion of what the intruder is, the Dream Lord turns to Rory for his diagnosis, "And what about the gooseberry here, does he get a guess?" It immediately consigns Rory outside of the relationship between the Doctor and Amy, as part of the Dream Lord's attempt to destabilise all the relationships in the story. "Listen mate, if anyone's the gooseberry around here, it's the Doctor," he argues back. The Dream Lord's response of "there's a delusion I'm not responsible for," in diagnosing Rory's self-deception, parallels Ann Yeoman's depiction of Wendy's father, Mr Darling, in *Peter Pan* where she describes him in *Now or Neverland* as a man who "the more he denies the reality of Peter Pan, or an incursion from the unconscious, the greater his panic, the threat of falling apart" and where we see in him "grandiosity and 'lion courage' succeeded by feelings of failure and remorse." This kind of neurosis is triggered when Rory worries that his selection of the Doctor as 'gooseberry' may actually be false, "No, he is. Isn't he, Amy?" The question forms the nub of the Dream Lord's challenge to her and consequently, as he also represents the Doctor's shadow, it becomes the Time Lord's request too, "Oh, Amy, have to sort your men out. Choose, even." Even though she does reassure Rory of her choice, that "it's you, stupid," the seeds of doubt have been sown in him again. The Dream Lord re-eroticises the relationship between the Doctor and Amy, the spectre of which Rory had managed to banish in *The Vampires of Venice*, by suggesting he has seen her dreams and that "Blimey, I'd blush if I had a blood supply and a real face." His ability to articulate the workings of the Doctor's libido, the sexual desire he strives to keep hidden away, emphasises the Dream Lord's role as the shadow side to the Time Lord's designation as eternal, wise fool or trickster. The shadow and the trickster are not in binary opposition to each other but they merely, as Helen Bassil-Morozow in *Tim Burton: The Monster and the Crowd* suggests, "occupy different positions on... the trickster-shadow spectrum or the scale which 'measures' the degree of malevolence in the character's playfulness (or is it the degree of playfulness in the character's malevolent actions?)."

When they return to Leadworth, after the Dream Lord has issued his challenge to them to uncover which dream is real and which is false with the reward of "if you die in the dream you wake up in reality," Rory is again pushed into a state of infantilism. The Dream Lord says, "Ask me what happens if you die in reality." Rory falls for this ruse, asks him and is scolded with, "You die, stupid. That's why it's called reality," and this mockery indicates how much further along the spectrum of malevolence the trickster shadow of the Doctor is. As the Doctor works out the nature of their communal trance, Amy also defuses the Doctor's criticism, both of the village's dulling effect on his mind and of how their lifestyle has slowed them down, by pretending to go into labour. Male panic ensues, with the Doctor and Rory flummoxed about what to do in such a situation: "It's OK, we're doctors. What do we do?" She is still attached to the reality of her Leadworth idyll and rounds on the Doctor, "This is my life now and it just turned you as white as a sheet. So don't you call it dull again, ever.

121

OK?" The juxtaposition of the Doctor's life as the modern, well-travelled Time Lord with Rory and Amy's 'back to nature' retreat to Leadworth is a trope that is echoed in Simon Nye's comedy-drama *How Do You Want Me?* (1998-9). It similarly explored the 'fish out of water' tribulations of an urban man, Ian Lyons, who marries country girl Lisa Yardley and moves back with her to a rural village after living in London. He finds it impossible to fit in and understand the different values and pace of life in the village whilst she, back with her parents and family, blossoms. It again underlines the dualistic modes of culture as the contrast between the metropolitan, technological city life, or travels with the Doctor, and the less complicated, pastoral, return to Eden of village life, of Upper Leadworth.

Rory's empathy with the country life is symbolised in the hippy-like ponytail he sports in the Leadworth reality, simplistically marking how he has embraced the rustic aesthetic. Amy remains somewhat ambivalent about their life, using platitudes to defend it but not entirely embracing it. All of this is articulated in one of the key scenes in the dead TARDIS where Rory confesses to Amy, "I want the other life. You know, where we're happy and settled and about to have a baby." He emphasises this by mirroring an action from a similar conversation in *The Vampires of Venice* where Amy tentatively punched him and hastily withdrew. He does the same, very unsure that this life is what Amy wants. "But don't you wonder, if that life is real, then why would we give all this up? Why would anyone?" she asks, obviously much happier with her other life of exploration in the TARDIS. She reassures him that the Doctor will repair the dying, freezing TARDIS and alternatively he reasons that they will give up their travels with the Doctor because they are getting married. Her response of "We can still get married, some day," once again problematises the relationship, indicating that beneath it all she is still not ready for commitment. His frustration with her and his insecurity is given vent when he accuses her of running off with another man. "Not in *that* way," she clarifies, firmly refuting that her sexual desire had anything to do with her 'elopement' with the Doctor. "It was the night before our wedding!" he gasps. She is far more pragmatic and understands the complex life of time travelling with the Doctor better than he, stating, "We're in a time machine. It's the night before our wedding for as long as we want." This suggests that she wishes to postpone the consummation of their desire and their commitment to one another indefinitely. She wants to remain an adolescent for as long as possible, to hold back the process of maturation, to not become Mrs Darling to Rory's Mr Darling. Ann Yeoman sees *Peter Pan*'s Mrs Darling as compromised by "identifying with her mother's maternal values to the detriment of her own feminine initiative," whereas Amy would rather retain Wendy's "openness to the unknown of imaginative fantasy and the unconscious" and exploit her opportunities to travel in time and space, because marriage would deny "access to the magic shores of Neverland [that] seems to be barred to grown-ups." Rory, for all his blundering, knows precisely what must happen, and his statement, "We have to grow up eventually," illustrates an all too brief commonality that exists between the Doctor and his companions, where the Time Lord remains an eternal child and they must mature. "Says who?" demands Amy, ignorant to the fact that it will be the Doctor who says when it is time to leave Neverland, go home and grow up and when it will no longer be acceptable to wander in time and space as an excuse never to commit emotionally to one person, one place, one time.

Rory's dissatisfaction with life in the TARDIS is summed up by his grumpy attitude to what has become a dark, cold and inhospitable place, as their dream reveals, with the assistance of the Doctor's Heath Robinson contraption to activate the scanner, the ship drifting into a cold star. Amy attempts to rationalise the symbol of the cold star, by offering that scientifically it does not make sense and that "This must be the dream. There is no such thing as a cold star. Stars burn." However, the Doctor counters this, "No, ice can burn. Sofas can read. It's a big universe." Rory is very unimpressed with his travels so far, "I was promised amazing worlds. Instead, I get duff central heating and a weird kitcheny wind-up device." Talking of getting wound up, he has yet another dig at the Doctor as the Time Lord announces that they have little time to live and should stay calm as this "might be the battle they have to lose." "Oh, this is so *you*, isn't it?" snaps Rory, drawing our attention to the repetition of a well-used trope within the series itself, so recently demonstrated in *The Eleventh Hour*. "A weird new star. Fourteen minutes left to live and only one man to save the day? Huh? I just wanted a nice village and a family." Later, Rory's desire for the 'nice village and family' is highlighted back in the Leadworth reality when he observes that "nothing bad could ever happen here" at precisely the moment that the 'worm in the bud' and the evil living in the heart of his paradise is revealed. Significantly, it is depicted as both the doubt Amy articulates about Leadworth as "not really me" and the realisation that Mrs Poggit has vaporised the children in the playground. The Doctor concludes that, after his examination of the piles of dust left behind, "playtime's definitely over." Again, the Dream Lord makes them question this reality when, as the pensioners appear threateningly en masse, he asks Amy's opinion and the Doctor forcibly requests him to leave her alone. The Dream Lord exploits what he sees as the combative anxiety between Rory and the Doctor by comparing them to each other, positively fawning over the Doctor whilst stoking the fires of Rory's inadequacy with "you're not quite so impressive." Whilst he puts Rory down, he salaciously exposes Amy's misdirected desire for the Doctor, telling her he knows "where your heart lies," and using a spiteful double entendre with "Listen, you're in there," suggesting she still could have the Doctor, in a sexual way, and that she also remains part of his subconscious, as a fantasy or a desire. After all, "He loves a redhead, our naughty Doctor," gossips the Dream Lord and he suggestively dishes more dirt, conflating the virginity of Elizabeth I and the idea of the Doctor as a Lothario in, "Has he told you about Elizabeth the First? Well, she thought she was the first..."

The failure to connect, a major theme in the story, is underlined by Amy as both she and Rory manage to escape from the marauding pensioners, leaving the Doctor behind to take shelter in their cottage. "We just ran away. We just abandoned the Doctor. We don't see him for years, and somehow we don't really connect anymore and then, then he takes a bullet for us." She sees loyalty and friendship as a vital component in their relationship with the Doctor, and a sense of shame in their both running away from what they fear the most (in this case, ironically, the augmented pensioners as symbols of encroaching maturity), despite having not seen him for five years in the Leadworth dream. Rory's reply, as another example of a script full of Nye's wordplay and double meanings, "He'll be fine. You know the doctor. He's Mr Cool," confirms not only the Doctor's charisma as a heroic figure but also how he literally becomes frozen in these alternate realities, fighting off the unconscious threats inside the icy TARDIS and the butcher's meat fridge. The imagery of his frozen consciousness is bound up with the story's links to fairy tales explored later in the chapter. The Doctor freezing in the meat fridge is symptomatically reproduced as a definite drop in temperature felt by Amy when she reawakens inside the TARDIS. Their disconnection is exacerbated when all three of them simply fail to agree which reality is false and which is true after the Doctor demands that they "have to agree which battle to lose. All of us, now." However, this attempt to agree is entangled in the competitiveness between the two men, where Rory clearly wants the Leadworth dream to be real and the Doctor prefers his choice of the dream in the TARDIS. These choices become analogous to their relationship with Amy. Rory wants the pregnant Amy of Leadworth to be real whilst the Doctor requires likewise of his companion in the TARDIS. When Amy asks them what they are competing over, they simultaneously turn and look at her, not saying a word. She rolls her eyes and turns away, disappointed at the immaturity her "boys" are displaying. This competition reaches a crisis when the temperature in the TARDIS becomes so cold that both men fear for the efficacy of the most vital symbols of their masculinity, their manhood. "I can't feel my feet... and other parts," states the Doctor. "I think all my parts are basically fine," boasts Rory. It reflects the similar scene in *The Vampires of Vampires* where Rory and the Doctor also symbolically compare their male prowess in the lighting implements they take into the Calvierri school. The Doctor has only one reply: "Stop competing." Eventually, Amy's own solution to this clash of male egos is to return them to a state of childlike acquiescence by making each man his own poncho and, restating her motherly role first established in *The Vampires of Venice*, by referring to them again as "my boys" but further embellished in this instance as "my poncho boys. If we're going to die, then let's die looking like a Peruvian folk band."

However, her ministrations do not prepare her for the spectre of abandonment, a fear she has borne with her since childhood that the adults she becomes attached to will leave, now sent to haunt her again by

124

the Dream Lord. He reappears just as the Doctor suggests it may be a good idea to try and divide up and have a presence in both dreams. The Dream Lord sees this as an opportunity to possess Amy for his own purposes and tells the Doctor he can keep Rory, or "Pointy Nose", for eternity instead. As the Doctor and Rory slump into unconsciousness, Amy is left alone once more. Again, as Roger Salerno demonstrates in *Landscapes of Abandonment*, the fairy tale is put to service in the narrative where it "reaches the child at a primitive level of awareness. They are frequently bridges between dreams and reality – existing in a twilight of both. Children often receive subtle threats and sometimes not so subtle ones through the use of such stories." The story in *Amy's Choice* certainly unfolds on the borderland between two dreams that are very real to the individuals that inhabit them. The Dream Lord sadistically manipulates the three friends and the story reflects Salerno's view of Grimm's fairy tales where they "support a popular psychoanalytical contention that abandonment disrupts the child's healthy individuation." Taunting her with "Poor Amy, he always leaves you, doesn't he? Alone, in the dark. Never apologises," the Dream Lord emphasises the dark, cold dream of the TARDIS as the primal scene of a chaotic, non-world in which she feels utterly lost. It is one in which writer Nye's ambition to explore the emotional framework of the series is exposed, often through humour, in a story that tackles fear, anger, isolation, responsibility, bitterness, connectedness, manipulation and, ultimately, forgiveness.

Amy believes the Doctor has no need to apologise to her. "That's good. Because he never will," spits his alter ego. "Now, he's left you with me. Spooky old not-to-be-trusted me. Anything could happen." With that unsubtle suggestion of sexual impropriety, the Dream Lord perhaps symbolises the lascivious wolf encountered by Red Riding Hood and his libidinous directive is emphasised by his transformation into the spectacle of the predatory seducer wearing a shirt slashed to the navel and flaunting a medallion. She bravely offers that the Doctor always explains everything to her and although he has not yet told her who the Dream Lord is, she is certain he will. However, the Dream Lord, as an alter ego of the Doctor, confronts her about the very scrap of knowledge that separates her from any intimacy with the Doctor. It is knowledge that exists only in the closeness that River Song, as far as we are aware in *Silence in the Library*, has shared with the Doctor. "The one girl in the universe to whom the Doctor tells everything?" he intimates, followed by a demanding, "So what's his name?" The Dream Lord underlines the major theme of making moral choices in this episode, reflecting Joe Winston's view of fairy tales and similar narratives in *Drama, Narrative and Moral Education* where they act as the "location of morality within the social world; the fact that the social world will provide different roles and relationships for each of us to fulfil; and that these roles and relationships will bring different moral pressures to bear on us, non of which may be any the less binding than another." Here, the dark shadow of the Time Lord states the proposition within the narrative, and to an extent within the series as a whole, "Now, which one of these men would you really choose? Look at them. You ran away with a handsome hero. Would you really give him up for a bumbling country doctor who thinks the only thing he needs to be interesting is a ponytail?" His terms are set within the moral principles of storytelling, where fairy tale is a myth that can be revised and retold and where such tales function as a communal experience rather than a private one. She is offered a solution to her dilemma, to negate the conflict between her loyalties: "Then, maybe it's better than loving and losing the doctor? Pick a world and this nightmare will all be over. They'll listen to you. It's you they're waiting for. Amy's men. Amy's choice." The private torment between Amy, Rory and the Doctor is staged within a series of realities, of moral possibilities, where Winston suggests that *Doctor Who*, as a television programme watched by millions, serves the original reception of such stories where "tales were part of a shared, public process, more akin to a dramatic performance than a private, literary reading, and... they were adaptable to change, historically and geographically, to address the needs and concerns of particular communities which constituted the audience." The challenges for Rory and Amy are not necessarily rooted in Leadworth but are to be mythically played out in the vast, monster-filled environs of time and space.

The development of the mature hero in *Amy's Choice* reaches its apotheosis both in Rory's 'self-emasculation' where his removal of the ponytail signals his subsequent death, and Amy's final choice where she can no longer live without him. "I want to do something for you," he says to Amy, cutting off the hair that is for all intents and purposes an emblem of the dream Leadworth and his aspirations for "a nice village and a family." The ponytail is all that remains of Rory in the dream Leadworth, itself suggesting that this version of Rory is just a man of appearances, of surface charm. As Marie-Luise von Franz explains in *The Interpretation of Fairy Tales*, lockets of hair "preserved as keepsakes are believed to connect one individual with another over a distance," and "cutting the hair and sacrificing it often means submission to a new collective state – a giving up and rebirth." The ponytail is Rory's concession to Amy's desire, even though she half-heartedly suggests she was starting to like him wearing it, that they simply be themselves, their lives not dominated by Leadworth or the Doctor's travels in the TARDIS. It is highly significant that immediately after he surrenders that part of his dream she begins her labour and this time it is 'real', not an act or a false alarm. "Would I make it up at a time like this?" she states. His response of "Well you do have a history of... being very lovely," suggests that the removal of the ponytail, that restriction of his hair, is connected to a freeing of his inhibitions, an ability to deal with her on a more sensual and intuitive level. The symbolic rebirth he undertakes parallels the birth of his child and is embellished by his death, the man slipping through Amy's hands simply because she could not see his true worth, in the Leadworth reality. It is a necessary sacrifice because it finally reinforces the object of Amy's desire, underlines her choice and is the catalyst to the destruction of the Leadworth fantasy created by the Dream Lord. This choice is also brokered by the Doctor's inability to rescue Rory. "Save him. You save everyone. You always do. It's what you do," she demands of the Doctor. When he admits that he is not always able to do so, she no longer sees him as a potential love object and finds a flawed hero hiding beneath that once desirable surface. As she discovers that the Doctor is not her object of desire and does not function as her hero, her deluded objectification of him is framed by her angry denouncement, "Then what is the point of you?" She clutches the totemic ponytail and announces, "This is the dream. Definitely this one. If we die here then we wake up, yeah?" and her question raises the possibility that Rory's death may also have resulted in his waking in the TARDIS reality. "Unless we just die," the Doctor reminds her. "Either way, this is my only chance of seeing him again," she reasons and her emphatic "Because if this is real life, I don't want it. I don't want it," becomes a rejection of the way of life in Leadworth, with no Rory in it and full of ageing and death.

This leads to the decision to use the camper van to smash into the cottage, an act that will kill the Doctor, herself and her unborn child. "Be very sure," warns the Doctor, "this could be the real world." "It can't be. Rory isn't here," she replies, now sure that his absence is not her idea of reality, and the loss of his love has been a profound revelation for her: "I didn't know. I didn't. I didn't. I honestly didn't until right now. I just want him. I love Rory and I never told him but now he's gone." This revelation is so profound that she is willing to sacrifice their unborn child to prove that Leadworth is not the real world. Admittedly, she has been troubled with doubt about this reality and her role in it since she saw the children reduced to dust in the playground and now she is sure she wishes to be rid of it altogether. It is a disturbing sequence, but Nye and director Morshead do find a moving, emotional core to the characters that the series has been demanding for some time and it is fully realised in the magical aftermath of the crash when Amy wakes up in the ice palace version of the TARDIS and reaches out for the sleeping Rory. This gesture is accompanied by the rising strings of Murray Gold's incidental music, suggesting that the sacrifice has been worth it as we see Amy, her defences melting away, embrace the man she could not bear to lose. The Dream Lord admits his defeat, "So you chose this world. And you got it right. Fair's fair." His agreeable "Let's warm you up" emphasises the thawing of older, less convivial relationships and begins the reintegration of their personalities, the individuation process that Jung believed led to the fullest actualisation of the self. Amy's physical intimacy here is genuine compared to her guardedness in *The Vampires of Venice* and even Rory can tell the difference, "This is good. I am liking this. Was it something I said? Can you tell me what it was so I can use it in emergencies? Maybe birthdays?"

The changes in Amy, the result of the consequences of their actions in the dream reality, are reproduced in Rory when he discovers that he was dead and the camper van crash destroyed the Leadworth dream. "O... K... But how did you know it was a dream? Before you crashed the van, how

127

did you know that you wouldn't just die?" Amy confesses that she had no idea if she and the Doctor would live or die and he realises that she took a risk, took a leap of faith and made a huge sacrifice to demonstrate her choice. He passionately kisses her and the episode finally shifts all the relationships into their proper orbits. The Doctor applauds as they embrace and kiss. "So. Well then, where now? Or should I just pop down to the swimming pool for a few lengths?" Significantly, he has assumed Rory's earlier role of 'gooseberry'. For Rory, the Leadworth dream is not where he will necessarily be the happiest. "Anywhere's good for me. I'll be happy anywhere. It's up to Amy this time. Amy's choice."

## "I've always been able to see through you, Doctor"

The story's examination of the impetuousness of adolescence in contrast to the maturity of adults also finds expression in both Nye's use of the pensioners as the monsters that must be defeated in the Leadworth reality and in the symbol of the cold star into which the TARDIS is plunging. In one reality, youth is being destroyed, turned to dust by the Eknodines that live inside the old people, and in the other reality, the TARDIS becomes a frozen monument to the retreat of their own warm, living consciousnesses and personalities as the Dream Lord undermines them. The Doctor, Amy and Rory are all representative of the masculine and feminine aspects of both a life and a society that struggle to find their own connections. The curse of losing consciousness, of falling into a deep sleep, of being frozen, finds its parallel in *Sleeping Beauty*, where the story's curse symbolises the feminine, feeling side of life becoming lost in the unconscious. Nye's story also echoes the narrative of the fairy tale *The Snow Queen*, where an evil troll, perhaps representative of the devil and in *Amy's Choice* personified as the Dream Lord, makes a mirror that distorts everything reflected into it. All the good and beautiful aspects of people are replaced by its magnification of all their badness and ugliness. The mirror is shattered and shards of it are blown around like snow and when it gets into everyone's eyes and hearts only the darkest things can be seen in people. The Dream Lord is the distorting mirror of the Doctor himself, reflecting back the shadowy nature of the nine-hundred-year-old alien onto his two companions, symbolically rooted in that final glimpse reflected in the TARDIS console at the end of the episode.

The idea of the aged occupants of Leadworth turning feral again taps into the common fears that children and young adults have of the elderly and of ageing itself. In *Ageism: Stereotyping and Prejudice Against Older Persons*, Jeff Greenberg, Jeff Schimel and Andy Martens, perhaps describing the segregation of the aged in Leadworth, offer in 'Ageism: Denying the Face of the Future' that "the separation of the elderly in this way may also be a form of proximal defence against thoughts about old age and death." The Sarn nursing home (a little nod to *Doctor Who* continuity, with the planet Sarn featuring in *Planet of Fire* and a character of that name appearing in *Time and the Rani*) could be described as a place where "there may exist a cycle of psychological defence and increased fear of the elderly in Western culture: the more the elderly remind us of our mortality, the more they become potent reminders of death." The focus on Mrs Poggit, who turns children, and Rory himself, into the dust that, in death, we must all become, is a reminder of our childhood fear of the stereotypical crone or witch as a symbol of repulsive femininity. She is the witch who devours fattened up children in *Hansel and Gretel* or the stepmother that forces young *Cinderella* to slave away cleaning her house, and she is another expression of Moffat's exploitation of an armoury of childhood anxieties in the series. This fear is also embellished by the images of armies of pensioners physically attacking the Doctor, Amy and Rory, killing postmen and besieging the younger inhabitants of the village. The imagery that Morshead uses, particularly of the aged slowly marauding their way across the fields of Leadworth, is evocative of the zombies wandering across the post-war American landscapes of suburbia in George Romero's *Dawn of the Dead* (1978). These visions turn the initial depiction of the elderly in the nursing home, typified in the sentimentality of Mrs Poggit knitting jumpers and trying them out on the Doctor, into a palpable terror. They become a dark but witty threat where "playtime's definitely over" for the younger inhabitants of Leadworth and, by extension, for Amy and Rory who must eventually destroy this fantasy in order to grow up. This destruction not only involves bashing Mrs Hamill with a plank of wood ("I can't hit her," admits Rory. "Whack her!" yells Amy) and knocking Mrs Poggit off a rooftop, but also inevitably the death of Rory's youthful dream and a return to mature reality. In April 2010 even Nye rationalised this choice in *Doctor Who Magazine*'s preview of *Amy's Choice*: "Given the choice between creating – or being – a nice, meek pensioner, or a deliciously crazed old maniac, I know which one I'd go for. I did, initially, make various sensitive points about aging, but they were cut from the script when we realised they weren't funny, clever or dramatic." The pensioners are also representative of the doppelgänger, as Helena Bassil-Morozow explains in *Tim Burton: The Monster and the Crowd*: "The real enemy is inside not outside. But the crowd perceives it in its external, 'dehumanised' form – alien, yet distinctly and suspiciously, recognisable." Nye not only turns meek pensioners into a deadly army attempting to drive out youthful non-conformists, but he also expands their role by revealing them to be a race of aliens, the Eknodine.

When the Eknodine are revealed in the standoff with the Doctor, Rory and Amy, they become the ultimate symbol of the monstrous, sporting a green, slimy-looking tongue complete with an eye on the end that alludes simultaneously to a phallus and the *vagina dentata*. The aged are shown as not only a site of haunted decay but also, through an alien possession, as a representation of the inhuman, complete with tongues ejaculating green bile, that Roger Dadoun describes in 'Metropolis: Mother City – "Mittler" – Hitler,' his chapter of *Close Encounters: Film, Feminism and Science Fiction*, as "various libidinal investments around the mouth,

producing a sexual syncretism (mouth as anus, urethra and phallus)."
Rory both verbalises the audience's reaction and introduces the final layer
to this syncretism: "That is disgusting. They're not going to be peeping out
of anywhere else are they?" These inner demons, archetypal monsters
from the id, are then used by Nye to wittily comment on the series's own
master narrative built around alien invasions. As the Doctor interrogates
the Eknodine inhabiting Mrs Poggit, the Dream Lord literally puts words
into their mouths and the Doctor completes each sentence that the
Eknodine starts while their origin and plan to dominate and punish other
life forms is revealed. "OK. Makes sense I suppose. Credible enough,"
comments the Doctor, summarising the viewer's own suspension of
disbelief required to watch and enjoy much of *Doctor Who* itself. This
familiarity of *Doctor Who*'s tropes is also commented on as the pensioners
cease their attack, self-aware enough of the reality created by the Dream
Lord to know it will end with the camper van gambit. It is a recognition
that the Doctor notes, "Either because this is the dream or because they
know what we're about to do."

When the Doctor announces in the TARDIS, "Something, somewhere
is overriding *my* controls," it alerts us to the fact that he is not just
referring to the mechanism of the time machine but he is also aware that
his shadow side, the Dream Lord, has taken control of this reality. The
Dream Lord instantly seeks to dismiss the Doctor and uses all manner of
jibes and insults to inflame his insecurities. "Honestly, I'd heard such
good things. Last of the Time Lords, The Oncoming Storm. Him in the
bow tie," mocks the shadowy trickster. The figure of the Dream Lord is
also visually analogous to that of the Doctor. They both wear jacket and
bow tie ensembles, a form of dress and style that the Dream Lord sees as a
cabaret act complete with "madcap vehicle, the cockamamie hair, the
clothes designed by a first-year fashion student. I'm surprised you haven't
got a little purple space dog." They are clearly vitriolic attacks on the
TARDIS and his costume and a veiled insult to K9. The looks on Rory and
Amy's faces suggest that, in part, some of this is true. In essence the
Doctor does tend to overcompensate, with the repeated "bow ties are cool"
meme part of a repertoire that the Dream Lord sees as an effort to "ram
home what an intergalactic wag you are." After issuing his challenge to
them, all three wake up in the abandoned Sarn nursing home. He
reappears to them as a physician brandishing a set of x-rays, claiming of
the Doctor, "This is bad, very bad. Your brain is completely see-through.
But then I've always been able to see through you Doctor." Amy senses
that this Dream Lord is someone who is more than familiar to the Doctor.
"Always? What do you mean always?" she asks and then poses further
questions to the little man, "Have you met the Doctor before? Do you
know him? Doctor, does he?" He invokes the spectre of sexual jealousy
here, knowing full well from his sharing of the Doctor's subconscious that
Amy desires the Doctor. "Now, don't get jealous. He's been around, our
boy." The Doctor claims not to know who he is and suggests he is yet one
more manifestation of evil in a big universe. He also believes, because the

Matt Smith (the Doctor) and Karen Gillan (Amy Pond) shooting the Eleventh Doctor's debut THE ELEVENTH HOUR on the Cathedral Green in Llandaff, Cardiff, in October 2009. Above: © Alun Vega / Below: © Scott Frankton

Above: Matt Smith, Karen Gillan and Arthur Darvill (Rory) during filming of THE ELEVENTH HOUR in Llandaff in October 2009. © Lee Tucker

Below: Bill Paterson (Bracewell) on top of the Glamorgan Building, Cardiff University, for VICTORY OF THE DALEKS in August 2009. © Scott Frankton

Filming at Southerndown Beach (Ogmore Vale, Bridgend) for THE TIME OF ANGELS, with Matt Smith, Karen Gillan and Alex Kingston (River Song) and the new-look TARDIS on 20 July 2009 - the first day of filming on the fifth series. © Scott Frankton

The residents of the Sarn retirement home advance on the Doctor, Amy and Rory in AMY'S CHOICE, during filming at Skenfrith, Monmouthshire in February 2010. © Catherine Cranston

Above: Filming at St Gwynno's Church, Llanwonno in the Rhondda Valley in October 2009 for THE HUNGRY EARTH. Below: Alaya the Silurian (Neve McIntosh) emerges from the mist. © Scott Frankton

Above and below left: More filming for THE HUNGRY EARTH © Scott Frankton

Below right: Matt Smith, Tony Curran (Van Gogh) and Karen Gillan filming in Roald Dahl Plass, Cardiff for one of the final Paris-set scenes in VINCENT AND THE DOCTOR in January 2010. © Scott Frankton

Above: More filming in Cardiff for VINCENT AND THE DOCTOR. © Scott Frankton

Below: Matt Smith dons his kit for the football match in THE LODGER, filmed at Victoria Park, Canton, Cardiff in March 2010. © Lee Tucker

Above left: Daisy Haggard (Sophie), Matt Smith and James Corden (Craig) filming THE LODGER in Westville Road, Cardiff in March 2010. © Alun Vega

Above right: Matt Smith during filming of THE LODGER © Scott Frankton

Below: Filming at Stonehenge for THE PANDORICA OPENS © Gareth Price

Dream Lord has no physical form, he must be suffering from a form of Napoleon complex and is taking it out on the three of them as, unlike him, they can "touch and eat and feel."

The Dream Lord adopts various identities, often reflecting some aspects of the Doctor's own persona. After appearing as a physician, he turns up outside the castle in Leadworth as a 'lord of the manor' figure, referring to the three of them as "peasants," and as a butcher in a shop that the Doctor takes shelter in. This might refer to Davros's comment about him having "butchered millions" in *Journey's End*. His line "Oh, I love a good butcher's, don't you? We've got to use these places or they'll shut down," comments on the fact that, as he rummages around in the Doctor's subconscious, he is making the Doctor face up to his insecurities and his less pleasant characteristics and by failing to acknowledge them his persona will remain incomplete. It will "shut down." For the Doctor to complete his process of individuation he must accept the shadow part of his nature and subsume these darker aspects of himself into his personality in order to function properly. The Doctor's strength of character is a particular target that the Dream Lord aims for and in the butcher's shop he directly compares the Doctor's weaknesses with meat-eating, "Oh, but then you're probably a vegetarian aren't you, you big flop-haired wuss?" and makes a particularly bad pun, "We've got lots of steak here this week. Lots at stake. Get it?" as the gang of pensioners burst into the shop in pursuit. He also taunts the Doctor with a limerick, "There was an old Doctor from Gallifrey, who ended up throwing his life away, he let down his friends..." but then exclaims that he has run out of time to complete it, subtly referring to the way time was running out in *Flesh and Stone* when the crack in the universe devoured the Weeping Angels. There is also his attempt to seduce Amy as a Lothario figure, symbolising the Doctor's hidden sexual desires, and a final appearance as a racing driver as the Doctor speeds along to Amy's rescue, where the Dream Lord questions his need to find his friends. "Friends, is that the right word for the people you acquire? Friends are people you stay in touch with. Your friends never see you again once they've grown up. The old man prefers the company of the young, does he not?" brings to the surface the constant issue of the Doctor's age and immortality in relation to his companions where as he changes, and outwardly remains younger, they will always grow up, grow old and eventually die. It also mocks the Doctor's claim to Amy and Rory at the beginning of the episode, after his initial arrival in Leadworth, "I don't just abandon people when they leave the TARDIS. This Time Lord's for life." The Dream Lord knows this is somewhat untrue because the Doctor rarely revisits those that have long since left a life of travelling in the TARDIS. It certainly refers back to some of the issues raised in *School Reunion* when he encountered former companion Sarah Jane Smith after many decades. However, he genuinely believes that his choice of Amy and Rory as friends is instrumental in preventing the Dream Lord's further feeding off the darkest aspects of their personas. "The darkness in you pair? It would have starved to death in an instant. I choose my friends with great care. Otherwise I'm stuck with my own company and you know how that works out." This darkness is obviously something the Dream Lord admires amongst the Doctor's physical and character strengths, beneath the "tawdry quirks." When the Doctor growls at him to leave Amy alone after the Dream Lord suggests to Amy it would be a good idea to jump under a bus to end the Leadworth reality (prefiguring its eventual destruction using the camper van), the little man says admiringly, "Do that again. I love it when he does that. Tall, dark hero, '*Leave her alone!*'"

It is intimated that the Doctor knows who the Dream Lord is by the time they confront the pensioners in Leadworth. After the Dream Lord teases Amy about the Doctor's preference for redheads, the Doctor angrily rounds on him, "Drop it. Drop all of it. I know who you are. No idea how you can be here, but there's only one person in the universe who hates me as much as you do." This begins to crystallise the idea that the Dream Lord is the Doctor's alter ego, representative of the double or doppelgänger and a classic element in the horror film genre. Steven Jay Schneider in *Horror Film and Psychoanalysis: Freud's Worst Nightmare* suggests that "most theorists and psychologists define doubling as the experience of seeing or otherwise sensing, feeling, or believing that there exists another 'you' from inside your own self." The classic texts that *Amy's Choice* emulates here are Robert Louis Stevenson's *Dr Jekyll and Mr Hyde* and Oscar Wilde's *The Picture of Dorian Gray*, where in the former the scientist Jekyll uses his alter ego Hyde to bear his own deeply buried, evil, physical impulses and in the latter an aesthete sublimates his criminal behaviour within a mirror-like portrait. The Dream Lord character is also reminiscent of the Valeyard, that distillation of the Doctor's evil side, as seen in *The Trial of a Time Lord* and in which the shadow trickster figure is represented by a dark version of the Doctor somewhere between his twelfth and thirteenth regenerations. Indeed, there was much fan speculation that the Dream Lord and the Valeyard were one and the same when the episode was transmitted. Symbolically, the Valeyard also takes on the similar role of the double and both characters depict the Doctor as if he is suffering from a monothematic delusion where his doppelgänger, just like Stevenson's Hyde, is operating independently of him. When the Doctor understands the Dream Lord's ability to "see right through" him, he also realises that the Dream Lord concedes too easily after the eradication of the Leadworth reality. He can now "see right through" his evil counterpart. "Notice how helpful the Dream Lord was? OK, there was misinformation, red herrings, malice and I could have done without the limerick, but he was always very keen to make us choose between dream and reality." Even though Rory and Amy believe that the frozen TARDIS is reality rather than dream, the Doctor astutely sees that the TARDIS's own double, the cold star into which they were about to plunge, is also completely unreal. "Star burning cold? Do me a favour. The Dream Lord has no power over the real world. He was offering us a choice between two dreams." Amy questions, "How do you know that?" and the Doctor finally admits, "Because I know who he is." He blows up the TARDIS, foreshadowing its destruction in *The Pandorica Opens*, and returns them all to the true reality.

Nye clearly needs to explain what triggered this battle with the Doctor's darker impulses and he opts for one of the 'deus ex machina' solutions that Terry Pratchett criticised the series for overusing. There literally is an explanation lodged in the works of the TARDIS, a "speck of psychic pollen from the Candle Meadows of Karass don Slava. Must have been hanging around for ages. Fell in the time rotor, heated up and induced a dream state for all of us." Like the splinters of glass reflecting back all that was evil and that blew as snow into the hearts and minds of characters in *The Snow Queen* or the spores that infected and mutated Ruth Baxter in *Terror of the Vervoids*, the pollen functions as a similar parasite. "So that was the Dream Lord then? Those little specks?" asks Rory. "Sorry, wasn't it obvious? The Dream Lord was *me*. Psychic pollen, it's a mind parasite. It feeds on everything dark in you. Gives it a voice, turns it against you. I'm 907. It had a lot to go on." However, after the Doctor explains that Amy and Rory were not a big enough meal for the parasite, Amy is still concerned about the vitriol hurled at the Doctor by the Dream Lord. "But those things he said about you. You don't think any of that's true?" She cares not to believe that the Doctor harbours the unattractive attitudes and qualities the Dream Lord was keen to expose. The Doctor remains tight-lipped, suggesting that he is painfully aware that perhaps some or all of what was said reflects the shadowy areas of his nature into which the Dream Lord has simply retreated. Again it is apt that this was shown in the week that those other Dream Lord-id and Time Lord-ego sparring partners of Cameron and Clegg celebrated their own marriage to save England from the marauding spectre of the financial deficit. The Dream Lord works especially well as a foil for the Doctor here because actor Toby Jones plays the part with such relish and comes across as a more vindictive, fantasy version of the Truman Capote he played in *Infamous* (2006). That said, the Dream Lord, if he is an amalgamation of all the Doctor's repressed anxieties and traumas, should really have been more vicious. With nine-hundred-odd years of skeletons in the closet to exploit, he should perhaps have done some lasting psychological damage in a story that really only scratches the surface about the emotionally damaged Doctor and his companions.

*Amy's Choice* is a very witty and imaginative script from Nye, a seasoned television writer and an extremely well thought of translator of Molière and Dario Fo. When he was announced as a writer for the series, various alarm bells went off in the fan community about why the creator/writer of *Men Behaving Badly* (1992-8) was being commissioned to write telefantasy for a Saturday night BBC One audience. Judging by the completed episode, Nye successfully and succinctly grasps one of the central conceits of *Doctor Who* here – what makes the ordinary so extraordinary, the domestic so terrifying – and weaves a magical little tale about repression, guilt and deadly pensioners. The script unpacks the Doctor's darker aspects, especially in relation to his new companions Amy and Rory, without tipping the whole thing over into the hyperbole of the 'Time Lord Victorious' of *The Waters of Mars* and it follows in the tradition of lower-budget and often more atypical episodes such as the much-admired *Turn Left* and *Midnight*. Nye uses the fantastic to undertake a much-needed examination of Amy's childlike relationship to and dependency on the Doctor, her wavering love for Rory and the constant check that the Doctor keeps on his dual nature. The choice that Amy is forced to make, between Rory and the Doctor, life and death, reality and dream, including giving up the life of her unborn child, also alludes to Alan J. Pakula's film of *Sophie's Choice* (1982). The film's central character Sophie harbours the traumatic secret that, as an internee at Auschwitz, she was forced by a Nazi officer to make a choice over the survival of her two children, to choose life for one child and death for the other. He also evokes much genre hybridity too by emulating: *The Avengers*, with its use of a threatened and threatening English pastoral setting in a similar fashion to the other Leadworth-set episode *The Eleventh Hour*; the comedy horror of Peter Jackson's *Braindead* (1992); and the reality versus dreamscape mind-games of *Doctor Who*'s own *The Edge of Destruction*, *The Mind Robber* and *The Deadly Assassin*. The great script is somewhat hampered by average execution, with some quite disappointing direction from the usually reliable Catherine Morshead. It is a literate script, very dependent on wordy exchanges, puns and double meanings, and Morshead fails to inject enough energy into the finished episode with many scenes feeling rather visually inert. The quirkier style of director Adam Smith would perhaps have better suited this material.

Nye's script establishes well the two realities of Leadworth and the frozen TARDIS and manages to generate suspense and tension in those settings very consistently throughout the episode, leaving the viewer and, to an extent the characters, with a guessing game as to which reality is true and which is false. The denouement, that posits a third reality whilst revealing that both the other settings were dreams, is clever. However, the resolution of the plot using the pollen undermines this somewhat. Despite the weakness of the psychic pollen as an explanation for the psychedelic trip through the backwaters of the Doctor's personality, Nye's script serves a vital purpose. It humanises the Amy Pond character to such a degree that her less palatable, rather forced spikiness and feisty cynicism is ameliorated. Much of this relies on Karen Gillan's superb performance, certainly her best given in the series at this point, and the story's overall examination and development of Amy's relationship with Rory. As a viewer, this comes as rather a relief from the alienating effect that the character of Amy Pond has inadvertently created through her disconnection with the audience's expectations. In progressing through the series, Amy has tended to become less likeable and as much as she has distanced herself from her husband-to-be Rory, she has also, for me personally, become estranged from us as viewers. While it is clear that the testing of both companions by the Dream Lord is, in effect, a series of challenges set by the Doctor too, Amy's love for Rory and her need for him to be part of her world overrides her role as mother-to-be. The series of choices she is given also include the sacrifice of a child, a choice that is reliant on her faith that the reality in which she is pregnant is just a wish fulfilment plucked from Rory's mind by the Dream Lord. It is a harsh choice to make and the script rather avoids a moral debate in which to contextualise her decision, meaning she again, despite Nye's efforts to the contrary, comes across as rather uncaring about the baby's fate, be it a real or fantasy child. Potentially, Nye rescues the character from the audience's disaffections and is assisted in this by the inclusion of Rory Williams. A complete charmer, bumbling but brave, insecure but loyal, he is a character you warm to instantly and Arthur Darvill deftly manifests his idiosyncratic attractions. Rory is a 'giver', wanting emotional security in return, and Amy is often seen as rather aloof, pushing Rory away just as he tries to get closer to her. *Amy's Choice* finally demonstrates that Amy and Rory actually do love one another (and it takes Rory's fantasy death for Amy to realise this) and it successfully ring-fences their relationship in opposition to the previously ill-defined, 'will they, won't they' dynamic between Amy and the Doctor. Rory's death scene, tragic as it is and wonderfully performed by the cast, seen in the wider context of how Amy has treated Rory so far, does not completely fulfill its emotional potential. There is always a sense of doubt surrounding Amy's intentions and affections where we question her motives based on the inconsistency of the choices and emotions she has displayed in the past. The choice for Amy, deciding that Leadworth's English idyll is a false reality and life is not worth living without Rory, is a great way of finally exposing the humanity of her character and making her 'grow up eventually' but it begs the question as to whether Nye's script comes too late in the running order of the series to change our hardened opinions of the character.

Chapter Seven

# THE HUNGRY EARTH
# COLD BLOOD

Written by: Chris Chibnall
Directed by: Ashley Way
First broadcast: 22 & 29 May 2010

## "Humans, you're so nostalgic"

Nostalgia haunts *The Hungry Earth* and *Cold Blood*. Chris Chibnall's story embraces the act of longing for the past, one that here informs the present and shapes the future in the narrative, where the viewer is encouraged to knowingly seek comfortable recognition in both the recycling of narrative and visual tropes of a bygone era of *Doctor Who* and the creation of nostalgia for the events that occur in Cwmtaff in 2020. The characters of Rory and Amy see themselves revisiting present events and their future selves have, as the Doctor ironically points out, "Come to relive past glories, I'd imagine." Silurian leader Eldane provides a melancholic view in his voiceover, looking back from a thousand years in the future presumably as the hibernating Silurians wake up, to suggest the less than favourable outcomes of the present-day story. "This is the story of our planet, Earth, of the day one thousand years past when we came to share it with a race known as humanity. It is the story of the Doctor who helped our races find common ground and the terrible losses he suffered. It is the story of our past and must never be forgotten." Observed both from within and without the frame of the television screen, by both viewer and character, this aesthetic is perhaps indicative of the way Alec Charles, in *Time and Relative Dissertations in Space*, 'The Ideology of Anachronism: Television, History and the Nature of Time', sees television itself as a "confusion between the old and the new, the archived and the live [that] has dissolved the distance between the past and the present." The two episodes are bookended with moments where a character or characters inside the narrative witness or recall past events, even though they are experienced in the present, albeit a 2020 one, by both the audience and the same characters.

Nostalgia is part of culture, often bound up within the art of storytelling and is that which Jerry Herron calls in *Electronic Media Criticism: Applied Perspectives*, "the longing we imagine others would feel if they only realised the value of things they never knew about, but now seem disastrously to have 'forgotten'." His definition summarises the impending tragedy at the heart of the story, in Ambrose's failure to find her humanity beneath her xenophobia and in Rory's forgotten sacrifice to

137

the erasing light of time. It is consistent with the overall idea that Moffat is keen to address in the 2010 series, one of remembering the past and not forgetting those who lived in it, and becomes more relevant than ever in the conclusion of *Cold Blood* with the subsequent death of Rory and Amy's failure to remember him. Chibnall, however, is not only telling the story within Eldane's thousand-year eschatology, but he is also exploiting a particular longing for the past within *Doctor Who* devotees, dissolving 'the distance between past and present' history of the series itself, in his enthusiastic borrowing from an era of *Doctor Who* which had its heyday some thirty years ago. By doing so he creates an abstract pastiche of the Jon Pertwee era, described by John Tulloch and Manuel Alvarado in *Doctor Who: The Unfolding Text*, as "the SF discourse of the empirical present interrupted suddenly and fearfully by alien invaders... by threats from the interior and/or past of the Earth." Not only does the story significantly evolve out of Malcolm Hulke's *Doctor Who and the Silurians* and reiterate much of its settings and characters, bringing back and reinterpreting the titular 'monsters' from his serial, but it also plays freely with a number of other familiar idioms that have become synonymous with the Pertwee era. The drilling project run by geologist Nasreen Chaudhry (an amusing performance from a somewhat underused Meera Syal) in the Welsh hills of Cwmtaff is presented as a conflation of various Pertwee era settings, including: the Stahlman project in *Inferno*, which features an operation to drill into the Earth's crust to tap new energy reserves; the Welsh mining setting of *The Green Death*; and the isolated village of Devil's End in *The Daemons*, cut off from the rest of the country with a heat barrier that is here reproduced when the Silurians erect an invisible energy barrier around Cwmtaff. There are also a number of shots that director Ashley Way employs of the drilling area showing the modern drill head adjacent to the old pit head and winding gear of a disused coalmine that specifically evoke the setting of *The Green Death*. This comparison practically symbolises the story's own attempt to blend the modernist iconography of scientific progress with the relics of the past, captured in Robert Sloman's serial with his clash between Global Chemicals and the traditions of coalmining in the area. When Tony Mack (surely with the surname paralleling how Hulke was himself often addressed as 'Mac'), played by Robert Pugh, reveals the spreading infection from Alaya's venom, his infected green veins are simply another example of Chibnall's substitutions, recalling both *The Green Death*'s visions of diseased miners succumbing to the poison of the giant maggots and an allusion to the mutagenic green slime that transforms humans into Primords in *Inferno*. The Pertwee era is also emphasised in dialogue too, and the Third Doctor's role as scientific advisor to paramilitary organisation UNIT, suffering the necessary evil of working with government and the establishment, is humorously commented on when the Doctor introduces himself to Nasreen as the 'man from the ministry', from a "Ministry of Drills, Earth and Science. New Ministry. Quite big, just merged." The Third Doctor's ambivalent relationship to Brigadier Alistair

Gordon Lethbridge-Stewart, the commander of UNIT, is emphasised particularly well in *Doctor Who and the Silurians* when, to the Doctor's horror, and despite his overtures to peace, the Brigadier blows up the Silurians at the end of Hulke's story. In *Cold Blood*, when the Doctor is introduced to Restac in the Silurians' underground city, Chibnall alludes to this uneasy collaboration. "Restac. Military commander," she barks, much to the Doctor's dismay, and his response summarises his attitude to the many encounters with UNIT, the tactics of its commanders and the military in general, with "Oh dear. Really? There's always a military, isn't there?"

The events of the Pertwee-UNIT era take place in serials transmitted in the early 1970s, but the stories have always been accepted as set in a predicted near future of Britain. *The Hungry Earth* and *Cold Blood* play with this convention, setting the story ten years hence, in 2020, and suggest visually, in the opening scene at least, that the country has been affected by climate change. While the story perhaps acknowledges the tone of the Pertwee era's relationship with, and reflection of, the Britain of the 1970s, its attempt to mimic Hulke's own political discourse in *Doctor Who* rather underachieves in its examination of the global, twenty-first century social and political debates affecting Britain. Looking back at the *Doctor Who* of 1970, James Chapman, in *Inside the TARDIS: The Worlds of Doctor Who*, sees the Pertwee era as "an uncomfortably sinister projection of the society Britain might become." Not only does the series move into colour in 1970 and embrace a 'realism' in its narrative and aesthetics hitherto unseen, but it is regarded as commentary on the rise of new social movements such as feminism and environmentalism, the impact of the economic and industrial recession with its resulting strikes and blackouts, the rise of corporate culture and the loss of Empire. The depressing scenario of the present, the end of the liberalism of the 1960s, is a subtext seen through the refracting mirror of an alternative, future Britain with its own space programme, development of nuclear power and drilling projects as emblematic of a country that still believes it is a thriving world power. With *Doctor Who and the Silurians* there is an emphasis on the public mistrust of science and the establishment, and Chapman also reflects on Nicholas J. Cull's reading, suggested in 'Bigger on the Inside... Doctor Who as Cultural History' in *The Historian, Television and Television History*, of both *Doctor Who and the Silurians* and *The Sea Devils* as commentaries on the ongoing political and religious crises, of the time, in the Middle East and in Ireland, and suggests, "the belligerent factions amongst the Silurians and the Sea Devils stand for the PLO and the IRA: groups claiming to represent those dispossessed and displaced inhabitants who resort to violence to assert their territorial claims." In Chibnall's story, the narrative conventions of the afore-mentioned Pertwee stories struggle to become little more than a generic longing for that era in what becomes his primary re-reading of the original Malcolm Hulke story. *The Hungry Earth* and *Cold Blood* attempt to engage with similar political debates but the results are a vague and simplistic reading of the continuing dispute over territory between Palestine and Israel. As *Cold Blood* was transmitted, this conflict escalated with the Israeli attack on a flotilla of ships carrying aid and attempting to break Israel's blockade of the Gaza strip. The politics of the area is highly complex, certainly more so than the disputes of the 1970s, and *Cold Blood*'s negotiation scene between the Silurians and humanity is a naïve distillation of an often very violent struggle between Arabs and Jews over land, water, borders, security and the fate of refugees from the 1948 war. Unlike Hulke, who succinctly tapped into the zeitgeist of unrest in the 1970s, Chibnall misses an opportunity to place this latest chapter of the Silurian saga within much wider debates about the European economic crisis, globalisation and the environment. Instead, as we will discuss later, his agenda is more concerned with individuals.

Chibnall's nostalgic desire to emulate the Doctor's earlier attempts at brokering peace with *Homo reptilia* in *Doctor Who and the Silurians*, *The Sea Devils* and, to a lesser extent, the later *Warriors of the Deep* is nowhere better illustrated than in the "first meeting of representatives" seen in *Cold Blood*. Taking its cue from the Pertwee era's own discussions about colonialism and federalism, in stories such as *The Mutants* and *The Curse of Peladon*, the conversation about land rights between Eldane, Amy and Nasreen is somewhat optimistic to the point of absurdity. Rigorous politicking was never the overall intention of the series in the early 1970s and inevitably the views on racism, colonialism and the environment lacked sophistication, but it comes as something of a surprise that the scripts for *Cold Blood* are equally unsophisticated, barely raising the issues beyond a basic good-versus-evil binary opposition view of Silurians and humans that the story posits. The Pertwee serials managed, if somewhat clumsily, to depict the morally grey areas of such conflicts of interest by examining, for example, xenophobia in *The Ambassadors of Death*, the science-military schism of Silurian society in *Doctor Who and the Silurians* and eco-catastrophe in *The Green Death* with a degree of sympathetic refinement. The conference scene in *Cold Blood*, with its heart no doubt in the right place, does descend into a form of 'equal opportunities' racism, contained in certain remarks from Nasreen, that even the BNP would be proud of. "Yes, fine, but what happens when their population grows and breeds and spreads?" she argues after Amy suggests that the Silurians could occupy deserted areas of the Earth such as the Sahara desert, the Australian outback and the Nevada plains. Even Amy's own solution to the sharing of the planet conjures up the spectre of colonial guilt and subsequent apologia over the way that white European-American expansionism displaced the indigenous populations of America and Australia. It is little wonder then that the Silurians relish the opportunity of mitigating this sense of guilt with the beguiling offer of propping up Western capitalism with their superior technology, sources of energy and scientific advances. This eagerly anticipated rise in Silurian stock, a peace dividend if you like, alludes to what Naomi Klein, in *The Shock Doctrine*, saw as the failure of the Oslo Accords between Israel and the PLO in 1993 to "push ahead with the 'peace of markets'... by flinging open the borders and joining the globalization juggernaut." This scenario was ultimately derailed by assassination and suicide bombings. Granted, Nasreen does articulate the potential for resistance in her claim: "Nobody on the surface is going to go for this idea. It's just too big a leap," but this notion is never really explored in much depth again. The triteness of the scene is heightened by the way the Doctor acts as broker for world peace, his pomposity hand in hand with a naïve belief that humans and Silurians can overcome the evil within themselves. His address, "bringing things to order – the first meeting of representatives of the human race and *Homo reptilia* is now in session. Never said that before, that's fab," unfortunately echoes some of Tony Blair's own righteousness and over-sincerity when, in the final Prime Minister's Questions in the House, in June 2007, he announced his appointment as envoy to the Middle East and devoutly believed it was his mission to prioritise a two-state solution to stability and peace in the area. The Doctor's role as mediator is made distinctly untenable when, in a later scene, he praises the Silurian scientist Malohkeh without questioning the immoral nature of the creature's activities, accepting what might be classed as his war crimes as part of the settlement process. The Doctor's lack of moral outrage is distinctly out of character as Malohkeh reveals that, as well as performing vivisection on human beings and presumably stealing the bodies of the dead from the village churchyard, he has also been kidnapping children ("taking samples of the young") to study their growth and evolution. This is in complete contradiction to the Doctor's attitude towards Tony Mack when, earlier in *The Hungry Earth*, he rules out the suggestion of any such disassembling ("No dissecting! No examining!") of Silurians visiting the surface. Yet he seems to positively condone the activities of this Silurian version of Josef Mengele (even his name, Malohkeh, sounds similar), based principally on one scientist relating to another's line of scientific enquiry, of actions committed in the name of science. While he demands non-violence from Ambrose with: "No, no weapons. It's not the way I do things," and dutifully fulfils his role as the catalyst for human and Silurian peace, his ethical approach to suffering in the name of science and research are coupled with the moral vicissitudes of Chibnall's script to reveal a rather hypocritical Doctor.

Another problem here, in this yearning to replicate the politics of Hulke's stories, is that the attempt to develop a moral and ethical underpinning of the story, particularly the idealistic two-state solution that Eldane, Amy and Nasreen confer over, takes place in a complete vacuum. Like the invisible energy barrier that seals off Cwmtaff from the rest of the country, Chibnall animates his characters, and their respective moral positions, within a non-referential world. The events in both episodes are literally cut off from the real world beyond the hills of Cwmtaff. The story intimates that it is a community in decline and that mobile and internet communication is poor, but if a record-breaking attempt by scientists to drill into the Earth is taking place then where are the media and the establishment? Many of the Pertwee-era stories, whilst gently mocked by fan critics for their parochial depiction of alien invasions occurring in the Home Counties with alarming regularity, do at least acknowledge figureheads and institutions with a relationship to the establishment mores and political debates of a world beyond the confines of the Doctor's consultancy work with UNIT. The alien incursions in the stories we have highlighted all, more or less, happen within a national, and often international, space that actively involves such emblems of the establishment's moral order as the police, the regular army and UNIT's troops and officers, the Navy, the government (including several ministers and civil servants), as well as other scientists and the media. There are reporters all over the meteorite landings and the Doctor's own arrival on Earth in *Spearhead from Space*, and correspondents like John Wakefield, Alastair Fergus and real-life BBC reporter Alex MacIntosh cover *The Ambassadors of Death*, *The Daemons* and *Day of the Daleks*, respectively. In Chibnall's story, the drilling project seems to be progressing in a place and time of its own. There is no media frenzy when Nasreen announces that they have achieved their target of drilling twenty-one kilometres into the Earth's crust. She simply hugs Tony Mack and cheers along with her colleagues. They are not even seen going to the pub to celebrate. The lack of real-world verisimilitude such as a press conference, a visit from a local MP, or the return of Russell T. Davies's own symbol of global affairs reportage – AMNN television bulletins with newscaster Trinity Wells – emphasises the failure to connect the events in Cwmtaff to the audience's own experience of a media-saturated global village. The peace negotiations between Eldane, Nasreen and Amy, a scene used by Chibnall as yet another example of how the Doctor likes to empower the humans he encounters ("Come on. Be extraordinary," he says to Nasreen), take place with no reference to the outside world. Its ultimate outcome, to prepare the world for the awakening of the Silurians a thousand years hence, is to be disseminated by the survivors of this encounter through legend, myth and questionably, considering the allusion to the Israel-Palestine conflict, as a form of religion. When our world is depicted taking Dalek invasions and Gallifrey materialising in the skies above Earth in its stride, then this seems a rather atypical and unreliable way of spreading the news. This is perhaps Chibnall's interpretation of Moffat's desire to steer the series away from Davies's own mixing of the political thriller genre with the melodramatic flourishes of soap opera. Davies reconfigured the Pertwee era's sense of scale and actuality in his use of the Downing Street setting of *Aliens of London* and the election of Harold Saxon that culminated with the return of the Master in *The Sound of Drums*. These action and thriller elements, including the re-emergence of UNIT as a global force complete with aircraft carrier Valiant in *The Sontaran Stratagem*, all pay homage whilst also taking care to use a form of social realism to ground the characters and emotions within the spectacle. As Matt Hills explains in *Triumph of a Time Lord*, Davies's work reflects the idea that "social realism is not just about the details of ordinary life, however; as an explicitly political form of drama it relates micro-structures of everyday life to macro-structures of economics, politics and... 'social inequality'." There is a sense that Moffat, and by extension Chibnall, are still partially concerned with the 'micro-structures of everyday life' in the emphasis on the relationships between parents and children in the story, here writ large in the destabilising anxiety of a mother, Ambrose (a powerful performance from Nia Roberts), separated from both her son Elliot and her husband Mo. However, Chibnall's attempts to marry this with the 'macro-structures' that Hills describes, and to simultaneously capture a 'retro' sense of nostalgia for the Pertwee era, lead to the problems in the narrative detailed thus far. As Elizabeth E. Guffey suggests in *Retro: The Culture of Revival*, during her discussion of memorialising the past, this homage to classic *Doctor Who* "revisits the past with acute ironic awareness" but also "pillages history with little regard for moral imperatives or nuanced implications." While *The Beast Below* successfully used the nostalgia for a mythical British nationalism within the framework of political satire and *Victory of the Daleks* explored the same nationalism, rather jingoistically, via the prism of the 'myth of the Blitz' and the character of Churchill, it is the lack of actuality, the sense that the events are taking place beyond the effects of our media-saturated, politically ambivalent world, that is one of the contributing factors to the lacklustre generic efforts of *The Hungry Earth* and *Cold Blood*. That said, the strength of Chibnall's scripts can be found in the relationships of the aforementioned parents and children, the lovers Nasreen and Tony, and the sibling warmongers Alaya and Restac. However, the 'gunboat diplomacy' discourse, describing the mistrust and conflict between Silurian and human, articulates itself by depending on an underdeveloped re-creation of Hulke's original Silurian story, in the use of contentious, somewhat unrealistic political allusions and uncharacteristic moral turpitude from the Doctor.

Since its return in 2005, *Doctor Who* has obviously embraced melodrama and social realism, particularly in the use of the emotional and family lives of characters such as Rose, Martha and Donna, and offering these as attractive dramatic tropes within spectacular science fiction and fantasy narratives. This enables a wider audience, one not necessarily au fait with *Doctor Who* and science fiction drama in general, to connect and empathise with believable characters. However, Chibnall's nostalgic remounting of *Doctor Who and the Silurians* in particular, while attempting to provide a family setting as a basis for audience empathy, could also be seen employing a process that Lynne Joyrich in *Re-viewing Reception: Television, Gender and Postmodern Culture* describes as "artificially contrived plots [that] vacillate between both the compression and extension of time as old plots and stereotypes are frequently recycled or rehearsed rather than being fully developed." In essence, *The Hungry Earth* and *Cold Blood* offer a much cruder replication of story elements and characters from the series's past to inform the emotional content of Chibnall's script. The danger is that dramatic content becomes

143

subservient to little more than self-reflexive commentary on genre in *Doctor Who* itself. Joyrich sees pastiche and recycling of formula as "the nostalgic mode of postmodern culture" and, ironically, Chibnall's desire to re-create what he may see as 'authentic' *Doctor Who* becomes a self-fulfilling prophecy of his own critique of the original series from 1986. His then regard for the authenticity of *Doctor Who*, as a fan rather than a writer, saw him infamously criticise the show on the BBC's *Open Air* programme as "clichéd, it was very routine running up and down corridors with silly monsters." In 2010, he stages 'authentic' *Doctor Who* as a blatant revival of the Pertwee milieu, and not only attempts to match its complex and often contentious view of the decline of Empire, colonialism and nationalism, but also operates within the very mode he holds up as an example of 'inauthentic' *Doctor Who*. The Silurians, the underground city and the various chase sequences in the two episodes could be seen as nothing more than 'routine running up and down corridors with silly monsters,' absent of, what John Storey refers to in his 'Postmodernism and Popular Culture' chapter of *The Routledge Companion to Postmodernism* as, "the shared pleasure of intertextual recognition, the critical effect of play with narrative conventions, character and cultural stereotypes and the *power* rather than the passivity of nostalgia."

The power of *Doctor Who* as nostalgia, so often provided by knowing references scattered throughout many episodes of the current revival, is present in some of the incidental details as well as Chibnall's recycling of tropes from the Pertwee serials. Ambrose's son Elliot codifies the TARDIS itself as a potent symbol of nostalgia, referring to it as "a bit retro" and defining it as a "portable crime lab." When Rory is mistakenly taken for a plain-clothes policeman by Ambrose and Elliot after he emerges from the TARDIS, the allusion to Jago and Litefoot's own assessment of the Doctor's vehicle as a "portable police station" in *The Talons of Weng-Chiang* is complete. The Holmesian pastiche of *The Talons of Weng-Chiang* is also noted in Elliot's deduction of the grave robbing. He observes Holmes's credo of "whatever remains, however improbable, must be the truth," as Rory assumes an investigative role assigned to him when Ambrose demands an explanation for the empty grave. Splitting up the companions is also a familiar *Doctor Who* trope and the Doctor's remark to Amy – "You're sure Rory will catch us up?" – not only underlines this but also highlights the fact that Rory is still a novice crew member in the TARDIS and prefigures the 'catching up' he has to make in *The Big Bang* as he guards the Pandorica for two thousand years. Later, as the Doctor arrives in the Silurian city, Chibnall even manages to mention the restorative qualities of celery last mooted in *The Caves of Androzani*. The passing effects of nostalgia certainly go some way to explaining the reimagining of the Silurians. Without criticising Neve McIntosh's exceptional performance as Alaya and Restac, the decision to let the prosthetics serve the script's depiction of the more human-like Silurians has both positive and negative repercussions. Neill Gorton, whose company Millennium FX creates many of the prosthetic effects for the series, explained that the intention was to update the original James Ward design from the 1970 serial which first featured the iconic appearance of the Silurians. Illustrated in *The Brilliant Book of Doctor Who*, Gorton's original maquette for the Silurians beautifully updates the design whilst retaining most of its distinguishable characteristics, including the creature's third eye. As the design's most instantly recognisable detail, the third eye could psycho-kinetically control doors and instruments and inflict devastating heat rays on inanimate objects and human beings. Arguably, it is as distinctive to Silurians as the 'ears' are to the Cyberman helmets or the sink plunger to a Dalek silhouette. Gorton says, "I wanted to do them as a mixed effect, with the prosthetics around the performer's mouth, but with animatronic eyes. It was still a Silurian but sleeker and much more up-to-date, with a better design." In the end, Chibnall and Moffat requested a complete overhaul to the design, one that would favour the actor's ability to put emotional investment, through facial expression, into the dialogue. There is no doubt that Neve McIntosh achieves this, adding impressive physical ticks to the superbly crafted prosthetic makeup she wears, but her appearance as Alaya and Restac is far removed from the Silurian design that James Ward conceived and that Gorton brought to life in his own initial concepts. The design used in these episodes simply turns the creatures into *Doctor Who*'s version of the lizard-like Jem'Hadar from *Star Trek: Deep Space Nine* (1993-9) or the reptilian Narn of *Babylon 5* (1993-8) and they become the generic 'rubber-headed' aliens seen in countless similar science fiction shows. Nostalgia, in recalling the iconic appearance of the Silurians, does actually matter and in the reworked design eventually used they lose what makes them distinctive, especially with the omission of the all-important third eye. Sadly, the Silurian design seems to be at the mercy of the law of diminishing returns after a less than successful redesign for their previous appearance in the 1984 serial *Warriors of the Deep*. Whilst the design of the new Daleks indicates that deliberately exaggerating their qualities to redefine their appearance is problematic, then the reverse seems to be true of the Silurians and less is definitely not more in this case.

## "The future pivots around you"

In the aftermath of *Amy's Choice*, it seemed that the bond between Amy and Rory had not just been repaired but also strengthened. However, in *The Hungry Earth* and *Cold Blood*, the relationship between them suggests a regression to the fragile nature of their attraction and Amy's distance from Rory as exposed in the earlier episodes of the series. The characters seem to retreat rather than progress and Chibnall's script creates more a sense of doubt about their newly acquired intimacy than a context for further opportunities to build upon the secure resolution of the previous episode. This insecurity is perhaps a way of recontextualising the imagined death of Rory in *Amy's Choice*, where Amy actualises her love

145

for Rory through her choices and only after he is 'dead', in order to make his actual death more of a profound experience. The problem here is that there is a sense of repetition about Rory's impending death while Amy, again, goes through a very familiar rediscovery of her true attraction and love for him. It seems excessive to put both characters through the same emotional wringer in successive stories. Chibnall again emphasises the depiction of male characters as perpetual underdogs, a trait Moffat often employs, with men having to prove to the women in the series that they are worthy of their trust, friendship and love. As we discussed in the previous chapter, to make Amy a more empathetic character it was crucial, in Simon Nye's script for *Amy's Choice*, to explore and understand the bond between her and Rory and how their relationship fitted into life aboard the TARDIS. Without that development in *Cold Blood*, Amy is an unsympathetic character and Rory's actual death at the end of the episode has less emotional impact, both external of and internal to the narrative, on the viewer outside and on characters within the drama. Oddly, both Amy and the Doctor react as if the imagined death of Rory was of little traumatic significance and the crisis they face in *Cold Blood* is one that is seemingly experienced as free of that context.

The episodes are framed by that strange moment where Amy, Rory and the Doctor observe, in the opening of *The Hungry Earth*, the future Amy and Rory on the hillside. Later, at the conclusion of *Cold Blood*, it is Amy and the Doctor who see only Amy waving back at them from the hillside. This device is primarily a way to emphasise Amy's loss of Rory, both in the physical sense of his death at the hands of Restac and the diminishing memory of him after he has been erased from history by the time-devouring crack in the universe. It also demonstrates that events can be changed by the occupants of the TARDIS whether they visit either the past, present or the future. As the Doctor explains to Amy in the peace negotiations, changing the circumstances of the present they inhabit can create different realities: "There are fixed points through time, where things must always stay the way they are. This is not one of them. This is an opportunity, a temporal tipping point. Whatever happens today will change future events, create its own timeline, its own reality. The future pivots around you. Here. Now." His statement about fixed points in time reflects his own actions and their consequences in both *The Fires of Pompeii* and *The Waters of Mars*. In the former, at Donna's insistence, he rescues Caecilius's family from the eruption of Vesuvius without apparently affecting the timelines, while in the latter, his hubris prevents the deaths of Adelaide, Mia and Yuri in Bowie Base One, but Adelaide commits suicide to return history to its proper course after she realises that an all-powerful Time Lord with control over the fate of both the influential figures of history and insignificant "little people" is wrong. It is curious that he seems to know what these fixed points in time are and that he sees certain events in time as a variation of Malcolm Gladwell's theories in *The Tipping Point*. Perhaps in much the same way that he understood Adelaide's life and death as important to history remaining on

146

its proper course, he sees Amy, Nasreen and Eldane as examples of Gladwell's "connectors", "mavens" and "salesmen", those individuals who act as agents of change, with their social interactions creating the momentum for future events at certain points in history. The negotiations between the humans and the Silurians clearly break down in *Cold Blood* but the force for change is unleashed, the tipping point represented by Nasreen and Tony's decision to go into hibernation with the Silurians, Ambrose's moral lesson and the myth of a shared planet with the Silurians that she and her family will try to perpetuate. Therefore, there is also a suggestion in *Cold Blood* that this change has had long-term consequences because, in his voiceover, it is intimated that Eldane has woken and emerged a thousand years later into a very different set of circumstances on Earth.

The idea that time can be unwritten, can be changed, is also central to the major story arc of the series. Rory's death in *Cold Blood* demonstrates, in a specific way, what the real stakes are for the future of the universe. When we see Rory absorbed by the time field, we are also seeing, on a small scale, another of those tipping points, one that will lead to the erasure of the whole of existence in *The Big Bang*, and consequently how his death is inextricably bound up with its recovery. The optimistic view of the future, as symbolised in Rory and Amy waving to their counterparts from the hillside, vanishes by the end of *Cold Blood*. When they both express a wish to meet their future selves, the Doctor clearly understands the consequences, perhaps referring to the Blinovitch Limitation Effect introduced into the series with *Day of the Daleks*, mentioned again in *Invasion of the Dinosaurs*, and demonstrated narratively in both *Mawdryn Undead* and *Father's Day*, where the dangers of predestination paradoxes and crossing your own time stream are depicted. "No, best not, really best not. These things get complicated very quickly, and..." he says, breaking off to deliberately distract them with the view of the drilling operation: "Oh, look! A big mining thing. I love a big mining thing." However, Amy is more incredulous about the fact that she and Rory are "still together in ten years?" suggesting that this relationship with Rory is not something she ever expected to last. Again, this underlines her fear of abandonment and what she sees as the inevitable deterioration in adult relationships. "No need to sound so surprised," says a vexed Rory. Security is important to Rory and, unimpressed by the Doctor's inability to get them to Rio, he worries that they will never get home. Amy is more optimistic and the sight of their future selves is an indication to her that: "It all works out fine." However, Rory reflects on this, as many of the Doctor's companions often do in the latest series, with: "After everything we've seen, we just drop back into our old lives? The nurse and the kissogram?" and this echoes many of Sarah Jane Smith's slightly bitter sentiments upon encountering the Tenth Doctor in *School Reunion*. Symptomatic of her treatment of Rory, Amy is not interested in his concerns and wanders off after the Doctor. The boundaries that divided them before *Amy's Choice* are still in position, despite the events of that previous episode, and Rory's "after everything we've seen" suggests he views these experiences in time and space as a catalyst for change. When Rory notices that she is wearing the engagement ring he has since given her, a positive signal that the relationship has actually progressed, he is scared, rather typically for him it has to be said, that she will lose it whilst participating in their adventures. He is also fearful that if the ring is lost, by extension, she also will lose him and her commitment to him will no longer be valid. "I thought you liked me wearing it," she protests, before he takes the ring from her and returns to the TARDIS. The irony is that, of course, even after he puts the ring into safekeeping, she loses him in the most complete way imaginable. Here, Chibnall commences a series of narrative set-ups, the prime purpose of which are expectation and inevitability allied to the generation of jeopardy and tragedy. Much of this is achieved with the symbolic use of the countdown, and his tendency is to overuse this mechanism, with at least three different countdowns in the story: one that heralds the achievement of the drilling record; one noting the arrival of the Silurians at the surface; and a final one to accompany the destruction of the drill. They prefigure and then condition the audience to expect unavoidable disaster and in *Screening the Past: Memory and Nostalgia in Cinema*, Pam Cook sees tragic inevitability as something that "resists the progress of history, giving us a perspective on how it affects the lives of human beings caught up in it, and enabling us to see certain truths about our own lives. This means it can be mobilised politically, to ask questions about the 'positive' aspects of progress, but it can also be used to confirm our feeling that human beings are the victims of social forces, over which they can never exert control." Chibnall marshals these forces and certainly uses much of *The Hungry Earth* as an opportunity to fulfil Anton Chekhov's old maxim, "One must not put a loaded rifle on the stage if no one is thinking of firing it." In what might be construed as *Doctor Who*'s version of *Uncle Vanya*, a string of repetitive designations are littered throughout the script. Rory's return to the TARDIS with the engagement ring is very clearly going to demand the ring has a role in the resolution of the story, a symbol of the tragic fate that awaits the Amy and Rory relationship. Another example is the door that keeps sticking as the humans take refuge inside the church and set up a perimeter in the village to detect the arrival of the Silurians. As Chibnall constructs the bonds between the characters, especially those between Elliot and the Doctor, the sticking door tells the audience it is inevitable that someone will get trapped on the outside of the building to either be captured or killed by the Silurians. As soon as the Doctor takes his eye off Elliot, the drama's sense of expectation is fulfilled and it is clear what will happen before it actually does. Taking the Doctor's idea of defending herself quite literally, Ambrose loads her van with an assortment of weapons, including a Taser specifically isolated by director Ashley Way in his interior shot of Ambrose's van and Ambrose's brief reaction to it. It is a literal allusion to 'Chekov's Gun', making it very clear she is a woman who is more than expected to act upon Alaya's prophecy to the Doctor, "I know apes better than you know yourselves. I know which one of you will kill me. Do you?" The audience already has the answer to that question and we are hardly surprised when Ambrose uses the Taser and kills Alaya. The problem with setting up all these repetitive designations is that they are often, by their very nature, completely predictable. *The Hungry Earth* functions as a series of recognisable set-ups that the audience already knows the payoffs to. Granted, the trajectory of Ambrose's character does offer us, as Pam Cook suggests, the "punishment and suffering... built into the tragic struggle," and despite the clichés, the story of her fall from grace leads to a partial redemption for her at its climax. The character of Alaya is the ultimate symbol of this tragic inevitability, entirely self-conscious about her role in the conflict as soon as she is introduced, and as Ambrose arrives to kill her, she states, "I knew it would be you. The one with the most to lose and the weakest." She confronts Ambrose as the inevitable victim awaiting her fate, positioning the frightened woman as the inevitable victimiser, the reactionary who uses the justification of keeping her family together and safe to defend the use of violence. However, their roles as victim and victimiser are in flux, with each character often assuming both.

Rory is once again the male character who perhaps represents a certain masculine ambivalence and insecurity about women, in a story where much of the power is exorcised and traded by female characters. This once more reflects a certain attitude on Moffat's part, something that permeates his writing, where his male characters are often subjected to a certain amount of victimisation by stronger female characters, perhaps because he sees male heroes in a post-feminist world as characters generalised by their ability and willingness to accept emasculation, but only where self-deprecation and an awareness of their own vulnerability can be exploited to appeal to independent women. When Rory goes to investigate the empty graves in Cwmtaff because Ambrose believes he is a plain-clothes police officer, he goes through the motions and mimics what he thinks the Doctor might do in the same situation, listening to her story about the missing bodies, but is relatively unsure about what to do. Even Elliot, the dyslexic boy spouting quotes from Sherlock Holmes, seems to have already beaten him to some kind of deduction. When Amy is swallowed up by the bio-programmed earth, his mettle reasserts itself and he gets actively involved in preparing for the Silurian incursion. We see that he values loyalty and trust above anything else. He angrily projects his own inadequacy back at the Doctor, when it is revealed that the Doctor tried but failed to prevent Amy's disappearance, and berates him for not keeping Amy safe. "Well, you should have tried harder," he demands of the Doctor. The Time Lord understands that Rory needs the security that Amy often teases or refuses him because she desires an independent, free-thinking man and not a needy, vulnerable one. "I'll find Amy. I'll keep you all safe, I promise," comforts the Doctor. He begs Rory tenderly, "Come on, please. I need you alongside me." Under the Doctor's tutelage, he actively sets about establishing the detection zone around the village and even when Elliot is kidnapped and he is confronted by Ambrose accusing him of lying about being from the police, he responds with: "I'd trust the Doctor with my life. We stick to his plan." Rory has come a long way in his relationship with the Doctor, and whilst he may often feel inadequate and face difficulties in adjusting to his new lifestyle, his faith in the Doctor has grown substantially. Unfortunately, as we see at the end of *Cold Blood*, that faith is not powerful enough to help Rory brave the perils of the universe. Chibnall emphasises the tender, caring side of Rory by at least remembering that he is a nurse with a certain set of skills and that these can come in handy when venomous Silurian warriors attack people.

Meanwhile, Amy is once again yelling at authority figures after they have lived up to her expectations of limiting her freedom. Trapped in the Silurian decontamination chamber, she screams, "I'm alive in here, let me out! I know you're out there. My name is Amy Pond and you'd better get me the hell out of here or so help me I am going to kick your backside!" Perhaps this is an example of the attitude she demonstrated to those four psychiatrists she bit during her treatment in Leadworth, especially when the masked Silurian hisses at her through the door of the chamber and she retorts, "Did you just shush me?! *Did you just shush me?!*" The Silurians have obviously dealt with her type of primitive ape before and the masked figure promptly gases her. This throwback to the pre-*Amy's Choice* version of the character, whilst accurate in and of itself, often sits uncomfortably with Chibnall's rather clichéd depiction of Amy as the damsel in distress, the woman in peril who needs rescuing, first seen disappearing into the earth and then seen strapped into the decontamination area about to be dissected by Malohkeh. She also seems to have acquired an amazing propensity for knowing exactly what she is looking at when she and Mo go wandering around the corridors of the Silurian city. Her eye for detail is now so attuned that her immediate conclusion upon finding the immobile Silurians is that they are all in suspended animation and are standing on powered transport discs that could provide their escape back to the surface. In *Cold Blood*, Chibnall also undoes a great deal of Amy's development in Simon Nye's script by having her utter the worst possible response to Rory as he agrees to assert his responsibility with his nomination of "I speak for the humans" when the Silurians make contact with him and the others above ground. His joyful, "Amy, I thought I'd lost you!" at seeing her alive again is cut down by her defensive, mean and spiteful remark, "What, because I got sucked into the ground? You're so clingy." Any self-confidence he might have had at that point surely withers away in an instant, and with an attitude like that it is little wonder than an audience might have difficulty empathising with her loss at the end of the episode and may feel that, in fact, she gets her just reward for treating the object of her love with such disloyalty. When Restac mortally wounds Rory, and he dies in Amy's arms, his faith in the Doctor and in his own future disappears. "I don't understand. We were on the hill. I can't die here," is his incomprehension at the different fate that now awaits him as a time traveller. The final ignominy lies in the fact that not only is he shot down by Restac, but he is also physically, psychically and spiritually removed from existence, and Amy's rather ignorant treatment of him is now emphasised, while he is actually being wrenched away from her, by her fate of never being able to remember him again. In this separation, she will never come to regret the lost chances for an emotionally and physically fulfilling life together. As the light of the devouring time field consumes him, she rather poetically states her case to the Doctor with, "That light, if his body's absorbed, I'll forget him. He'll never have existed. You can't let that happen." Her demands of the Doctor take us back to the similar requests she made in *Amy's Choice*, except of course this death is real whilst that in Leadworth was a dream. The Doctor restates the major theme of the series and her final, rather mournful plan of action, "Keep him in your mind. Don't forget him. If you forget him, you'll lose him forever." He tells her why she must remember him when she questions that, as a time traveller, she was able to remember the Clerics on the Byzantium, "They weren't part of your world. This is different, this is your own history changing." In trying to fix Rory in her mind and to follow the Doctor's advice of "Remember Rory. Keep remembering, Rory is only alive in your memory. You must keep hold of him. Don't let anything distract you. Rory still lives in your mind," she experiences a second-hand testimony to the authenticity of her and Rory's relationship, or what Pam Cook refers to as "prosthetic memory." We see imagery of Rory and Amy from a number of previous stories and unseen footage of intimate moments between them, as the Doctor hugs her and demands, "Tell me about Rory. Fantastic Rory. Funny Rory. Gorgeous Rory." As scenes from *The Hungry Earth* and *The Vampires of Venice* dissolve into nothingness and an image of Rory's face is overlapped onto the Doctor's head in the TARDIS, John Storey's assessment of the power and the passivity that nostalgia offers us is reiterated in Pam Cook's suggestion that "prosthetic memory" engages us in a process whereby "reconstructions of the past produce replacement memories that simulate first-hand experience," and that it produces "'false' memories or at least memory scenarios whose veracity, or relationship to the real, are impossible to determine." In *Cold Blood*'s climax, Amy is desperate to hold onto the real Rory and conjures up these images of him in a bid to authenticate their love. Cook's view of "prosthetic memory" sees this memorialising of him as mourning "the loss of reality" and the "authority of history itself." Amy's attempt to recall Rory before he is lost forever is a perfect definition of nostalgia being the essence of something that is irretrievable but much longed for and in never being fully retrieved it eventually ceases to be real. When the TARDIS encounters turbulence, the Doctor and Amy are both knocked to the floor and the engagement ring, the 'loaded rifle on the stage' that Chekhov wrote about, lands on the floor in the Doctor's direct line of sight. Only he acknowledges its real value after Amy recovers and we assume he removes it before she can see it. Rory is erased and is gone, destroyed instantly in the countdown to the exploding drilling project, and his absence changes the future when Amy returns to the TARDIS and waves to her future self on the hillside. "Are you OK?" asks the Doctor and she, momentarily troubled by that absence, says, "I thought I saw someone else there for a second." She even refers to the plural when she responds to the Doctor's desire to fix the TARDIS lock, with her "You boys and your locksmithery" evoking a memory of 'her boys' from *The Vampires of Venice* and *Amy's Choice*.

## "Now, who loves you more than me?"

Chibnall's story and characters are inspired, in the main, by Hulke's serial from 1970, *Doctor Who and the Silurians*. Ironically, on the surface there are many similarities between them but, as the story shifts its focus to the underground city of the Silurians in *Cold Blood*, there are some striking differences worth noting. The comparisons between the two stories include the drilling project that wakes the Silurians as analogous to the Cyclotron nuclear reactor, the isolated village of Cwmtaff standing in for Wenley Moor, and the Silurian sting inflicted upon Tony Mack as a variation of the virus that they release in Hulke's story. The opposing arguments for peace with mankind are also replicated, with different factions of Silurians and humans involved in an internal power struggle. However, where Hulke's story is driven forward by a majority of male, establishment figures, including the Doctor, Chibnall seeks to ground the story emotionally by changing the gender dynamics. The all-male world of civil servants, scientists and the military in 1970 only peripherally involves female characters, in the figures of Liz Shaw, Miss Dawson and Doris Squire. Liz Shaw and Miss Dawson are scientists and are representative of the establishment too. With both the Doctor and Dr Quinn, they form the story's internal debate about the hubris of scientific discovery and scientists 'playing God'. Doris Squire is overtly positioned as the anonymous female victim of a Silurian attack. Miss Dawson, her hatred for the Silurians heightened by their murder of Dr Quinn, becomes Ambrose in Chibnall's script, and the scientific ambition of Dr Quinn and Dr Lawrence is therefore represented, in much simpler terms, by Nasreen and Tony. The Doctor's debates with the Old Silurian and Young Silurian in Hulke's story are also repositioned in the discussion he has with the captured Alaya and the talks he brokers between Eldane, Amy and Nasreen.

The difference here is not just, as pointed out earlier, that the story takes place in something of a social and political vacuum in its relationship to the wider world, but that the antagonist roles are all gendered as female. There are more female characters participating in the drama in Chibnall's scripts, with Alaya and Restac positioned as commanders of the Silurian military, one that appears to be composed of female warriors, in opposition to the belligerent human Ambrose. Nasreen is clearly an independent woman, capable of persuading the Doctor to take her in the TARDIS with him into the world below, and as previously noted Amy is not only her usual bellicose self but also actively takes part in the settlement talks. These are active and, in part, aggressive female roles dominating the narrative. Their domination also raises the question about the violence that the female characters inflict or threaten to inflict upon each other and, by extension, the violence in which their respective races may become entangled. It is interesting to view how the female characters and their use of force in *The Hungry Earth* and *Cold Blood* relate to post-feminist discourse in film and television. The revenge motif that binds Ambrose, Alaya and Restac together, where Ambrose kills Alaya in an attempt to retrieve her son and husband, and Restac, mourning the death of Alaya, then seeks retribution by attempting to kill Ambrose, affects character development to lesser and greater degrees. Alaya and Restac are more or less the same character, defined by their slightly different prosthetic makeup, but Ambrose's journey is one in which revenge comes at a bitter cost and demands of her a period of self-abnegation. Lisa Coulthard sees violence in the revenge fantasies of modern cinema, in 'Killing Bill: Rethinking Feminism and Film Violence', her chapter of *Interrogating Postfeminism: Gender and the Politics of Popular Culture*, as "not tied to character arc, development or psychology; instead the revenge film offers a series of murders and/or scenes of torture linked through a loose narrative of revenge." This view is certainly true of the scene in which Ambrose tortures Alaya to death. It precipitates Restac's desire for revenge, symbolised by her mobilisation of the military, her attempt to kill Ambrose, the murder of Malohkeh and the threat to usurp Eldane. The significant difference here is that the revenge narrative is also positioned as a duel between two families: the human, nuclear family headed by Ambrose ("First you take my son, now you hurt my Dad. I'm just protecting my family here. That's all") and the genetically bonded sisters Alaya and Restac (Malohkeh reminds Restac, "It's fine to show concern you know, she's part of your gene chain") who command an extended line of female *Homo reptilia*. The clash between two races becomes a very personal and feminised dispute and one that, as Coulthard suggests in her analysis of revenge films, focuses on "closure, narrative containment, the personal (often familial) nature of public acts of violence and the rampant individualism of the quest narrative." *The Hungry Earth* and *Cold Blood*'s view of strong female characters, with their use of violence as revenge, and their deliberate distancing from the patriarchal figures of the Doctor, Eldane, Tony and Mo, is reflective of some common narrative tropes and characters found in films and television series such as *La Femme Nikita* (1990), *Kill Bill, Vols I & II* (2003-4), *Buffy the Vampire Slayer* (1997-2003), *Xena: Warrior Princess* (1995-2001) and *Alias* (2001-6), and the mother-protector figures of Ripley and Sarah Connor in James Cameron's *Aliens* (1986) and *Terminator 2: Judgement Day* (1991), respectively.

The familial is heavily codified in the narrative and the desire for retribution becomes all-encompassing for Restac and Ambrose, while a more gender-neutral attempt to frame the resolution of the conflict within a discourse of ethical and social justice is made between the Doctor,

Eldane, Nasreen and Amy. Ambrose's maternal recovery of Elliot and Mo therefore becomes the melodramatic and emotional heart of the story. Whilst she is, inadvertently, the catalyst for a collective effort from both Silurian and human to put an end to the escalating violence, resulting in Eldane forcing Restac's troops back into hibernation and Nasreen agreeing to blow up the drill and remain with Tony in the Silurian city, her belligerence is seen as so unacceptable that even her own son is repulsed by her. Tony attempts to contextualise Ambrose's actions for Elliot, "You mustn't blame her. She only did what she thought was right." The Doctor, who all along has been trying to show Ambrose that aggression is not the way to deal with the Silurians, delivers a specific moral lesson to her at the conclusion of the episode: "An eye for an eye. It's never the way. Now, you show your son how wrong you were. How there's another way. You make him the best of humanity... in the way you couldn't be." This is the culmination of the story's reversal of Hulke's original depiction of a male, and militarily achieved, solution to the crisis at Wenley Moor. In that story, violence is predominantly achieved through male aggression and force, ending with the Brigadier's decision to blow up the caves where the Silurians are hibernating, much to the Doctor's outrage. Here, the male characters are overtly passive. Mo and his son Elliot are imprisoned and Mo's only attempt to resolve the conflict at gunpoint is easily counteracted by the aggressive Restac. The Doctor's pacifism is highlighted throughout the story and, whereas he actively tried to broker the peace between the Silurians, the Sea Devils and the humans in his previous encounters, this time he defers to a council of human females in the form of Nasreen and Amy. This is, of course, a reflection of his desire to inspire humans to greatness. Eldane is an analogue to both the Old Silurian and to the Doctor and, as his name suggests, he is old and wise and sees war and aggression as a childish activity, dismissing Restac with "Now go and play soldiers." The physically imposing Tony Mack allows the crisis to reveal his deeper feelings for Nasreen, but is manipulated by Ambrose into restarting the drill. He finally becomes a potential symbol of human and Silurian hybridity when it is shown that Alaya's poisonous sting is in fact mutating him rather than killing him. These images of sober, thoughtful, rational and pliable masculinity have a tendency to make Ambrose, Alaya and Restac appear as symbols of irrational female hysteria that need to be defused and contained. Malohkeh is, however, probably the one morally dubious male character. Initially, he calmly claims that the Silurians are "not monsters." On one hand he is sensible enough to wake Eldane when he fears that Restac and Alaya's aggression is about to get out of hand, but on the other he is guilty of kidnapping living and dead human beings, violating their bodies in the name of science. Even though Restac sees Malohkeh as enough of a pacifist to kill him, his principles are not criticised when the Doctor uncovers Elliot's eventual fate. While Ambrose is charged by the Doctor to change her ways, he does not take the opportunity to deliver the same lesson on morals and ethics to the Silurian scientist, perhaps sticking to the letter of his earlier admonition to the humans on the surface that the Silurians are "Not monsters, not evil. Well, only as evil as you are."

Finally, it is worth noting how Chibnall uses the influence of Steven Spielberg in the codification of the family and its construction. This is definitely symbolised by the character of Elliot who literally acts as a parallel of the Elliott character in Spielberg's *E.T.* (1982). Elliot/Elliott is a lonely, naïve but imaginative child who struggles to bond with parental figures. Elliot's dyslexia in *The Hungry Earth* is initially seen as a problem when the boy refuses to read along with his father from *The Gruffalo* but is then later seen as an asset when the Doctor requires him to create a map of the sensors around the village. Elliot resignedly offers, "I can't do the words, I'm dyslexic." The Doctor, unlike perhaps his mother and father, does not see this as a handicap: "That's all right. I can't make a decent meringue. Draw like your life depends on it, Elliot." There is an emphasis on visual communication as an alternative to using words, qualified by the Doctor with "Dyslexia never stopped Da Vinci or Einstein, it's not stopping you." With the Doctor as his friendly extraterrestrial, Elliot is also able to prepare for a confrontation with the monsters hurtling towards the Earth's surface, "Is it monsters coming? Have you met monsters before?" The Doctor confirms that he has, and Elliot clearly needs to displace his fear of them: "You scared of them?" "No, they're scared of me." As far as fairy-tale allusions to childhood fears go then *The Gruffalo* is an interesting allegorical choice for this episode. Julia Donaldson's story about the mouse that exploits fear of a mythical beast to scare away predators conjures up a number of ideas and themes. It is traditionally a book that parents and children read together, often amongst the first books used to teach a child to read, and Chibnall's use of it suggests that these episodes of *Doctor Who* can also be digested by the same company of children and parents and skews the series to the more child-friendly end of the audience spectrum. *The Hungry Earth* opens with Elliot and Mo reading *The Gruffalo* in a garden, complete with wind turbine, that is not too dissimilar from the fantastic space in which young Amelia's first encounter with the Doctor occurred. The central child character Elliot, whose father has been swallowed up by the earth, is then allowed to go wandering about unchaperoned in the dark by a Doctor who is as much a child himself when it comes to facing dangers and who fails to understand the concept of child-minding, just as the monsters have started skulking around the equally eerie and fairytale-like confines of the graveyard. *The Gruffalo* is also the prompt, later in the episode, for Mo's descent into the underworld, swallowed up by the dark fears residing in the unconscious areas of the mind. The journeys undertaken by the humans between the recognisable human environs of Cwmtaff and the underground world of the Silurians perhaps suggest the requirement of myth and fairy tale for the hero to leave home and explore the wilderness as a symbolic act of facing your fears and growing into maturity. The discovery of the hidden Silurian city made by the Doctor and the residents and workers of Cwmtaff is perhaps the same symbolic exploration that

Margery Hourihan, in *Deconstructing the Hero: Literary Theory and Children's Literature*, sees when "Sherlock Holmes leaves the domestic comforts of 221b Baker Street to venture into the dark places of the criminal underworld. Peter Pan has left Kensington for Neverland." The childhood fears of parental abandonment also loom large in this episode and the overprotected Elliot is eventually separated from both his mother and father in the story. It evokes some very Gruffalo-esque qualities in the Doctor. Surely, the Doctor is the mouse who, like a Zen master using his antagonists' aggression against them, reassures the child that he has met monsters before and they are usually the ones afraid of him. By his very nature, the Doctor is the tallest of all tall stories (especially now that he's played by the gangly Matt Smith) and this Zen-like approach to confronting one's fears, where *The Gruffalo*'s suggestion that no matter how gruesome the monsters are that children create in their own minds, they are never as bad as they imagine them to be, is given strength by the Doctor's encounter with Alaya where he first removes the fearsome mask from her face. The mask is another symbol of the deception of appearances, here the monstrous and warlike hiding the Silurian's true image and reflecting the idea that the most fearful things are not always what they seem. "You are beautiful," he opines at the sight of her natural form, much as he did with the appearance of the werewolf in *Tooth and Claw*, and, like the liberal Englishman he is, pulls up a foldaway chair, crosses his legs and calmly gets behind her interrogation defence.

With Mo missing, Elliot's prime objective is to be reunited with him and he immediately enquires of the Doctor, "Will you really get my Dad back?" "No question," retorts the unfazed Time Lord. As Dean A. Kowalski confirms in *Steven Spielberg and Philosophy: We're Gonna Need a Bigger Book*, the Elliott of *E.T.* learns a vast amount about parenthood, friendship and love in the film and "E.T. teaches... the child the hard lessons of life. The young boy has to watch his friend die (at least it appears that way for a while), learns to love for purely altruistic reasons and, ultimately, must say goodbye." In *Doctor Who*, Elliot must cope with the anxiety of separation from his father, understand his mother's motives for killing Alaya and say goodbye to his grandparent, Tony. The scene in which he says farewell to Tony is also visually an allusion to the separation of E.T. and Elliott in Spielberg's film, with Tony touching Elliot on the heart and reassuring him, "I'm here, always." It emphasises the importance and restoration of the father-son relationship. Elliot's estrangement from his mother at the end of *Cold Blood* also underlines Mo's definition of his own fatherly love for Elliot in the opening of *The Hungry Earth* as "who loves you more than me?" This is cruelly and ironically illustrated in Ambrose's actions, where her devotion to her son, a love that seems so much more powerful than that of his missing father, is literally her undoing. Her earlier critique of the Doctor's parenting skills when he inadvertently takes his eye off Elliot, leading to the boy's capture, is also a rather subtle way of reminding him of his own responsibilities to his travelling companions. The anxieties of parental bonding with children is, of course, a reflection of the themes attributed to the character of Amy, where the separation and loss of parents inform her refusal to commit to Rory and her fear that the fantasy father figure of the Doctor will also disappear out of her life.

Overall, *The Hungry Earth* and *Cold Blood* offer the most traditional expression of the *Doctor Who* format in the 2010 series, but Chibnall's drive for the authenticity and nostalgia of past *Doctor Who* adventures and the bland realisation of the Silurian prosthetics are the story's weakest elements. There is also a lack of consideration about the character of Amy with much of the scripts making her seem like the Amy of the earlier episodes, seemingly unaffected by the events of *Amy's Choice*. There is also a climax that shows Rory torn from her side yet again, but this major calamity in her own timeline seems to have very little effect on her as a person. If Rory is such a vitally important part of her life, and his childhood spent play-acting for her as the Raggedy Doctor indicates he was, surely his erasure from history would affect her own development as a person and we would see a completely altered Amy at the end of *Cold Blood* rather than the one who is desperate to still have that trip to Rio? Very little is forthcoming about this in the script. The reappearance of the crack in time and the Doctor's knowledge of it, particularly the sequence where he recovers shrapnel from "some sort of space time cataclysm. An explosion, maybe? Big enough to put cracks in the universe" and reveals it as a burnt remnant of the TARDIS, is intriguing and develops the mystery of the overall story arc. However, that both he and Amy are constantly being haunted by it and that "The Angels laughed when I didn't know. Prisoner Zero knew, everybody knows, except me!" might telegraph to him that he should now turn his attention to finding out exactly what is going on instead of, after nine episodes, ignoring it.

## Chapter Eight

# VINCENT AND THE DOCTOR

Written by: Richard Curtis
Directed by: Jonny Campbell
First broadcast: 5 June 2010

---

"Yes, well they are not my favourite flower"

The announcement that Richard Curtis was writing a script for the new series of *Doctor Who* was greeted with much the same mixed reaction that his fellow writer, Simon Nye, received. While some commentators welcomed such an experienced writer to the fold, many were very cautious, citing the sentimental, melodramatic excesses and the often slapstick humour of his small- and big-screen 'feel-good' comedy-dramas, such as *Four Weddings and a Funeral* (1994), *Notting Hill* (1999), *Love Actually* (2003), *The Vicar of Dibley* (1994-2007) and *Mr Bean* (1990-5), as qualities that would be seen as incongruous in a *Doctor Who* adventure. Curtis has a reputation for manipulating his audience's emotions and his work in British cinema, whilst hugely successful, is often derided for its idealised depiction of British culture. The lacklustre performance of his last film, *The Boat That Rocked* (2009), certainly triggered much debate on the poor quality of current British films. In *Vincent and the Doctor*, Curtis does trade on his penchant for sentimentality in reaching for a somewhat overwrought climax to his story, but the journey towards it is a provocative, and often humorous, examination of creativity, loneliness, the pain of depression, our attitude to, and commodification of, modern art, and the postmodern use of history and high culture in the series. Richard Curtis himself partially suggests this intent in David Bailey's preview of *Vincent and the Doctor* in the May 2010 edition of *Doctor Who Magazine*: "I was immensely interested in Van Gogh for two particular reasons. One, this amazing fact of his lack of success while he was alive – very few great artists in any form have been so unacknowledged in their own lifetime – he only sold the one painting, and that to a sister of a friend. So that's very intriguing. And then I'm gripped by the idea that someone who was in such much mental pain could produce works of such radiant beauty."

In my analysis of *Victory of the Daleks*, *The Vampires of Venice*, *The Hungry Earth* and *Cold Blood*, I have offered that *Doctor Who*, particularly in its post-2005 form, is comfortable using and re-creating specific recognisable periods and iconic moments in history, including some from its own televised canon, as both a form of postmodern pastiche and self-reflective commentary on our view of cultural figures and

159

historical events in television drama discourse. Of late, we have seen narratives using the Blitz with Winston Churchill, the backdrop of sixteenth-century Venice to reappropriate the vampire genre, and a direct homage to the series's own era of the 1970s in *The Hungry Earth* and *Cold Blood*. These developments not only reflect the production's relationship to history as a genre, and to *Doctor Who*'s own fictional history, but also define how it situates itself in the realm of 'quality television', where the aesthetics of such stories reinforce how Britishness and British television is globally contextualised and received, together with the high cultural cachet implied by period dramas and their attendant production values. For Daniel O'Mahony, in *Time and Relative Dissertations in Space*, it would seem that *Doctor Who*, as it defines itself in its use of history and historical figures, mutates as a series from one "where *Doctor Who*-as-history... demands a previewed familiarity on the part of the audience to tell the story" to one "where it becomes subservient to *Doctor Who*-as-genre... [in which stories] resemble history but they speak the default language of SF." This takes us from the original series's attempted educational remit of the 'pure historical' in stories such as *Marco Polo* and *The Aztecs* through to the 'pseudo historical' stance of most period-set stories in the post-Hartnell era. At that point the perceived desire to educate diminished in favour of stories that used specific historical locations or characters as a form of "pageantry" in a determinedly science fiction narrative. After *Doctor Who* returned in 2005, historical and cultural "pageantry" became the operating modes of stories that featured Charles Dickens, Queen Victoria, William Shakespeare and Agatha Christie. Each story used the audience's knowledge and familiarity of such figures, particularly with the majority being literary figures where the scripts played on a familiarity with their literary works as well as the commonly known details of their lives. Their roles in the stories also underline the global importance of British cultural figures as part of the series's power to, as Shawn Shimpach describes in *Television in Transition: The Life and Afterlife of the Narrative Action Hero*, "keep adapting to new conditions – to keep regenerating – [that] strikes a nationalist chord, casting the essence of the programme as quintessentially British for many." *Doctor Who*'s current desire to equate iconic moments and figures of history with the high cultural aspirations of quality television has, for Shimpach, "meant a focus on signifiers of "national heritage" and/or small contained narratives readily read as allegories of the state of the nation," to support the BBC's public service remit and manage its drive towards quality television production practices. For Matt Hills, in *Triumph of a Time Lord*, this also throws open a debate about the programme's cultural worth and how, in his exploration of *The Shakespeare Code* in relation to David Tennant's casting in Gregory Doran's RSC production of *Hamlet*, the series vacillates between opposing binaries of "quality versus popular, theatre versus TV, and Shakespeare versus *Doctor Who*."

With these observations in mind, how does *Vincent and the Doctor* present the life and works of Vincent van Gogh and reflect some of these debates? If we emulate the set of relationships established between quality and popular referred to by Hills, then *Vincent and the Doctor* may well be situated along the axes of Van Gogh versus *Doctor Who*, major London gallery retrospective versus TV, and the authentic, 'original' work versus the aesthetics of television reproduction. To begin with, Van Gogh moves the goalposts slightly in the way that the series deals with its cultural icons. Instead of a quintessentially British figure, we are involved in a narrative that features a globally significant cultural name, an artist recognised the world over who arguably eclipses the achievements of Agatha Christie and potentially carries as much, or perhaps even more cultural weight than the British icons of Shakespeare and Dickens. As Dr Black (a controlled and effective cameo from Curtis regular, Bill Nighy) stridently confirms at both the opening and conclusion of the episode, Curtis is in the business of re-mythologising Van Gogh and his iconic imagery. Jonny Campbell's opening montage confidently sets the visual tone for this ongoing process, giving the episode a visual splendour that cleverly captures the intensity of Van Gogh's work, reproducing many of the signature works with a great deal of knowing wit and care. It is a beautifully designed and lit production and the use of the Trogir (Croatia) locations is effective in depicting the inspiration for his major paintings. In the opening, Van Gogh is in the wheat field, painting, with the correlation between the eye of the observing artist and the disrupted landscape (presumably the invisible Krafayis disturbs the crows) reproduced on the canvas. The camera pulls back from what is easily recognisable as Van Gogh's 'Wheatfield With Crows' (painted in July 1890) and the noise of the crows, seen disturbed in the field, is suddenly cut off as Dr Black appears and informs us that, as one of the last paintings made, it emerged from a period where "those final months of his life were probably the most astonishing artistic outpouring in history." The subtitles confirm that we are now in the 'high art' location of the Musée d'Orsay in Paris and Dr Black is the gallery guide. They are symbols of the bridge between high culture, mass popularity and the depiction of the artist as a tragic, frustrated unknown. Black emphasises the comparison between Van Gogh's creative "outpouring" and the series's previous use of Shakespeare as a cultural manufacturer in the line: "It was like Shakespeare knocking off *Othello*, *Macbeth* and *King Lear* over the summer hols." Curtis suggests that, even though the Doctor may well have hobnobbed with Dickens, Shakespeare and Christie in the last few years, here he is about to meet the ultimate, misunderstood artist who struggled with his vision in "no hope of praise or reward." Black is essentially a Greek chorus to the episode, providing the biographical context to Van Gogh's reputation in the art world where, as Gary J. Bamossy suggests in 'Star Gazing: the Mythology and Commodification of Vincent van Gogh' in *Inside Consumption*, "Vincent van Gogh emphasises the personalization of artistic greatness... the misunderstood genius, *peintre maudit*,

161

paradigm of the modern artist, saint, martyr, hero, an enduring and evolving icon of popular culture" and as Black confirms, an artist whose work, now valued as high culture, "is worth tens of millions of pounds." These are the parameters provided for the audience to generate meaning as they form their connection to the painter. They are the familiar historical and cultural tropes attached to him as an instantly recognisable globally famous artist. This pattern reflects O'Mahony's contention that the formation of the historical or the cultural icon in *Doctor Who* "is, in the words of *1066 and All That*, 'what you can remember.'" Commonly known facts are the basis of reactions from children visiting the gallery, picked up by the Doctor simply because he thinks they are talking about him. "Who is it? It's the doctor!" is heard as he turns to wander through the paintings in the gallery. We then hear and see two children, stood in front of a painting, deliberately contextualising it for us, describe the 'Portrait of Dr Gachet' as "he was the doctor who started to take care of Van Gogh when he started to go mad." Ironically, one of the two answers back, "I knew that," much as a knowledgeable audience might respond while absorbing the cultural details in the episode. It underlines Curtis's unloading of Van Gogh's biography as information that is generally accepted by an audience even vaguely aware of the painter's life, as a democratising 'art is for everyone' effect. It also prepares the viewer for the journey back to 1890.

This chorus of Dr Black and the young gallery visitors then evolves into recognisable behaviour repeated endlessly over time, the world over, when consumers of art are confronted by the authenticity of high culture. They compare it to the postcard just purchased in the gallery shop. Amy drags the Doctor over to one of the paintings with a cry of, "Look! There it is, the actual one." Here, she is cast as the typical consumer of, what John Walker confirms in his essay from the August 1976 edition of *Art and Artists*, as the "The Van Gogh Industry." Amy, like many of us, is seized by the power of his painting and "its emotional impact [that] impresses even those who are generally unmoved by art" and she reacts to seeing the original work, the authentic Van Gogh, in relation to the reproduction of his images, seen on everything from postcards to tea towels, that "must run into millions and [where] Van Gogh can confidently be placed among the top ten most popular artists in terms of postcard sales: one hundred and eleven of his pictures are currently being reproduced." To emphasise this, she holds the postcard of 'The Church at Auvers' next to the original and the Doctor comments, "You can almost feel his hand painting it right in front of you, carving the colours into shapes." Amy's enthusiasm for Van Gogh is a far cry from Romana's dismissive appraisal of the 'Mona Lisa' as "quite good" in *City of Death*, that other *Doctor Who* story exploring artistic legitimacy. Not only does the Doctor's observation highlight the authenticity of the craft of an artisan, formalised in the knowledge and use of pigment and the labour involved, but it also foreshadows the day in 1890 when they will actually watch the painting being created. Van Gogh will prepare his canvas as they await the reappearance of the Krafayis that, aping his overview of the dire situation in *Flesh and Stone*, the Doctor now sees in the painted window of the church as "something not very good indeed." The democratisation of art and culture, through the deification and commodification of his work in the Musée d'Orsay, the postcards and Black's biographical commentary, is reflected in the Doctor and Amy's attitude to meeting Vincent. They experience the alleged reality of his life and his own attitude to the preciousness of his work after they see "our nasty friend" lurking in the painting and visit 1890. As the Doctor so succinctly puts it, "Art can wait. This is life and death," and they both set off to explore what Walker sees as "the mass replication and commercialisation of Van Gogh's art" and the problem this creates in "that it destroys what [Walter] Benjamin termed the 'aura' of artworks: their authenticity and uniqueness as originals, their historical specificity." Their mission is to "recuperate the particular meaning of a Van Gogh painting and for whom it was intended" as part of Curtis's attempt to strip away the dead wood of commercialism from the man's life and works and get to the heart of the matter, to understand artistic vision through a simulation of the conditions under which the paintings were created. As Walker underlines it, Curtis must "isolate the man from the myth, to disentangle the primary objects from their husk of secondary imitations, and to reconstruct in imagination their historical and social context."

The difficulty here is that *Vincent and the Doctor* is obsessed with playing with the 'secondary imitations' as it, quite tenderly, sets out to explore Van Gogh's damaged soul. When that human tragedy is projected onto an alien creature, it also underlines the uneasy relationship between the use of historical figures as representational of high culture and the science fiction genre as popular television while attempting to present a recognisable version of history. The danger is that Amy and the Doctor's journey to the France of 1890 descends into nothing more than a cultural tour of the locations that Van Gogh painted, a series of reproductions of his most recognised works that are nothing more than the equivalent of the postcards bought in the gallery shop. This tour evolves from Amy and the Doctor meeting Vincent for the first time in the production team's skilful re-creation of Van Gogh's celebrated 'Café Terrace at Night', their standing in awe in the cluttered reproduction of 'The Bedroom in Arles' and, significantly, to the moment when Amy actively suggests he paint the sunflowers she has arranged for him. These, and many other visual references to his work, are part and parcel of the mythology that Bamossy sees as "the various discourses that not only *create* knowledge about Vincent's life and works, they also become the *reality* they appear to describe." Curtis's aims are honourable, with a sensitive exploration of creativity and its link to manic depression resonant as a concern to us today perhaps more so than in the nineteenth century. However, his expression of Van Gogh's schizophrenic or manic-depressive personality is entangled within the episode's culpability in perpetuating the accepted cultural myth of Van Gogh, the one that mixes together the reputable and authentic high art icon, whose work now sells for millions of pounds, the tragic sociopath suffering from manic depression, with the commodification of his images as "the co-opted endorser for products, services, kitsch." The episode skates very closely, in its playful devotion to reassembling his paintings and a knowingness on the part of the Doctor and Amy about his relationship to art history and commerce, to what Fabio Cleto sees, in *Camp: Queer Aesthetics and the Performing Subject*, as a "camp historicism that abolishes the concreteness of its object of desire, its referent." After the TARDIS lands in 1890, the Doctor describes to Amy the location where they are likely to find Van Gogh: "Probably be in the local café, sort of orangey light, chairs and tables outside." Pointedly, this is said in voiceover as Amy's hand flicks through her book of postcards to the painting 'Café Terrace at Night'. The director Jonny Campbell holds the reproduced postcard image in close-up and Amy says, "Like this?" and the Doctor approves. "Or indeed like that?" suggests Amy as director Campbell then cuts to a wide shot of another reproduction of the scene, this time staged on location in Trogir, Croatia. Historical re-enactment becomes a visual slippage between one version of the Van Gogh painting and another. In the café scene, this process is taken further when Van Gogh barters a self-portrait for one drink with the maître d' of the establishment. Notions of authenticity are codified in the Doctor's conversation with the waitresses where he asks them if they know of Van Gogh. The reply, "he's drunk, he's mad and he never pays his bills," their derision when the Doctor attempts to correct this character assassination with "good painter, though, eh?" and the maître d' criticising the poor quality of the painting and vocalising his desire to "protect my business from madmen" all confirm a reality built upon the mythology of the painter's life, mental health and lack of success. The Doctor and Amy's privileging of their version of art history over Van Gogh's recognition of his own failure, one that places the value of art in direct relationship to the life of the man who creates it, is illustrated when the maître d' holds up the self-portrait next to Vincent's face. At the same time, the Doctor and Amy silently express their astonishment and delight, through a mimed exchange, that they are sitting in the café with *the* Van Gogh whose work they had been admiring only moments before in the twenty-first century.

The combination of the production's re-creation of the original paintings and this playfulness with what the audience, the Doctor and Amy know about Van Gogh is highlighted in later scenes. When the Doctor and Amy return with Vincent to his home, the room is not only a faithful reproduction of the 'Bedroom in Arles' but its "clutter" is also an analogue to the twenty-first-century gallery seen at the beginning of the episode by dint of its own, rough catalogue of his major works, including the 'Portrait of Dr Gachet' that was seen previously hanging in the Musée d'Orsay. The difference here is that only Vincent and his awestruck houseguests admire his oeuvre and there is a sense of irony throughout the episode about the Doctor's comment, "Art can wait. This is life and death." Van Gogh's art clearly does not "wait" because the Doctor and

Amy are so concerned for its preciousness, as a freshly produced commodity and art object, and the need for Van Gogh to deliver the painting that signals the danger they have come to investigate. The episode is littered with references to making paintings and to the value of art. "Dark night, very starry," notes the Doctor as they arrive at Vincent's home, both a passing acknowledgement to Van Gogh's 'Starry Night' and a foreshadowing of the episode's key depiction of the shared artistic vision between him, the Doctor and Amy. The bedroom scene itself is introduced by Vincent's aside of "Watch out, that one's wet," referring to a canvas hanging out to dry, that causes Amy to pause in front of it and provide a key moment for director Jonny Campbell to overlap the image of 'Bedroom in Arles' with the room they then enter. "I've come to accept that the only person who is going to love my paintings is me," says Vincent as the camera slowly pans around the room, positively relishing in the familiar Van Gogh canon both as modernist masterpieces and as a dream of capitalist investment. As Van Gogh prepares coffee and rests the coffee pot on one of the canvasses littering the room, the Doctor nervously suggests, "You know, you should be careful with these... they're... they're precious." Is the Doctor concerned for their safety because they represent either the revered "artistic outpouring" from Impressionism's stereotype of starving artist, rebel, nonconformist, outsider and existentialist or their worth of "tens of millions of pounds" to the art market and to the commercial exploitation of his imagery. When Van Gogh denies their value as "precious to me, not precious to anyone else," Curtis is adamantly in favour of the former interpretation of authorial authenticity in the work, especially when Van Gogh is seen to promote the virtues of the artist's struggle with the natural realm and his vision as an extension of his mental health. The damage done to paintings during the story is also symbolic of our perception of their worth. Later, in the interweaving of artistic vision, of seeing the hidden, dark half of the artist's nature, as expressed in Van Gogh's battle with the Krafayis, Amy is briefly seen peering through a torn canvas. When the Doctor asks Vincent to draw what he sees, requesting a representation of the Krafayis to enable him to identify it, the artist takes one of the many 'Irises' paintings and immediately paints over it. "Oh, no! Noooo!" cries the Doctor as Vincent sets to work. Vincent remains nonplussed, clearly used to recycling and reusing canvasses and is not precious about his work, simply because he sees in it no worth beyond it being a channel through which he can express himself. After challenging the Doctor's outrage, the Doctor can only sheepishly respond, "It's just... that... that was quite good," painfully aware of its financial value as well as attempting to give Vincent a critical perspective on his work. This devaluing, deconstruction and destruction of historic works of art is central to the episode's use of cultural settings and iconography to explore history as the simulated reality of Van Gogh's life and work and how, as a cultural producer, he hovers on the border between modernism and postmodernism. Fredric Jameson, in *The Cultural Logic of Late Capitalism*, compares Van Gogh's authenticity as an artist, his sheer physical and mental toil, with Andy Warhol's work, seen as representative of "flatness or depthlessness, a new kind of superficiality," and sees Van Gogh's modernism as the "whole metaphysics of the inside and the outside, of the wordless pain... that 'emotion' then projected out and externalised." In *Vincent and the Doctor*, there is a sense that Van Gogh has been co-opted by postmodernism's own obsession with the marketplace, epitomised in Jameson relating Van Gogh to Warhol's role as the artist/commodity commenting on the mass media surrounding him. It underlines the episode's emphasis on the value of art, how Van Gogh's own work and images have been democratised, through mass media and mass production, within consumer society. It reflects, in a minor way, the satirical view about the 'authenticity' of art works, both classical and modern, in *City of Death* where the sequence in the Paris gallery, featuring John Cleese and Eleanor Bron as a pair of art critics, is seen by John Tulloch and Manuel Alvarado, in *Doctor Who: The Unfolding Text*, as "a play on notions of artistic 'authenticity' and criticism... on recognisable 'academic' discourses designed to appeal to the large number of adult viewers with considerable 'intellectual capital'." *Vincent and the Doctor* flirts with this postmodernist discourse, setting out to replace hierarchies and traditions, truth and reality with allusion, mimicry, irony and parody and a self-conscious mixture of forms and styles, epitomised in actor Tony Curran's physical similarity to Van Gogh and the series of simulations of the paintings and the places in which he lived, that are then blurred together with science fiction tropes of invisible monsters and time-travelling police boxes.

The complex fluidity between the modernist and postmodernist, rationalism and existentialism, in *Vincent and the Doctor* is also found in the Doctor and Vincent's understanding of the power of art. The Doctor returns to the TARDIS with Van Gogh's drawing of the Krafayis and uses a science fiction gadget, a technological mash-up of Jules Verne and post-war 1950s design, to identify the beast. The Van Gogh image of the Krafayis is wrongly identified as a parrot, then a polar bear and the Doctor is as exasperated as many of us when confronted by modern art's modes of decentralised perception and representation. "No, definitely not. This is the problem with the Impressionists – not accurate enough! This would never happen with Gainsborough or one of those proper painters. Sorry, Vincent." The debunking of Van Gogh's inaccurate vision results in the Doctor throwing the image of the Krafayis over his shoulder and consigning a Van Gogh original to the status of disposable art. The machine's registration of the Doctor's face is so accurate that it can detect all aspects of his identity and show the images of his various incarnations. The Doctor puts his tongue out when looking into the mirror of the machine, an image that cleverly acknowledges Matt Smith's admission that he found inspiration for the role of the Doctor in the image of Einstein putting out his tongue in Arthur Sasse's celebrated portrait taken in 1951. The Doctor's face is reproduced as images of both the First and Second Doctor, printed out from a typewriter on the console. This use of "photo-mechanical reproduction to challenge the uniqueness of the art image and its specific 'aura'," as Tim Woods describes the postmodern use of appropriation in contemporary culture in *Beginning Postmodernism*, suggests that the codifying of Einstein as 'mad scientist' and the mechanical rationalism of the Doctor, his dependency on technology and science to reveal the hidden areas of the universe, is contrasted with Van Gogh's intuitive, emotional and physical connection to nature. Art is Vincent's tool of choice when it comes to analysing the Krafayis, emphasised in the close-up of the brushes and easel he selects and carries on the way to the church as they prepare to await the Krafayis's return. The Doctor's preference for intellectual rigor and accuracy in art, for clear reproduction, is further emphasised in his recollection of Picasso, "what a ghastly old goat. I kept telling him 'Concentrate Pablo, it's one eye either side of the face.'" It is also a reminder of the argument between Romana and the Doctor in *City of Death* where she believes that Gallifreyan computers are far better at producing accurate likenesses than the one the café artist draws of her. Her reaction causes the Doctor to take her to the Louvre to show her one of the finest examples of Renaissance painting, the 'Mona Lisa'. In essence the Doctor leans toward the Romantic tradition of an empirical, accurate and rational representation of reality and rather sees artists like Van Gogh and Picasso as a potential threat to this coherence. Vincent's expression, perception and emotions, the qualities that Curtis personally identifies with in his story, seem to baffle the Doctor. In Van Gogh's conflict with his inner demons, and its projection via the medium of paint, Curtis also seems to hint at something of the divine mystery of the universe, forces beyond the rational knowledge of the Doctor, and expressed in Vincent's own attitude toward the sunflowers that Amy surrounds him with. He admits to her, "I find them complex. Always somewhere between living and dying. Half-human as they turn to the sun. A little disgusting. But you know, they are a challenge." Robert Farrar Capon, in *Hunting the Divine Fox: An Introduction to the Language of Theology*, expresses this conflict between the Doctor's desire to rationalise the universe and Vincent's drive to express its mysteries, "We are so impressed by scientific clank that we feel we ought not to say that the sunflower turns because it knows where the sun is. It is almost second nature to us to prefer explanations... with a large vocabulary. We are much more comfortable when we are assured that the sunflower turns because it is heliotropic. The trouble with that kind of talk is that it tempts us to think that we know what the sunflower is up to. But we don't. The sunflower is a mystery, just as every single thing in the universe is." At the same time, Curtis is unable to resist a further tongue-in-cheek reference to how popular and recognised the paintings of sunflowers will become, after Amy suggests "I thought you might like, you know, possibly to perhaps paint them or something? Might be a thought." It is a creative challenge the Doctor knowingly acknowledges to Vincent as "one I'm pretty sure you'll rise to."

Finally, Curtis removes Vincent from his own time, plunging him into the twenty-first century, and acknowledges that his history is something we can never actually know in full and that Van Gogh is mythically constructed out of various texts. This construction is partly seen in both Amy's determination that "time can be rewritten, I know it can," in order to extend Vincent's life and enable him to produce more paintings and thus perhaps stave off failure, and in Dr Black's eulogy where Vincent is believed to have "transformed the pain of his tormented life into ecstatic beauty. Pain is easy to portray but to use your pain and passion to portray the ecstasy and joy and magnificence of our world – no one had ever done it before. Perhaps no one ever will again." This perhaps suggests the transformative power within the iconic figure of Van Gogh, one with the potential to inspire someone to change history in their favour and one where the artist himself is transformed, and sanctified, by a life lived. As Nathalie Heinich's *The Glory of Van Gogh: An Anthropology of Admiration* indicates, he is formed from a multiplicity of interpretations and texts and belongs in "art history and criticism, which are concerned with the construction of artistic greatness... belongs to the history of religion, which is concerned with the sacrificial construction of greatness; to the biographical and hagiographical tradition, which is concerned with systems of admiration and heroisation; to psychiatry, psychology and anthropology, which are concerned with deviance and singularity; to economics which is concerned with the moneterization of the value attributed to the work; and to the sociology of religion, which is concerned with the status of relics, pilgrimages and atonement." This is probably the closest that the current series has ever got to telling a fiction about a single recognisable historical figure without recourse to the use of science fictional trappings that codify it as *Doctor Who*. Daniel O'Mahony sees the likes of *Marco Polo* also as a synthesis of fictions, where writer John Lucarotti's "entire narrative line, on which he hangs historical detail and his own fiction, may itself be fictional" because the source he based his script on, *Il Milione*, is itself inauthentic. Curtis must also recognise that his simulations of Van Gogh are informed by yet further textual meaning where his life and work have been commodified in other dramatic forms. Our knowledge of him therefore also comes from what Gary Bamossy sees as:

> "the substantial and direct visual impact that stemmed from the growing popularity of cinema and television. The prominent list of cast members and directors, particularly from the Hollywood genre of Van Gogh films, is impressive: Directors Robert Altman (*Vincent and Theo* 1990), Kurosawa Akira (*Dreams* 1990), and Vincente Minnelli (*Lust for Life* 1956); actors Kirk Douglas as Vincent, and Anthony Quinn's supporting actor academy award winning role as Gauguin, and Martin Scorsese as Vincent in Kurosawa's fifth *Dream* sequence. *Lust for Life* is perhaps the most influential Hollywood film on Van Gogh, and presents the major components of the legend and myths of Vincent as a

suffering genius and mad artist, using powerful visual images and dramatic characters."

Curtis also announces that he is a fully paid-up member of the Van Gogh fan club in the way that he uses the narrative to sentimentalise the myth of the misunderstood artist. By retrieving the artist from his own past and allowing him momentarily to understand that his work lives on and is loved by millions, Curtis provides atonement for the failure of Van Gogh's generation to recognise the painter's genius in his own lifetime. Bamossy again understands how the postmodern works in context with the figure of Van Gogh:

> "Postmodernists would argue that parodies and (mis)approp-riations of images result naturally and necessarily through the breaking away from the canons of normal representation. Van Gogh represents the *sine qua non* of this break for artists and their works, and for historical figures generally. The thousands of 'low art' and 'kitsch' reproductions of Vincent, and of his paintings provide many consumers with crude and transient images of who he was, and what he created. It may be that these postmodern representations of Van Gogh and his work, provided by the advertising industry and delivered via mass media, help lead the way to a shift in some consumers' contemporary needs for myth, and ultimately, to their understanding of the man and his works."

While *Vincent and the Doctor* is full of postmodern skepticism, because, as Julian Barnes insists in *A History of the World in 10 1/2 Chapters*, "We all know objective truth is not obtainable, that when some event occurs we shall have a multiplicity of subjective truths which we assess and then fabulate into history, into some God-eyed version of what 'really' happened," it still remains a beguiling, complex vision of one artist's mythological presence, one that is finally communicated to us on a very emotional and spiritual level.

## "Art can wait. This is life and death"

In *Vincent and the Doctor*, Curtis uses the Krafayis as a symbolic 'other' to explore a number of ideas related to the boundary between creativity and madness. The cliché is that there is a fine line between the genius and the madman and that is certainly one aspect of Curtis's portrayal of Vincent's turmoil and depression. He also links his illness and painting to the act of seeing, of perceiving the unseeable, of knowing the unknowable. Creativity and madness, rationalism and existentialism are all highlighted in the dynamic between the Doctor and Vincent. Anthony Storr, in *The Dynamics of Creation*, sees creativity "as one mode adopted by gifted people of coming to terms with, or finding symbolic solutions for, the internal tensions and disassociations from which all humans suffer in varying degrees." Not only does Vincent produce paintings at a furious

169

rate, suggesting some kind of self-imposed time limit in his duel with nature and his desire to capture, for all intents and purposes, a sense of the divine before madness claims him completely, but Curtis also manifests the darker, fragmented parts of his psyche as a monster, as a blind phantom. The Krafayis, as alone, blind and anxious as Vincent is in his psychotic episodes, is also Vincent's coping mechanism, a projection of his inner turmoil that only he can see. The painter's battles with himself are intrinsically bound together with his perception of the world. When Vincent despairs and struggles to find a way to see and encapsulate nature, he collapses into depression and rejects those that come to help. The Krafayis is that rejection and anger anthropomorphised for him, as an enemy to be conquered. It has to be sublimated successfully within Vincent's persona to allow him to be creative. Storr sees the relationship between creativity and psychopathology as one where this sublimation is either exorcised through painting or through symptoms of neurosis as, "one of the reasons that creative people are apt to be labelled neurotic even when they are not is that their psychopathology is also showing, but it is showing in their works and not in the form of neurotic symptoms. The work is a positive adaptation whereas neurosis is a failure of adaptation." Curtis clearly delineates Vincent's struggle for 'adaptation' throughout the story and it is a process that Amy certainly believes she and the Doctor can affect, to the extent that neurosis, in the form of the Krafayis, can be alleviated to such a degree that Vincent will not consider suicide.

The plotting of Vincent's neurosis, the way he perceives it and it is manifested, is initially framed in the conversation with the Doctor. The Doctor is an interesting figure to contrast with Vincent. They are both described as 'madmen' and certainly the Doctor has been codified in the series as 'the madman with his box'. Equally, Vincent is regarded as a madman by the local population, perhaps 'the madman with his easel' and is mocked at the café, attacked in the street ("Get that madman out of here," screams the mother of the murdered girl Giselle, "You bring this on us, your madness, you!") and blamed for the murders committed by the alien Krafayis. Curtis is also providing a critique of our attitudes to the 'other', suggesting that the actions of the villagers resemble our treatment of the mentally ill in society. The locals may be deeply suspicious of Vincent simply because he is seen to have a connection with his own inner psyche and is able to depict it, whether for ill or good, as the forces of nature in his painting. His pulsating and energetic view of the world, of the raw power of nature, is probably quite alien to them. It is also interesting to note that the Krafayis physically disassembles humans in much the same way that it, represented as Vincent's debilitating neurosis, fragments his personality and destroys his ability to paint and fix his vision to the canvas. When the Doctor, Amy and Vincent return to the painter's humble home, Vincent is puzzled by the Doctor's eagerness to find the church in 'The Church at Auvers' canvas and to know when Vincent will paint it. The church later becomes a battleground between them and the Krafayis, taking on a semi-religious symbolism, and suggests it as a physical site of the civilising power of Van Gogh's Christianity over the pagan, merciless 'other' of the rampaging alien. Momentarily, Vincent identifies a kindred spirit in the Doctor's fixations and deflects these from the Doctor and back to Amy, "Seems to me you never talk about anything else. He's a strange one." The Doctor changes the subject and asks him what he is most interested in. The following sequence is the episode's first real indication of what drives Vincent's obsessions to the point of neurosis when he, at first, philosophises about his art and then the reverie rapidly becomes a psychopathological diatribe about how he perceives nature. "It seems to me there is so much more to the world than the average eye is allowed to see. I believe, that, if you look hard, there are more wonders in this universe than you can ever have dreamed of," he offers the Doctor. The idea of using perception to find the hidden details in the universe is, of course, something that is recognised in the Doctor's curiosity and it is a gift that he always passes on to the companions that journey with him. "You don't have to tell me," acknowledges the Doctor. However, Vincent suggests a form of visual and aural inspiration that puzzles the Doctor, "It's colour. Colour holds the key. I can hear the colours. Listen to them," and this puzzlement is in his reaction, to try and "hear the colours" that Vincent talks about, cocking his ears to see if he can hear them too. Director Jonny Campbell emphasises this mania in Vincent by simply and effectively holding a close-up on Vincent's claw-like hand because, after all, his perception is translated into paint through that physical appendage. Finally, Vincent issues the challenge to his neurosis, and perhaps the Krafayis itself, in "Every time I step outside, I feel nature is shouting at me. Come on, come and get me. Come on. Come on, capture my mystery!" For Vincent to be free of his pain, albeit momentarily through the act of painting, he must freeze nature with his vision, capture it before it disappears. Ironically, as they engage in this debate and the Doctor tries to calm him down, Amy vanishes from the field of vision. "Amy? Where's Amy?" requests the Doctor as she screams and the Krafayis, the shadowy genie released from the bottle as Vincent works himself into a manic episode, is manifested outside the cottage.

In the attack, precipitated by Amy looking at the paintings outside ("when something hit me from behind") and suggesting that the raw power of nature has somehow leapt out of the canvasses, only Vincent can see the Krafayis. The Doctor and Amy are worried when Vincent picks up a pitchfork and hurtles toward them and only assess the outward symptoms of Vincent's violent reaction: "Amy, get back. He's having some kind of fit. I'll try to calm him down." The episode's fascination with seeing and not seeing, with internal and external perception is signified in the way Campbell allows only Vincent and the audience to see the Krafayis. As the Doctor explains that no one else is there and that it is just he standing in front of Vincent, the point of view in the scene becomes Vincent's as a tail lashes out and strikes the Doctor down. As Amy, peering through the symbolically shredded canvas, like the shreds of Vincent's mind, shouts "I can't see anything. What is it?" she further opens up the story's discourse about perception and the dichotomy between rationalism and existentialism. It is also a dichotomy where the Doctor uses science to identify an alien beast and Vincent uses art to conquer, temporarily, his Krafayis, the shadow of himself that is the synthesis of his loneliness and rejection, the fragmentation of his self-esteem. Rather like Morbius in *Forbidden Planet* (1956), whose own id is manifested as an invisible monster, the Krafayis is metabolised in an invisible force when Vincent's creative impulses lose control. After the Doctor and Vincent drive off the invisible monster, having witnessed the physical presence of the beast during the fight, the Doctor has already rationalised that this is not just a permutation of Vincent's manic-depressive state. The release of the monster from the id is rather humorously referred to in the Doctor's instructions to Amy. "Right, Amy, make Mr Van Gogh comfortable. Don't let any invisible monsters through the front door." By implication, he warns her not to let the Krafayis attack by any normal route and that she should also prevent, by an unseen 'back door' route, Vincent's manic episodes reoccurring.  She is rather concerned about what is outside rather than inside, "It could be outside... waiting." "What's the worst that could happen?" queries the Doctor and she simultaneously suggests, with "You could get torn into pieces by a monster you can't see," that he will be subject to the predations of the 'monster of the week' and meet the same disassembling fate meted out to the villager Giselle, death at the hands of a collective madman or bogeyman conjured up by the fears of the villagers. This is also a reflection of the themes of the shadow 'other' that the Doctor, in his travels, must conquer in order to become a fully individuated person. Here, he is faced with what Helena Bassil-Morozow, in *Tim Burton: The Monster and the Crowd*, calls, "a summation of individual hatreds directed against another group of individuals," where the villagers blame Vincent and his strange friends for the Krafayis's own violent fear of isolation, rejection and loneliness.

The Krafayis is reconfigured from the symbol of Van Gogh's inner turmoil into something more akin to the 'monster of the week', where *Doctor Who* prefers to blur the historical and science fiction genres to reiterate the long tradition that the Doctor must fight monsters, must rationalise their extraordinary disruption into ordinary reality and find the truth of them rather than simply provide a straight re-reading of historical events. The invisible Krafayis is eventually classified as "you poor thing. You brutal, murderous, abandoned thing" in the Doctor's analysis from the mirrored device. The device is an allusion to Alice's discovery of the Jabberwock creature while reading the nonsense poem 'Jabberwocky' in Lewis Carroll's *Through the Looking Glass*. The Jabberwock is contained in a 'looking glass' book where everything is printed backwards but acquires a true and sensible reading when reflected in a mirror. Only by looking beyond reality and into the mirror, incidentally one provided to him by a Carroll-esque two-headed, dull godmother with bad breath (twice), can the Doctor identify the creature and, likewise, does director Campbell offer a mode for the audience to get a clear view of the being. Therefore the Krafayis functions as a generic monstrous, alien 'other' found in traditional science fiction, a manifested symptom of Vincent's precarious state of mind and Curtis's own concerns about how mental illness is codified in our society, that Sander Gilman in *Disease and Representation: Images of Illness from Madness to AIDS* classifies as, "the fear of collapse, the sense of dissolution that contaminates the Western images of all diseases, including elusive ones such as schizophrenia. But the fear we have of our own collapse does not remain internalised. Rather we project this fear onto the world in order to localise it and, indeed, to domesticate it. For once we locate it, the fear of our own dissolution is removed. Then it is not we who totter on the brink of collapse but rather the Other. And it is an-Other who has already shown his or her vulnerability by having collapsed."

When the Doctor 'localises' the Krafayis for Vincent, the mission to remove the creature, now categorised as an "individual, utterly merciless, utterly abandoned Krafayis" that will "kill until they're killed. Which they usually aren't. Because other creatures can't see them," is also seen as a potential opportunity to prevent Van Gogh's mental disintegration. The Doctor pointedly suggests that they are in a unique position "to end this reign of terror" and by that we take him to mean not just the rehabilitation of the Krafayis and the Doctor's desire to return it home, but also to treat the cause of Van Gogh's own internal despair and sense of abandonment. The Doctor raises the question, "Feel like painting the church today?" because he knows this chance will only occur if Vincent gets to the church and paints it. Vincent asks about the monster and the Doctor rationalises the situation: "Take my word for it. If you paint it, he will come." The beast is both classified by the Doctor and mythologised by Vincent and their positions mimic the legacy of the Enlightenment where the late nineteenth century embraced the drive towards rationalism and science and the Romantic tradition's values of emotion, feelings and the autonomy of the artistic experience. These classifications reflect how the episode outlines the systems that the Doctor and Vincent employ to make sense of their own place in the world, where Vincent's painting is integrated into the adaptive process that Anthony Storr sees as the artist's "need to reunite himself with the world from which he feels alienated and thus come to build bridges between the subjective and objective." However, the Doctor understands a number of risks inherent to this project. Vincent could be killed by the Krafayis, shredded to pieces just as Giselle was, or he could be swamped by his neurosis, devoured by the shadow side of himself. Either way, his fragmentation could result in, as the Doctor explains, "the brutal murder of the greatest artist who ever lived. Half the pictures on the wall of the Musée d'Orsay will disappear. And it will be our fault." The threat of erasure from, or altering the course of, history as a result of their actions is a theme common to the time travel scenarios in *Doctor Who* and certainly highlights the overall theme of this particular series. Unfortunately, the Doctor overlooks a key factor in

173

Vincent's psyche and his casual remark, "I promise you, we'll be out of your hair by this time tomorrow," is the trigger for another moment of manic despair for the artist, foreshadowed in Vincent's brief pause in the doorway as the Doctor says this. At heart, he is desperately lonely, isolated and feeling abandoned, much like the Krafayis, and at the first indication of the loss of friendship and companionship he plunges back into his shadow world, takes to his bed to struggle with his anxieties. Van Gogh's torment is to reconcile these troubles with the external world because, as Storr offers, "we all possess inner worlds that are, to varying degrees, at odds with the external world," and only through his creative acts can he have any possibility of this reconciliation. The melancholic Vincent's cry, to the Doctor, of "It's so clear you cannot help. And when you leave – and everyone always leaves – I will be left once more with an empty heart and no hope," not only parallels the similar fears that fuel the Krafayis's violent reaction to the world it finds itself in, but it also underlines Amy's own fear of abandonment. Her anxiety is one that the Dream Lord signified in *Amy's Choice* and is also symbolised in her own psychopathological state as a child, abandoned but deeply affected by the Raggedy Doctor's visit, resulting in her parents seeking psychiatric help for her. The Doctor is shown to be rather ineffectual in this crisis. Dealing with violent emotions is not something he has much expertise with and his forlorn, "My experience is that there is, you know, surprisingly, always hope" does little to salve Vincent's anguish. "Then your experience is incomplete," accuses Van Gogh and it perhaps suggests that the incomplete Doctor, the lonely Time Lord, mirrors some aspects of the fragmented personality of both Vincent and, with the recent loss of Rory, Amy. Vincent seems sure of the imminence of his own death and fears his creative outpourings will not be his saviour, "I know how it will end. And it will not end well." His reappearance, in a highly deranged state, in *The Pandorica Opens* with the painting of the exploding TARDIS also offers a coda to this prescience about 'how it will end' for the Doctor and the rest of the universe. All three characters express something of the alienation inherent in the modern condition and Erich Neumann in *Art and the Creative Unconscious: Four Essays* relates this to the way modernism in culture has superseded the formally traditional, something that the Impressionists had a huge influence on, where "The disappearance of the certainty once conferred by the cultural canon shows itself primarily in a sense of isolation, of forlornness, of homelessness and alienation," and he sees an artist like Van Gogh as "a world in himself, endeavouring alone to ward off the chaos that menaces him or to give it form, each with his own characteristic of desperation." Here we also understand why the Doctor needs his human companions as a very necessary way of relating to the rest of the world, with the closeness of a friend to help deal with the loneliness and isolation.

The Doctor recognises the delicate balance of Vincent's mind, where he is destined to die at his own hand, and decides that he must deal with the Krafayis on his own. Amy, although she clearly knows Vincent's fate, would rather disavow its inevitability, and her admonition, "Don't say that, please," reminds us of her own denial, on two occasions, of Rory's death. The inevitability of history, of events and people shackled to an unavoidable fate and destiny, is symbolised by the Doctor's brief glance at Van Gogh's painting 'The Prisoner's Round' as they prepare to leave for the church. The circle of prison inmates in the picture implies the continuous cycle of time and the monotonous, slow path of prison life, as well as Van Gogh's own experiences, during the vicious alternation between madness and lucidity, as a self-imposed internee of the Saint-Remy asylum. Vincent's death is again foreshadowed on the road to the church when they pass Giselle's grieving mother with the bearers and her daughter's coffin. The coffin, draped with sunflowers, is a visual allusion to fellow painter Emile Bernard's description of Van Gogh's funeral: "A plain white cloth was draped on the coffin and there were a great many flowers – sunflowers, which he was so fond of." In another rather effective moment of visual symbolism, Campbell catches Amy and the Doctor, as they leave for the church, in the looming shadow cast by Vincent and suggests, along with specific shots of brushes and easel, he is the equivalent of a knight preparing to slay a dragon. Later, as Vincent sets to work on the canvas of 'The Church at Auvers', the idea that he has regained the powers of his art in order to banish the debilitating despair he felt in the bedroom are formalised in the Doctor's attempt to get him, as in a patient-doctor confessional, to open up. After asking him to alert them of the presence of the Krafayis, Vincent counters with "I may be mad, but I'm not stupid." The Doctor attempts to remove the stigma with "No, quite. And to be honest, I'm not sure about mad either. It seems to me depression is a very complex..." but he is abruptly silenced. "Shhh. I'm working," demands Vincent. His creativity and concentration is holding the depression at bay and as if to acknowledge this, the Doctor agrees, "Well, yes. Paint. Do painting." This conquest over his manic episodes is symbolised further when, as the Doctor enters the church to stun the Krafayis, there is a long, slow pan up to the lintel above the door onto a carving of an angel, probably Michael, slaying a serpent or dragon. Not an uncommon composition in Early Christian art, its depiction symbolises the Doctor and his detection device about to do battle with the Krafayis and more potently Vincent's triumphant spearing of the creature. In *The Crooked Path Journal, Issue 2*, Robin Artisson, in the article 'The Dragon and the Dragonslayer' suggests that this image is "the symbol of the particular psychology of Christianity moving itself into a dominant position over the psychology of the earlier earth-centred faiths; a symbolic triumph of 'reason' over 'irrationality', and 'civilisation' over 'savagery'." There is also a hint here of the mythical hero's journey outlined by Joseph Campbell in *The Hero with a Thousand Faces*, in which he delineates the stages and common elements found on the hero's journey as a form of transformative psychotherapy. This transformation can also be linked to Van Gogh's acceptance of the Doctor as "the first doctor ever to make a difference to my life." The coffin on the road, headed by a crucifix-bearing priest, the Christian iconography above the lintel and the use of the church as the final confrontation are also brief acknowledgments of Van Gogh's own religious faith in his art when dealing with reason over irrationality. Michael Roth, in *Rediscovering History: Culture, Politics, and the Psyche*, suggests Van Gogh's painting "transposed religious conflict into image-making and it illuminates some of the distinctive historical texture of Van Gogh's psychological being." When Vincent literally uses art, in the form of the easel, to slay the Krafayis, the scene is an apotheosis of the episode's depiction of artists using their vision to adapt the turmoil of their inner world and perhaps temporarily ameliorate its effects. It is also a crude symbol of his Christian faith triumphant over the savagery of nature, the challenge of capturing nature that Van Gogh was so agitated about earlier in the story. The mythological aspects of the duel with the Krafayis, of Vincent's battle with depression and of the Doctor's ongoing eternal struggle against the monsters, is later emphasised, back in the Musée d'Orsay, as the Doctor, Amy and Vincent mount the stairs to the gallery. The Doctor poses by and imitates a classical statue of Perseus slaying the Medusa, one in the manner of sculptor Cellini, the mythology of which author John Barth suggests, in his novel *Chimera*, is about creative power being used, where Perseus becomes the master of his own story and myth, to banish maladies and monsters. There are also parallels between the Doctor seeing the Krafayis in a mirror and the Perseus myth. Perseus can only 'see' the Medusa when she is reflected in his polished shield, thus allowing him to approach and kill her.

The stalking and slaying of the Krafayis also reiterates the episode's fascination with perception, where the creature compensates for its blindness with a heightened sense of hearing. It is when Vincent explains to the Doctor that the creature is feeling its way around the room, with Amy alluding to the Krafayis's desperation with her confession "I can't see a thing," that the Doctor realises that it is actually blind. As Vincent wounds the beast, he understands that the creature, like him in his manic episodes, "wasn't without mercy at all. He was without sight." The monster is signified as not monstrous and is simply "afraid" and again Vincent can see himself as a human configuration of the Krafayis. "He was frightened. And he lashed out. Like humans who lash out when they're frightened. Like the villagers who scream at me. Like the children who throw stones at me." The series again emphasises that appearances can be deceptive and that, indeed, the intentional or accidental slaying of monsters does not necessarily lead to an expected sense of triumph. The Doctor, perhaps reflecting the fact that in *The Beast Below* he almost killed the Star Whale, unhappily summarises this with "Sometimes winning... winning is no fun at all." Ultimately, the most powerful scene in the episode is the moment when Vincent, for a moment, gets to share his vision of the world with the Doctor, Amy and the audience. As they lay on the ground, holding each other's hands and gazing into the night sky, the sequence that follows corresponds to the 3D trailer that promoted the series in February 2010 which, in a strikingly analogous bit of marketing, was shown before screenings of Tim Burton's *Alice in Wonderland* (2009). The trailer opens with the Doctor and Amy lying on the ground and stargazing, then takes them on a journey into a vortex filled with the monsters they will encounter during the series, with the Doctor voicing the tag line, "All of time and space, everywhere and anywhere, every star that ever was... where do you want to start?" As the trailer synthesises the modus operandi of the eternal-child figure of the Doctor, then Vincent proposes a similar journey and one that opens us up to his interpretation of "all of time and space." As he narrates to both audience and his friends, the scene cuts to a vista of the night sky and gradually it changes into a blazing simulation of 'Starry Night'. "Hold my hand, Doctor. Try to see what I see. We're so lucky we're still alive to see this beautiful world. Look at the sky. It's not dark and black without character. The black is in fact deep blue. And over there, lighter blue. And blowing through the blueness and the blackness, the wind swirling through the air and then shining, burning, bursting through – the stars! Can you see how they roar their light? Everywhere we look, the complex magic of nature blazes before our eyes." It is a sublime moment where music, visual effects and performance come together to provide us with a shimmering manifestation of Van Gogh's ability to fuse the nineteenth-century tradition for depicting reality with his wilder Romantic passion to imbue what he sees with transcendental values. The act of seeing beyond reality, of finding the extraordinary in the seemingly ordinary, is also not too dissimilar to the way *Doctor Who* presents the universe to us. The swirling, blazing imagery of the stars is analogous to the climactic scene of *The Pandorica Opens* where the reverse of this is seen as the stars and galaxies contract into total blackness, symbolising the loss of our ability to perceive the wonders and mysteries of nature. For the Doctor and Amy it is as if they are seeing the energies that bind the stars and planets together for the first time, without the use of technology as a frame of reference. The Doctor acknowledges Vincent's perception of the universe and its majesty and power that transcends all the earthly concerns of history and modernity: "I've seen many things, my friend. But you're right. Nothing quite as wonderful as the things you see."

For Vincent, the sharing of 'Starry Night' as a visual experience is also a symbol of their friendship. This friendship is one that Amy, particularly, hopes will change Vincent's outlook on life and that may lead to new paintings, a longer life. Curtis does not resist one last opportunity to include a dig at the values attached to appreciating and owning art when Vincent offers the Doctor 'Self-Portrait with Straw Hat' and nonchalantly says, "I only wish I had something of real value to give you." Campbell again lines up the portrait with Tony Curran's face and returns the episode to its simulation of the historic in the café scene. There is an underlying sadness in the scene, especially when Vincent grasps the Doctor's hand and proudly announces, "Doctor, my friend, we have fought monsters together and we have won. On my own I fear I may not do as well."

Campbell's close-up on Matt Smith's face, as the Doctor and Vincent hug, is a perfect summation that these victories are only temporary, despite the TARDIS's trip into a future where Van Gogh is venerated and the determination on his return that "this changes everything. I'll step out tomorrow with my easel on my back a different man."

## "How come I'm the crazy one? And you two have stayed sane?"

For Amy, the events of *Vincent and the Doctor* prove to her that the fixed points in time will always remain so despite her efforts to alter them. It is clear that she has a desire to see Van Gogh avoid his destiny and believes that their experiences with him are enough to change the outcome. Her journey through the story runs in parallel to Van Gogh's attempts to adapt to his manic episodes and control them through his paintings. Beginning in the Musée d'Orsay, it is obvious that the Doctor has brought her to the gallery in an attempt to assuage his guilt over the death of Rory. She has noticed his efforts and is rather suspicious of them. "You're being so nice to me. Why are you being so nice to me?" she asks the Doctor and he bristles at her "I'm always nice to you" in order to cover up that, in effect, he is mourning Rory on her behalf. She is alarmed when he insists that there is nothing to be suspicious about. "I was joking! Why aren't you?" It is perhaps a signal of the Doctor's growing awareness of the seriousness of the situation now that the crack in the universe has claimed the life of Rory and still remains a worrying mystery. Her humour, he feels, is perhaps not quite as appropriate as it was. Later, his feelings seem to be justified when, on the road to the church, Amy and Vincent not only touch on this guilt but also highlight that a perception as powerful as Vincent's makes Amy's inner sadness very apparent, despite the effects of the crack in time to wipe away her memories. "I'm sorry you're so sad," says Amy, walking arm in arm with him. "But I'm not," he replies. "Sometimes these moods torture me for weeks, for months. But I'm good now. If Amy Pond can soldier on then so can Vincent van Gogh." She is puzzled by this remark. "I'm not soldiering on. I'm fine." Clearly a reference to the loss of Rory, both a person and an event she is unable to recall, Vincent understands that, deep within, a memory of him still persists. "Oh, Amy. I hear the song of your sadness. You've lost someone, I think," he sympathises. "I'm not sad," she reassures him. "Then why are you crying?" he asks, as she wipes away a tear she did not know she was even shedding. It suggests an inner turmoil that perhaps Vincent is attuned to and he acknowledges with "It's all right. I understand." She is baffled as to why she is crying, unable to fathom this inner tragedy: "I'm not sure I do." It is perhaps indicative of her ability in *The Pandorica Opens* and *The Big Bang* to recall Rory and to bring back the Doctor.

The episode again amusingly plays on Amy's nationality, here as part of a witty explanation for the lack of French and Dutch accents when they travel to France in 1890. The scene in the café proposes that the TARDIS perhaps translates non-English languages into regional accents then recognisable to the speakers. "That accent of yours. You from Holland like me?" asks Vincent. "Yes" says the Doctor, "No" says Amy, unaware that her Scottish accent has been translated by the telepathic field of the TARDIS. "She means 'yes,'" corrects the Doctor. The joke certainly deflects any criticism from viewers about the less than authentic accents or language in the story. The encounter between Amy and Vincent, with them almost wooing each other, bathed in orange light and complimenting each other on their orange hair, positions the Doctor as the 'gooseberry' of *Amy's Choice* again and his restlessness and discomfort allows him to cut to the chase as to when Vincent is likely to paint the church. The obsession with ginger hair is also later reflected in Amy's comments at the end of the episode about her and Vincent's potential offspring being the "ultimate ginge" and "brighter than sunflowers" as she gazes at the painting of sunflowers dedicated to her in the Musée d'Orsay. However, these scenes could be a rebuttal to the criticism from some parents who detected an 'anti-ginger' agenda in *Doctor Who* after noting Matt Smith's first lines in the series. When the Doctor regenerated in the concluding part of *The End of Time*, the Eleventh Doctor was saddened to discover "I'm still not ginger," which in turn reflected a similar line from the Tenth Doctor to Rose in his debut story *The Christmas Invasion*, "Aww, I wanted to be ginger. I've never been ginger." Peculiarly, this seems to have been construed as encouraging the bullying of ginger-haired children.

The Doctor once again assumes the role of authority and of rationalism. In the meeting with Dr Black, the gallery's bow tie-wearing analogue to the Doctor that repeats the series's contention that "bow ties are cool," he flashes the psychic paper and declares a "Routine inspection. Ministry of Art and... Artiness." In another example of the serendipity in this episode, it is amusing to see Bill Nighy, an actor mistakenly announced as taking on the role of the Ninth Doctor by the *Daily Mail* on the same morning of 20 March 2004 when it was officially announced that Christopher Eccleston had won the part, now guest starring as Dr Black. He still gets to play *a* doctor, at least, rather than the definite article. Here again, the Time Lord rationalises the details around him, using his perception to spot the Krafayis in the window seen in the painting and setting up the detection device to classify the beast. When he hands the picture from the device to Vincent, one created mechanically rather than through the application of oil on canvas, he defines the species for him, "They travel in space, they travel as a pack. Scavenging across the universe. Sometimes one of them gets left behind and because they are such a brutal race the others never come back." Amy seems to have an emotional affinity for this situation, having felt left behind by the Doctor in *The Eleventh Hour* and never having had a life with her apparently non-existent parents. The Krafayis is as abandoned as she was. The Doctor's intuition is sensitive enough that, later, as they lie in wait for the appearance of the Krafayis, he instinctively feels that "there's something not right. I can't quite put my finger on it." Amusingly, as Vincent paints

'The Church at Auvers', the Doctor perceives the passage of time from a very different perspective, a reminder of what he experienced as 'the slow path' with Madame de Pompadour in *The Girl in the Fireplace*, with "Is this how time normally passes? Really slowly. In the right order." The fact that he is progressing through his day in the right order also reflects the opposite state when he keeps meeting River Song in the wrong order. He also believes that technology will win the day, and that "Overconfidence, this [he pats the suitcase containing his godmother's present] and a small screwdriver" confirms that he's "absolutely sorted" to face the Krafayis and all it will take is to "find the right crosactic setting and stun him" with the sonic screwdriver. His claim that the "sonic never fails" is, in this case, erroneous and it takes Vincent, his easel and brute force to fatally wound the creature. The conclusion he makes is that "in future, I'm definitely just using this screwdriver for screwing in screws." Technology is also little help in communicating with the creature, even though he acknowledges that the TARDIS telepathic field is allowing it to understand him, and it takes the Doctor's physical approach and his appeal to the Krafayis to understand its side of the story, to temper its irrational behaviour. "I also know that no one's talked to you for a pretty long stretch but please... listen. I also don't belong on this planet. I also am alone. If you trust me I'm sure we can come to some sort of, you know, understanding," implies an olive branch from a fellow survivor and one who understands, like Vincent and, to an extent, Amy, the sorrows of loneliness.

When Amy casually ignores the Doctor's instructions not to follow him into the church, Vincent really admires her courage and declares, "I love you." His growing affection for her eventually results in a marriage proposal. The marriage proposal is a defining theme in all of Curtis's romantic comedies and he is unable to resist including one more here, extending the notion of the perils and pleasures of romantic courtship and the art of wooing that Nigel Mather describes in his critique of Curtis's films, *Tears of Laughter: Comedy-drama in 1990s British Cinema*, as "a comic and potentially tragic business (the object of one's affection may leave, die or fall in love with someone else) but [where] the attempt to seek... empathetic states with other characters will always be applauded." Significantly, when Vincent asks, after returning from the journey into the future, "You are sure, marriage is out of the question?"Amy adamantly reiterates her phobia to commitment, demonstrated in the first half of the series, as "Hmm, this time. I'm not really the marrying kind." The loss of Rory, his erasure from history, has also expunged her desire to settle down. Rory's name is inadvertently mentioned whilst they regroup during their encounter with the Krafayis and the Doctor suddenly realises that in the confusion he still thought Rory was by their side. "Right, here's the plan. Amy, Rory..." rallies the Doctor. "Who?" asks Amy and the Doctor hastily corrects himself, "Sorry... um... Vincent."

When the Doctor takes Vincent to the Musée d'Orsay of the future, with the proviso of "Now you know we've had quite a few chats about the possibility there might be more to life than normal people imagine?"

acknowledging Vincent's own ability to see beyond the limits of his own life and use his imaginative powers, it is also a trip that is predicated on a false premise. Both the Doctor and Amy know they are unable to affect his life and death, and so this indicates that the Doctor is also attempting to teach Amy a lesson about their relationship with time. Uncannily, the flaming fragments of the street posters pasted onto the TARDIS, still burning on the side of the time machine after their journey through the vortex, allude to the burnt shrapnel of the police box that the Doctor plucked from the crack in *Cold Blood* and prefigure the exploding TARDIS of *The Big Bang*. It is also not entirely clear if the Doctor fully realises that the trip in the TARDIS for Vincent may not necessarily be of benefit to such an unstable mind, with the contention here that the reaffirmation of his genius in the Musée d'Orsay only provides a temporary moment of lucidity before he plunges back into his manic-depressive state. Upon entering and exploring the dimensions of the TARDIS, itself a visual conundrum befitting Vincent's transcendental perception, the painter astutely acknowledges the precarious balance of the mind when faced with such a vision, "How come I'm the crazy one? And you two have stayed sane?" However, the sequence where Vincent visits the gallery full of his paintings and hears Dr Black's enthusiastic eulogy is extremely moving if rather over-sentimentalised. It is typical of Curtis's desire to provide a 'feel-good' conclusion and where, on the one hand, it effectively strips away the playful allusions to Van Gogh, his work as commodity and reproduction to concentrate on the man and his spectacular vision, on the other, it is hampered by the mawkish lyrics and elegiac pomp of Athlete's track 'Chances' that presumably the writer, director and producer felt adequately fulfilled their music's objective to manipulate the emotions of the audience. The scene is carried by the wonderful performances of Tony Curran and Bill Nighy and only needed a light touch in the use of music. Curran's achievement is his ability to convey a certain amount of Vincent's torment without it becoming too disturbing for a family audience. There is no doubt that a great deal of visual license is taken here and the Vincent we see is definitely a kinder representation of the desperately ill man that spent his final days in Auvers. He portrays the man's unhinged state more through subtle performance rather than through the typical visual and physical attributes that the likes of Kirk Douglas and Tim Roth provided in *Lust for Life* and *Vincent and Theo*. Perhaps the Vincent seen here lacks some of the dramatic edge of those performances but Curran should be rightly praised for what he manages to achieve. On this occasion, I unhappily concur with the Doctor about the treatment of this climactic scene in the episode, "Vincent? Sorry, I'm sorry. Is it too much?" and the BBC's public service announcement at the end of the episode, asking "if you've been affected by the issues raised in this programme" and offering a helpline, while clearly well meaning, sensitive and supportive to those with mental health issues, could easily be misconstrued as slightly patronising after such a heavy dose of sentimentality. The Musée d'Orsay scene stands out as one of the more moving sequences in the revival of the series and yet it seems both a generous and a cruel thing for the Doctor and Amy to show Vincent his future, with the Doctor knowing that tragedy will not be averted and Amy believing it can, before he walks into that wheat field and shoots himself. It is perhaps better to remember the more effective, philosophical conclusion where Amy and the Doctor return to Paris after leaving Vincent in 1890. Amy is triumphant and is certain that "Time can be rewritten, I know it can," echoing the Doctor's observations of temporal flux in *Flesh and Stone* and the proof that time can be changed as evidenced by the scene on the hillside in *Cold Blood*. The Doctor knows that Vincent's life is a fixed point in time and Amy's hopes that he lived longer and produced hundreds of new paintings will be dashed. Dr Black acknowledges that Van Gogh committed suicide as history stated and Amy angrily sees that the Doctor also knew this would be the outcome, "So you were right. No new paintings. We didn't make a difference at all." The Doctor elegantly sums up the situation for her, possibly out of his guilt over the loss of Rory, and for Vincent and his short life, "I wouldn't say that. The way I see it, every life is a pile of good things and bad things. The good things don't always soften the bad things. But vice versa, the bad things don't necessarily spoil the good things or make them unimportant. And we definitely added to his pile of good things." History then reveals, as the Doctor explains, "a couple of little changes" where the 'bad things' such as the Krafayis in the painting have been erased in favour of the 'good things', with one of the sunflower paintings now bearing a dedication to Amy. It seems a fitting conclusion to the episode's discourse, suggesting that if you look at something intensely enough you may see something that is beyond the normal range of perception. It suggests other dimensions and realms, both in the artist's mind and, as the Doctor and Amy discover, physically existing within the real world.

# Chapter Nine

# THE LODGER

Written by: Gareth Roberts
Directed by: Catherine Morshead
First broadcast: 12 June 2010

---

"Has anyone ever told you, you're a bit weird?"

When Russell T. Davies depicted the character of Vince Tyler as a gay man who also happened to be a *Doctor Who* fan, in his drama *Queer as Folk* (1999-2000), he was confirming what many in fandom were already widely aware of. As Vince, alone after a night on the town in Manchester, was seen watching episodes of the series, his overt familiarity with them signified in his recital of lines from the cliffhanger ending of the first episode of *Pyramids of Mars*, Davies celebrated the fact that a large proportion of *Doctor Who* fans, at the time, were gay, white and male. Paul Cornell, in *Licence Denied: Rumblings from the Doctor Who Underground*, concurred with this in his introduction to 'Interactive Bits' where he acknowledged that *Doctor Who* had a huge gay following, one it still continues to attract to this day. In 1997, he speculated that the series, and a proportion of its fandom, could be codified as 'queer' because of the theory that the series's appeal to gay men was founded on the principle that "the Doctor is the only hero who saves the universe but (until the *TV Movie*) shows no interest in 'getting the girl'." Further to this, he also merged this 'queering' of *Doctor Who* and its fanbase, as a reflection that "the Doctor's pacifist, anti-authoritarian approach also lends itself to adoption by any number of countercultural and minority groups," with what he noted as the series's reading as 'camp' as a significant factor in gay fans' appreciation. *Doctor Who* as 'camp' provokes a multiplicity of readings, perhaps very simplistically traced along the axes that David Bergman describes in *Camp Grounds: Style and Homosexuality*:

> "First, everyone agrees that camp is a style (whether of objects or the way objects are perceived is debated) that favours 'exaggeration', 'artifice' and 'extremity'. Second, camp exists in tension with popular culture, commercial culture or consumerist culture. Third, the person who can recognise camp, who sees things as campy, or who can camp, is outside the cultural mainstream. Fourth, camp is affiliated with homosexual culture, or at least with a self-conscious eroticism that throws into question the naturalization of desire."

Camp and queer are thus conflated inside *Doctor Who*, implicated in its settings and characters, styles and performances, and outside, detected by those who view it and deconstruct its meaning and values. This detection should also not be seen as an exclusively gay reading of the series. Camp and queer are democratic positions, taken by a much broader community of viewers in their appreciation of the series.

The character of Vince was also clearly an analogue of Davies himself, a gay writer also a life-long *Doctor Who* fan, a symbol of the queer and camp cognoscente producer and consumer, who came to prominence in fandom during the interregnum between the end of the original series and the revival in 2005. Through his authorship of one of Virgin Publishing's *Doctor Who* novels, *Damaged Goods* (itself a narrative depicting LGBT characters) and his association with speculative revivals of the show, Davies gained a reputation as a writer who would be interested in working on any future incarnation of the series. Indeed, the success of *Queer as Folk* and his increasing media profile as its creator initially coloured the reception of the news, in certain papers, that Davies had been appointed as showrunner and executive producer for the revival of the series in 2005. "Doctor Who Ready to Come Out of the TARDIS" was the insinuating headline from *The Daily Telegraph* of 27 September 2003 that categorically linked Davies's drama about young gay men in Manchester and the forthcoming series of *Doctor Who*. A number of fans were also concerned about Davies's appointment and were worried that the show would become overtly gay in theme. During the period of Davies's tenure as producer, a perceived bias towards same-sex themes and characters was regarded by certain fans as an insidious 'gay agenda' being introduced into the series by Davies. In the first series, the introduction of the omni-sexual Captain Jack character in *The Empty Child* certainly raised a few eyebrows, particularly when Jack is seen flirting and admitting to same-sex relationships with British officers in the story. Steven Moffat himself rather playfully commented on this in a *New York Times* profile of the series in March 2006, "You come across the occasional nutter who will talk about Russell's gay agenda – I imagine he keeps it in a pink folder in a special leopard-skin safe – but this is possibly the most heterosexual Doctor [referring to Christopher Eccleston] we've ever had. Clearly, Russell's gay agenda is to turn everyone straight." Moffat's well-intentioned argument was that Davies certainly had no intention of making the Doctor gay, but suggested that the fluid nature of gender and sexuality in the twenty-first century was being acknowledged by the series. A number of queer characters, many of whom, by implication, are codified as homosexual or bisexual, have been referenced in the series to date and Gareth Roberts, the writer of *The Lodger*, has also included such themes or characters in previous episodes of his own, *The Shakespeare Code* and *The Unicorn and the Wasp*. In the former he wittily makes reference to the many debates in academia about Shakespeare's sexuality after the character flirts with both Martha and the Doctor, at which point the Doctor exclaims, "Fifty-seven academics just punched the air," and in the latter he specifically highlights a closeted gay relationship between Roger Curbishley and a footman, Davenport.

In hindsight there are two points to be made here. Firstly, as Davies himself remarked, in *The Writer's Tale: The Final Chapter*, his work is authorially connected to his gender orientation, much in the same way that Roberts's work for the series could be appraised, but it should never be a reason to criticise him for poor writing:

> "... it doesn't bother me at all, the gay thing. A lot of writers would die for a label! I'm proud of it, I really am, which is lucky because I reckon it's going to stick... I suspect I'll be left with the epitaph of *Queer As Folk*. The thing is, I think I *am* a Gay Writer, when I write anything. Most crucially, I don't think it's ever affected my commissions. I'm not aware of anyone ever having said, 'He can't write that, because he's gay.' Well, it might have been thought, subtly and insidiously. When people write off my scripts as 'lightweight' I think that's bound up with their perception of my sexuality, even if they aren't conscious of that. But there's always someone who's going to say they don't like my writing because of this, that or the other. Equally they might say, 'Gay or straight, I think you're rubbish.' Fair enough."

From this we could conclude that Cornell's codifying of the queer appreciation of the series is now also contained as experiences within the authoring of episodes by specifically queer writers, themselves seen as fans of the series. Secondly, *Doctor Who* has arguably now become part of a continuum of queerly coded television drama that appeals, beyond the values that Cornell ascribes, to a dramatically wider, and demographically more diverse, audience than the original series ever did prior to the revival in 2005. While the series has grown and sustained its appeal with minority groups, it has also been applauded for reinstating 'family' prime-time viewing by regularly bringing parents and children together to watch. This is achieved even though the series can still be construed as subversive in the way that it deals with contemporary ideas, themes, ethics and moralities. Its appeal has significantly shifted from, what was perceived as, cult viewing to mass appreciation, reflecting, and even outstripping, its former ratings glory of the mid 1970s.

That shift also frames a deliberate alteration and flexibility in the series's codification of the Doctor. Prior to the return of the series, and despite the then fan taboo-busting scene of the Doctor kissing Grace Holloway at the conclusion of *Doctor Who – The TV Movie*, the Doctor was regarded as an asexual alien with little time for romantic or emotional relationships with his companions or other characters. Even when the Ninth Doctor made his debut, he was firmly seen as rejecting the 'domestic' and melodramatic, emotional inclinations introduced into the series with the characters of Rose, her mother Jackie and boyfriend Mickey Smith. Greater changes occurred when David Tennant took on the role in 2006 where the relationship between the Doctor and Rose changed and was projected as a doomed, romantic, highly emotional one, positioning them both as stereotypical star-crossed lovers. The series, contrary to the claims of a 'gay agenda' being foisted upon it, clearly showed a female companion in love with the Doctor. The Time Lord was ordered, whether deliberately or not, as an object of romantic, heteronormative desire, rather than the sexually ambiguous hero of the classic series. This was emphasised particularly in Moffat's own *The Girl in the Fireplace* with its depiction of the affair between the Doctor and Reinette, suggesting that Davies had confounded his doubters by carrying out, in part, what Moffat had, tongue in cheek, suggested, "to turn everyone straight" as an effect of the alleged 'gay agenda'. With the possibility of romantic love between the Doctor and his female companions having become a reality in the series, it is interesting to see how Moffat has taken that idea, and with the introduction of Matt Smith, proposes that the Eleventh Doctor returns to a more innocent, eccentric, sexually ambiguous state. Whilst this may be by dint of Smith's own approach to the role, it is a theme that Moffat highlights in a number of episodes in 2010. The most blatant example of this is in Amy's attempted seduction of him at the conclusion of *Flesh and Stone* which, although it caused some concern with viewers about Amy's morals and behaviour on the night before her wedding, demonstrates that the Doctor has no interest in 'getting the girl' on this occasion. We also see in *Amy's Choice* that the Doctor represses, and can do so at will according to the Dream Lord, his desire for Amy, which is still coded as heteronormative but is one that only she acts upon. As a development of these alterations, Gareth Roberts takes his episode *The Lodger* further into the realms of queerly stratified television drama, shifting the heteronormative subtext onto other characters in the story, extending the Doctor's own actions in bringing Amy and Rory closer together through his encounter with Craig and Sophie and again blurring the Doctor as the subject and object of desire for characters and audience alike.

Before we examine how *The Lodger* evidences its own 'queerness' it is perhaps best to start with what we mean by 'queer' and 'queer television' in this context. Looking back at Cornell's observations and Davies's emergence as a major creative force within television, we can see that both were caught up in the cultural debates about identity politics, specifically enshrined in gay and lesbian studies, of the 1980s and 1990s where the pejorative term 'queer' was reappropriated as, what Mo Meyer describes as, an "affirmative, self-nominated identity label" in *The Politics and Poetics of Camp*, that opposed the assimilationist and reductive categories of gay and lesbian. Queer theory emerged, as Samuel Chambers explains in *The Queer Politics of Television*, "in distinction to lesbian and gay studies' effort to affirm and sometimes reify what it often took as some sort of *given* – namely gay identity or sexual orientation," and he sees queer theory as "an impulse to question, problematise or even disclaim the very idea of a fixed abiding notion of identity." For Chambers, 'queer', in the sense we intend to use it here, can mean both 'odd' and 'gay' whilst also acknowledging that its combination of the two is founded upon the activist politics of the late 1980s. Michele Aaron, in 'Toward Queer Television Theory' in *Queer TV: Theories, Histories, Politics*, emphasises that queer "is not merely an umbrella term for all that is positively not straight, or narrow. It is an oppositional stance intimately bound to an anti-normative trajectory" that she sees emerging from AIDS activism of the aforementioned period. For our purposes, in analysing *The Lodger*, it is David Halperin, in *Saint Foucault: Towards a Gay Hagiography*, who best sums up what queer represents in this brief examination of the queerness of *Doctor Who*:

> "Unlike gay identity... [which] is rooted in the positive fact of homosexual object-choice, queer identity need not be grounded in any positive truth or any stable reality. As the very word implies, 'queer' does not name some natural kind or refer to some determinate object; it acquires its meaning from its oppositional relation to the norm. Queer is by definition whatever is at odds with the normal, the legitimate, the dominant. 'Queer', then, demarcates not a positivity but a positionality vis-a-vis the normative – a positionality that is not restricted to lesbians and gay men but is in fact available to anyone who is or feels marginalised because of his or her sexual practices."

To emphasise this distinction, and to position heteronormative desire itself within this definition, Gareth Roberts uses the word 'normal' ten times in his script, all within the first thirty minutes of the episode. He proposes 'normal' as the benchmark against which a series of characters are relatively positioned in the story and as a way of both disputing and reaffirming the queerness of the Doctor and the drive towards heteronormativity as represented by the couple Craig and Sophie. Roberts also plays with the construction of gender in the episode, subtly exploring queerness in the perceived homosexuality and homosocial bonding between the Doctor and Craig and in his depiction of society's current crisis of masculinity. It is a crisis that Judith Kegan Gardiner, in *Masculinity Studies & Feminist Theory*, believes is a result of "the drive to maintain patriarchal entitlement and a sign of many men's legitimate search for new forms of vulnerability, responsibility, intimacy and maturity." The word 'weird' is also regularly used throughout the episode, often in opposition to the use of the word 'normal' and their use signifies a queer fluidity and ambiguity about gender and desire in the story that Eve Kosofsky Sedgwick describes, in her 'Queer and Now' essay in *Tendencies*, as "the open mesh of possibilities, gaps, overlaps, dissonances and resonances, lapses and excesses of meaning when the constituent elements of anyone's gender, anyone's sexuality aren't made (or can't be made) to signify monolithically." However, it is not just the pitches of gender and sexuality, the spectrum from homosexual to heterosexual, that are queered here. As indicated later it is also a mode that can be used to analyse the episode's sound effects, use of time, and visual symbolism, including set design and architecture.

For the episode, Roberts adapts a comic strip story of the same name, published in *Doctor Who Magazine* in 2006, which depicts the Tenth Doctor and Mickey Smith sharing a flat. In the television version of *The Lodger*, the 'odd couple' relationship between the Doctor and Craig is formalised at the end of the pre-titles sequence. The sequence has already set up the various subplots: the TARDIS malfunctioning and disappearing without the Doctor on board; the interrupted romance between Craig and Sophie; the expanding damp patch on the ceiling; and the 'man upstairs' luring his victims into Flat 76b, Aikman Road. As all these crises reach a climax, Craig decides to declare his love for Sophie when he assumes she has returned to the flat for her keys. Roberts cleverly subverts Oscar Wilde's demand for homosexual acceptance, 'the love that dare not speak its name', as the claim of a heterosexual one that refuses to be uttered by two people so undeniably in love with one another. This unspoken love is also symbolised by the set of keys, complete with pink bear and pom-pom key ring, that feature prominently in the story as the fluffy pink love object that, for Craig, stands in for the absent Sophie. Craig, gazing intently at Sophie's picture on the fridge, hears the doorbell to the flat ring, rushes to the door, determined once and for all to tell her "I love you." What we see and hear is an overlapping of his desire, its excess of meaning, transposed onto the Doctor, who is now standing on the doorstep as Craig flings the door open and tells him, "I love you." Immediately, the episode offers an ambiguous, humorous meaning to the meeting between the men which the Doctor confidently accepts as perfectly logical and rational, "Well, that's good, cos I'm your new lodger. Do you know, this is going to be easier than I expected?" Pointedly, the Doctor takes the keys, Craig's love object, from him. Craig is rather suspicious of this strange man who declares himself as "less of a young professional and more of an ancient amateur. But, frankly I'm a dream." The Doctor is not only restating his personification of the duality between Peter Pan and Captain Hook in Barrie's novel, of the wisdom of an older man realised through a younger body, but he is also intimating he is a 'dream' lodger, a projection of Craig's wish fulfillment and longing to escape from the dull reality of "pizza, beer and telly." It is a wisdom that the Doctor will share with Craig and Sophie, a youthful zest for life that will rub off on them. Embarrassed that he has admitted his love to a strange man he argues, "I don't know if I want you staying. Give me back those keys, you can't have those." He takes repossession of the symbolic Sophie and the exchange prefigures several scenes in which Sophie, and her desire, is exchanged between the two men as the Doctor precipitates Craig's crisis of masculinity by playing football and doing his job better than he can. The Doctor's definition of himself as "less of a young professional and more of an ancient amateur" not only restates our previous analysis of the Doctor as Peter Pan but it also confirms, in the pairing of Craig and the Doctor, what David P. Munns, in 'Peter Pan and the Queering of Popular Culture' *Second Star to the Right:*

*Peter Pan in the Popular Imagination*, sees as a modern queering of Barrie's character where, "No longer free of all sexuality, *Peter Pan* now serves as a vehicle to discuss ideas of developing sexuality and even developing alternative sexualities. Pan and Hook are tightly intertwined like youth and age. Through popular gay media, we see Peter is as much Hook as Hook is Peter. Both are obsessed with growing old and dying and both characters demonstrate the cultural capital, and power, and eternal appeal of youth." Matt Smith, as the youngest actor cast in the role of the Doctor, certainly epitomises the "appeal of youth" and he appears to have great cachet with a gay, male audience, having appeared on the cover of *Gay Times* twice in one year, promoting both *Doctor Who* and the film *Christopher and His Kind* (2010), where he plays gay writer Christopher Isherwood.

At this stage, we as viewers are not aware of the backstory that has led to this meeting. The episode initially positions the Doctor as contra to societal norms by dint of his status as a nine-hundred-year-old alien, emphasised in his ignorance of the true value of money in a rampantly capitalist society. "Yes, quite right. Have some rent," he blithely says as he hands over a paper bag containing three thousand pounds. "Is it a lot? I can never tell," he mutters, barging into the flat. The Doctor's gender, sexual orientation and social skills are confused as he takes Craig by the shoulders and provides him with two air kisses and offers, "That's how we greet each other nowadays, isn't it?" Not exactly the conventional way that two men, nominatively heterosexual men it could be said, might greet each other, the Doctor further adds to the identity and gender confusion, the comic homoeroticism, with, "I'm the Doctor. Well, they call me the Doctor. I don't know why. I call me the Doctor too. Still don't know why." It supposes a fluidity of identity on the Doctor's part, a blurring of his essence, a reclaiming of the queerness of his mysterious name. Craig's bizarre and exotic encounter with the Doctor is presented in opposition to the alleged normalcy of 'the man upstairs' whom Craig describes as "Just some bloke. Normal, he's very quiet." As he says this there is a loud crash from upstairs and Craig qualifies this with "usually" and reminds us that the characters in the story have yet to discover what the audience already knows. The scene begins to formulate the normative versus the weird, the odd and the queer, with 'the man upstairs' regarded as someone who has established his pattern of living and social interaction as 'normal' in opposition to the Doctor's clearly unorthodox negotiations with social etiquette and masculine behaviour. Roberts uses the Doctor to interrogate simultaneously what we would perceive as being normal and how he interprets that normality by sharing the flat with Craig. The script further escalates the oscillation between these opposite positions in relation to Craig and Sophie's undeclared desire. The Doctor praises Craig's decor in a rather exaggerated way, "This is the most beautiful parlour I have ever seen, you're obviously a man of impeccable taste." It is yet one more performance of queer identity, of perhaps the Doctor's difference from the other 'straight' men that Craig has social contact with. It could also be

191

read, on the other hand, as an attempt by the Doctor at camp bitchiness, an ironic comment on how poor Craig's taste actually is and his lack of aesthetic awareness. He begs Craig to let him stay and when Craig points out that he has not yet seen the room that is available, the Doctor eagerly, delightedly, and rather provocatively, demands, "Take me to my room!" The Doctor's queer performance becomes an affect of the homosocial bonding between him and Craig, with the parlour and the bedroom defined as spaces where the spectrum of masculinities and sexualities they represent can have free reign and expression. The queerness in the story powerfully prescribes the flat as a site where "a variety of sexual identities can take shape" to usurp the "the sexual conservatism and inherent heteronormativity of suburbia" that Phil Hubbard describes in 'Between Trangression and Complicity (Or Can the Straight Guy Have a Queer Eye?)' in *Geographies of Sexualities*. Roberts continues to subvert the queer reading of the scenes in the flat when Craig and the Doctor go to look at the room. They hear another crash from 'the man upstairs' and the Doctor, clearly sensing that he must get on and begin his investigation, licks his finger and waves it in the air in front of Craig's face. It is a gesture, both provocative and comic, that reiterates the Doctor's eccentric penchant for analysing his environment through the senses: combinations of taste, touch, sight and smell, and contrasts the Doctor's queer, weird performance with the normal, domestic setting of a suburban flat. Innuendo can also be found in the Doctor's knowing acknowledgement of his references, where "Ah, you want to see my credentials?" comes across as sexual euphemism as well as a presentation of the symbols of normal, bona fide citizenship, an NHS number and National Insurance number, that are then destabilised by the reference from the Archbishop of Canterbury. An unusual reference to present, indicative of the Doctor's vanity for name-dropping, and one that the Doctor codifies rather strangely in his remark, "I'm his special favourite," followed by a finger to his lips to tell Craig that it must remain a secret between them.

The scenes in the flat continue to map out male sexuality and bonding primarily as reference to what the media has referred to in the last two decades as 'metrosexuality'. Both men do invite questions about their sexuality, even though Craig is clearly in love with Sophie, with the Doctor seizing the role of domesticated male, one he would normally have baulked at, and cooking for Craig while confirming the diagnosis of unrequited love between his flatmate and Sophie. When Craig responds to the Doctor's question ("Girlfriend?") about the photo of Sophie on the fridge with "Friend who's a girl. There's nothing going on," the Doctor emphasises the relationship that now exists between him and Amy. "Ah, that's completely normal. Works for me," he concludes and Roberts repositions the roles of the Doctor and his companion along the same, non-romantic, platonic lines that Moffat has been striving to reclaim since *Flesh and Stone* and ever since the introduction of Rory. For the Doctor it seems that "nothing going on" is now his normal state. Craig's sense of inadequacy as a man is also seen in his worries about work. The failure to get his solution to the company's problems heard and his claim, "I know what they should do. I got a plan all worked out but I'm just a phone drone. I can't go running in saying I know best," reflects the similar lack of imperatives in his love life. The theme of communication and miscommunication, shown between Craig and his boss, Sophie, the Doctor, Amy and with 'the man upstairs', is a major thread in the episode and Roberts ironically symbolises it all by having Craig and Sophie work at a call centre, victims lured into the house through a flat intercom, and Amy and the Doctor scrambling their conversation through his ear pod. After their meal, the Doctor and Craig sit in the flat chatting. The Doctor's queerness is emphasised in the description of his time-out-of-joint lifestyle, which has been a common theme highlighted in the current series, that forms his response to Craig's enquiry about where he acquired his culinary skills: "Paris. In the eighteenth century. No, hang on, that's not recent is it? Seventeeth? No, no, no. Twentieth. Sorry, I'm not used to doing them in the right order." The idea that the Doctor's life and identity is bent out of shape by time itself is another aspect of the queerness of Roberts's narrative and is one which Craig recognises, "Has anyone ever told you, you're a bit weird?" Again the normal and the weird are placed in binary opposition and even the Doctor acknowledges "they never really stop" telling him about how odd, how queer he really is. Craig simply accepts this with, "You're weird and you can cook, that's good enough for me," before he takes the Doctor aside to give him the keys to his room. He also offers that the Doctor only needs to let him know if he should ever want to bring someone round. "If you ever need me out of your hair, just give me a shout. OK?" he says, winking at the Doctor. The Doctor winks in return, presuming that this is normal, manly banter and behaviour, but then asks, "Why would I want that?" Craig codifies the Doctor with his reply, assuming that the Doctor perhaps swings both ways, his supposition of the Doctor's sexual orientation now blurred, with "In case you want to bring someone round... a girlfriend or [he stops and looks the Doctor up and down] a boyfriend?" The Doctor also misunderstands Craig's idea of 'giving him a shout' as literally an instance of yelling at him across the room when this scenario should potentially arise.

The Doctor's efforts to blend in, to act in what he sees as a normal fashion, are revealed to be a means to an end, a way of discovering what 'the man upstairs' is up to and why he is able to prevent the TARDIS from landing, from performing its own normal functions. For him, "It is vital that this man upstairs doesn't realise who and what I am," just as much as Craig and Sophie should never actually know who or what he is. Normality is for him a form of drag, something he must wear temporarily, where his objective is to 'pass' in heteronormative cultural systems. All he has "got to do is pass as an ordinary human being. Simple." However, he can never quite achieve this and his 'weird' behaviour is sustained even in the performance of what we would see as a heteronormative daily life. "C'mon Amy. I'm a normal bloke, tell me what normal blokes do," he asks, clearly out of his depth, his bravado telling us he is not a normal bloke and never can be. She suggests that he ditch the bow tie, the symbol that actually defines his queerness for her, while he repeats again that "bow ties are cool." When she offers a litany of stereotypical male behaviour for him to enact, "They watch telly, they play football and they go down the pub," he is challenged to perform these, to create them anew. Even though he spent some formative years in exile on Earth, he seems to have forgotten how to do these things. Even when gelling his hair, wearing sunglasses indoors, playing football, taking a shower, having a quiet drink in with Craig and Sophie, he is performing a version of normality that he believes will be authentic enough, As he does so he subtly deconstructs each of them to emphasise his unpredictable, odd and queer behaviour to us and vice versa. Layered on top of this are extremes of performance, including his late-night sojourn with the shopping cart, the construction of the bric-a-brac scanning device and the recruitment of, and psychic connection with, a cat.

Another interesting aspect of this non-essentialist performance is the way that the episode presents the Doctor's body as spectacle, an object of desire appealing to the complete spectrum that defines men, women, straight, gay and queer. Roberts knowingly takes his cues from recognisable sources in the scene where the Doctor is seen taking a shower. We very rarely see the Doctor indulging in such a private moment and, as he showers, we hear a rendition of what sounds like 'La donna e mobile' from Verdi's *Rigoletto*, and ironically one that describes the inconstancy of women that perhaps mirrors Sophie's indecisiveness and Amy's banishment to the TARDIS, that then comically blends into a version of the vaudeville classic 'Ta-ra-ra Boom-de-ay'. This recalls several similar scenes in which the newly regenerated Third Doctor also takes time out to have a shower in *Spearhead from Space* and later where he also sings the same Verdi aria in *Inferno*. When the Doctor becomes concerned about Craig's decision to try and find out why 'the man upstairs' is causing a disturbance, he falls out of the shower after trying to hold on to the curtain. As much a parody of Hitchcock's infamous 'shower scene' in *Psycho* (1960), a film about which there will be more discussion when we look at the depiction of the flat in this chapter, it is also, as Caroline Evans and Lorraine Gamman suggest in 'Reviewing Queer Viewing' in *Queer Cinema: The Film Reader*, the spectacle of the male body as a voyeuristic, polysemic image that can "make many forms of address to more than one audience and allow the possibility of multiple identifications by the spectator." This is also true of Craig and Sophie's reaction to the Doctor's half-dressed body. Initially, the Doctor's nakedness is codified, along with his Stan Laurel shock of hair and his defence of Craig with a toothbrush rather than his sonic screwdriver, as odd and comic. When the Doctor asks him about 'the man upstairs' and enquires, "You spoke to the man upstairs? What did he look like?" Craig gazes at the Doctor and laughs, "More normal than you do at the moment, mate." He clearly finds the Doctor's appearance amusing and non-threatening whereas, after Sophie has met him, half naked, on the stairs and he has greeted her with another double air kiss, she admits to Craig, out of the Doctor's earshot, "You didn't tell me he was gorgeous." In the kitchen, after Craig has persuaded the Doctor to come and play football and complete their squad for the league, providing the episode with yet another symbol of their homosocial bonding, Craig strokes the Doctor's face and adds, "You saved my life." This acknowledges the mock defence on the stairs with the toothbrush and the completion of the football team, and it prefigures both the Doctor nursing him to health after contact with the poisonous damp patch and the climactic scene at the end of the episode. The Doctor also copies Craig's act of physical contact, gently stroking the man's face. Again, this is all emblematic of the episode's need to demonstrate the fluidity of the Doctor's gender and to an extent how his body is the centre of various gender-specific gazes and actions.

Caroline Evans and Lorraine Gamman also argue that the heterosexual subject position, which the Doctor is attempting to emulate within the episode, is equally as queer, "as fluid in terms of gender identifications as homosexual or lesbian subjectivities... and recognises we too might be queer, if not personally then theoretically... that all sexuality is a construct and sexual categories and definitions impinge on us all." The Doctor agrees with the idea that "blokes play football" because Amy holds it up as the normal activity for the male role he intends to perform. However, he has an expectation and assumption that Sophie plays the sport too when he asks "Do you play, Sophie?" He can see beyond the stereotypes that inform his performance, perhaps as a consequence of his innocence of the complexities of human subcultures and socialisation. The Doctor, and his 'fish out of water' position, in relation to heteronormative human society, resembles the equally bemused efforts at assimilation made by Jeremy Paul's character Dominick Hyde in *Play for Today*'s witty and subversive science fiction drama *The Flipside of Dominick Hyde* (1980). Hyde, a traveller from the future of 2130, similarly explored the social and sexual mores of his own ancestors on the Earth of 1980. The Doctor might accept that normal blokes play football but his own match etiquette once again positions him contrary to that expectation. Amy's delight that the Doctor's attempt at assimilation now includes football as a mark of being 'normal' is then confounded by his impression that the game "is the one with sticks." His habit of greeting men with double air kisses continues unabated when Craig introduces him to the rest of the all-male team. The Doctor's grasp of the game implies he sees it as an activity that can be played multi-dimensionally. "Where are you strongest?" asks Sean. "Arms," replies the Doctor. Craig corrects him with, "No, he means, what position? On the field?" This underlines the Doctor's perception of the rules of the game and the episode's agenda of showing the Doctor attempting a performance of the normal, of what he thinks is the correct human behaviour. It is a performance, a 'passing' for normal, that Judith Butler sees as an element of drag in her essay 'From Interiority to Gender Performatives' in Fabio Cleto's *Camp: Queer Aesthetics and the Performing Subject*, where the Doctor's gender performance "reveals the imitative structure of gender itself." His negotiations with other men and women such as Sean, Craig and Sophie – symbolised in his evolving "The front, the side? Below?" positions as a football player – describe "a fluidity of identities that suggests an openness to resignification and recontextualization." The Doctor's 'performance' here is also given an extra layer with the visual wit of the number eleven shirt he dons for the game and the knowledge that Matt Smith's intention was to become a professional footballer before a back injury initiated his acting career. The game itself is a conflict of emotions for Craig and Sophie with the Doctor's natural aptitude relegating Craig to the sidelines, in much the same way that Sophie is sidelined as a mascot, fuelling his feelings of inadequacy as a virile man and exposing him as a failure in front of the woman he desires. The Doctor claims all the glory, shows off his quickly acquired skills and is rewarded with the physical pleasures of homosocial bonding with his team mates. His cry of "I love this game," after he scores several goals, proposes that not only is he enjoying the football but that he is also finding satisfaction in his game of passing as human and normal. Sophie clearly sees Craig is jealous of the Doctor's success and makes a point of encouraging him, taking on the role of mascot that earlier they both denied that she represented. Director Catherine Morshead isolates Craig visually, he is seen alone on the field, disappointed and deflated as the crowd cheer on the Doctor and his team gather round the new man in his life. There is a lovely moment where, at the end of the game, Sean discusses tactics for the next game, threatening to annihilate the next team they play against. The Doctor slips out of his role as Craig's flatmate and back into his identity as a Time Lord that fights evil in all the dark corners of the universe: "Annihilate? No, no violence, understand me? Not while I'm around. Not today, not ever. I'm the Doctor. The Oncoming Storm. And you basically meant beat them in a football match, didn't you?" This moment occurs just as 'the man upstairs' claims another victim. The shape of linear time and the flight of the TARDIS are queerly disrupted again and the Doctor's own shifting between roles distorts his apparent normalcy in front of the other players. The time loop repeats the actions of the group, witnessed by the Doctor in isolation, and emphasises their everyday modes of performance, their normality that includes laughter, cheering and the opening of beer.

The repetitious nature of the modes of normality, found in the mores of everyday human socialisation, are summarised by Sophie in her conversation with the Doctor. He plays 'gooseberry' again to a heteronormative couple, as he did in Amy's connections to Rory and Vincent van Gogh. She only sees the "work, weekend, work, weekend" rut of a normal life whereas the Doctor sees a much bigger picture of how you relate to the rest of the world. Yet, even as he uses cruelty as a form of kindness to motivate her, his queer, almost childlike behaviour comes to the fore when he takes a gulp of wine and then immediately spits it back into his glass. When the Doctor activates the scanner in his bedroom and relates the readings to Amy, the diagnosis of "too normal" contextualises what the Doctor and the 'the man upstairs' represent, where both of their attempts at assimilation actually highlight how abnormal, weird or queer they both are. As Amy, in exasperation of the scanner's results and the Doctor's frustration, remarks, "Only for you could too normal be a problem." For Craig, the Doctor's aberrant behaviour reaches a crisis point. The Doctor supplants him in a planning meeting when Craig is poisoned after touching the damp patch on the ceiling. His boss is full of praise for the Doctor's handling of the meeting and his interaction with Craig's difficult customers, "Leave off the Doctor. I love the Doctor. He was brilliant at the planning meeting." Again, this demeans Craig as a man incapable of handling his own work/life balance and, despite the Doctor's very tender ministrations in helping him recover from the poisoning, he decides that the "too normal" Doctor has to go, especially in light of Sophie's decision to follow her aspirations to work with animals. The Doctor's conversation with a cat, the feline recruited to spy on 'the man upstairs' and now reporting back to him, distresses Craig further. The Doctor, assured he has been the epitome of the average man, wonders why Craig is throwing him out. "For a start, talking to a cat. Everybody loves you and you're better at football than me, and my job, and now Sophie's all 'Oooh, monkeys, monkeys!' and then... there's that," Craig yells as he opens the door to the Doctor's room and reveals the bric-a-brac scanner. Amusingly, Roberts has the Doctor defend it as a piece of modern art, with its ironic title reflecting the domestic crises he has landed himself in, "It's art! A statement on modern society. 'Oh, ain't modern society awful!'" Craig sums up his experience of living with the Doctor with, "You've only been here three days. The three weirdest days of my life," which succinctly casts doubt on the Doctor's ability to pass as normal. "Your days will get a lot weirder if I go," counters the Doctor, raising the spectre of the unfinished business with that other impersonator, 'the man upstairs'. It is only by a literal knocking of heads, where the Doctor headbutts Craig, that any sense can be made of the situation. Craig immediately discovers the true identity of the Doctor, provided in another flashback of previous incarnations, monsters and companions, and with a second blow the Doctor apprises him of the situation where the Doctor found Craig's advert for the flat share, Amy is trapped in the TARDIS and he is here to prevent 'the man upstairs' from piloting his time ship. James Corden's reactions in this scene are superbly judged and highly amusing, with the character accepting all the weirdness of the situation immediately now that he can see the Doctor's point of view and even understanding the scanner as an oddity of "the non-technological technology of Lammasteen." The reveal of the Doctor's true identity and origin is the effective outcome of direct, if somewhat violent, communication, similar to the way the Doctor used his abrasiveness and bluntness, in earlier scenes, to shock Craig and then Sophie out of their complacency.

The 'weird' and the 'normal' are better balanced by the conclusion of the episode. Sophie and Craig have found each other, the Doctor no longer needs to pass as normal, 'the man upstairs' is discovered to be nothing of the sort and is neutralised and Amy is no longer trapped in the TARDIS as the victim of the queer effects of time.

In exploring the queer role of the Doctor in relation to the heteronormative metrosexuality of Craig and Sophie, the episode provides a conclusion that falls between two stools of analysis. On the one hand, the Doctor's queerness, his operating outside of normality, functions in bringing Craig and Sophie together, particularly to facilitate the heteronormative aspiration for reproduction and childbearing that the Doctor suggests with, "Now then, 6,000,400,026 people in the world. That's the number to beat." Lee Edelman, in *No Future: Queer Theory and the Death Drive*, sees queerness "positioned and defined as its separation from reproduction... working against the ideological role that reproduction occupies as a familial and heterosexual discourse." Yet the Doctor's queer function and their happy reception of it, as suggested in Craig's symbolic gift of the keys to the flat before he departs, is a position in the story, as Judith Butler suggests, where "gender reality is created through sustained social performances" with the effect of "proliferating gender configurations outside the restricting frames of masculinist domination and compulsory heterosexuality." We see these "sustained social performances" between the men and women in the story, as part of the fabric of their everyday work and leisure pursuits. Edelman's strict binary opposition between queerness and heterosexual reproductive ideology does not take into account that much of the Doctor's queerness, used in an attempt to mimic male heterosexual performance here, haunts his own origins and reproductive potential, where we are aware of an oft-mentioned 'family' and Susan as his 'granddaughter', and the true nature of Time Lord reproduction and the Gallifreyan concept of family are in flux and do not easily conform to such an ideology.

## "What is he doing up there?"

76 Aikman Road is a very queer house indeed. As we discussed earlier, *The Lodger* expresses a queer sensibility throughout in the way that the Doctor performs as 'normal' in relation to the ordinary, everyday lives of Craig and Sophie. However, there is another occupant of the building who figures prominently in the story and sustains the queerness that Roberts brings into the script. 'The man upstairs' is initially proposed to us as "just a bloke" and as normal as anyone else living in the house. The audience however are privy to the various abductions and murders that 'the man upstairs' commits. His identity, qualified as male in the first such sequence, suggestive of sinister sexual connotations when it appears that an older man lures a young teenage boy into the house, eventually shifts through various genders and ages. 'He' lures several women into the house on the proviso that a child is looking for her mother or needs an adult to help because there has been an accident. It is the appeal from a little girl that eventually draws Sophie upstairs and precipitates the climactic revelation that the very structure of the upper storey of the

house is as weird as its occupant. The blurring of identity and gender used by 'the man upstairs' again denotes a form a drag, of impersonation and simulation, in order to 'pass' and acquire the victims of its murderous impulses. Caryl Flynn, in 'The Deaths of Camp' in *Camp: Queer Aesthetics and the Performing Subject*, sees these impersonations as a form of camp that attempts "to take the signs of human identity and place them into a performative situation, distancing them from their 'original' sites, or indeed, the notion of an original or natural condition at all." The idea that the people we see at the top of the stairs have no "original or natural condition at all" is confirmed when the Doctor confronts 'the man upstairs' and discovers that 'he' is the emergency crash program of the time engine ("someone's attempt to build a TARDIS") that now constitutes an equally non-natural, queerly dimensioned, upper floor of the house. The program is a figure partly analogous to the Doctor in the way that they both have to perform as artificial selves in order to complete their functions. For the Doctor it is to prevent the TARDIS from spinning off into the vortex and for 'the man upstairs' it is a quest to find a pilot to launch the time ship. Even when the Doctor approaches the program to fathom its intent, he is required to perform as "Captain Troy Handsome of International Rescue," a brief nod to *Thunderbirds* (1965-6), to elicit the correct response.

The interior of the house, including the staircase and the room containing the time engine on the second floor, also suggests a queer architecture in the story. This 'queer' space is accompanied by a sense that time is also behaving oddly, queerly folding back on itself, disturbing the modes of natural behaviour. Linear, normal time and space are bent completely out of shape in *The Lodger* and symbolically match the way that characters are misshaped too, where everyone, from the Doctor, Craig and Sophie to Amy in the TARDIS, are at the mercy of the architecture of the house and the freefalling fluctuations in linear time that occur whenever the emergency program attempts to find its pilot for the ship. It can only use a person to pilot the ship who desires to leave the normality around them. We can only use conjecture to understand the reasons why the young man and the women it brings into the house wish to break free of their normal lives, but when Sophie is encouraged by the Doctor to leave and take a voluntary position with an animal sanctuary, this is clearly the catalyst for the program to try and use her as a pilot. It wants people who aspire to look beyond their ordinary lives, who perhaps want to exist in a mode of queerness that Judith Halberstam describes as, "alternative temporalities [where] their futures can be imagined according to a logics that lie outside of those paradigmatic markets of life experience – namely birth, marriage, reproduction and death," in *In a Queer Time and Place: Transgender Bodies, Subcultural Lives*. The Doctor's codification as a queer hero is understood when we see that he too exists outside of the norms of human experience where his role as asexual outsider and wanderer continues to mark out his appeal to queer audiences. Halberstam also sees lives led in the queer subculture as distinctly separate from sexual identity and the episode seems to reflect the way "queer uses of time and space develop... according to other logics of location, movement... as a result of strange temporalities, imaginative life schedules and eccentric economic practices." What then are Amy and Rory's journeys in the TARDIS with the Doctor other than an attempt to avoid the "work, weekend, work, weekend" schedule that Sophie dreads? By bringing Sophie and Craig together and making them realise that they can achieve this without the benefit of mad adventures in time and space, the Doctor offers them a way out of "quotidian temporality."

The TARDIS and the time engine allude to each other in the story. Both are fantastic, multi-dimensional architectures existing in another dimension, therefore operating outside of linear time and space. In this story, both have 'crashed', with the TARDIS spinning out of control through the vortex and the time engine grounded above Craig's flat. Amy is attempting to pilot the former while the emergency program of the latter slaughters innocent people in its search for a suitable crewmember. Their operations affect the normal flow of time in the lives of Craig and Sophie. Whenever the time engine burns up another human being it throws the TARDIS off course, creating these disturbances in time. Their malfunctions are accompanied by queer noises both where the signature sounds of the TARDIS in flight are so aurally dissonant that the Doctor describes them to Amy as "Ooh, nasty" and the emergency program's burning up of potential pilots fills the house with crashing and exploding noises that prompt Craig and Sophie to gaze at the ceiling and ask, "What is he doing up there?" These noises signify something odd and abnormal that is then underlined by visual flourishes in the house, itself a space full of Gothic atmosphere, including the flickering lighting at the top of the stairs and from behind the door where 'the man upstairs' lives, the gloomy staircase and the very odd portraits on the walls. In the TARDIS, the fluctuating lighting of its interior is punctuated by explosions and turbulence, its instability emphasised by director Catherine Morshead's pitching camera moves. Last of all, both time machines require piloting and navigating. The localised time distortions, created each time a victim is used by the time engine to attempt a launch, continue to frustrate the TARDIS's attempts to materialise. "Whatever's stopping her is upstairs in that flat. Go upstairs and sort it!" yells Amy, as the Doctor declares that, "Anything that could stop the TARDIS landing is big, scary big." To combat the effects of the fluctuations, the Doctor instructs Amy to use the 'zig-zag plotter'. The device obviously functions to plot these random courses through space and time, delivering an abnormal trajectory to avoid the time distortions, following a queer geography that only the Doctor can plot into the machine in a specific way. Note how he gives her very detailed and idiosyncratic operating instructions for the zig-zag plotter that entail standing in a particular way at the console, operating certain controls in an unorthodox manner. One of the biggest zig-zags in the story's depiction of time is related to us in the flashback that we see when the Doctor knocks Craig on the head to impart the "specific detail" of the situation to him. During the flashback we see a postcard, written by Amy, telling the Doctor which flat share ad to look at in the paper shop window. However, the Doctor brandishes the card after Craig confirms that he put the ad in the window and adds, "Yes, with this right above it. Which is odd because Amy hasn't written it yet. Time travel, it *can* happen." Not only does this convince Craig that what the Doctor has revealed to him is true, but it also foreshadows all the predestination time paradoxes of the following story in *The Pandorica Opens* and *The Big Bang* and builds on the theme of time being erased and rewritten in the series. At the end of *The Lodger*, the Doctor states that he and Amy need to go back in time in order for her to "go to the paper shop and leave that note for me," thus clarifying that what we have just watched was the effect of this cause. Time becomes queer again, a zig-zag that folds back on itself and places the Doctor and Amy outside of the linear temporal progression of the narrative. Worryingly, this also alerts us to the fact that if the Doctor is now so aware of specific events, of his role in them and can jump into them at any point to effect new causes, dramatic tension is potentially at risk in such stories. This is something that comes back to haunt the series in Steven Moffat's finale.

In Craig's flat the effects of this disturbance are realised in the ever-growing damp patch on the ceiling. The damp patch is a sign that the rest of the house, quite different in atmosphere and tone and representative of the illusion created by the time ship, is invading Craig's light and airy bachelor pad and that something odd and threatening is encroaching on the normal space that he occupies. "Ah, I suppose that's... dry rot," observes the Doctor of the ceiling bearing the mark of the victims' remains after their encounter with 'the man upstairs'. Perhaps the rut that Craig and Sophie are in, a relationship that never seems to get started and where life is dominated by work, is also the rot on the ceiling where its increasing size signifies the distance they have to overcome. The Doctor however can spot something rotten straight away. His claim of, "I'll fix it. I'm good at fixing rot," notifies us that he has taken on the role of Craig's flatmate in order to investigate the strange goings-on in the house. He has detected the abnormalities at the heart of the domestic scene, literally and symbolically. This form of housekeeping, and Craig's own offer of "I'll get someone to fix it," is, as Jack Morgan in *The Biology of Horror: Gothic Literature and Film* emphasises, "a primal imperative, part of our warding off of abjection – of decay, rot, squalidness." The corruption of Craig's modern flat, its invasion by the poison leeching in from 'the man upstairs', is "very much in the Gothic tradition, the environment as counterpart to human life," where the rot may not just represent the menace upstairs but also the anxieties between Craig and Sophie, particularly after the Doctor arrives and begins to undermine Craig's confidence. Morgan sees such corruption as a force setting out to "subvert human vitality, aesthetic sense, or civic-cultural order."

The queer architecture of the house, and the title of the episode *The Lodger*, alludes to the cinema of director Alfred Hitchcock in specific ways. In *The Wrong House: the Architecture of Alfred Hitchcock*, Steven Jacobs proposes that "specific architectural motifs such as stairs and windows are closely connected to Hitchcockian narrative structures, such as suspense, or typical Hitchcock themes, such as voyeurism." In *The Lodger*, director Morshead emphasises the gloomy staircase and its flickering light, using low camera angles to contrast small human figures against what looks like a vast staircase. The staircase bears a great resemblance to the one in the Bates mansion seen in *Psycho* (1960) and Morshead's visual style resembles the film's "twisted dolly shots... used for narrative purposes [that] also function as visual extensions of Norman Bates' trapdoor spider view of life." When Amy declares to the Doctor, after finding the architectural plans of the building in the TARDIS data banks, that "you cannot be upstairs, it's a one storey building. There is no upstairs!" Morshead punctuates this with a very low shot from the bottom of the stairs, gently pulling back from the much smaller figures of Craig and the Doctor. Jacobs notes that as "dynamically and spatially fragmented structures, staircases are often places of crisis and their perspectival effects seem to isolate and confine characters. Furthermore in Hitchcock's films, staircases lead to trouble since they accompany the cognitive hubris of the characters. Inquisitiveness drives characters upstairs or downstairs." The repetition of Gothic visuals, such as the figure behind the closed door that greets Craig or those that meet various victims in silhouette on the stairs beneath the flickering light bulb, are also connected to Hitchcock where "the motif of the closed door... relates to the theme of a secret hidden within the house... activating a dialectic of concealing and revealing" that can be found in *Rebecca* (1940), *Spellbound* (1945), *Notorious* (1946), *Strangers on a Train* (1951), *Dial M for Murder* (1954), *Psycho* and *The Birds* (1963). Hitchcock was also fond of using keys symbolically in conjunction with doors and *The Lodger* reflects this. The fluffy pink keyring attached to Sophie's keys become a fetishised object for Craig and they are the first clue that the Doctor is given about their relationship. In the climactic moment when the Doctor and Craig rush upstairs to finally uncover what has been going on, Morshead uses a very Hitchcockian cutaway from Craig to his viewpoint of Sophie's keys hanging from the flat door, signalling to him that it is Sophie's intrusion upstairs that has caused the recent noises and time disturbances and that she is now in danger. Finally, we discover that not only is there no upper storey to the house but that its presence is the effect of a perception filter, altering memories and disguising the transdimensional interior of the time engine, which bears a striking resemblance to Richard Hudolin's design for the TARDIS console room featured in *Doctor Who – The TV Movie*. Once more, the series uses motifs of invisibility, disguise and perceiving the truth that we have seen accompanying similar uses of perception filters in *The Eleventh Hour* and *The Vampires of Venice*.

"Oh, monkeys, monkeys!"

*The Lodger* returns the series to the familiar domestic settings of contemporary Earth and harks back to the discourse of melodrama that was such a prominent feature of the Russell T. Davies era. Essentially a 'love story', *The Lodger* also explores the contemporary burdens upon masculinity and the crisis of male identity from an essentialist point of view, one that presumes that there was, and still exists, a relatively stable masculine 'essence' that defines men and distinguishes them from women. As we have discussed, this essentialism is subverted by Roberts's script and the fluidity of gender roles and sexual identity add interesting dimensions to the depiction of Craig as the metrosexual 'caring' man struggling with his sense of self-esteem and a severe case of unrequited love. The central relationship between Craig and Sophie, and their own crisis of commitment is framed in their first conversation. "That's your mission in life, Craig – find me a man!" demands Sophie after Craig tells her about advertising for a flatmate. The double meaning here is of course that they eventually find the Doctor, the man who will fix things for them, and that the man she is looking for is under her very nose. Craig mockingly adds, "Yeah, otherwise you'll have to settle for me," and Sophie bashfully concludes, "You'll have to settle for me first." This outlines the inevitable trajectory of the romantic drama and the interruptions to it. When Sophie has to cancel their "pizza, booze, telly" evening (clearly the social ritual from which the relationship has developed) after other external disputes erupt ("a Dylan crisis on top of a Clare crisis" that her friend Melina drags her into), as a result we see the pair of them reluctant to dip their toes in the choppy waters of the urban, metrosexual, and often dysfunctional, roundelay that surrounds them.

A reluctance and fear to commit to each other is a running theme in the episode, informed by the traditional tropes of male behaviour where Roberts uses the differences between the Doctor and Craig to deconstruct some of the masculinities on display and the wider questions of change and continuity in contemporary identities. Craig, too reluctant to share his feelings with her, increasingly feels his chance has simply gone. The Doctor has already demonstrated that he is better at being a man and, crucially, has opened Sophie's eyes to wider horizons and an escape from her suburban rut. Much of this is also concerned with communication, the inability of Craig and Sophie to say what they mean and tear down the closet that surrounds their desires, hopes and dreams. When Sophie leaves and Craig rehearses his proposal to her and as the Doctor cooks for Craig, the camera lingers over images of the couple tacked to the fridge, next to fridge magnets of monkeys and plastic letters that spell out 'Craig Rocks' (there is also a neat bit of continuity with a postcard displayed for the Van Gogh exhibition featured in *Vincent and the Doctor*). The fridge door initially tells us (and the Doctor) more about their ideals than they do – Craig wants affirmation from Sophie and his boss; Sophie wants to work with animals. They are telling each other the things they want known but in a very subliminal way. The omelette the Doctor cooks not only shows off his culinary skills, an instinctual ability to throw basic food stuffs in a pan and produce something good to eat, but it also symbolises the need to 'break a few eggs' in order to knock down the walls preventing any kind of physical and spiritual compatibility between the couple. The Doctor, in contrast, has no concept of sparing anyone's feelings and, after their meal when he reveals that he learnt to cook in Paris, he asks if Craig has ever been there. "Nah, I can't see the point of Paris. I'm not much of a traveller," he confides (by the end of the episode this will have reversed, after his declaration of love to Sophie, to "I could see the point of Paris if you were there with me"). The Doctor cuts to the chase and damns him with, "I can tell from your sofa. You're starting to look like it," suggesting that in fact Craig has such little confidence in himself, in his desire for Sophie and in finding the will to live his life and see the world, that he is disappearing, merging into the background. The motif of Sophie's keys with their pink, fluffy key ring is repeated here as the Doctor notices how vigorously Craig is stroking them. "No, I like it here. I'd miss it. I'd miss..." argues Craig, and what he fails to say is 'Sophie' at the end of that admission. "Those keys. You're sort of... fondling them," observes the Doctor. Craig sublimates his desire for Sophie, acting out by proxy the physical intimacy he would like to be capable of having with her. There are other moments where, through confused or double meanings, both Craig and Sophie deliberately erase any suggestion that they are a couple seeking romantic love. When Craig describes Sophie as his mascot and says that "she just stands on the sidelines" as he recruits the Doctor for the football match, he both validates her presence but also places her firmly to one side, not wishing to admit that they have feelings for each other. He also denies her the potential to actually play in the football game rather than simply observe it. Craig is a little uncomfortable but continues to reveal more, "It's a football match. I can't take a date." This suggests a very narrow view of what is permissible in the all-male world of the amateur football league. It is obviously a space only for male homosocial bonding and women do not enter into that sphere, either as dates or players. "I didn't say I was your date," adds Sophie. They confirm their mutual denial of all inferences in this exchange as Craig finishes with "Neither did I." The Doctor, meanwhile, has been observing this, his eyes darting back and forth between them, waiting expectantly for one of them to openly admit their feelings. It seems very obvious to him as a rational observer that their irrationality is symptomatic of their unspoken love. He summarises the whole situation by keenly observing that Sophie possesses two sets of keys to the flat. "You've got two sets of keys to someone else's house?" he asks. "Yeah," she qualifies, not quite comfortable with where this line of questioning is going. He immediately conflates Craig's reluctance to explore the world with her ownership of the keys. "You must like it here too." This slippage and obfuscation of meanings in conversations reflects the long-distance communication between Amy, now apparently stranded in the TARDIS, and the Doctor, happily blending in with his flat share.

The Doctor, on a mission to discover what prevented the TARDIS from landing, has pinpointed the cause to 76 Aikman Road. As Craig and Sophie talk on their mobiles, with Craig believing the Doctor to be "a bit weird. Good weird, y'know" and Sophie concerned that 'the Doctor' is just his just his drug-dealer name, Amy relates the problems of the TARDIS to the Doctor via an earpiece com-link. Their conversation is also scrambled into gibberish in an ironic form of the miscommunication or the failure to communicate that Craig and Sophie endure. To impart your true feelings or to just get your message across is all part of the episode's queering of space and time.

Craig's initial discomfort with the Doctor's arrival switches to a sense of defeat when the Doctor goes on to demonstrate that he is better at the things Craig does – the things that define him as a man. The Doctor might be weird and wear a bow tie but in the end Craig is left feeling inadequate as the Doctor discovers his abilities as a footballer, working for Craig's company and, finally, as another man who can seemingly relate to women with openness and honesty, convincing Sophie of her potential. Craig decides to stay in with Sophie for "pizza, booze, telly" and almost plucks up the courage to finally suggest they should get together. The Doctor, playing the 'gooseberry', intervenes and Sophie begins to pour her heart out to him as he constructs the scanner. "Cos life can seem pointless, Doctor. Work, weekend, work, weekend. And there's six billion people on the planet doing pretty much the same," she observes. His task, described as "reconnecting all the electrics," on the one hand is to build the scanner in his bedroom to detect what 'the man upstairs' is attempting to do, and on the other is about reconnecting Sophie to her aspirations in life, bringing her together with Craig in the process. It reflects his efforts to reunite Amy and Rory in *The Vampires of Venice*. "It's a real mess," he states, fiddling with a mountain of wires, cleverly getting Sophie to understand that she has failed to live up to her potential. The Doctor goes for the jugular and is clearly exasperated at the way human beings conduct themselves: "Six billion people. Watching you two at work I'm starting to wonder where they all come from." Sophie is rather taken aback but he asks her what it is she really wants out of life. "I want to work looking after animals. Maybe abroad. I saw this orangutan sanctuary on telly," she admits. He rejects Craig's excuses ("She can't. You need loads of qualifications" and "What's wrong with staying here? I can't see the point of London") and uses their negativity against them, "Well, perhaps that's you then. Perhaps you'll just have to stay here secure and a little bit miserable until the day you drop. Better than trying and failing, eh?" Sophie is again rather shocked that the Doctor would think she is likely to fail. "Perhaps in the whole wide universe, a call centre's where you should be?" he taunts, finally triggering a rise out of her. "I'm not staying in a call centre all my life. I can do anything I want!" she rails. The Doctor smiles at her and she realises, brightens, "Oh... yeah! Right!" They clash knuckles as if to confirm that the message has finally been received, that communication has been achieved. "Oh, my God. Did you see what he just did?" she asks Craig. However, Craig has not really been paying any attention and has been staring at the festering damp patch on the ceiling and asks, "No, what's happening? Are you going to live with monkeys now?" The Doctor highlights everything that, deep down, they have long acknowledged but have failed to realise by not taking the necessary action: "It's a big, old world, Sophie. Work out what's really keeping you here, eh?" Sophie ponders this and Craig remains silent, both of them aware that their denial of a commitment to each other is holding them back, is preventing them from achieving their dreams.

The whole issue of men and their relationship to the work/life balance is explored with Craig's job. In a culture of recession, downsizing and market-driven policies, he also represents the rising occupational insecurity and sense of precariousness in the male workforce, especially when he finds the Doctor sitting in his office, implementing the very ideas that he intended to present at the planning meeting. There is a sense that when Craig turns up for work after the Doctor's gentle, feminised and caring administrations to the sickness brought on by the poisonous damp patch, that he is further emasculated by the Doctor's interruption into his working life. He has seemingly usurped Craig, is clearly using his intellect and charm to influence company policy and tell awkward customers the way things will be from here on in, and is generally being praised by Craig's boss. Perhaps doing all the things that Craig himself has long since secretly desired. The episode also explores further notions about men, fear and weakness. Craig puts a brave face on the world, disowning his fear of rejection and yet he is weak enough to capitulate to it when faced with affirming his relationship with Sophie. He regresses from intimacy as much as she does and this is only resolved at the end of the episode when their survival relies completely on the expression of their desire for each other. The regression and repression, the apologia for refusing to change, that Craig is acting out is also the very thing that protects him from the time engine's search for a pilot. His seeming contentment with the status quo is at first challenged by 'the man upstairs' when the noise of what he does to his victims disturbs the flat share with the Doctor, but he is symbolically rejected ("Thank you, Craig. But I don't need your help") by the threat as not suitable to be the pilot, the man in charge. The time engine and its pilot emphasise his entanglement in the roots of suburbia and his lack of ambition beyond "pizza, booze, telly." The conclusion of the episode effectively questions whether he is man enough to become the pilot. The only way he can do that is to want to move on, to demand change, to be 'the man upstairs' who wants to escape the crashed time ship. He must also recognise that a man who can communicate his feelings and desires is not necessarily connotative of a weaker man but is actually a positive aspect of the way heterosexual men are being redefined in what Ron Becker concludes, in 'Guy Love' in *Queer TV: Theories, Histories, Politics*, is a "post industrial culture where sexuality is increasingly integrated into a commercial economy, where erotic pleasures become ends-unto-themselves." Roberts potentially reflects something of this transformation, albeit in a very metaphorical way, in *The Lodger* but does safely return the couple to a heteronormative if somewhat more enlightened state. It occurs when Sophie herself begins her journey to self-fulfillment under the Doctor's influence and, finally, when Craig understands that 'the man upstairs' is threatening her. Even she still questions her surroundings and requires some direct talking to at the very moment of her peril in the final scenes. "Seriously, what is going on?" she asks as Craig and the Doctor struggle to switch off the emergency program's need to absorb them. "Oh, for goodness sake, the top floor of Craig's building is in reality an alien spaceship intent on slaughtering the population of this planet. Any questions? No? Good," shouts a flustered Doctor. Thus Craig is spurred on to undertake what could best be described as a 'heteronormative coming out' where the defeat of 'the man upstairs' and the destruction of the time ship rely on a 'love conquers all' confession from him. "Craig, what's keeping you here?" yells the Doctor, slapping him on the face. "Sophie, I don't want to leave Sophie. I can't leave Sophie. I love Sophie!" he reveals and upon this admission, it is clear that Sophie feels the same about Craig. The Doctor and Amy implore them to enact the 'hero gets the girl' climax of scores of romantic comedies and adventure stories by demanding of Craig, "For God's sake, kiss the girl!" as the time ship threatens to explode and, amusingly, as their conversation mirrors earlier moments of doubt and insecurity and briefly pauses the action. Ironically, it is the sort of 'getting the girl' climax that Cornell held up as anathema to the Doctor's own role as adventure hero, a role that he felt appealed to a queer audience. Amy's reaction to this is interesting because she obviously gets rather frustrated with the romantic declarations, even feigning vomiting as Craig and Sophie get to celebrate their love. However, their defeat of 'the man upstairs' is vitally important in freeing the TARDIS and her continued survival. One of the problems with the script is that this is a fairly rushed ending. The time ship and its unknown occupant do come across as just a device through which to articulate the inner desires of the characters and the notion of relationships lost and found. As Craig and Sophie are finally brought to their senses by the Doctor, Amy discovers the engagement ring and perhaps starts to recall her relationship with Rory that has been wiped from time. For all the 'fish out of water' humour, the Doctor's reasoning and behaviour is possibly at its most illogical here, with his delaying tactics, resulting in a rising death count, as significant as the delay that has been inflicted, over the series, on his primary investigation of the crack in the universe. The script tantalises, rather infuriatingly, with the mystery of the TARDIS-like time engine and its unknown owner or owners but then explains no further. Despite these problems, the setup is interesting and the threat from 'the man upstairs' is wonderfully evocative and visually arresting as he or it lures in his victims one by one. The episode is also blessed with three outstanding lead performances from Matt Smith, James Corden and Daisy Haggard. Corden confirms here that he is very comfortable in drama and that perhaps it is time he left the outmoded 'New Laddism' of sketch shows, horror film pastiche and football punditry behind him. Later, as the Doctor says farewell to Craig and Sophie and departs in the TARDIS, Amy again raises the question of her own abandonment and commitment issues, praising the Doctor as a "right little matchmaker" in bringing the couple together, and then evokes memories of the lost Rory with her request, "Can't you find me a fella?" The Doctor, with his stethoscope on, tinkers with the TARDIS and ignores her. Roberts and Moffat are building up to something here and in the previous scene director Morshead has revealed the presence of the crack in the universe behind Craig's fridge (now declaring in plastic letters 'The Doctor Rocks') and it returns, with a visual flourish that fills the screen with light, just as Amy recovers the engagement ring from the Doctor's pocket. A timely reminder then that this business has not yet been dealt with and the 'Next Time' trail reinforces these concerns and prefigures their urgent resolution, with Rosanna's speech about the crack and the silence from *The Vampires of Venice* used in voiceover, as a succession of clips feature the crack as it appeared in each story across the series.

208

## Chapter Ten

# THE PANDORICA OPENS
# THE BIG BANG

Written by: Steven Moffat
Directed by: Toby Haynes
First broadcast: 19 & 26 June 2010

"The girl who waited"

The series's finale, written by Steven Moffat, slowly brings together all the themes and ideas that have marked out the progress of the major story arcs. As well as the repetition, meme-like, of the notions of remembering and forgetting, the fluxation of time and the malleability of history often represented by the effects of the cracks in the universe, there is a very specific trajectory for the characters of Amy and Rory. The series has described the path along which they have travelled, from a childlike state of immaturity to a destination that sees them emerge from transitional adolescence to physical and sexual maturity, as symbolised by the wedding at the end of *The Big Bang*. The event has constantly been held at bay by Amy, her fears of abandonment and commitment preventing the achievement of this maturation, where her identification with the Peter Pan-like figure of the Doctor has, according to Ann Yeoman in *Now or Neverland: Peter Pan and the Myth of Eternal Youth*, forced her to perform "the conflictual dynamics of adolescence, that turbulent period where one is caught between two worlds, and one's whole being seems to hang on the slender thread of the chance remark or decision of the moment. We may see the tensions and conflicts of our teenage years reactivated in any period of change and growth." Her relationship with Rory and the Doctor certainly sees her acting spitefully and impulsively as she shifts towards and away from emotional commitment. By the conclusion of *The Lodger*, this lack of emotional contentment, fleetingly within her grasp during *The Vampires of Venice*, *Amy's Choice*, *The Hungry Earth* and *Cold Blood* when Rory accompanied her and the Doctor, is symbolised by the recovery of the engagement ring from Rory, hidden away in the pocket of the Doctor's jacket. In *The Pandorica Opens*, the first image of Amy presented to us is of her alone, in the depths of the TARDIS, staring at the ring, rapt in concentration, attempting to recall its significance. As Yeoman explains, she is "in No-Man's land, betwixt and between the old and new orders, the previous and future sense of self." She is waiting for her memory, an important theme in the finale, to yield up the new order. Various messages, carried across history, take her and the Doctor to an encounter with River Song. Stories, legends, histories,

211

myths and fairy tales probably acquire their strongest effect within Moffat's narrative here and the construction of the self, via the telling of stories, is a crucial form of liberation for Amy, Rory and the Doctor as the events of the finale play out.

Amy as a character at the centre of storytelling, of myth-making, has been seen before, notably in *The Eleventh Hour*, where her obsession with the Raggedy Doctor has spilled out into a frenzied fictional re-creation in the form of drawings, models and role-playing. She is a companion who has already been performing the role of the companion in her childhood fantasies, through the relationship with an imaginary friend. What we discover in *The Pandorica Opens* and *The Big Bang* is that the expressiveness of this young woman, and her fantasies, shapes her worldview, relocates the meaning of her self and the sense of her identity onto the narrative. Upon arrival in Roman Britain, she mentions that this period was a favourite topic at school, libidinously codifying it as "invasion of the hot Italians." When she, the Doctor and River Song access the 'underhenge' and uncover the Pandorica, Amy recalls the Doctor's description of the device as "a box, a cage, a prison" and his theory that it contains "the most feared thing in the cosmos" and immediately relates it to the story of Pandora's Box. The Doctor queries her reference and she reminds him, "The story. Pandora's Box with all the worst things in the world in it. That was my favourite book when I was a kid." She again reflects on her childhood experience of storytelling and narrative. It is a connection that the Doctor spots with "your favourite school topic, your favourite story? Never ignore a coincidence." The box is a symbol, according to *The Penguin Dictionary of Symbols*, of "the unconscious, of a highly charged imagination, of the power to realise our heart's desire but a power which is illusory and the source of all of our woes," and here the Pandorica is both representative of the folly of the alien alliance who use it to trap the Doctor and instigate the total collapse of the universe and of its eventual resurrection as the Doctor uses its restoration field to reboot all of existence. Amy's concerns are alerted by this coincidence and she worries that the prophecy ("Is that going to happen?") of Vincent van Gogh's painting, the image of the exploding TARDIS that has passed through the hands of Van Gogh, Churchill, Liz 10 and River Song, will come true. The exploding TARDIS, the threat of the unknown about to be released from the Pandorica, transmitted as a warning across the centuries to "everyone, everywhere" and powerful enough that "even poor old Vincent heard it in his dreams," and the engagement ring sealed in its box are all redolent symbols of the exploration of mystery and enigma, of Amy's feminine curiosity about her own buried desire, about the mystery she herself personifies. She confronts the Doctor with the ring, after he has claimed he could give them an extra half an hour before the alliance fleet requisitions the Pandorica and he innocently mentions fruit flies that live for twenty minutes and yet do not mate for life. His point obliquely made, she sees this as a cue to ask, "So, are you proposing to someone?" While this may prefigure the comic proposal between him and River at the end of *The Big Bang*, it is more likely that the symbol of the ring, proposing a circle or cycle of continuous rebirth, and her question is related to the desperate need to recall her memories, the part of her life with Rory that the crack in the universe, in her bedroom wall, "has been eating away at... for some time." The Doctor actually underlines its value with "No, no, no, no... that's er... a memory. A friend of mine. Someone I lost," and simultaneously implies that it is kept in memory of Rory but also as a reminder of the Amy he knew, perhaps a more fulfilled woman, before Rory died. "It's weird. I feel... I don't know, something," she says, looking at the ring. The Doctor presents a number of themes in his reply. "People fall out of the world sometimes, but they always leave traces," alludes to both his earlier encounter with her younger self, Amelia, and how he affected the girl's life as the Raggedy Doctor, and Rory and his death, falling through the crack in time. "Little things we can't quite account for. Faces in photographs, luggage, half-eaten meals... rings. Nothing is ever forgotten, not completely. And if something can be remembered, it can come back," defines the direction that the story is being taken in, the themes of remembering and forgetting reinforced here and throughout *The Pandorica Opens* and *The Big Bang*. His emphasis to her of this concept will result in the return of Rory and her parents, and the Doctor's rescue from the void between worlds after he plants myth-making memories about himself in her mind. "So, was she nice, your friend?" Amy assumes it was a she, not really aware that it is Amy and her relationship with Rory he is referring to here. He seizes his chance to try and evoke further memories, reminding us of their resonance as the series's versions of Peter Pan and Wendy. "Remember that night you flew away with me?" he enquires, "and you asked me why I was taking you and I told you there wasn't a reason. I was lying." She is suddenly concerned and asks him to explain. Here, the setting of *The Eleventh Hour*, the sinister atmosphere of Amy's home, is addressed again, "Your house. It was too big, too many empty rooms," and he suggests that the crack in her bedroom wall has gradually emptied out her life, taken away her memory, made her incomplete. Before they are interrupted by the dismembered Cyberman, that other symbol of the fragmented individual looking for reconstitution, his question, "Does it ever bother you Amy, that your life doesn't make any sense?" is both an indication of her splintered personality and the extremely tangled journey through time that she will make back to 1996. There, upon greeting herself as the young Amelia, she will pronounce, "OK, kid. This is where it gets complicated."

The Cyber arm and head that attacks first the Doctor and then Amy not only recalls the booby traps of dank, dark catacombs from Spielberg's *Indiana Jones* films but, like the Pandorica, is a machine that seeks to devour human hosts. As the Cyber head turns into a set of jaws that repeatedly snap after Amy as it coils its trailing, snake-like terminals around her, she is punished, as the Doctor will be later, for attempting to violate the taboo of the Pandorica, to get past its "layers and layers of security protocols" to confront the "fear that went into the making of this box," just as similar material in Spielberg's adventure films "rapidly triggers an avalanche of primal fears and phobias. If one does not get you then the next one will; fears of the dark and unseen... fears of the body being penetrated, violated or crushed... fears of the dead – decaying corpses, mummified bodies and skeletons," according to Andrew Gordon in *Empire of Dreams: the Science Fiction and Fantasy Films of Steven Spielberg*. Amy is eventually rescued by Rory, now a Roman centurion but only after she slips into unconsciousness, as if in a dream, when the self-repaired Cyberman tranquilises her with a dart. The notion that the characters have entered a dream is something that is repeated throughout the episodes. The Doctor talks to Rory, blatantly ignoring the fact that Rory is alive ("No, I'm missing the obvious, Rory! Something big, something right in front of me! I can feel it") and then suddenly realising that Rory should actually be dead. "Yeah, I know. I was there," Rory points out and the Doctor questions how he can be here. "I don't know. It's kind of fuzzy. I died and turned into a Roman. It's very distracting." The revenant Rory is more concerned with the unconscious Amy. "Did she miss me?" Before he can get a reply, the Pandorica opens and light pours from it, and the mystery of the object, about to be revealed, supplants the intimate question. *The Pandorica Opens* offers a series of slippages between the emotional condition of the central characters and, in their relationship to non-human technologies, a posthuman determination. In *Cyberculture, Cyborgs and Science Fiction: Consciousness and the Posthuman*, William S. Haney's view of posthumanism, seen here in Rory's Nestene programming, the Cyberman attack on Amy and River struggling with the wilful TARDIS, can be equated to signs that "the intersubjective dimension of human nature has begun to lose its aura and is in peril of being phased out by electronic components." The posthuman has already resulted in Rory's consciousness being trapped in plastic and subject to Nestene dehumanisation, and the story sees the opening of the Pandorica restrain the subjectivity of both the Doctor and Amy and the TARDIS emergency protocols trap River in a time loop. Intimate and revelatory moments that seek the recovery of memory or the validity of subjectivity are curtailed by technologies. As a simulation of himself and not yet fully identifiable as an Auton, Rory struggles with his existence within the spectrum of human and non-human. It is especially difficult for him because he can only exist if others have a past awareness of him. "How can she not remember me?" puzzles Rory. "Because you never existed," claims the Doctor. He explains to Rory that the TARDIS is exploding and creating the cracks in time and if anyone gets too close "you fall out of the universe." "So I fell through a crack and now I was never born?" he responds and the Doctor agrees but asks him what he remembers. "I was dying and then I was just here, a Roman soldier. A proper Roman. Head full of Roman... stuff. A whole other life. Just here, like I'd woken up from a dream. Started to think it was a dream. You, Amy and Leadworth." This parallels the dream state he fell into during *Amy's Choice* where the Dream Lord provided him with a fantasy life as a doctor and a father-to-be. For Rory then this is perhaps another facet of his personal crisis of masculinity. Outwardly, he is the epitome of the soldier, strong, powerful and driven, but he is also an inhuman puppet of the Nestenes. Inwardly, he is the same Rory, troubled and trying to come to terms with his new role, still seeking the respect of Amy. He is the civilised self in contradiction to a non-civilised 'other'. The Doctor throws him the engagement ring, after Rory despairs that Amy seems not to remember who he is, and orders him to "go get her." "But I don't understand. Why am I here?" The Doctor's response is to invert the rational for some kind of supernatural occurrence or miracle, unaware that in fact there is a rational, scientific reason for Rory's reappearance, and this pathology of the miraculous to later explain the many temporal causes and effects featured in both episodes itself suggests that Moffat is well aware of the sleight-of-hand effects he is building into the narrative. "The universe is big. It's vast and complicated and ridiculous," summarises the tautologies and paradoxes that drive the narrative in *The Big Bang*, and "sometimes, very rarely, impossible things just happen and we call them miracles" best describes some of the setups we see later. The words 'complicated' and 'ridiculous' – repeated on several occasions – are apt categorisations for many of the later incidents in the story. Rory, however, turns out to be neither impossible, ridiculous, nor a miracle. The Doctor reminds him of Amy's libidinous, flirtatious and confrontational nature with "Now get upstairs. She's Amy and she's surrounded by Romans. I'm not sure history can take it." This also suggests that the Doctor has achieved further accommodation in his acceptance of her nature.

While Rory attempts to rekindle Amy's memories of him, the TARDIS takes River back to Amy's house on the night of 26 June 2010, the evening before her wedding. The house, like the 'underhenge' containing the Pandorica, is in darkness and is a cold, uninviting space. As River investigates, she discovers that the domestic space has been invaded, the front door hanging off its hinges, the rooms and landing, familiar to us from *The Eleventh Hour*, all cold, forgotten and frozen. Director Toby Haynes provides a point-of-view shot of Amy's dressing table littered with the drawings and models of the Raggedy Doctor and his TARDIS. The fictions of Amy's life, her creations, are supplemented with two books: one *Roman Britain*, the cover of which reproduces the Roman General who River met in the legion's camp, and the other *The Legend of Pandora's Box*, an exploding Pandorica depicted on it. River realises that events are being woven from the contents and images of Amy's childhood memories, from the drawings and books that visually represent her feelings and thoughts. She warns the Doctor, "They're not real. They can't be. They're all right here in the storybook. Those actual Romans. The ones I sent you, the ones you're with right now. They're all in a book in Amy's house, a children's picture book." Fictions have been made real and the Doctor concludes that "something is using her memories, Amy's memories" and that whoever it is that visited the house "could have used her psychic residue. Structures can hold memories and that's why houses have

215

ghosts." Perhaps there is also a ghost in the machine, a TARDIS haunted by the repeated shibboleth of 'silence will fall', heard once as River leaves the TARDIS when the details of her destination on the scanner screen are split apart by the familiar pattern of the crack in time and then again when River struggles to control the machine on her return journey. Rory too is a haunted structure, a simulation of the Rory that River sees in a photograph of him, dressed in fancy dress as a centurion with Amy in her policewoman outfit. David Morgan, in *Visual Piety: a History and Theory of Popular Religious Images*, explains how images and memory "operate iconically in the sense that [they attempt] to recapture and hold on to certain features of the past, to re-present what is past by making it appear to happen again." They are crucial to Amy and Rory's validation of their inner lives, the alliance's reconstruction of her childhood to trap the Doctor and, fundamentally, her memory of the Doctor's myth of origin. When Amy brings the Doctor back from the void, "the act of remembrance is magical because it repeats the past in mental imagery and in the sensations, time and place, and material forms that act as a kind of sensory trace." The idea that memories act as a "sensory trace" and can "cancel the temporal difference between past and present" is a very strong theme in both episodes, achieving an apotheosis in Amy's remembering of the Doctor, symbolised in the aide memoir mantra of "something old, something new, something borrowed, something blue." The sensory trace of Rory is, as the Doctor assumes, one of the many "projections or duplicates" that now surround him in the cavern, with his former companion now projected as his own doppelgänger or shadow amongst the many created from Amy's school-book memories. He is a deadlier version of the aide memoir and another example of how appearances can be deceptive. The Roman soldiers are real as far as River is concerned because they behaved as predicted under the influence of her hallucinogenic lipstick. "They might think they're real. The perfect disguise. They actually believe their own cover story. Right until they're activated," reasons the Doctor, demonstrating to us that Rory, as a facsimile Roman soldier housing the memories of the dead companion, is "activated" in different ways. Obviously, he is the unwilling Auton, but he overcomes his programming and in doing so gets Amy to remember him.

John Fiske, in *Television Culture*, delineates the gender roles that are developed in *The Pandorica Opens* and *The Big Bang*. The story sees the Doctor and Rory "develop a more centred subjectivity" where "the masculine narrative tends to deal with more singular goals and achievements, feminine narrative more with people and relationships." The goal here is to become the individuated hero. Rory demands to protect the Pandorica containing Amy and does so for two thousand years, finally 'getting the girl' he has been attempting to marry since the start of the series. The Doctor plunges the Pandorica into the sun, ending the chaos of a rapidly shrinking universe through an act of self-sacrifice, his resourcefulness successfully creating the universe anew. They both determine closures to major narratives. Amy and River are more

216

concerned with feelings, dealing with intimacy, the power of nostalgia and family and they "emphasize the process over the end product, whereas the masculine gives the product priority over the process." There are exchanges of power throughout the story where the female characters act upon the masculine aspects of their own lives, from little Amelia's tenacity in following the Doctor's clues to the museum, to River's killing of the stone Dalek. Similarly, there are very intimate moments where Rory and the Doctor express their feelings to Amy and River. As we discussed in *Flesh and Blood*, the Doctor and River behave like a married couple, emulating the pairings in classic Hollywood romantic comedy and this is evident again here when River, attempting to return to the Doctor in the TARDIS, warns him that there is "Something wrong with the TARDIS, like something else is controlling it," but he takes it as an opportunity to criticise her piloting skills. "You're flying it wrong," he tells her but she has the perfect comeback, paying off a joke that Moffat set up in *The Time of Angels* about who taught her to fly the TARDIS, with "I'm flying it perfectly. You taught me." Later, in *The Big Bang*, she mysteriously reappears at Amy's wedding and teases the Doctor about their relationship with a mock marriage proposal before intimating that all will be revealed about who she really is. She assumes the role of femme fatale, described in Frank Krutnik's *In a Lonely Street: Film Noir, Genre, Masculinity*, as symbolic of *film noir*'s "feared, but fascinating, women [who] tend to represent conflicting currents within male identity" and where, typically in Moffat's use of female characters, she represents "the dislocation of men from their former sense of being the prime movers of culture."

Amy, on the other hand, continues to shed tears without fully understanding why, repeating the moment she experienced in *Vincent and the Doctor*, either because of an overwhelming sense of happiness or out of deep despair. The story sees her both connecting and disconnecting with the men in her life and in each instance, in each moment of transcendence, she cries either tears of sadness or tears of joy. The presence of Rory, sitting with her under the night sky, induces her to involuntarily caress his face. "I don't know why I'm doing that," she claims as he then pleads with her to recognise who he is, "It's me. Amy, please..." he begs. She begins to cry, baffled by this act because, as she says, "it's like... it's like I'm happy," and he believes that she is beginning to remember him but still she denies him, "But I don't know you. I've never seen you before in my life." However, at the very moment that the memory of him is sparked in her, the Nestene programming overwhelms him and he struggles with his own identity and motivations. Just at the moment of her acceptance, he rejects her out of a real fear of hurting her and shouts, "I'm not going! I'm Rory!" Denying the shadow side of himself, represented by the Nestene protocols, is part of his self-realisation as the hero. The schizophrenia of his nature, where he shouts "I'm a thing. I'll kill you! I'm Rory..." and she completes this with "... Williams," is the catalyst to Amy's act of reclamation: "Rory... Williams, from Leadworth?

My boyfriend. How could I ever forget you?" Moffat's irony, at the centre of this tragedy, is that Rory's sense of identity slips away just as she closes in on it, reflecting many of the scenes in which her rejection of him has been central to the relationship with Rory. "You've got to run. I can't hold on... I'm going," he warns her, but she is, finally, sure of him and wants him, "You are Rory Williams and you aren't going anywhere, ever again." The symbol of their union, the engagement ring, is reintroduced when she asks about it and then demands he display it to her. "The ring. Remember the ring? You never let me wear it in case I lost it," reminds us of his determination to keep it safe in the TARDIS at the start of *The Hungry Earth*. He shows her the ring and she confirms his identity and place by her side, "There it is, you remember. This is you. And you are staying." However, the Nestene programming possesses him and he kills her. What follows are three sequences, all in slow motion, that demonstrate that the heroes of the story are being engulfed by the massing of their dark, chaotic selves, the shadows they must battle with. Rory is conflicted by his inhuman nature, the Doctor is faced with all of his 'others' in the forms of Daleks, Cybermen, Sontarans, Judoon et al. and enters the Pandorica, and River is subjugated by the mysterious force that has taken over the TARDIS. Haynes intercuts these sequences and Murray Gold scores them in the 'epic television' mode of J. J. Abrams's *Lost* (2004-10), his themes redolent of those by composer Michael Giacchino, where climactic moments in the drama are heightened by cross cutting, slow-motion and scoring. Visual expression of the epic in *The Pandorica Opens*, where "slow-motion sequences are usually used to aestheticize – to make beautiful and instil significance into their subject" according to Graeme Turner in *Film as Social Practice*, also suggests that the major characters are trapped in a dream-like state from which there seems to be no escape. After the Doctor attempts to reason with the assembled alliance but is sealed away in the Pandorica, the music rises to a crescendo, River flings open the TARDIS doors and finds her way blocked by a wall. "I'm sorry my love," she offers before the console room explodes and Haynes accentuates and connects the intimately tragic with the grand-scale epic in his pull back from Rory cradling Amy's body, up through the Earth's atmosphere and into space, where we see the universe wink out of existence as galaxies explode in a scintillating homage to Van Gogh's vision of 'Starry Night' and his prophetic image of the TARDIS exploding.

In *The Big Bang*, we return to the fairy-tale garden outside Amelia's house, with Haynes duplicating precisely the pan across the scene that formed the introduction in *The Eleventh Hour*, complete with the symbolic toy windmill to signify that time has moved on. It is one thousand, eight hundred and ninety-four years later, or the year 1996 to be precise. The same night, as seen in *The Eleventh Hour*, where Amelia says her prayer for Santa and the dialogue about dolls, pencils and fish is repeated verbatim. The crack is still in her wall and she is afraid because she can hear voices coming from it. She asks him to send someone to fix it. In *The Eleventh Hour* the Doctor arrives and their adventures begin. In

*The Big Bang,* he never arrives, now that he is locked away in the Pandorica, and she seems to pause, perhaps concerned about a memory that existed from another time line, still half expecting him to arrive. The absence of the Doctor, the Time Lord now long forgotten by everyone, is noted by Amelia, the symptoms of which Amy later describes to Rory as "Do you feel like you've forgotten something really important? Do you feel like there's a great big thing in your head and you feel like you should remember it but you can't?" Amelia's nostalgia for him is symbolised in the painting of the stars, her own version of 'Starry Night' and a memory of a universe that not only used to contain stars but also was home to the Doctor. *The Big Bang* is perhaps more of a sequel, rather than claiming to be the second part of a story, to both *The Pandorica Opens* and *The Eleventh Hour.* Their themes about memory are something that Carolyn Jess-Cooke, in *Film Sequels: Theory and Practice from Hollywood to Bollywood,* sees as part of their function as much as their narrative: "By creating both a new ending and a retrospective interpretation of a previous production, the sequel encroaches upon the memory of a prior text and infringes upon spectatorial agency to imagine what may have happened next. The sequel makes the past re-present, and in so doing creates a secondary version of the past that is marked by its repetitions of and differences from an 'original'." Here, Amelia's narrative trajectory begins again, following the one set out in *The Eleventh Hour,* even suggesting that her obsession with the stars now absent from the sky will become as pathological to her as her previous fixation with her imaginary friend, the Raggedy Doctor. Her Aunt Sharon and Christine, presumably a psychiatrist as a nod to the psychiatric help Amelia reputedly received in *The Eleventh Hour,* both tell her, "You know this is all just a story, don't you? You know there's no such things as stars." Still, she does have a friend in Richard Dawkins, with Moffat ironically positioning the noted atheist, well known for his belief that religion is a delusion, as the leader of a cult. Christine the therapist is overheard relating some detail about this system of belief: "Quite common, actually. Throughout history, people have talked about stars in the sky. God knows where it comes from." Amy's Aunt simply does not "want her growing up to join one of those Star Cults. I don't trust that Richard Dawkins." Amelia is, however, a child steeped in imagination, using the power of stories, legends and myths to inhabit a form of dynamic and independent role-play that has been highlighted in all three episodes.

Messages directed at the young Amelia, 'Come along Pond' and 'Stick around Pond', mirror the way that Van Gogh's painting of the exploding TARDIS gave the Doctor and his companions the coordinates for Stonehenge in Roman Britain. Of course, Stonehenge itself is yet another of those iconic historic monuments that signify Britishness to the television audience, particularly one of an international scope. As the Doctor, unseen for much of this sequence because we are ostensibly being teased as to whether he has escaped from the Pandorica or not, leaves a trail of messages for the young Amelia, *The Big Bang* swerves away from the epic scale of *The Pandorica Opens*. Moffat's homage to Spielberg is abundantly clear in the massing of the alliance's spaceships above Stonehenge which, in its freewheeling joy at the sheer spectacle of referencing many familiar vessels previously seen in *Doctor Who* and in having them burst into the frame, is a direct reference to the approach and landing of the glowing, multicoloured UFOs at the Devil's Tower in *Close Encounters of the Third Kind* (1977). The celebration of visual spectacle, exaggerated in the explicit bravado of the uplifting challenge from the Doctor of, "the question of the hour is, who's got the Pandorica? Answer, I do. Next question, who's coming to take it from me?" and by Murray Gold's rousing theme for the Doctor in the scene, is close to Nigel Morris's analysis, in *The Cinema of Steven Spielberg: Empire of Light*, of the Devil's Tower sequence in *Close Encounters* where "As a public event *Close Encounters* shares elements of an ancient literary genre, the *menippea*. This 'broke the demands of historical realism or probability' and was linked with carnival – a ritualised festival where 'everyone is an active participant, everyone communes...' The carnival life is life drawn out of its usual rut, it is to a degree 'life turned inside out', 'life the wrong way round'." Essentially, *The Big Bang* becomes more of a character study, a reflection on the psychological journey that Amy and Rory now get to complete at the end of the series, overturning both the brash, bold, crowd-pleasing special effects sequences created for the alliance's gathering above Stonehenge and the indulgent 'carnival' of monsters that line up in front of the Pandorica to gloat in slow motion as the Doctor is thrown bodily into its innards. In *Problems of Dostoevsky's Poetics*, Mikhail Bakhtin sees Menippean satire as one of the classical "serio-comic" genres where the "use of the fantastic... is internally motivated by the urge to create extraordinary situations for the testing of philosophical ideas" and is "a special kind of experimental fantasticality... full of abrupt transitions and shifts." Morris observes this in Spielberg's cinema as a postmodernist "multiple discursiveness, inter- or transtextuality" and in Terry Gilliam's fantasy films as "clashes between an idiosyncratic, anarchic and spectacular vision and realist conventions." Moffat jettisons the expectations of the epic and settles for a complex and witty exploration of time travel, predestination paradox and destiny in *The Big Bang*. It is "experimental fantasticality" as opposed to the visual showmanship of the previous episode and where "life turned inside out" is the operating mode for the narrative set in a museum that houses the fossilised relics of the epic in the form of the stone Daleks. The "fantasticality" provides a stark contrast between the line-up of iconic *Doctor Who* monsters positioned as the threat to the Doctor, where they simply gloat as the Doctor is thrown into the Pandorica, and the single Dalek that stalks the four characters of the Doctor, Amy, Rory and River in the museum and, eventually, shoots down the Doctor. There is a sense of containment to *The Big Bang* after the vamping of *The Pandorica Opens* and, while there are some action and effects set pieces in the episode, it is very exposition heavy. All four characters are left to deliver large sections of the plot and explanations.

## "The boy who waited"

When Amelia finally frees the adult Amy, the episode's signature narrative is initiated. Not only does Amy acknowledge the 'complicated' nature of time travel that is about to unfold in the story, but we also begin to see the final stages of her journey in this drama of individuation, where, as J. P. Telotte notes in *Science Fiction Film*, "we learn to live in a complex world by drawing together, in the process of maturation, the various elements of the self." By the end of the episode, her role as Wendy to the Doctor, as a version of Peter Pan, reflects many aspects of Barrie's book concerned with memory and storytelling. As Amy emerges from the Pandorica, the title card on screen takes us back one thousand, eight hundred and ninety-four years and to Stonehenge. The Doctor has also been freed from the Pandorica, visually linking the past with the events in 1996, but to his dismay discovers that Rory has murdered Amy. "Oh, Rory!" sighs the Doctor, before the anxious Nestene duplicate, the so-called "lump of plastic with delusions of humanity," adamantly reinforces that he is who he is now and "whatever was happening has stopped. I'm Rory!" The Doctor regards any signs of humanity as just "software talking" and arrogantly dismisses any effort to help Amy with "Your girlfriend isn't more important than the whole universe." In counterpoint to the many humiliations that both the Doctor and Amy have subjected to him, he symbolises his newfound sense of identity and strength by punching the Doctor. "She is to me!" he yells and the Doctor, rubbing his sore chin, is triumphant that this test of character has paid off. "Welcome back, Rory Williams! Sorry, had to be sure." In effect, Rory's sense of his changing masculinity is displayed as the character shifts its location from fantasy to action genres. As a putative hero, we see him transform from the man always trapped in the act of becoming, a transmutability that prevents him from being little more than a lover, to one who is loyal, solid and dependable and takes decisive action. The Doctor acknowledges this as they place Amy in the Pandorica, using the box's regenerative field to return her to life. Again, he highlights the importance of memories and dreams in defining human characteristics: "Memories are more powerful than you think and Amy Pond is not an ordinary girl. Grew up with a time crack in her wall. The universe pouring through her dreams every night. The Nestenes took a memory print of her and got a bit more than they bargained for. Like you. Not just your face. But your heart and your soul." Rory, however, understands that his transformation is not complete. His subjectivity remains in question and he wishes to aspire to many of the qualities of manliness that J. A. Mangan and James Walvin describe in their 'Introduction' to *Manliness and Morality: Middle Class Masculinity in Britain and America*: "as embracing physical courage, chivalric ideals, virtuous fortitude with additional connotations of military and patriotic virtue." When he demands to stay and protect the Pandorica for the next two thousand years, to keep Amy safe (mirroring her own demand of him, "You aren't going anywhere, ever again"), the Doctor warns him that he will never sleep, will be conscious the entire time. His selflessness and integrity will drive him mad. "Will she be safer if I stay? Look me in the eye and tell me she wouldn't be safer," he argues. "Yes, obviously," the Doctor agrees. "Then how could I leave her?" The Doctor finds it a rather irrational stance for him to take and in exasperation, perhaps recognising in Rory some of the missing aspects of his alien self, complains "Oh, why do you have to be so... human?" Pointedly, Rory acknowledges his desire for completeness, his craving for the heroic soul while trapped in a plastic body, "Because right now I'm not." As Rory takes up his guard duty outside the Pandorica, becoming the man who waits for Amy in parallel to her as the girl who waited for the Doctor, Haynes cuts back to Amy in the museum. Here the interpretation, through video, still images and narrative, of the exhibition's display of the Pandorica and the fate of "the centurion [who] would be there guarding it" picks up the story. Amy refers to it as "a very long story" after meeting her younger self and discovering, via storytelling, what happened to the box and Rory. The box is a symbol of linear time and of history unfolding in a straight line but it is also emblematic of Rory's loyalty and courage, the centurion full of "military and patriotic virtue" as he is last seen dragging the Pandorica from the flames of the Blitz in 1941 (another instance of British fortitude in the series) and allegedly dies in the blaze in "one last act of devotion." Amy sheds tears for a self-evident, justifiable reason and knows precisely why she is sad, murmuring "Rory, oh, Rory" in much the same way the Doctor had when he discovered she had been slain.

Rory triumphantly appears, disguised as a museum security guard, and reasserts his heroic, chivalrous masculinity. As the reactivated stone Dalek detects his presence and declares "Intruder unarmed," Rory begs to differ ("Do you think?") and, amusingly, he disables the threat with his Auton wrist gun. Amy and Rory are passionately reunited, with him apologising for killing her with "I'm sorry. I couldn't help it. It just happened," while Amy tells him to shut up as she smothers him with kisses. As their desires take control, the Doctor, as 'gooseberry' once more, interjects, "Yeah, shut up! Because we've got to go!" but Rory reiterates his honourable deed, seeking validation from her with "I waited. Two thousand years I waited for you." "Oh, still shut up," she gasps, maintaining her place in the hierarchy of their relationship. Rory may well have found his inner courage and performed very competently as the hero, but she still seems to enjoy keeping him in his place. The Doctor is confounded by this outpouring of desire, taking on a childlike disposition, advising them to "break" and "breathe" during their extended clinch and observing that "somebody didn't get out much for two thousand years." Again, this places the Doctor, rather like Peter Pan, outside this expressive sphere of desire and symbolised as an eternal father figure who does not wish to be troubled by such things. When the young Amelia requests a drink, the Doctor playfully highlights both the intense, heteronormative mouth-to-mouth contact and the child's thirst, "Oh, it's all mouths today, isn't it?"

When the Doctor from twelve minutes in the future materialises and apparently dies, Amy makes a prophetic statement, capitalising on her own faith in the Time Lord, "He won't die. Time can be rewritten. He'll find a way. I know he will," but Rory is concerned, not fully aware of the cumulative effects of the time-jumping narrative he finds himself in. "We can't leave you here dead!" he says to the Doctor. The Doctor snipes at Rory, still not quite comfortable with his newfound outspokenness, while also highlighting the bigger problem they face, "Oh, good! Are you in charge now? So tell me what are we going to do about Amelia?" During this conflagration, the young girl has vanished, devoured by the shrinking of history that is taking place around them. "There is no Amelia. From now on, there never was. History is still collapsing," observes the Doctor. Time and storytelling are compressing simultaneously. On the roof of the museum, they encounter the exploding TARDIS, now seen burning up as a sun, hanging in the sky. Rory detects River's voice when the Doctor uses a satellite dish to prove to them that the sun is the TARDIS, picking up its familiarly odd materialisation noise. "Trust the plastic," suggests Rory when Amy claims she does not hear anything. His augmentation, as Auton and hero, is demonstrated in these exceptional senses and the willingness to defend them with his wrist-gun. River's looped line of "I'm sorry my love" is like a heartbeat and proposes again that she is someone who has managed to get closer than anyone else to the enigmatic Doctor's hearts. As she is at the heart of the explosion so she is at the heart of his life, and the circle of the sun, created by the exploding TARDIS, is perhaps the cycle of time that their lives overlap along. Trapped by the emergency protocols of the TARDIS, that have sealed her in to save her, the Doctor uses the vortex manipulator to break the time-loop and rescue her. There is also another confirmation of their husband-and-wife 'relationship' in the aping of the post-war American domestic scene where the Doctor announces "Hi, honey. I'm home!" and River looks at her watch and scolds him with "And what sort of time do you call this?" A witty allusion to these tropes also becomes a tongue-in-cheek reference to the 'sort of time' that Moffat is endlessly playing with, particularly in the use of temporal loops, in *The Big Bang*. It also nods to the sub-genre of husband-and-wife action-caper films like *Grosse Point Blank* (1997) and *Mr and Mrs Smith* (2005) that, as proposed by Lachlan MacDowall in 'Professional Killers at Home' in *Heroes of Film, Comics and American Culture*, derive "comic effect from the collision between the spheres of labor and home life, and the related genres of action and romantic comedy." This mode is extended into the scene where Amy and River effectively gang up on the Doctor, in rather the same way they demeaned him in *The Time of Angels*, to steal the fez off his head and destroy it, putting an end to his delusion that "fezzes are cool" and where River, out of past experience, assures Amy she is onto a good thing by having a relationship with a Nestene duplicate because, for her, a "swappable head did keep things fresh." Rory's depiction as a piece of dumb plastic, reflecting some of the deprecating attitudes towards his intelligence seen earlier in the series, is highlighted in "No, too fast. I'm not getting it," as the Doctor explains the complexities of how the Pandorica can probably restore the universe. However, we laugh with Rory at this moment because by now the plethora of temporal loops and the mechanics of rebooting the universe are equally as befuddling to a large proportion of the audience.

The Pandorica here becomes the 'Peter Pan-dorica', bestowing wellbeing and youth upon Amy, reviving the Doctor to the point where he can fly it into the heart of the explosion to re-create the whole of the universe, the Neverland that all the characters play in. There are also a lot of religious metaphors present in the story at this point. The Doctor allegedly dies but is resurrected ("Rule one. The Doctor lies"), his use of the Pandorica creates the universe anew (River pointedly describes the process as "Let there be light"), and he undertakes a biblical journey into the sun, symbolised as the 'son of man' and dies again to save us. The Christ metaphor can be extended to include Amy, Rory and River as the disciples who carry the word forward and revive him. As the dying Doctor takes control of the Pandorica and prepares to fly it into the sun, Haynes dissolves from an image of the sun seen through the skylight into a close-up of the Doctor's head and shoulders, the slippage between the two momentarily suggesting a glowing halo around his head. Amy and Rory once again rehearse the dynamics of their relationship as the sun burns through the skylight of the museum, awkwardly facing up to the loss of the Doctor. "Are you OK?" asks Rory. "Are you?" replies Amy, and after he tells her "No" she snaps angrily at him, "Well, shut up then." Like Rory, she is still not complete from the journey, disavowing both their feelings about the likelihood they will never see the Doctor again. However, she realises she has been cruel and turns to him as he enfolds her in his arms. The taciturn Amy is still dealing with abandonment and she demands an explanation from River. Emphasising the dream-like nature of the story and the patterns of remembering and forgetting that litter the series, River offers that they will all wake up where they ought to be, that none of the events they are witnessing will ever happen and they will never remember them. The Doctor will be "purged from the universe" and he never will know River, Amy and Rory. Amy, sure of the closeness between River and the Doctor, asks her why the Doctor wants to talk to her and not to River. "He doesn't really know me yet," she says, emphasising that this event is taking place early in the time line of their relationship.

The conversation between the Doctor and Amy that follows prefigures the end of the episode and much of the complexity of Amy's heritage. The Doctor understands that her attitude towards life has been coloured by the loss of her parents and this scene is probably the first to provide a more satisfying explanation of what happened to them. "Amy, your house was too big. That big, empty house. And just you," he explains, suggesting the importance of the house as a visual analogy to her own incomplete psychological state. "Where were your mum and dad? Where was everybody who lived in that big house?" he asks. She claims to have lost her mum and dad but does not even remember where they went or what happened to them. There is an inference that the alliance, who used her memories to trap him in the Pandorica, had some influence on his need to solve the mystery. "Amy Pond, all alone. The girl who didn't make sense. How could I resist?" he suggests. Amy is baffled by how she could forget her parents and the Doctor tells her that, "Nothing is ever forgotten, not really. But you have to try. Try to remember your family and they'll be there." This last statement mirrors the Second Doctor's own process of recollection. In *Tomb of the Cybermen* he tells Victoria, who is missing her father, that in order to remember his family, "I have to really want to – to bring them back in front of my eyes. The rest of the time they... they sleep in my mind, and I forget." Amy struggles to understand how she could bring her parents back if they never existed in the first place as a result of the cracks in the universe. "Because you're special. That crack in your wall, all that time, the universe pouring into your head. You brought Rory back, you can bring them back too. You just remember and they'll be there," he explains softly. She remonstrates with him that he will not be there, but he knows that it is time for her to leave the Raggedy Doctor behind, to grow up and move out of adolescence. She must substitute him for Rory and her parents: "You'll have your family back. You won't need your imaginary friend anymore." Amy cries again, the prospect of the severance of emotional connections with the Doctor representative of her leaving behind his Neverland of the adventures in the TARDIS, no longer free to explore the universe. "Ah, Amy Pond, crying over me, eh? Guess what?" he observes. She queries him and he simply says "Gotcha" as the doors to the Pandorica slide shut and it shoots through the roof of the museum, struck by lightning in the same manner that the TARDIS is bombarded in the opening titles to the series. "Gotcha" is, of course, that indication of sympathetic emotional resonance between the two of them first declared in *The Beast Below*, where each recognises previously hidden aspects of the inner life of the other.

The Doctor is seen to reverse down his own time stream with Haynes throwing together familiar and unfamiliar sequences, including a previously unseen moment in the TARDIS interior where he momentarily distracts Amy from her trip to Space Florida and where she puts the card in the paper shop window before the events of *The Lodger* unfold. The speculation over the short scene in *Flesh and Stone* that divided eagle-eyed fans about whether Moffat was being very clever by dropping a 'future' Doctor onto the Byzantium to talk to Amy or had overseen a significant continuity error is also put to rest here when Haynes includes the scene, emphasising its significance ("Now, listen, remember what I told you when you were seven?") to the last stop he makes as his time line is "unravelling, erasing... closing." After he arrives in Amelia's house on "the night she waited," he finds her in the garden asleep next to her packed suitcase. Picking up "the girl who waited" and then watching over her as she sleeps, the Doctor begins the process of creating his own myth, the story of himself that will enable her to remember him in the form of words and, crucially, bring him back from the other side of the void into which he must disappear. He also gives her the gift of her parents, ensuring she remembers them as space and time are returned to their proper place. "When you wake up, you'll have a mum and dad... and you won't even remember me. Well, you'll remember me a little. I'll be a story in your head. But that's OK. We're all stories in the end. Just make a good one, eh? Cos, it was you know. It was the best." Not only is he speaking about the adventures that he and the adult Amy had or never had ("The Doctor and Amy Pond. And the days that never came") but he is also re-creating the myth at the heart of *Doctor Who* itself, the very story that began in 1963 with "a daft old man who stole a magic box and ran away. Well, I borrowed it. I was always going to take it back. Oh, that box, Amy. You'll dream about that box. It'll never leave you. Big and little at the same time. Brand new and ancient. And the bluest blue ever." This of course ties into her act of remembrance at the wedding and the familiar good luck saying, dating back to the Victorian era, attached to the giving of gifts and the bride's outfit. The Doctor knows that these symbols of continuity, of the new future, of faith and loyalty are important. "In your dreams, they'll still be there," he tells the sleeping Amelia. Before he decides to prevent any further progress back into his own time line by voluntarily entering the crack in her bedroom wall, he departs, kissing her on the head in a gesture we have seen in a number of previous episodes, with "Live well, love Rory. Bye bye Pond."

Briefly, Amelia stirs and looks around the empty bedroom. Haynes pans up to her bedroom window and we see that the stars have returned to the night sky and he slowly dissolves this into a brilliantly blue, sunlit morning, suggesting it is the following day. However, when he cuts back to the bedroom, it is the adult Amy sleeping there and time has advanced to the day of her wedding, the day after she originally flew off with the Doctor in the TARDIS in *The Eleventh Hour*. A slow pan across her dressing table reveals that the original Amelia's experiences and memories of the Raggedy Doctor have become the memories of the adult Amy, now living in the restored time line. His key words and the story that he planted in her head have survived in the drawings and models of the TARDIS and the Doctor that litter the table. This is odd because she then phones Rory and claims that she has forgotten "something really important" when all the evidence is more or less in front of her. Rory is the proud groom, still slightly scared of "the girl who didn't make sense." It is only when River, symbol of the Great Mother and the ambiguous femme fatale, walks past the window of the hall hosting the reception and looks at her momentarily that Amy's memories are triggered. Amy spontaneously cries again and she is puzzled because, contrary to Rory's opinion that it must be because she's so happy ("Happy Mrs Rory. Happy, happy, happy"), she actually feels very sad. This ties in with previous sequences of tearfulness related to the once-absent Rory, consumed by the cracks in the universe, and she worries, "Why am I sad?" as Rory nervously contemplates his future marriage to a very sad wife. She is distracted by the sight of River's diary, the colour, design and shape of the TARDIS but now blank because the Doctor and his adventures have ceased to exist, left as a "present" that Rory assumes correlates with "the old saying. The old... wedding... thing." As she grasps at the "great big thing in your head... you feel like you should remember," her gaze captures visual fragments of the Doctor in aspects of her wedding guests – a bow tie here, a pair of braces there – and then in the blue book held in her hands. A teardrop falls onto the diary. In mythology, tears are often supposed to have a redeeming and healing effect, to provide life-giving power and wisdom. Here, it is symbolic of the restorative energy of Amy's imagination and the words and memories the Doctor has specifically provided. Her inner, fantasy life has also been seen by her parents as a troubling, psychological issue. As she stands, telling her father to shut up, and begins to remember that imaginary Doctor, her father is in the middle of a story (yet another myth-creating tale about little Amelia), where she, at the "age of six, announced her new head teacher wasn't real because she looked like a cartoon." Amy announces, "There's someone missing. Someone important. Someone so, so important," and when Rory shows his concern she continues with, "Sorry, everyone, but when I was a kid I had an imaginary friend." Her mother clearly recalls the four psychiatrists that she sent Amelia to, with her "Oh no, not this again. The psychiatrists we sent her to!" connecting the return of her parents in this new life with Amy's background in *The Eleventh Hour*. Amy's assurances that "The Raggedy Doctor. *My* Raggedy Doctor. But he wasn't imaginary. He was real" begin to cement together the memories of that first encounter in Amelia's garden when the TARDIS crash-landed and she met the Doctor. In her analysis *The Secret Garden*, with particular reference to the classic children's story by Frances Hodgson Burnett, Margaret Eileen Meredith connects together the psychology and rich symbolism associated with gardens and secrets, the reality of the psyche, the importance of symbols, imagination and play in the pursuit of self-knowledge. She describes this individuation as "a process that fosters a relationship between the ego and unconscious material generated by the self in the form of dreams, art, fantasy and active imagination, so it can be contemplated and possibly integrated into the personality. Gradually one connects with previously unknown facets of the personality that enrich or restart the flow of life." It is clearly demonstrated in Amy's cry of, "I remember you! I remember! I brought the others back and I can bring you home too. Raggedy man, I remember you and you are late for my wedding!" and in how she imagined her parents and Rory back into existence. It is also a humorous reflection on the Doctor's dreadful sense of punctuality, with the fourteen-year hiatus to return to Amy at the beginning of the series a specific example. The power of the creative impulse is framed in her tribute to the Doctor's origin story, "I found you, I found you in words, like you knew I would. That's why you told me the story... the brand new, ancient blue box. Oh, clever, very

227

clever," and Haynes uses a tracking shot that closes in on Amy and simultaneously foregrounds the couple on top of the wedding cake, symbolising the various permutations of 'marriage' that are being formulated here and that include: Mrs Rory and Mr Pond, the Doctor and Amy, Rory and Amy, and River and the Doctor.

The TARDIS materialises as she literally casts a spell, an enchantment of "Something old, something new, something borrowed, something blue," that reflects, in shorthand, the tale of "a daft old man who stole a magic box." As that familiar blue box appears, Rory remembers, "It's the Doctor. How did we forget the Doctor?" and, as the Doctor emerges, he is overheard to say to his wedding guests, "I was plastic. He was the stripper at my stag. Long story." All of the events from the previous episodes have not been erased or forgotten and Amy's very act of recalling them back into life leaves the Doctor "completely astonished" as he grandly announces to the reception guests, "Hello everyone, I'm Amy's imaginary friend. But I came anyway." Amy demands he "absolutely, most definitely may kiss the bride," but this time the Doctor offers a firm and definitive rebuttal, sealing her lips with his fingers as she approaches him and specifically addressing her with the non-diminutive of her name, as her child self: "Amelia, from now on I shall be leaving the kissing duties to the brand new Mr Pond." Here, Amy is like Wendy attempting to kiss Peter Pan, but like Peter Pan in Barrie's book, the Doctor remains perplexed by this and would rather his sexual ambiguity remain intact. When Allison B. Kavey, in *Second Star to the Right: Peter Pan in the Popular Imagination*, describes Peter as "an enchanting image of everlasting youth, a runaway, an irresponsible adolescent, a lost child, a sexual object, and an action hero," this also surely summarises the Doctor. Like the adult Wendy keeping the memory of Peter alive for her children through storytelling, Amy has perpetuated the myth of the Doctor, keeping him alive in her imagination and dreams, to facilitate her own process of maturation. Moffat reuses self-deprecating humour and his trademark dynamic between strong, independent women and inadequate men to restate the roles he established in *The Vampires of Venice*, where Amy, previously the mother to 'her boys', is now a variation of wife and mother as Mrs Rory/Mrs Pond. Rory corrects the Doctor with "No, I'm not Mr Pond. That's not how it works," but the Doctor dismisses this, acknowledging in his "Yeah, it is" that it is Amy who will always be in charge of this relationship. Clearly, Rory accepts this arrangement and is now more secure about how the marriage will continue in the flux of their active and passive roles. Moffat also blurs the connotation of his long-accepted euphemism for sex and when the Doctor states, "I only came for the dancing," here he really does mean dancing and we see him entertaining the guests with some very suspect moves on the dance floor, where a previously empty house is now full of warmth, love and friendship. This and his concluding appraisal of Rory in "Two thousand years. The boy who waited. Good on you, mate," determinedly position the Doctor outside the realm of their marriage and relationship (where the girl who waited meets and marries the boy who waited) and to a certain extent away from the murkier depths of desire and sexuality.

However, when the Doctor returns to the TARDIS, now parked again in Amy's garden, River re-connotes 'dancing' in their conversation. "Did you dance? Well, you always dance at weddings, don't you?" she observes, suggesting that she and the Doctor will attend such an event in the past or the future. "You tell me," he replies and she can only delay our curiosity further with her trademark response of "Spoilers." He hands her back the diary, telling her that all of their history has been returned to its pages, the myths and legends of the Doctor and River restored as a result of Amy recalling him from the void. Time has literally been rewritten but he "didn't peek" at his own future. Mimicking the proffering of an engagement ring, he hands her the vortex manipulator and asks, "Are you married, River?" "Are you asking?" she returns, clearly intent on tripping him up and then succeeding in confusing him into thinking he was proposing to her. "No hang on, did you think I was asking you to marry me, or... or asking if you were married?" She double bluffs him with a simple "Yes" and this coquettish little game spirals on with his "No, but was that 'yes' or 'yes'?" and she breathily concludes with "Yes." When he asks her who she is, Moffat prepares us for the next chapter in their saga and she acknowledges this, the mood changing from playful romance to deep regret, "You're going to find out very soon now. And I'm sorry but that's when everything changes." With that, the morally ambiguous good/bad witch disappears. This episode, like much of the series, plays with concepts of faithfulness, the importance of family and the richness of a fantasy life and, in her appraisal of *Peter Pan*, Kavey sees such stories as "meaning different things to all of us at different moments in our lives" and it is possibly true that *Doctor Who*, like *Peter Pan*, "reveals the nastiest aspects of childhood, rather than simply genuflecting at the altars of innocence and youth." As he prepares to leave in the TARDIS, Amy and Rory reappear at the door. She wonders where he is off to, upset that they have not "had a snog in the shrubbery" and is unable to resist goading Rory with "Shut up, it's my wedding," to which he emphatically declares "*Our* wedding." The Doctor is concerned about the safety of space and time, setting up another subplot because "the silence, whatever it is, is still out there" and one the next series is being set up to address. A phone call about "an Egyptian goddess loose on the Orient Express, in space" prompts them all to say goodbye, but it is goodbye once again to Leadworth and a return to Neverland. Amy, Rory and the Doctor, the prince and princess with the good wizard in the TARDIS, all elope together. The end of *The Big Bang* proposes that the Doctor, Amy and Rory have achieved the ability to straddle both the earthly confines of Leadworth, now populated with a warm and loving family for Amy, and the dark, wonderful but threatening vastness of the universe. Kavey sees Peter, the Lost Boys and the Darling children imbued with the same capacity to "move between their cozy beds and Neverland which makes it more possible for us to move with them, leaving our nightlights behind for the eerie twilight of London and the Technicolor dawn of Neverland."

## "Hello Universe, goodbye Doctor"

*The Pandorica Opens* and *The Big Bang* are an unbridled and playful execution of history, temporal tautology, time-loops, cause and effect, flashes and recaps both forward and backward. Moffat effectively picks up where *Flesh and Stone* left off and its proposal that the expanding time field of the cracks in the universe would completely devour everything in the *Doctor Who* universe. His use of time travel to miraculously perpetuate the narrative's cause and effects is complex and often confusing. It is certainly the case that *The Big Bang* is a distinctive series finale, very different from the expansive, comic book brushstrokes that an audience came to expect from Russell T. Davies, a formula Moffat pays homage to to an extent in the first part of the story with its vicarious, fan-pleasing thrills of spaceships and monsters. For the second part of the story, his attention is focused on the resolution to the character arcs for Amy and Rory and the consequences of "total event collapse" after the cracks in the universe erase everything in existence. The ideas and how those are communicated to the audience seem to be his concern here and *The Big Bang* is heavy on exposition, delivered in more or less two or three locations by four characters. There are no massed armies of the Doctor's enemies and no pitched battles, no roll call of past companions, no crossover with either *Torchwood* or *The Sarah Jane Adventures*. Instead, we get a battery of concepts and ideas, many of which need to be unpacked long after the episode is seen, and which have a tendency to make this finale a little too cerebral and often quite static.

In director Toby Haynes, Moffat evidently has someone who is extremely skilful at getting these concepts onto screen through a mixture of well-composed visuals, editing, music and stand-out performances from Matt Smith, Karen Gillan and Arthur Darvill. Sadly, Alex Kingston, as entertaining as she is in this story, is not given a huge amount to do simply by dint of the fact that the narrative is not really about River Song. She is superb in the few notable scenes that she gets, particularly her face off with the stone Dalek in *The Big Bang* that adds a cold-blooded and merciless quality to the morally ambiguous River. Haynes starts as he means to go on and reflects Moffat's legerdemain with time travel concepts with a complementary style that uses flashback, jump cuts and dissolves to mark both the graceful forward passage of time and the dizzying jumping back and forth in various time streams that mark out the narrative. The 'history' of the current series is presented as recap in the opening montage of *The Pandorica Opens*. The story revisits a number of previous episodes to establish the idea that a message for the Doctor has been transmitted through time and space and has been forwarded on from Vincent van Gogh. As the sequence returns to the location of *Vincent and the Doctor*, takes us to the Stormcage Facility in the fifty-second century, back to Churchill and Bracewell and then to an encounter with Liz 10, it parallels the literal unspooling of the entire series that Hayne offers in the finale. Here, in the pre-titles, we see how history has progressed since the Doctor departed. Vincent is in the throes of his manic depression and appears to be attended by Dr Gachet, immortalised in the painting seen in the Musée d'Orsay, and Madame Vernet. Vernet, possibly in a tongue-in-cheek moment of self-deprecation from Moffat about his own script, glances at Vincent's latest work and declares, "Look at this, even worse than his usual rubbish." As Vincent's screams intensify, Haynes cuts to the Cabinet War Rooms in 1941 where presumably Bracewell returned to work at Churchill's side as it is he that brings the painting to Churchill's attention and states, "It's obviously a message and you can see who it's for." Churchill attempts to phone the Doctor but the vagaries of the time vortex see his call diverted to the Stormcage Facility where River, at a point earlier in her time stream than in *The Time of Angels*, uses her hallucinogenic lipstick to escape and travel to the Royal Collection to steal Van Gogh's painting. There she meets Liz 10, who seems to have lived to a ripe old age since we last saw her on Starship UK in 3295. River is on the slow path until she visits the Maldovarium, a colourful homage to Mos Eisley and the cantina sequence from *Star Wars*, and acquires the vortex manipulator ("fresh off the wrist of a handsome time agent," that implies a reference to either Captains Jack or John from *Torchwood*). The Doctor, meanwhile, takes Amy to Planet One, the "oldest planet in the universe," to look at a cliff of pure diamond that displays a message from the dawn of time in letters fifty feet high. Another homage, this time to Douglas Adams's *The Hitchhiker's Guide to the Galaxy*, the message on the cliff is translated by the TARDIS as that characteristic greeting, last seen on the Home Box relic in *The Time of Angels*, of 'Hello Sweetie'. Presumably the coordinates the Doctor uses to travel to Britain in 102 AD are the High Gallifreyan hieroglyphs underneath. In a tent in a Roman encampment, River, disguised as Cleopatra (and she is later reminded by the Roman General that in fact Cleopatra is in Egypt and dead), presents the painting to the Doctor. The image of the TARDIS exploding, in the style of 'Starry Night', is "some kind of warning," says River and shows that "something's going to happen to the TARDIS?" All this happens in the first seven minutes of the episode and its convolutions back and forth in history prepare us well for the complexities ahead.

Haynes then intercuts the horse ride to Stonehenge with more exposition in the tent, compressing time in his editing, and explaining why they are travelling to the monument. "Date and map reference on the door sign," indicates River, perhaps reflecting back to the section of the door sign that the Doctor recovered as shrapnel from the time crack in *Cold Blood*. When she reveals that the title of the work is 'The Pandorica Opens' and that the Pandorica is "a box, a cage, a prison. It was built to contain the most feared thing in all the universe," the Doctor is in denial and claims it to be "a fairy tale, a legend. It can't be real." She reasons that "if it is real, then it's here and it's opening. And it's got something to do with your TARDIS exploding." Its location remains hidden but the Doctor suggests that "if you'd buried the most dangerous thing in the universe, you'd want to remember where you'd put it." These references tie in with the series's themes of remembering and forgetting, myth, legend and fairy tale and, as Haynes pans across to Stonehenge in the distance, we are also reminded that the circular monument is considered to be a solar observatory concerned with the cycle of time through the heavens. It is the circle of time that bothers Amy about River's warning on Alfava Metraxis where "last time we saw you, you warned us about it, after we climbed out of the Byzantium. You told the Doctor you'd see him again when the Pandorica Opens." River warns her with "Spoilers" and suggests that this is earlier in her personal time line and that the events of the crash of the Byzantium have not yet happened to her. "Maybe I did, but I haven't yet. But I will have." The mystery of what is in the Pandorica allows the Doctor to initially propose a number of possibilities from "it contains the mightiest warrior in history" to something more akin to himself, or at least, the shadow aspect of himself, as "a goblin. Or a trickster, or a warrior. A nameless, terrible thing, soaked in the blood of a billion galaxies. The most feared being in all the cosmos. And nothing could stop it, or hold it or reason with it. One day it would just drop out of the sky and tear down your world." This is probably how the alliance of his enemies, who end up imprisoning him in the box, actually see him. When Amy asks how this trickster ended up inside, the Doctor invokes the realm of fantasy in "You know fairy tales. A good wizard tricked it." His *Harry Potter*-esque descriptor is pointedly commented on by River: "I hate good wizards in fairy tales. They always turn out to be him," recalling how the Doctor was presented as a transdimensional Merlin in *Battlefield*.

Stonehenge turns out to be a vast communications array, "broadcasting a warning to everyone, everywhere, to every time zone... 'The Pandorica is Opening.'" Its message is bringing ten thousand starships from across time and space, bearing a huge gathering, emblematic of *Doctor Who*'s own history on television and in print, of Daleks, Cybermen, Sontarans, Terileptil, Slitheen, Chelonian, Nestene, Drahvin, Sycorax, Haemo-goth, Zygon, Atraxi, Draconian. A carnival of monsters and according to River, "Everything that ever hated you is coming here tonight." Later, River contrasts this massing of alien superiority with the barbarianism of the Romans, little knowing that they are in fact Nestene duplicates, to offer the General a salutary lesson in real world politics, "When you fight barbarians what must they think of you? Where do they think you come from? Your world has visitors. You're all barbarians now." The Doctor also highlights the effectiveness of superior and inferior technologies and observes the dismembered Cyberman sentry, "Probably got himself duffed up by the locals. Never underestimate a Celt." When the Doctor addresses the fleets of his enemies he rather presciently admits that "Who takes the Pandorica takes the universe," and although he thinks it is a weapon it is in fact a cage, designed by his enemies, to house his own personal universe and where his incarceration will result in all that he represents being erased from time.

As River sets off in the TARDIS to bring the Doctor necessary equipment, she notices that something is wrong with the ship as it dematerialises. As the TARDIS is hurled through the vortex, struck by lightning, the Doctor begins to explain to Rory that his non-existence is the consequence of "a huge explosion in the future, on one particular day. And every other moment in history is cracking around it." When Rory asks "What exploded?" the Doctor reflects for a moment and Haynes inserts a flashback to *Flesh and Stone* that first depicted the origin of the explosion, the so-called "base code of the universe," as 26 June 2010 ("Amy's time") and a brief recap of the Doctor recovering the shrapnel of the TARDIS from the crack in *Cold Blood*. The clues, together with Van Gogh's painting, all point to the one conclusion that the TARDIS is the cause of the explosion. The Doctor warns Rory, "The cracks are everywhere now. Get too close and you fall out of the universe," and this not only indicates that Rory fell out of the universe but it also prefigures the Doctor's own fate when, at the end of *The Big Bang*, he sacrifices himself, never to be born, to the crack in Amelia's bedroom. The TARDIS takes River to Amy's house in 2010 and Moffat suggests a new mystery as a crack shatters the scanner screen and a voice utters "Silence will fall." It is one that suggests the "external force" dragging the TARDIS off course may be connected to the alliance's trap for the Doctor, a "scenario you'd believe, to get close to you" according to River. Haynes again underlines this unseen and powerful threat with another flashback, where the Roman General's appraisal of the barbarian mind to comprehend the origin of the gods as "a place more deadly, more powerful and more impatient than their tiny minds can imagine" also provokes a similar comparison between the Doctor and this new threat. As she attempts to return back through time to Stonehenge, her difficulties with the TARDIS increase and, just as she informs the Doctor of the ominous date and he implores her to escape to another time zone, the Nestene programming is activated. He concludes that "the TARDIS exploding is what causes [the cracks in time] but we can stop the cracks ever happening if you just land her." The Pandorica splits open, bathing him in light, and he still believes that a force is about to emerge from it, "Well now, ready to come out, are we?" when, in fact, the alliance are preparing to imprison him in it, on the understanding that "all projections correlate. All evidence concurs. The Doctor will destroy the universe." The Doctor pleads with them that they have made a mistake and they little realise that their predictions of the deletion of the universe will, ironically, include them. He attempts to reason with them, advising that the TARDIS is exploding and will cause "Total event collapse! Every sun will supernova at every moment in history! The whole universe will never have existed." River finally manages to fling open the TARDIS doors but discovers her way is blocked. She resignedly utters, "I'm sorry my love" (the words that will later, in *The Big Bang*, signify her survival in a time loop), as the TARDIS is destroyed and the screen fills with bright white light. Haynes ends the episode with the Earth alone in the heavens, gradually fading out to black and accompanied by a Murray Gold musical crescendo that abruptly ceases as the Earth disappears from the screen.

The opening of *The Big Bang* follows the similar structure of the pre-titles to *The Pandorica Opens*. Starting with a seven-minute sequence, Haynes uses a title card to inform us that we have moved forward in time from the climax of the last episode. It is 1996 and, as previously noted, he replicates precisely the sequence in *The Eleventh Hour* with the slow pan across Amelia's garden, including the symbol of the turning toy windmill, and Amelia's prayer to Santa. There is only a gust of wind outside her bedroom window as the merest suggestion of what once was and yet has never been. Moffat's look into alternate time depicts an Earth and moon alone in the cosmos, the black sky devoid of stars. Aunt Sharon and the psychiatrist Christine take Amelia outside to demonstrate to her that her vision of stars in the sky is "all just a story" rather than the trace memory of a previous life in a previous version of the universe. However, the past slowly beings to impact upon the present and a leaflet through the door directs Amelia and Aunt Sharon to the National Museum where the relics of that alternate universe are on display. Time is out of joint and the Pandorica is the centre of a group of exhibits, the anomalous evidence of an altered time line, depicting stone Daleks, penguins in the Nile (which the young Amelia knocks over when she later emerges from hiding), Egyptians in the Himalayas, and dinosaurs in ice. As she gazes upon the Pandorica, the drink she is carrying is suddenly snatched from her hand and, when she turns her head away, a note appears on the side of the box that advises her "Stick around Pond" and ironically comments on the fact that the, as yet to be revealed, adult Amy has been doing so for two thousand years. Haynes uses a series of dissolves at this point, visually compressing time, as Aunt Sharon desperately searches for the missing Amelia in a gradually emptying museum. It prefigures the later erasure of Amelia and the museum's exhibits as history itself continues to shrink. After touching the Pandorica, she stands back and Haynes builds up an expectation that the Doctor will be found inside because that is where he was imprisoned the last time we saw him. This is confounded when the adult Amy, another anomaly of the past, looks at her and the audience and alerts us that *The Big Bang* is "where it gets complicated." It is a self-awareness on Moffat's part that the concepts of time travel, temporal paradoxes and non-linear narratives are central to the story and he requires the audience to pay attention as soon as the series's title sequence finishes.

Another title card tells us that we are now in 102 AD, the scene opening with Rory and the apparently dead Amy at Stonehenge. Rory mournfully tells her "So the universe ended," indicating that it was not just the cosmos that winked out of existence but their personal lives, where "you and I never get born at all. Twice in my case. You would have laughed at that." His moment of self-deprecation is movingly emphasised when he begs the dead Amy to "Please, laugh!" Recalling the Doctor's rationale about Rory's own illogical survival, he sees his place in a "huge and ridiculous universe" where "sometimes there were miracles." His wish for a "ridiculous miracle about now" is a self-reflexive moment where Moffat acknowledges the illogical nature of Rory's own time paradox. The Doctor suddenly appears, like a genie let out of bottle, brandishing a mop akin to a fairy godmother waving a wand and wearing a fez that suggests he is the story's equivalent of accident-prone magician Tommy Cooper. Moffat's paradox, a chicken and egg causality dilemma, is founded on the principle that the future Doctor, who has just appeared in front of Rory, must travel back in time to rescue his past self, currently sitting inside the Pandorica, in order to generate a future version of himself that will then rescue his past self and so on and so forth. This only works if you consider the future Doctor and the past Doctor as separate versions with their own time streams which they bounce across back and forth to release the Doctor of the alternate time line and produce a number of other instances of cause and effect. "Time travel. You can't keep it straight in your head" best describes the Doctor's relationship with temporal causality and reflects the queer nature of time that we discussed in the chapter on *The Lodger*. What we see back in 102 AD are the after-effects of a future Doctor's causal activities that take place in 1996 and these, with the other complex manipulations of time in the story, suggest a form of what Benjamin K. Bennett, in 'Strindberg and Ibsen: Toward a Cubism of Time in Drama' in *Modernism in European Drama*, calls "cubist drama." He sees the painterly abstraction of Cubism, expanding our perception of dimensions and awareness of space, as analogous to drama where "the temporal aspects of an object or event will include its past, present and future." The Doctor rescuing himself is "the fusion of present and past" and "reminds us of our moral freedom, our ability to break the apparently unbreakable causal relation between past and present. The past is still with us... and yet it has in a sense been 'undone', for it is no longer a distant and unalterable determinant of the present... but rather it has become fused with the present, thus subject to our will, our moral decisiveness, after all." Rory frees the past Doctor from the Pandorica with the sonic screwdriver and when the Doctor asks him "How did you do that?" he indicates that he is using the sonic screwdriver that he just gave him. The Doctor produces the sonic screwdriver and claims, "No, I didn't," but when the two screwdrivers touch there is an explosion that invokes the Blinovitch Limitation Effect, a plot device introduced in *Day of the Daleks*, where a time traveller is unable to reconfigure an act that they have previously committed and a dangerous release of energy will occur if two temporal versions of the same person come into contact. Yet, we see Amy and Amelia, the past and future Doctors all interacting without any difficulties. Succinctly, the Doctor partly explains this effect, and the paradox of a future and a past Doctor, as "Temporal energy. Same screwdriver at different points in its own time stream. Which means it was me who gave it to you. Me from the future. I've got a future. That's nice." As he looks around the 'underhenge' at the petrified remains of the stone

Dalek and a Roman centurion, he proposes that "history has collapsed. Whole races have been deleted from existence. These are just like after-images" and these traces, akin to the remains at Pompeii or the shadows left after a nuclear blast, are "echoes. Fossils in time. The footprints of the never-were." Rory is baffled and asks, "How can we be here? What's keeping us safe?" and the Doctor emphasises their temporary status in this aftermath of total event collapse, reminding us of the fade into black at the end of *The Pandorica Opens*: "Nothing. Eye of the storm, that's all. We're just the last light to go out."

Rory and the Doctor place the "mostly dead" Amy in the Pandorica, where as another symbol of the anomalous past, of the history prior to total event collapse, she and her memories will be kept in "statis-lock". The Doctor notes that "all it needs now is a scan of her living DNA and it'll restore her" and with this the connections are formed with 1996 and the reason why young Amelia was coaxed to visit the museum and see the Pandorica. After the Doctor telepathically provides her with a message of what has happened to her, in a parallel to his implanting of his own myth in the mind of the sleeping Amelia at the end of the episode, Haynes cuts back to Amy's recovery in the museum. The memories that Amy and Amelia share are obviously not synchronous here because Amelia does not know the Doctor when Amy mentions him and points to her head, "He's in here. Left a message in my head like an answer phone." The problems of meeting your younger self are highlighted when Amy looks around and realises where she is, "National Museum, right? I was here once when I was a little... [here she realises that little Amelia is her younger self] ... yeah, complicated." Ironically, it also suggests that as a young girl she was psychologically complicated too, by the disappearance of her parents and in her own history by the arrival of the Raggedy Doctor. The sudden revival of the stone Dalek precipitates the arrival of both the Doctor and Rory in the museum and initiates the series of jumps back into time, explaining the logistics of how the fez and mop were acquired and the little journey that the sonic screwdriver makes through time. Haynes deftly edits these sequences together, replaying most of the Doctor's encounter with Rory in 102 AD to knit together these temporal strands, and for good measure he also confirms Amelia's observation that this is all "magic" by showing the Doctor bouncing back and forth in her own time line like a demented Tommy Cooper. We see him engineer her visit to the museum, leave the notes for her on the Pandorica and take the drink out of her hands only to give it back to her later in the narrative when she complains of being thirsty. It is a breathlessly energetic bit of cleverness that also sets up the death, some twelve minutes later, of the Doctor and pays off his realisation that the Dalek's restoration has been caused by the light leaking from the Pandorica. However, this to-ing and fro-ing in time begs the question as to why the Doctor does not simply travel back to a point before the total event collapse and prevent it from occurring. An ambiguity that is perhaps reasonable to accommodate when it is clear that nothing prior to the total event collapse now exists and therefore the vortex manipulator is unable to make that journey. It suggests the history of time and space as we know it is no longer accessible.

After the 'death' of the future Doctor and the various strands of the narrative are gathered up, the impetus of the episode is focused on the collapse of history. When young Amelia is erased from the time line, the Doctor is quick to point out the terrible urgency of their situation, "There is no Amelia. From now on, there never was. History is still collapsing." Amy, puzzled, asks "How can I still be here, if she's not?" and the Doctor again explains that they are the vestiges of the past, at the centre of a rapidly shrinking reality. "You're an anomaly. We all are. We're hanging on at the eye of the storm but the eye is closing." This imagery again reflects the fade to black at the end of *The Pandorica Opens* and proposes the closing down or the loss of consciousness on a cosmic scale. Even death itself is seen as progress in this realm because, as the Doctor points out, "Reality will never have happened. Today, just dying is a result." As they get to the rooftop, night has rapidly become day and is another sign for the Doctor that "History is shrinking. The universe is collapsing. We don't have much time." The erasure of history and the flux of time are full of implications. William Bogard in 'Baudrillard, Time and the End' in *Baudrillard: a Critical Reader*, highlights how even the production's construction of the episode informs many of the conceptual meanings of history and time within it. Jean Baudrillard posited that "time in general, any-time whatever, is reproduced on [the] screen – future, past, present, all can be repeated or played back, and moreover, this can be done at variable speeds (fast forward, slow motion, reverse motion, freeze frame, stop time)." Haynes's editing, use of flashback, flashforward, repetition, reverse motion and slow motion is prominent throughout both episodes and the majority of sequences that employ these techniques also demonstrate the story's depiction of the consequences and effects of time travel on the formation and erasure of history. Consequently, Moffat's idea that all of history will completely disappear into a void complements Baudrillard's own idea that "the end of history is also the end of the hierarchical regime of signs, and the beginning of the 'flat', homogenous regime of signals and codes." The hierarchy of signs is the universe of *Doctor Who* itself – the Doctor, the companions, the TARDIS, the monsters – and the black, empty void into which they disappear is akin to an anti-Neverland. When the Dalek announces, "Restore! Restore!" in the darkness of the museum, it is putting voice to the necessities of the plot featuring the Dalek and is symbolic of what will happen when the light of the Pandorica is eventually spread throughout time by the exploding TARDIS.

On the rooftop of the museum, Amy wonders why the TARDIS exploded and took the whole of the universe with it. Moffat deftly avoids the question and suggests that the answer will wait until the next series when the Doctor, as Moffat's proxy, determines it is a "good question for another day." Standing before the burning sun, the Doctor poses a more immediate conundrum: "Total event collapse means that every star in the universe never happened. Not one single one of them ever shone. So if all the stars that ever were are gone, then what is that?" He uses a rudimentary detector made from a satellite dish and deduces that the sun is the burning TARDIS and "that's what's been keeping the Earth warm." A star in the morning sky, the burning TARDIS is figuratively both the way back to and the restoration of Neverland, especially if we follow Peter Pan's own navigation to it as "second star to the right, and straight on till morning" from the 1953 Disney film version of Barrie's book. After rescuing River from her time loop in the TARDIS, the subsequent Dalek attack prompts some further questions about the nature of the Pandorica's powers. "How can that Dalek even exist? It was erased from time and then it came back? How?" asks the Doctor. He comes to the conclusion that the Pandorica is "a perfect prison and inside it, perfectly preserved, a few billion atoms of the universe as it was. In theory you could extrapolate the whole universe from a single one of them." The episode advances the idea that a physical and temporal extrapolation of the universe could be made, and all the associated events, races, planets and history that formed it could be re-created "like cloning a body from a single cell." The aim of rebooting the memory of the universe contained in the Pandorica sounds very similar to Moffat's premise in *Forest of the Dead* where the Doctor rescues the four thousand and twenty-two survivors of the Vashta Nerada's attack on the Library because they could be rebooted from data storage in the main core of the planet-sized computer. This process implies that the temporality of the universe, where history would be returned to the right order in the time stream, would also be corrected and repaired. "Doctor, you're being completely ridiculous. The Pandorica partially restored one Dalek. If it can't even reboot a single life form properly, how's it going to reboot the whole of reality?" argues River and he posits the theory that the infinite power of the TARDIS can transmit "the light from the Pandorica to every particle of space and time simultaneously." In short, reality can be restored to the moment before the TARDIS exploded on 26 June 2010, in Amy's time. The absurdist notion is again questioned by River but the Doctor knows how ridiculous and miraculous the universe can be and believes it is not impossible, only "almost completely impossible." When River confronts the Dalek, creating a diversion for the wounded Doctor to use the vortex manipulator to get to the Pandorica, she understands first hand that the restoration field can do what he claims. The Dalek is able to consult its records and it recognises her as an "associate of the Doctor's" and that she "will show mercy." She tells the Dalek, "I'm River Song. Check your records again" and, presumably because she has previous history with the Daleks, it begs for mercy. The threads of time and space can be rejuvenated.

As the not-quite-so-dead Doctor prepares to fly the Pandorica into the burning heart of the TARDIS, River notes that reality continues to collapse and the museum and its contents are slowly vanishing and "history is being erased." The Doctor manages to tell River that he has set the box, the biggest representation of 'cubic drama' in the story, to deliver

"Big Bang Two." River explains to Amy and Rory that "a restoration field powered by an exploding TARDIS, happening at every moment in history," will clearly return everything to its rightful place and time. They will awake from unconsciousness, returning to space and time as it was on 26 June 2010, and "none of this ever happens and we don't remember it" predicts River, but the Doctor will be "at the heart of the explosion. All memory of him will be purged from the universe. He will never have been born." The problem with this idea is that as the Doctor is erased then the indications are that history will be restored but there will surely be consequences as many of the events and people he affected will produce an alternate history. Surely the Earth would be a different place to the one that Amy eventually returns to? Or does his history remain as it is? It is suggested that his entire timeline is unravelling as he returns to Leadworth and little Amelia. It remains ambiguous until the adult Amy recalls him from the void and one presumes that his shaping of, and involvement in, history and events is also reconfigured by her remembrance of the myth of the Doctor. Moffat has indicated that this was a deliberate aim of the script and in an interview with *Doctor Who Magazine* in July 2010 he was asked if "all bets were off as far as *Doctor Who* history as we know it?" His reply suggests that the familiar universe has shifted in the aftermath of *The Big Bang* and "history has wibbled. Without being too explicit about it we can have characters surprised at the existence of aliens again." He does not sound too precious about it, though: "... don't expect any 'history has wibbled' scenes. This is just a way for us all to justify continuity errors to ourselves." As the Doctor travels back down his own time stream, Haynes gets the opportunity to add in some unseen sequences as well as indulge in Baudrillard's "spectacle of time's immolation." The Doctor decides that as soon as he has engineered his own myth to become part of Amelia's subconscious, that he does not "belong here anymore" and, as noted, he sacrifices himself to the void to "skip the rest of the rewind" because he hates "repeats" and would prefer not to see the rest of his personal history absorbed by the cracks in the universe. Whether he circumvents his own unravelling by being absorbed into the crack at this point is again left rather ambiguous. He is dissolved by the crack in time and for Baudrillard is "thrown into the depths of an unnameable, unspeakable timelessness" as, simultaneously, the stars are seen to be back in the night sky, signifying the "disappearance of territories followed in turn by a reterritorialization, a replication of territories in simulation" that still promulgates a slightly altered *Doctor Who* universe, perhaps one that is so subtly changed that we may never completely grasp the reality of it or, indeed, the full meaning of this two part-finale.

From the grandstanding visions of a sky full of spaceships above Stonehenge and the alliance of monsters with their rather contrived plan to trap the Doctor in the Pandorica, Moffat turns the story inward in *The Big Bang* to focus on four people chasing around a museum whilst the universe shrinks outside the window. Moffat's indulgent use of temporal

239

puzzles certainly fulfils Bakhtin's criteria of *menippea* as "the urge to create extraordinary situations for the testing of philosophical ideas." However, this synthesis of a carnivalesque ambivalence for logic and an irreverent desire to break the rules and cross narrative boundaries only succeeds intermittently. Sometimes it works spectacularly – not just in terms of visual spectacle but also in narrative complexity – and sometimes it just offers a way for Moffat to avoid some of the implications of his ambition and refuse to answer questions left dangling by many of the preceding episodes. Testing our ideas about time and the use of empirical and metaphysical paradoxes in the science-fiction genre, however amusingly Matt Smith performs these sequences, amounts to more grandstanding, including the revitalisation of the Dalek as a token monster to chase our heroes down corridors, and deliberately delays the story getting to the roof of the museum and resolving the fate of the Doctor, the Pandorica and the TARDIS. *The Big Bang* tells us about the threat to the universe but never actually reveals why it is there in the first place, why it is happening and who caused it. It is an unsatisfying finale because we never have a villain emerge to provide a major conflict in the story, so the Doctor spends most of *The Big Bang* fire-fighting while Moffat brings the story of Amy full circle. In *The Pandorica Opens* money has clearly been spent on the Stonehenge locations and the visual effects. By the time we get to *The Big Bang* the Stonehenge location is gone, as is the visual misdirection of the massing alliance space fleet, and what was *indicated* as the threat has, ironically enough, become as fossilised as the remaining Daleks. The dilemma for the Doctor, Amy, Rory and River is contained in a self-referential bubble, with the effects of the conflict on those outside the bubble all referred to off screen. We are told about or shown the consequences of the shrinking universe upon the Doctor, Amy and Rory but we never really fully grasp how it actually affects other people. These are powerful concepts that Moffat is creating but having four people successfully carry the episode's exposition alone tends to reduce the action to lots of standing around and talking, when very strong, very identifiable supporting characters could better assist in the switch from the broadest to the narrowest world view and convince an audience that the apocalypse is not always taking place off screen.

Of more interest are the binary oppositions between men and women. Amy truly is the fairy-tale figure of the mysterious Little Red Riding Hood that the series has been constructed around. She is not only the absent woman in search of her self, on a journey from troubled little girl (the adorable Caitlin Blackwood returning as Amelia) to impending womanhood and *that* wedding, but the story is also a science-fiction satire about getting the bride to the church on time, about getting the adolescent Amy married off. Rory is that most human of non-humans, embodying the crisis of subjectivity at the heart of his struggle with the Nestene programming and his conflicted human emotions. Just as Amy evoked the same contradictions in the Daleks' android Bracewell in *Victory of the Daleks*, she helps Rory reaffirm his love for Amy, but only for him then to destroy the object of his feelings. That this death takes place simultaneously with the Doctor's capture and imprisonment in the Pandorica, the destruction of the TARDIS and the death of the universe, offers the spectacle of *The Pandorica Opens* a much-needed emotional grounding. *The Big Bang* is also more satisfying emotionally, with the conclusion of the series-long Amy arc. An outstanding scene is one between the Doctor and Amy as he prepares to hurtle into the heart of the burning TARDIS and it underlines the subtext about remembering and forgetting that has been drip-fed into stories from the beginning of the series. Moffat's story arc, in which all of history is erased and then rebooted, in which the very act of remembering is both a macrocosmic event (the key to saving the universe) and a microcosmic event (bringing back your long-vanished parents), is a main tenet in fairy tales. Amy's Red Riding Hood journey through time, symbolised very powerfully in the forest scenes in *Flesh and Stone*, is one about avoiding the threat of being devoured wherein the hungry wolf of the old fairy tale is now the crack in the bedroom wall. But like many readings of fairy tales, is this also a story about a girl's desperate avoidance of womanhood, delaying her impending marriage to Rory, and to remain forever a child by jumping aboard the TARDIS? The interesting thing about Red Riding Hood and other fairy tales is that they are concerned with the control of women, the control of desire. Amy as a Red Riding Hood princess, whose final trajectory is marriage, is a fascinating reading of the transgressive woman, often recklessly acting on her own desires but who in the end must be rescued by two friendly male figures – Rory and the Doctor – the husband and the father. River, cycling through a number of identities and appearances – from earth mother to seductress – is positioned here as literally the figure of the old wives' tale, the woman as storyteller and an analogue to Scheherazade, as one who spins her narrative ("spoilers") throughout the Doctor's timeline. As ever, Matt Smith completely steals the show and is particularly impressive in *The Big Bang*, giving us a mesmerising range of performances within one episode, capturing ancient wisdom and youthful exuberance in one big eccentric package. He truly is the biggest success in this year of transition for *Doctor Who* and remains as a major incentive for continuing to watch the show. Now, only time will tell how effective the dynamic of the newlyweds travelling in the TARDIS with the Doctor will prove to be.

# SELECTED BIBLIOGRAPHY

Aaron, Michele, 'Toward Queer Television Theory,' in Glyn Davis and Gary Needham (eds), *Queer TV: Theories, Histories, Politics* (Taylor & Francis, 2009)

Bakhtin, Mikhail Mikhaïlovich, *Problems of Dostoevsky's Poetics* (University of Minnesota Press, 2004)

Bamossy, Gary J., 'Star Gazing: the Mythology and Commodification of Vincent van Gogh,' in S. Ratneshwar and David Glen Mick (eds), *Inside Consumption: Consumer Motives, Goals, and Desires* (Routledge, 2005)

Barnes, Julian, *A History of the World in 10 1/2 Chapters* (Cambridge University Press, 1995)

Bassil-Morozow, Helena, *Tim Burton: The Monster and the Crowd – A Post-Jungian Perspective* (Routledge, 2010)

Baudrillard, Jean, *Simulacra and Simulations* (University of Michigan Press, 1994)

Baxendale, John, 'You and I – All of Us Ordinary People: Renegotiating 'Britishness' in Wartime,' in Nick Hayes and Jeff Hill (eds), *Millions Like Us? British Culture in the Second World War* (Liverpool University Press, 1999)

Becker, Guy, 'Guy Love,' in Glyn Davis and Gary Needham (eds), *Queer TV: Theories, Histories, Politics* (Taylor & Francis, 2009)

Bennett, Benjamin K., 'Strindberg and Ibsen: Toward a Cubism of Time in Drama,' in Frederick J. Marker and C. D. Innes (eds), *Modernism in European Drama: Ibsen, Strindberg, Pirandello, Becket* (University of Toronto Press, 1998)

Benshoff, Harry M., *Monsters in the Closet: Homosexuality and the Horror Film* (Manchester University Press ND, 1997)

Bergman, David, *Camp Grounds: Style and Homosexuality* (University of Massachusetts Press, 1993)

Bignell, Jonathan, *Postmodern Media Culture* (Aakar Books, 2007)

Bignell, Jonathan, and Andrew O'Day, *Terry Nation* (Manchester University Press, 2004)

Bogard, William, 'Baudrillard, Time and the End,' in Douglas Kellner (ed), *Baudrillard: A Critical Reader* (Wiley-Blackwell, 1994)

Botting, Fred, *Gothic Romanced: Consumption, Gender and Technology in Contemporary Fictions* (Taylor & Francis, 2008)

Britton, Piers D., and Simon J. Barker, *Reading Between Designs: Visual Imagery and the Generation of Meaning in The Avengers, The Prisoner and Doctor Who* (University of Texas Press, 2003)

Butler, David, 'Introduction,' in David Butler (ed), *Time and Relative Dissertations in Space: Critical Perspectives on Doctor Who* (Manchester University Press, 2007)

Butler, Judith, 'From Interiority to Gender Performatives,' in Fabio Cleto (ed), *Camp: Queer Aesthetics and the Performing Subject: A Reader* (Edinburgh University Press, 1999)

Cannadine, David, *In Churchill's Shadow: Confronting the Past in Modern Britain* (Oxford University Press, USA, 2004)

Capon, Robert Farrar, *Hunting the Divine Fox: Images and Mystery in Christian Faith* (Seabury Press, 1974)

Chambers, Samuel Allen, *The Queer Politics of Television* (I.B. Tauris, 2009)

Chapman, James, *Inside the TARDIS: The Worlds of Doctor Who* (I.B. Tauris, 2006)

Charles, Alec, 'The Ideology of Anachronism: Television, History and the Nature of Time,' in David Butler (ed), *Time and Relative Dissertations in Space: Critical Perspectives on Doctor Who* (Manchester University Press, 2007)

Chevalier, Jean, Alan Gheerbrant and John Buchanan (eds), *The Penguin Dictionary of Symbols* (Penguin Books, 1996)

Cleto, Fabio, *Camp: Queer Aesthetics and the Performing Subject: A Reader* (Edinburgh University Press, 1999)

Clover, Carol J., 'Her Body, Himself - Gender and the Slasher Film,' in Barry Keith Grant (ed), *The Dread of Difference: Gender and the Horror Film* (University of Texas Press, 1996)

Coats, Karen, *Looking Glasses and Neverlands: Lacan, Desire and Subjectivity in Children's Literature* (University of Iowa Press, 2004)

Cobb, Kelton, *The Blackwell Guide to Theology and Popular Culture* (Wiley-Blackwell 2005)

Cook, Pam, *Screening the Past: Memory and Nostalgia in Cinema* (Routledge, 2005)

Cornea, Christine, *Science Fiction Cinema: Between Fantasy and Reality* (Edinburgh University Press, 2007)

Cornell, Paul (ed), *Licence Denied: Rumblings from the Doctor Who Underground* (Virgin Books, 1997)

Coulthard, Lisa, 'Killing Bill: Rethinking Feminism and Violence,' in Yvonne Tasker and Diane Negra (eds), *Interrogating Postfeminism: Gender and the Politics of Popular Culture* (Duke University Press, 2007)

Creed, Barbara, *The Monstrous-feminine: Film, Feminism, Psychoanalysis* (Routledge, 1993)

Creed, Barbara, 'Horror and the Carnivalesque - The Body-monstrous,' in Leslie Devereaux and Roger Hillman (eds), *Fields of Vision: Essays in Film Studies, Visual Anthropology, and Photography* (University of California Press, 1995)

Creed, Barbara, *Phallic Panic: Film, Horror and the Primal Uncanny* (Melbourne University Publishing, 2005)

Dadoun, Roger, 'Metropolis: Mother City - "Mittler" - Hitler,' in Constance Penley, Elisabeth Lyon, Lynn Spigel and Janet Bergstrom (eds), *Close Encounters: Film, Feminism and Science Fiction* (University of Minnesota Press, 1991)

Davies, Russell T., and Benjamin Cook, *Doctor Who - The Writer's Tale: The Final Chapter* (Random House, 2010)

Day, William Patrick, *Vampire Legends in Contemporary American Culture: What Becomes a Legend Most* (University Press of Kentucky, 2002)

Dery, Mark, *The Pyrotechnic Insanitarium: American Culture on the Brink* (Grove Press, 1999)

Edelman, Lee, *No Future: Queer Theory and the Death Drive* (Duke University Press, 2004)

Eller, Jack David, *From Culture to Ethnicity to Conflict: an Anthropological Perspective on Ethnic Conflict* (University of Michigan Press, 1999)

Elms, Alan C., *Uncovering Lives: The Uneasy Alliance of Biography and Psychology* (Oxford University Press, 1997)

Evans, Caroline, and Lorraine Gamman, 'Reviewing Queer Viewing,' in Harry M. Benshoff and Sean Griffin (eds), *Queer Cinema: The Film Reader*

Feagin, Joe R., 'Toward an Integrated Theory of Systemic Racism,' in Maria Krysan and Amanda E. Lewis (eds), *The Changing Terrain of Race and Ethnicity* (Russell Sage Foundation, 2006)

Ferguson, Donald N., *Masterworks of the Orchestral Repertoire: A Guide for Listeners* (University of Minnesota Press, 1968)

Fiske, John, *Television Culture* (Routledge, 1999)

Flynn, Caryl, 'The Deaths of Camp,' in Fabio Cleto (ed), *Camp: Queer Aesthetics and the Performing Subject: A Reader* (Edinburgh University Press, 1999)

Franz, Marie-Luise von, *The Interpretation of Fairy Tales* (Shambhala Publications, 1996)

Gardiner, Judith Kegan, *Masculinity Studies and Feminist Theory: New Directions* (Columbia University Press, 2002)

Gilman, Sander L., *Disease and Representation: Images of Illness From Madness to AIDS* (Cornell University Press, 1988)

Gordon, Andrew M., *Empire of Dreams: The Science Fiction and Fantasy Films of Steven Spielberg* (Rowman and Littlefield, 2008)

Greenberg, Jeff, Jeff Schimel and Andy Martens, 'Ageism: Denying the Face of the Future,' in Todd D. Nelson (ed), *Ageism: Stereotyping and Prejudice Against Older Persons* (MIT Press, 2004)

Guffey, Elizabeth E., *Retro: The Culture of Revival* (Reaktion Books, 2006)

Halberstam, Judith, *Skin Shows: Gothic Horror and the Technology of Monsters* (Duke University Press, 1995)

Halberstam, Judith, *In a Queer Time and Place: Transgender Bodies, Subcultural Lives* (NYU Press, 2005)

Halperin, David M., *Saint Foucault: Towards a Gay Hagiography* (Replica Books, 2001)

Haney, William S., *Cyberculture, Cyborgs and Science Fiction: Consciousness and the Posthuman* (Rodopi, 2006)

Harris, Jason Marc, *Folklore and the Fantastic in Nineteenth-Century British Fiction* (Ashgate Publishing Ltd., 2008)

Harris, Jose, 'War and Social History: Britain and the Home Front in the Second World War,' in Gordon Martel (ed), *The World War Two Reader* (Routledge, 2004)

Hartsock, Chad, *Sight and Blindness in Luke-Acts: The Use of Physical Features in Characterisation* (BRILL, 2008)

Hauke, Christopher, *Jung and the Postmodern: The Interpretation of Realities* (Routledge, 2000)

Heinich, Nathalie, *The Glory of Van Gogh: An Anthropology of Admiration* (Princeton University Press, 1997)

Hickman, Clayton (ed), *The Brilliant Book of Doctor Who 2011* (BBC Books, Ebury Publishing, Random House, 2010)

Hills, Matt, *Triumph of A Time Lord: Regenerating Doctor Who in the Twenty-first Century* (I.B. Tauris, 2010)

Holte, James Craig, 'Resurrection in Britain: Christopher Lee and Hammer Draculas,' in James Craig Holte (ed), *The Fantastic Vampire: Studies in the Children of the Night* (Greenwood Publishing, 2002)

Hornsey, Richard, *The Spiv and the Architect: Unruly Life in Postwar London* (University of Minnesota Press, 2010)

246

Hourihan, Margery, *Deconstructing the Hero: Literary Theory and Children's Literature* (Routledge, 1997)

Høyrup, Helene, 'Childhood as a Sign of Change,' in Thomas Van der Welt, Felicité Fairer-Wessels and Judith Ings (eds), *Change and Renewal in Children's Literature* (Greenwood Publishing Group, 2004)

Hubbard, Phil, 'Between Trangression and Complicity (Or Can the Straight Guy Have a Queer Eye?),' in Kath Browne, Jason Lim and Gavin Brown (eds), *Geographies of Sexualities: Theories, Practices and Politics* (Ashgate Publishing, Ltd., 2009)

Hudson, Dale, 'Vampires of Colour and the Performance of Multi-cultural Whiteness,' in Daniel Bernardi (ed), *The Persistence of Whiteness: Race and Contemporary Hollywood Cinema* (Routledge, 2008)

Hunt, Peter, *Children's Literature* (Blackwell Guides to Literature, Wiley-Blackwell, 2001)

Jacobs, Steven, *The Wrong House: The Architecture of Alfred Hitchcock* (010 Publishers, 2007)

Jaikumar, Priya, *Cinema at the End of Empire: A Politics of Transition in Britain and India* (Duke University Press, 2006)

Jameson, Fredric, *Postmodernism, or, the Cultural Logic of Late Capitalism* (Duke University Press, 1991)

Jess-Cooke, Carolyn, *Film Sequels: Theory and Practice from Hollywood to Bollywood* (Edinburgh University Press, 2009)

Joyrich, Lynn, *Re-viewing Reception: Television, Gender and Postmodern Culture* (Indiana University Press, 1996)

Kavey, Allison B., 'Introduction,' in Allison B. Kavey and Lester D. Friedman (eds), *Second Star to the Right: Peter Pan in the Popular Imagination* (Rutgers University Press, 2009)

Klein, Naomi, *The Shock Doctrine* (Penguin, 2008)

Krutnik, Frank, *In a Lonely Street: Film Noir, Genre and Masculinity* (Routledge, 1991)

Kynaston, David, *Austerity Britain - 1945-1951* (Bloomsbury, 2007)

Lambert, Kenneth, *Analysis, Repair and Individuation* (Karnac Books, 1994)

Le Gall, Michel, and Charles Taliaferro, 'The Recovery of Childhood and the Search For The Absent Father,' in Dean A. Kowalski (ed), *Steven Spielberg and Philosophy: We're Gonna Need A Bigger Book* (University Press of Kentucky, 2008)

Lundin, Ann H., *Constructing the Canon of Children's Literature: Beyond Library Walls and Ivory Towers* (Routledge, 2004)

Lustyik, Katalin, 'Going Global? Children's Television in Transition in Central-Eastern Europe,' in Lennard Højbjerg and Henrik Søndergaard (eds), *European Film and Media Culture* (Museum Tusculanum Press, 2006)

Macdonald, Hugh, 'Military Power and Arms Control: Towards a Reassessment,' in Lawrence S. Hagen (ed), *The Crisis in Western Security: Volume 1982, Part Two* (Taylor & Francis, 1982)

MacDowall, Lachlan, 'Professional Killers at Home: Domesticity and the Deregulated Subject,' in Lisa M. Detora (ed), *Heroes of Film, Comics and American Culture: Essays on Real and Fictional Defenders of Home* (McFarland, 2009)

Mangan J.A., and James Walvin (eds), *Manliness and Morality: Middle Class Masculinity in Britain and America 1800-1940* (Manchester University Press, 1991)

Mather, Nigel, *Tears of Laughter: Comedy-drama in 1990s British Cinema* (Manchester University Press, 2006)

Meredith, Margaret Eileen, *The Secret Garden - Temenos for Individuation: a Jungian Appreciation of Themes in the Novel by Frances Hodgson Burnett* (Inner City Books, 2005)

Meyer, Moe, *The Politics and Poetics of Camp* (Routledge, 1994)

Middleton, Jason, 'Buffy as Femme Fatale: The Cult Heroine and the Male Spectator,' in Elana Levine and Lisa Parks (eds), *Undead TV: Essays on Buffy the Vampire Slayer* (Duke University Press, 2007)

Moore, Ryan, *Sells Like Teen Spirit: Music, Youth Culture and Social Crisis* (NYU Press, 2009)

Morgan, David, *Visual Piety: a History and Theory of Popular Religious Images* (University of California Press, 1999)

Morgan, Jack, *The Biology of Horror: Gothic Literature and Film* (SIU Press, 2002)

Morris, Nigel, *The Cinema of Steven Spielberg: Empire of Light* (Wallflower Press, 2004)

Munns, David P., 'Peter Pan and the Queering of Popular Culture,' in Allison B. Kavey and Lester D. Friedman (eds), *Second Star to the Right: Peter Pan in the Popular Imagination* (Rutgers University Press, 2009)

Neumann, Erich, *The Great Mother: An Analysis of the Archetype* (Routledge, 1996)

248

Neumann, Erich, *Art and the Creative Unconscious: Four Essays* (Routledge, 1999)

Newman, Kim, *Doctor Who: A Critical Reading of the Series* (BFI Publishing, 2005)

O'Mahony, Daniel, "Now how is that wolf able to impersonate a grandmother?' History, Pseudo-history and Genre in Doctor Who,' in David Butler (ed), *Time and Relative Dissertations in Space: Critical Perspectives on Doctor Who* (Manchester University Press, 2007)

Orlik, Peter, *Electronic Media Criticism: Applied Perspectives* (Taylor & Francis, 2008)

Paasonen, Susanna, *Figures of Fantasy: Internet, Women and Cyberdiscourse* (Peter Lang, 2005)

Person, Ethel Spector, *Dreams of Love and Fateful Encounters: The Power of Romantic Passion* (American Psychiatric Pub, 2006)

Punter, David, *The Literature of Terror: A History of Gothic Fictions From 1765 to the Present Day* (Second Edition, Longman, 1996)

Punter, David, 'Introduction,' in David Punter (ed), *A Companion to the Gothic* (Wiley-Blackwell, 2001)

Rattigan, Neil, 'The Last Gasp of the Middle Class: British War Films of the 1950s,' in Wheeler W. Dixon (ed), *Re-viewing British Cinema 1900-1992: Essays and Interviews* (SUNY Press, 1994)

Rojek, Chris, *Brit Myth: Who Do the British Think They Are?* (Reaktion Books, 2007)

Roth, Michael S., *Rediscovering History: Culture, Politics, and the Psyche* (Stanford University Press, 1994)

Russell, Gary, *Doctor Who: The Inside Story* (BBC Books, 2007)

Salerno, Roger A., *Landscapes of Abandonment: Capitalism, Modernity and Estrangement* (SUNY Press, 2003)

Sedgwick, Eve Kosofsky, *Tendencies* (Routledge, 1994)

Schneider, Steven Jay, 'Manifestations of the Literary Double in Modern Horror Cinema,' in Steven Jay Schneider (ed), *Horror Film and Psychoanalysis: Freud's Worst Nightmare* (Cambridge University Press, 2004)

Shimpach, Shawn, *Television in Transition: The Life and Afterlife of the Narrative Action Hero* (John Wiley and Sons, 2010)

Smith, Allan Lloyd, *American Gothic Fiction: An Introduction* (Continuum International Publishing Group, 2004)

Spooner, Catherine, *Contemporary Gothic* (Reaktion Books, 2006)

Storey, John, 'Postmodernism and Popular Culture,' in Stuart Sim (ed), *The Routledge Companion to Postmodernism* (Routledge, 2005)

Storr, Anthony, *The Dynamics of Creation* (Penguin Books, 1991)

Tatar, Maria, *The Hard Facts of the Grimms' Fairy Tales* (Princeton University Press, 2003)

Telotte, J. P., *Replications: A Robotic History of the Science Fiction Film* (University of Illinois Press, 1995)
Telotte, J. P., *Science Fiction Film* (Cambridge University Press, 2001)

Tulloch, John, and Manuel Alvarado, *Doctor Who: The Unfolding Text* (Macmillan, 1983)

Turner, Graeme, *Film as Social Practice* (Routledge, 1999)

Weart, Spencer R., *Nuclear Fear: A History of Images* (Harvard University Press, 1998)

White, Eric, 'Case Study: Nakata Hideo's Ringu and Ringu 2,' in Jay McRoy (ed), *Japanese Horror Cinema* (Edinburgh University Press, 2005)

Winston, Joe, *Drama, Narrative and Moral Education: Exploring Traditional Tales in the Primary Years* (Routledge, 1998)

Woods, Tim, *Beginning Postmodernism* (Manchester University Press, 1999)

Yeoman, Ann, *Now or Neverland: Peter Pan and the Myth of Eternal Youth - A Psychological Perspective on a Cultural Icon* (Inner City Books, 1998)

Zipes, Jack David, *The Brothers Grimm: From Enchanted Forests to the Modern World* (Palgrave Macmillan, 2002)

Zipes, Jack David, *Fairy Tales and the Art of Subversion: The Classical Genre for Children and the Process of Civilisation* (Routledge, 1991)

## PHOTO CREDITS

Front cover © Scott Frankton
Back cover © Alun Vega
Page 6 © Alun Vega
Page 24 © Lee Tucker
Page 44 © Rob Clarke
Page 66 © Scott Frankton
Page 116 © Catherine Cranston
Page 136 © Scott Frankton
Page 158 © Scott Frankton
Page 184 © Lee Tucker
Page 209 © Scott Frankton

Also available from Classic TV Press...

# being human

## unofficial and unauthorised

## Joanne Black

"So, a werewolf, a ghost and a vampire decide to live like humans do. They get jobs, a house and a TV licence."

*Being Human,* created for BBC Three by Toby Whithouse, puts the supernatural firmly into the everyday world.

That cute, geeky hospital porter? A werewolf.
A flash of a sunny smile and some grey leggings? A ghost.
The dark-eyed Irish guy at the bar? A vampire.

George (Russell Tovey), Annie (Lenora Crichlow) and Mitchell (Aidan Turner) live in a pink house in Bristol and all they want is to be normal, to fit in – to be human.

As well as reviewing each episode from the first two series in detail, this book looks at the birth of the show and profiles the characters and the mythology behind them. Not forgetting – of course – the plots, the themes, the darkness and the humour, in fact just about everything that being human really means.

An affectionate, humorous, and occasionally slightly sarcastic, exploration of the world of *Being Human.* A must for all fans of the series.

"It's a lot to take in. I mean, werewolves, ghosts, vampires. I didn't even believe in homeopathy before this!"

With illustrations by Chris Wreford.

Format: Paperback (300 pages)
Published: December 2010
Recommended Retail Price: £14.99

Available from Classic TV Press at a discounted price of £12.99 (plus P&P)
www.classictvpress.co.uk

# THE COMPLETE SECRET ARMY

the unofficial and unauthorised guide to the classic TV series

## Andy Priestner

This comprehensive book, an essential read for any fan of the series, seeks to uncover how *Secret Army* was conceived and details its journey to our television screens. Each episode is reviewed in depth and accompanied by information on the actual historical events which inspired the series's gripping storylines. The book also includes many exclusive behind-the-scenes and location photos, cast and crew interview material, a comprehensive section on spin-off series *Kessler*, and much, much more.

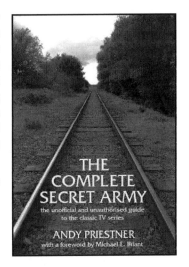

"You need to see *Secret Army* and you need to read this book." Gareth Roberts, writer - *Doctor Who*

Format: Paperback (672 pages)
Published: December 2008
Recommended Retail Price: £30.00

Available from Classic TV Press at a discounted price of £22.50 (plus P&P)

---

# WORLDS APART

the unofficial and unauthorised guide to the BBC's remake of Survivors

## Rich Cross

An examination of Adrian Hodges's re-imagining of Terry Nation's cult drama series *Survivors*, exploring its plots, themes and characters. As well as a detailed look at the making of the new series, Cross reviews the episodes in depth, recounts previous attempts to revive *Survivors* and describes the similarities and differences between the new *Survivors* and the original series. The book also includes cast and crew interview material, plus many exclusive behind-the-scenes and location photos.

Format: Paperback (310 pages)
Published: April 2010
Recommended Retail Price: £14.99

Available from Classic TV Press at a discounted price of £12.99 (plus P&P)

# ABOUT THE AUTHOR

*Doctor Who* has loomed large in the life of Frank Collins. A lifelong fan of the series, his earliest childhood memories recall the Patrick Troughton era, alas now under-represented in the BBC's archives, and images of the Yeti in the Underground, Cybermen hatching from space eggs and homicidal seaweed still fester away in his fevered imagination.

He has been writing 'proper stuff' about *Doctor Who* over the last two and a half years for the *Doctor Who Appreciation Society*'s magazine 'Celestial Toyroom' and is one of the team of contributors on the collaborative *Doctor Who* blog 'Behind the Sofa' where you will also find his opinions on the current series as well as the spin-off shows *Torchwood* and *The Sarah Jane Adventures*. He has also contributed reviews to the websites *Television Heaven* and *The Thumbcast*. On his own blog, *Cathode Ray Tube*, he continues to indulge his love of classic British television and cinema, obscure film and television soundtracks and regularly reviews the latest DVDs and books.

In his real life, he was educated at Newport School of Art and the University of Reading and has since followed an eclectic career path working for, amongst others, the British Market Research Bureau and the NHS, and has previously managed independent cinemas in both Surrey and Brixton. He currently works for the Design Initiative, a not-for-profit, charitable organisation that supports and promotes the work of designers in the North West of England.

This is his first book. He does not recommend writing a book while project managing a major design festival and hopes to heed his own advice if he ever gets the chance to write another one.